Mobilizing
Soviet Peasants

Mobilizing Soviet Peasants

Heroines and Heroes of Stalin's Fields

Mary Buckley

ROWMAN & LITTLEFIELD PUBLISHERS, INC.
Lanham • Boulder • New York • Toronto • Oxford

ROWMAN & LITTLEFIELD PUBLISHERS, INC.

Published in the United States of America
by Rowman & Littlefield Publishers, Inc.
A wholly owned subsidiary of The Rowman & Littlefield Publishing Group, Inc.
4501 Forbes Boulevard, Suite 200, Lanham, Maryland 20706
www.rowmanlittlefield.com

PO Box 317
Oxford
OX2 9RU, UK

HD
1536
.S65
B83
2006

British Library Cataloguing in Publication Information Available

Library of Congress Cataloging-in-Publication Data

Buckley, Mary (Mary E. A.)
  Mobilizing Soviet peasants : heroines and heroes of Stalin's fields / Mary Buckley.
    p. cm.
  Includes bibliographical references and index.
  ISBN-13: 978-0-7425-4126-9 (cloth : alk. paper)
  ISBN-10: 0-7425-4126-6 (cloth : alk. paper)
  ISBN-13: 978-0-7425-4127-6 (pbk. : alk. paper)
  ISBN-10: 0-7425-4127-4 (pbk. : alk. paper)
  1. Peasantry—Soviet Union. 2. Stakhanovite movement. 3. Soviet Union—Rural
conditions. 4. Agriculture and state—Soviet Union. I. Title.
  HD1536.S65B83 2006
  305.5'633094709043--dc22   2005033902

Printed in the United States of America

⊗™ The paper used in this publication meets the minimum requirements of American
National Standard for Information Sciences—Permanence of Paper for Printed Library
Materials, ANSI/NISO Z39.48-1992.

To Fergus, Brenda, Jennie, Andrea, Linda, and Paul

Contents

List of Tables

List of Figures

Acknowledgments

As usual, my debts are many. Huge gratitude is owed to the Economic and Social Research Council (ESRC) for a one-year grant without which the bulk of the research for this project would not have been conducted. It enabled me to be relieved of teaching and administration at the University of Edinburgh in order to read in archives in Russia. Preliminary research in Moscow that earlier enabled me to formulate the ESRC grant proposal was funded by the Travel and Research Committee of Edinburgh University and the Carnegie Trust for the Universities of Scotland. Subsequent trips to pursue more focused lines of inquiry in archives and to tie up loose ends were financed again by the Carnegie Trust and the British Academy.

Most of the sources upon which this book is based were found in Russia. Special thanks are due to archivists in GARF, RGAE, RGASPI, TsKhDMO, and TsGA RSFSR and to librarians in INION, the Russian State Library, and the State Public History Library. Galina Gorskaia in RGASPI, Elena Tiurina in RGAE, and Galina Tokareva in the former TsKhDMO merit gratitude for their backing and interest. Holdings in the libraries of the University of Glasgow and of CREES, University of Birmingham, provided useful Soviet secondary sources, Stakhanovites' autobiographies, and the Smolensk archive. I am also pleased to thank most warmly the women of the Vladimir Il'ich Collective Farm for their lively responses to my questions about life and work in the 1930s and after.

As a social scientist venturing into the conventional territory of historians, I especially valued indispensable feedback, critical comments, and advice from colleagues in the field. Bill Rosenberg and Lynne Viola gave extensive advice on the entire manuscript, offered wise reflections, and posed stimulating questions. I owe special thanks to them both. I am also grateful to Maureen Perrie and Sue Bridger for reading the entire penultimate draft, to Bob

Davies for commenting on selected chapters, to Wendy Goldman for thoughts on a related paper, and to Ian Blanchard for feedback on one section. I am particularly indebted to Bob Davies for prompting me to think about questions that were hard to answer and tempting to avoid. Mention is also due to Malcolm Anderson who labored to read an early draft far outside his general field of interest and to John Holloway for remarks on two chapters. Gerry Smith suggested sensible translations of eight words pertaining to rural life, particularly to dung, which were not found in dictionaries. I also wish to record thanks to those anonymous reviewers who made constructive suggestions.

More diffuse comments and advice, but nonetheless indispensable, were provided at seminars and conferences. Papers on the material of this book were given in the 1990s and into the new century at the University of Bath; CREES, University of Birmingham; at two annual conferences of BASEES in Cambridge; at the University of Strathclyde; in the History and Politics Departments at Edinburgh University; at the fifth and sixth ICCEES Conferences in Warsaw and Tampere; at St. Antony's College, Oxford; at the University of Durham; at a Russian studies conference at the University of Aberdeen; at a World Congress on Stalinism in Sigriswil, Switzerland; and at CamCREES, University of Cambridge.

Warm thanks are also due to the Centre for Research in the Arts, Social Sciences, and Humanities (CRASSH), of the University of Cambridge, for kindly hosting me from April to June 2004 on one of its nine-week Visiting Fellowships during which I put the finishing touches to this book whilst working on human trafficking. For its hugely welcoming atmosphere, professionalism and fun to be in, I am grateful to Ludmilla Jordanova, John Morrill, David Feldman, and the other visiting fellows. To Hughes Hall, particularly to Peter Richards, I owe thanks for an ongoing visiting fellowship.

Among those who in small ways pointed me in productive directions or who triggered elaboration of given points are Lynne Attwood, John Barber, Terry Cox, V. P. Danilov, Peter Gatrell, Michael Kaser, Hans Löwe, Maia Pankratova, Richard Stites, Stephen Wheatcroft, Mariia Zezina, and Iurii Zhukov. I am indebted to them all for their remarks and helpful suggestions, many of which probably seemed obvious to them at the time and have most likely been long forgotten. Needless to say, I alone am responsible for the arguments, flaws, and mistakes in this book.

Some of the material cited here has been published elsewhere: "*Krest'yanskaya gazeta* and Rural Stakhanovism" in *Europe-Asia Studies* 46, no. 8 (December 1994): 1387–1407; "Was Rural Stakhanovism a Movement?" in *Europe-Asia Studies* 51, no. 2 (March 1999): 299–314; "Why Be a Shock Worker or a Stakhanovite?" in *Women in Russia and Ukraine*, ed. Rosalind Marsh (Cambridge: Cambridge University Press, 1996), 199–213; and "Categorising Resistance to Rural Stakhanovism," in *Politics and Society under the Bolsheviks*, eds. Kevin McDermott and John Morison (London: Macmillan, 1999), 160–88. I am grateful to editors and publishers at Taylor and Francis, CUP, and Macmillan for kind permission to use selected published material.

This book was inevitably long in the making. It required numerous visits to Russia, slow work in archives and libraries (with much written out by hand), and a sifting of multiple sources at a time when I was writing more about the Russian present than about the Russian past. I firmly believe that all periods of Russian history teach us about others, whether looking backward or forward; yet although multiple projects enrich each other, they nonetheless slow the larger ones down. Final thanks on the text are due to John King of Essex for his expertise in converting twenty-six Amstrad disks to personal computer.

Fond debts are owed to good friends for humoring my endless reflections on Russian peasants or for simply being there when I needed them. I am delighted to thank Peter Aeberli, Rosalind Bieber, Barbara Buckley, Martin and Ruth Clark, Sally Cummings, Phil and Peggy Dallman, Andrea Davies, Linda Downey, Giovanni Favata, Barbara Heldt, Riitta Haino, Richard Harding, Bob and Rowena Harrison, Craig and Claire Ihara, Paul Key, Sue Laurence, Alena Ledeneva, Natasha Lindemann, Jackie Little, Ulla Öhse, Gillian Maskens, Betty Mitchell, Cathy Porter, Anne and Ramon Prasad, Brenda Rowe, Jennifer Somerville, John Smith, Meg Trott, Fergus, Irene, and Mary Whitty, and Mariia Zezina. I am also immensely grateful to Susan McEachern and Jessica Gribble at Rowman and Littlefield for making the editorial process so pleasant through their enthusiasm, efficiency, and positive approach. Thanks should also be recorded to Janine Osif of the graphics team for her superb work, to Molly Ahearn as production editor, and to David Luljak for compiling the index.

For their kind, loyal, and generous friendships over the decades, this book is dedicated to Andrea Davies, Linda Downey, Paul Key, Brenda Rowe, Jennie Somerville, and Fergus Whitty.

Introduction

"We must go forward, all the time forward. Everyone who this year gave 500 tsentners per hectare will next year give 600 and those who gave 400 must give 500. We must bombard the country with sugar."

—Mariia Demchenko[1]

Eighteen years after the Bolshevik revolution, fourteen years after the end of the civil war between Reds and Whites, eleven years after Lenin's death, six years after the assault on the Soviet countryside to collectivize and transform agriculture, almost two years after the grim famine of 1932–1933, two years into the Second Five-Year Plan, and just months before the Great Purge of 1936–1938, a twenty-two-year-old peasant from the Comintern collective farm in Kiev oblast, Ukraine, called Mariia Safronovna Demchenko, stood up in November 1935 at a special gathering in the Kremlin and, in the words quoted above, urged those working in sugar beet to step up their pace and to bombard the country with sugar.[2]

This book sets out to introduce the neglected story of rural shock work and Stakhanovism of the latter part of the 1930s and early 1940s and to analyze its relevance for Soviet subjects, society, state, and propaganda. It presents a variegated picture of patterns of rural life which includes tales of peasants like Mariia Demchenko, heroines and heroes of Stalin's fields, who progressed in status from shock workers to Stakhanovites, were glorified in ideology and blazoned in the press as role models for others to emulate. Alongside these peasants who became icons of politically correct behavior, keen to participate in what leaders saw as the drive to modernize agriculture, were peasants who worked at average rates and also some rural villains who were either indifferent to Stakhanovisn or who mocked, belittled, threatened, and

1

harmed Stakhanovites. How Stakhanovism was received by peasants varied, as did reactions to it from local party organizations, collective farm chairpersons, and state farm directors. How high Stakhanovites aspired, whether they kept on course, and why, was not uniform either.

The general aim here is to capture something of the atmosphere surrounding rural Stakhanovism on farms, in conference settings, and on movie screens, to explore its packaging as "news" in editorial offices, and to discuss its handling within political structures from the Politburo and Central Committee party departments all the way down to the local party, procuracy, farm leadership, and families. The book explores the complexities of rural Stakhanovism by probing behind the ideological lines and jubilant cries of the movement's resounding successes into mechanisms of mobilization, backing, and criticism.

Study of rural Stakhanovism as a developing movement offers us a window onto the Soviet rural fabric of the late 1930s and its "cultural filters."[3] It reveals patterns of aspiration, personal sculpting, reaction, adaptation, accommodation, evasion, resistance, and challenge in response to exhortations, party orders, and ideological fanfare and also shows the party's developing feedback. It highlights tensions and consistencies within official policy as well as enthusiasm and conflicts in the countryside.

SHOCK WORKERS AND STAKHANOVITES

Mariia Demchenko, shown in Figure 1, was the famous instigator of the movement of 500ers (*piatisotnytsy*) in sugar beet, triggered at the Second All-Union Congress of Collective Farm Shock Workers held in February 1935. At this grand occasion in Moscow, Demchenko publicly pledged to Stalin that she would harvest 500 tsentners of sugar beet per hectare.[4] In November 1935, when successful 500ers came to Moscow to celebrate their achievements, Demchenko at the podium again called for targets to increase still further.

These hardworking 500ers were also known as shock workers, or *udarniki*. Shock workers fulfilled obligations over and above work assignments. They were diligent peasants on their farms who met targets and exceeded them. By early 1936, many former shock workers, like Demchenko, had become Stakhanovites, or *stakhanovtsy*, a status superior to that of shock worker. Although the difference between the two was sometimes rather blurred in the countryside, Stakhanovism officially surpassed shock work since it was defined as a movement to encourage maximum productivity, generally aided by technology. The achievements were meant to be greater and more dramatic — a Stakhanovite was a shock worker par excellence. Stakhanovites were sup-

Figure Intro.1. Mariia Demchenko after becoming a Deputy of the Supreme Soviet of the USSR. Source: *Adapted from* Krest'ianka, *no. 23–24, December 1939, p. 13.*

posed to produce much more than other peasants and shock workers, whether of sugar beet, cabbages, cotton, flax, milk, piglets, or lambs. Stakhanovites were lauded as shining examples of inspiration and dedication who imparted appropriate "lessons" to others in how to work better, whether through devising new feeding techniques, treating the soil better, developing a special understanding of their cows' needs, or through plowing in a more systematic way. Agricultural research institutes studied the labor patterns of individual Stakhanovites in great detail and compiled numerous papers and reports on those techniques worth emulating. A bureaucracy of "studying Stakhanovism" began to develop and with it a massive literature of statistical reports that both reflected and fed into attempts to radically reorganize and modernize the countryside.

For students of Soviet society and politics, the term "Stakhanovite" does not immediately conjure up pictures of sugar beet growers, milkmaids, shepherds, or cotton pickers. Rather, it triggers images of miners, like Aleksei

Stakhanov after whom the movement was named, and engine drivers, car workers, and textile workers such as Petr Krivonos, Aleksandr Busygin, and Mariia and Evdokiia Vinogradova. This is because Stakhanovism began in industry in August 1935, was most widespread in industry, and has mainly been discussed in Western literature in terms of its relevance to heavy industry, with minimal attention paid to its role in the retail trade and to its consequences inside labor camps.[5]

In fact, with mixed results, Stakhanovism spread to the countryside too and to other sectors. Rural Stakhanovism began in late 1935 as an imitator of industrial Stakhanovism. Its scope, characteristics, and problems took on distinctive features, however, which merit examination. Officially rural Stakhanovism embraced all aspects of farming, from grain and sugar beet to pig rearing. It was defined according to the amount per hectare of any crop gathered, the number of pigs born, the number which survived, the amount of milk produced from a given cow, or the size of the area plowed by a tractor in a given time. Careful preparation for work and speed were among its propagandized hallmarks, official prerequisites of good and exponential results— usually measured in quantity.

By 1936 Demchenko was but one name among many to see her own records outstripped. Khristina Baidich and Ekaterina Androshchuk in Ukraine soon overtook her and were promising 600 tsentners per hectare, themselves beaten by Anna Khoshevaia who instigated the "700ers" (*semisotnitsy*).[6] A year later, keeping up the momentum in true Stakhanovite style, Baidich (shown in Figure 2) and Androshchuk became "1,000ers" or *tysiachniki*.[7]

Figure Intro.2.   " In the kolkhoz fields of Vinnitsa oblast a struggle is waging for a large harvest. This is the link of Khristina Baidich which is fighting for 1,000 tsentners of sugar beet per hectare." Baidich is on the extreme right in the photograph. Source: Adapted from Krest'ianka, no. 13, May 1936, p. 11.

Consistent with this picture, the press portrayed a dynamic momentum of escalating achievements in rural output. Demchenko's followers were affectionately called *demchenkovtsy*.[8] Reporters described the "500ers," "700ers," and "1,000ers" in sugar beet spreading from Ukraine into Kursk and Voronezh oblasts in Russia. Their achievements met the regime's aim of higher food production through large-scale agriculture to overcome famines.

In all sectors of agriculture, shock workers and Stakhanovites were lauded by the regime and glorified in propaganda. In dairying, the press praised Natal'ia Tereshkova, Mariia Epp, and Elizaveta Kuz'menkova and depicted the Stakhanovite milkmaids Nadezhda Persiantseva and Ekaterina Nartova as "initiators" of "the All-Union movement of milkmaid-3,000ers" (*vsesoiuznoe dvizhenie doiarok-3 tysiachnits*).[9] In combine harvesting and in tractor driving, famous Stakhanovite names included Fëdor Kolesov, Konstantin Borin, Aleksandr Os'kin, Petr Gusev, Praskov'ia (Pasha) Angelina, and Dar'ia Garmash.[10] Those who emulated Kolesov and Gusev became known as the *kolesovtsy* and *gusevtsy*.[11] Other role models with acclaim were Vladimir Zuev and Tat'iana Daeva in pig rearing, Faizulla Iunusov and Mamlakat Nakhangova in cotton, and Evdokiia Iufereva and Alexandra Smertina in flax.[12] Anna Masonova and Klavdiia Epikhina were heroines of the potato fields and Ermolai Iudin became a renowned Stakhanovite shepherd.[13] Each sector of agriculture had its heroines or heroes, or both—official icons of the fields.

THE LITERATURE ON STAKHANOVISM

Notwithstanding a reasonably substantial Soviet literature on rural Stakhanovism, and despite the party's very loud efforts to extend Stakhanovism from the cities into rural areas, the topic has rarely been discussed in the West. This relative silence is partly due to a long-standing preoccupation with developments of the early 1930s in the countryside, namely collectivization and famine. The impact of collectivization on the countryside was immense and its consequences in the short-term horrific and far-reaching, meriting serious attention. R. V. Davies, Moshe Lewin, Robert Conquest, Sheila Fitzpatrick, and Lynne Viola have written seminal works addressing its economic, political, and social aspects.[14] And for considerable time, many historical silences about the second half of the 1930s persisted since, until recently, available primary sources were thin. Writing before the Gorbachev era, Jerry Hough bemoaned that the Stalin years had become "the neglected orphan of political scientists," leading to a deterioration in understanding of its subperiods.[15] Over the last fifteen years, the opening of the archives has resulted in a burst of fresh scholarship on the purges, the forced labor system, building Magnitogorsk, criminal law, popular opinion, daily life, private diaries, memoirs, and youth culture.[16]

Regarding the countryside, Sheila Fitzpatrick's *Stalin's Peasants* has covered the entire decade by looking at rural life after collectivization. Her focus is on different strategies that peasants adopted to cope with state-inflicted policies. Fitzpatrick argues that peasants adopted ideas about what the "minimum requirements of kolkhoz life must be" and that the 1930s can be understood as a "process of pushing and pulling as the various interested parties strove to define the kolkhoz to serve their purposes."[17] Drawing on the field of peasant studies more generally, Eric Hobsbawm, James C. Scott, and David Moon have held that peasants adopt low-profile techniques such as foot-dragging, evasion, false compliance, dissembling, feigned ignorance, lying, slander, and sabotage in order to reap "minimum disadvantage" from the system.[18] "Weapons of the weak" across peasant societies are various and generally include willful poor work and a refusal to overstrain.[19] Fitzpatrick, however, views rural Stakhanovism as a form of "active accommodation," a strategy through which some peasants embraced the new system and participated in approved positions of responsibility.[20]

The literature on Stakhanovism concerning heavy industry has prompted huge debates about whether Stakhanovism was effective or disruptive, whether it raised productivity or instead led to breakdown. Alexander Baykov, Alec Nove, Joseph Berliner, Solomon Schwarz, Francesco Benvenuti, Donald Filtzer, and others have been preoccupied with whether output increased or fell.[21] More recently, R. W. Davies and Oleg Khlevnyuk have argued that Stakhanovism did "not achieve a substantial change in economic performance" since output per worker before September 1935 was increasing rapidly anyway. In their view, the economic effects of Stakhanovism were "quite short-lived."[22] Debates among Filtzer, Vladimir Andrle, and Lewis Siegelbaum have also included questions concerning the creation of a privileged caste of industrial workers, workers' relations with management, labor discipline, and workers' harnessing of technology.[23] Whilst retaining the emphasis on industrial productivity, Siegelbaum's work broadened analysis to include cultural mythology, the process of "making" Stakhanovites, and the question of whether Stakhanovism was encouraged from above, inspired from below, or at a minimum nonetheless redefined and shaped from below.[24]

Here I argue that the dynamic of the Stakhanovite movement was set neither wholly "from above" nor "from below." The apex of the system interacted with multiple levels beneath it, simultaneously dependent upon them whilst attempting to direct them. At the lowest level of the system on the ground—the peasant—I contend that although some aspects of peasants' behavior were heavily reliant upon party sanction, nonetheless the party needed enthusiasm and initiative from below for a movement to grow at all. Without some keen peasants and willing farm leaders prepared to encourage and facilitate increases in output, rural Stakhanovism would have been impossible, whatever the desires of party leaders.

This book does not pivot around the question of whether output was systematically increased across regions and across agricultural sectors due to shock work and Stakhanovism, although the issue of productivity is briefly discussed. Rather, it focuses on the relevance of rural Stakhanovism to the daily life of peasants, to central and local politics, and to the propaganda machine. It is, however, worth noting that the potential for success in the fields was in many ways considerably less than on the shop floor due to rural conditions, environmental factors, and recent rural history. The distinctive features of rural shock work and Stakhanovism and the problems resulting from them must be understood in this context.

Viola has portrayed the harshness of grain procurements and collectivization as a "civil war" which "tried to transform the peasantry into a cultural and economic colony," and Fitzpatrick has dubbed collectivization a "second serfdom" which sought to eradicate "peasant culture and independence."[25] Mark Tauger has challenged them both on the grounds that collectivization was a reform to modernize rather than an attack, that peasant responses cannot be reduced to "resistance," and that there were significant differences between serfdom and collectivization.[26] Whichever perspective the reader finds most convincing, it remains to be explained how, why, and with what significance Stakhanovites arose in the aftermath of radical changes wrought to agriculture and rural life. This book asks what motivated Stakhanovites to be loyal to a state which had destroyed the peasant commune and traditional patterns of life.

GUIDING QUESTIONS, ORGANIZATION, AND ASSUMPTIONS

The chapters that follow pose a series of interrelated questions. Chapter one asks what were the main features of the agricultural, industrial, political, and social context in which rural Stakhanovism arose. This is an essential backdrop for understanding the nature of the mobilization. Chapter two moves on to examine the official version of how rural Stakhanovism began and how it was encouraged, as defined by institutions at the apex of the party and state. Study of archival documents and the press indicates what was said about

Stakhanovism, by whom, in which institution, to what audience, at which administrative level, when, and with what significance.

The weighty propaganda machine of the state socialist system constructed, packaged, and transmitted images, messages, and cues about Stakhanovism to its people through the media and popular movies. Chapter three asks what sort of images of rural Stakhanovites were projected in the press and in films, and chapter four looks more closely at the pressures editors put on rural correspondents in order to shape their articles. Study of rejection letters from editors at *Krest'ianskaia gazeta* (*Peasant Newspaper*) to reporters in the countryside enables us to see why stories were turned down, the reasons given, and the advice proffered. Chapter five goes on to explore what sort of Stakhanovite "lessons" were imparted in the press and asks why the agricultural research institutes gathered extensive information about Stakhanovism.

Rural society reacted to the exhortations, images, and lessons delivered to it in various ways. From an examination of procuracy reports, chapter six categorizes different forms of resistance to Stakhanovism on the farm, ranging from gossip through to threats and violence. Chapter seven carries on the theme of how Stakhanovites were treated by scrutinizing how farm leaders responded to them and suggests why heterogeneous patterns obtained. It also discusses the nature of agitprop mechanisms between newspaper editors, peasants, procuracy, party, and secret police that tried to press local organizations to investigate peasants' complaints. It was not always easy for collective farm chairpersons and state farm directors to give Stakhanovites the preferential treatment that they needed in order to fill their production pledges. Chapter eight assesses the actual conditions on the farm that inhibited or deterred Stakhanovism, ranging from insufficient feed to drunkenness.

If some peasants reacted negatively to Stakhanovites and if not all farm leaders were well-disposed to them, or able to help them, why did peasants aspire to Stakhanovite status? Chapter nine discusses what motivated Stakhanovites and chapter ten looks specifically at what led women to take this path and asks what significance this had for gender hierarchies in the countryside. Roberta T. Manning has already made the point that the majority of rural Stakhanovites were women, possibly as many as 80 percent in some districts.[27] In sectors such as milking this predominance was inevitable given that women performed the work. The chapter discusses what effect this had on local attitudes and on what Sheila Fitzpatrick calls "the balance of privilege."[28]

Chapter eleven tackles the thorny question of the broader significance of rural Stakhanovism and debates whether it was success or mere fiction. It examines various criteria of "success," taking into account peasants' aspirations, the number of Stakhanovites, and the size and spread of the movement. It indicates that the concentration of Stakhanovites varied across farms and districts, as did enthusiasm for socialist competitions. There were clear "success" stories, as well as failures, indicating a mixed picture across a huge landmass.

These tasks are predicated upon the assumption that there is an interaction between the system, its institutions, the sites of its propaganda, social contexts, and citizen/subject. I take subjects under Stalinism to be shaped by historical, political, ideological, social, cultural, geographical, generational, gender, and personality contexts and also to react to them, being actors as well as objects, agents as well as recipients (despite the constricted official spaces available for participation in a one-party repressive authoritarian state). It is worth noting that some subjects in the 1930s, however, had greater proximity to officials, party, and agitprop, and were more touched by them, than others. Genadii Andreev-Khomiakov's memoir reminds us that "In the steppe town, we could at times forget about the Party and the Party only occasionally remembered itself."[29] Moreover, among those with proximity, some were keener than others to embrace ideology and to become communist persons. I begin by assuming a diversity of subject within social classes and across gender divides.

By interaction, however, I do not mean that a situation of free-bargaining or unmediated negotiation took place. The notion of "negotiation" under Stalinism is found in some recent writings and semantically connotes a willing dialogue on the part of those involved, with a defined agenda, to reach an amicable settlement. Often no dialogue took place and outcomes were not always willingly reached. The interaction I refer to concerns administrative orders or decisions made in one part of the system, be it Politburo or the People's Commissariat of State Farms, transmitted to other parts, such as local parties, newspaper editors, or farm leaders. These latter parts interact with that order by following it, partially implementing it, ignoring it, or knowingly avoiding it. In turn, the initiators of the order respond to the range of reactions received. Over time, a process unfolds of multiple interactions that generate the contours of rural Stakhanovism. The movement was not static but evolving. So whilst some negotiations may have taken place on the farm over given issues, the broader picture of rural change and continuity was one which developed through sets of interacting behaviors and actions rather than through a series of agreements. In his study of the attempted Stolypin Land Reform of 1905–1914, George L. Yaney also argues that what unfolded in fact "emerged" from "interactions between officials and peasants in the countryside" rather than from the "guidance" of political leaders.[30]

The motivations of the actors involved with Stakhanovism varied at different points of the system and there was also diversity of drive within each level.

Political actors and subjects often had different priorities, interests, and understandings of what was the best way to proceed. A *prikaz* (order) from the Commissariat of State Farms on desired Stakhanovite output in sugar beet meant that those in the apex of state bureaucracy wanted the sugar beet harvest to exceed previous levels by a given amount. How state farm directors received and responded to this order depended upon a range of factors: whether enough keen peasants might step up their pace of work; whether the harvest might be a good one, partly linked to environmental factors such as climatic conditions that year and insect infestation; whether there was sufficient fertilizer and fuel; and whether the director himself was efficient, had respect from the peasants and was not a drunkard. Similarly, how individual peasants, took up the call to sculpt their actions into shock work or Stakhanovism depended upon their beliefs about work, upon whether or not they were ambitious, upon whether they believed the effort was possible or worth it, upon the reactions of other local peasants, upon the exhortations of the *politotdel* (political department), and also upon the character of their farm director.

Notwithstanding tenacious uniformities in the oppressive one-party Stalinist state, particularly in ideological messages and official party orders, quite what developed on the ground was not always predictably shaped, willingly malleable, or identical across farms, districts, or regions. Nor were peasants necessarily cognizant of what was "meant" to be happening. The peasantry was not homogeneous, and its members defined "self-interest" in different ways. As agents of change as well as recipients of policy, peasants behaved in ways most acceptable to them, which may or may not have matched party priorities or coincided with the views of farm leaders. The unintended consequences of policies were often more important to outcomes in the countryside than what was officially intended. One central argument is that several reactions to Stakhanovism developed which cannot easily be reduced to univariate explanations.

Because different actors in the story of rural Stakhanovism had interests and motivations and attempted to act in accordance with what was best for them as they understood it, it does not follow that I am referring here to a rampant "individualism." Russian society before 1917 and after was one of deeply entrenched collective values, quite distinct from the liberal individualism of North America where notions of "liberty" are arguably their most unfettered.[31] I make this point since one strand in recent scholarship of the USSR holds that individualism in this looser sense was developing. I prefer to argue that indeed individuals had dreams, goals, and fears, but that the political and social context in which they existed set the parameters of what was conceivable and possible. Individuals did of course have a "subjectivity" but depending upon proximity to propaganda and state control mechanisms, this was a not a liberal "freedom to" as described by Isaiah Berlin.[32]

The 1930s have been variously interpreted as years of continued revolution, consolidation of revolution, interrupted revolution, betrayed revolution, retreat from revolution, and civil war against the peasantry. Whichever characterization the reader finds most plausible, one conclusion remains steadfast. Rural Stakhanovism in this context was perceived by leaders as functional to the regime's stated goals, whatever its results. They perceived it as consistent with attempts to advance the state of agriculture, to increase productivity in order to guarantee more food, and to mobilize citizens around heroic goals. Stakhanovism as "idea" was integral to the perceived logic and momentum of massive transformations, both urban and rural, that occurred during the 1930s; however, Stakhanovism in practice approximated this idea in differing degrees across farms. The notion of Stakhanovism enjoyed some coherence in its official images; yet its realities, however, both coincided and clashed with official claims.

Thus my central contention is that rural Stakhanovism was a movement that was shaped by numerous interactions between national leaders, local officials, directors of machine tractor stations, collective farm chairpersons, state farm directors, newspaper editors, reporters, procuracy, and peasants on the ground. The processes that unfolded were the result of the relationship between policies and exhortations emanating from the party machine and their interpretation and implementation in the countryside. Among the interpreters were peasants and local leaders who variously supported rural Stakhanovism, partially backed it, ignored it, ridiculed it, or resisted it.

Stalinism can be usefully viewed as a "system in motion." It initiated policies and movements within a particular socioeconomic and political context, but in so doing needed the participation of local leaders, farm leaderships, and peasants. Thus how the movement performed on the ground depended to a large extent on the input of those involved in it and on the nature of reactions. The challenge for the regime lay in its unexpected results. Although opposition to Stakhanovism could be stamped on by the regime as going against official party policy, the criticisms made by Stakhanovites themselves were trickier to deal with since they were being expressed within newly permitted discourses. In short, their voices had been given legitimacy by the official policies that had created them.

Through using an interpretive approach, this book sets out to appraise ideological lines on rural Stakhanovism, to assess the reality which leaders and Stakhanovites confronted and created, and to capture something of the atmospheres in which they existed.

NOTES

1. "Priem kolkhoznits-udarnits sveklovichnykh polei rukovoditeliami partii i pravitel'stva," *Sotsial'isticheskaia Rekonstruktsiia Sel'skogo Khoziaistva*, no. 11, part 5 (November 1935): 15. A tsentner is 100 kilos and a hectare is 2.471 acres.

2. "Priem."

3. Moshe Lewin used "cultural filter" to convey the notion that social systems have their own complex and specific cultures which can reject policies handed down "from above" and redefine them. See his *Making of the Soviet System: Essays in the Social History of Interwar Russia* (London: Methuen, 1985).

4. Valentin Kataev, "Mariia Demchenko," in *V Budniakh Velikikh Stroek: Zhenshchiny-kommunistki geroini pervykh piatiletok*, ed. L. I. Stishova (Moscow: Politizdat, 1986), 295–96; *Kolkhoznitsa*, no. 11–12 (November 1935): 14–15; *Kolkhoznitsa*, no. 3–4 (April 1936): 3; *Krest'ianka*, no. 13 (May 1936): 3; *Krest'ianka*, no. 23–24 (December 1939): 13.

5. For the less discussed topics of Stakhanovites in retail trade and in camps, refer to: Amy E. Randall, " 'Revolutionary Bolshevik Work:' Stakhanovism in Retail Trade," *The Russian Review* 59, no. 3 (July 2000): 425–41; and Anne Applebaum, *Gulag: A History of the Soviet Camps* (London: Allen Lane, 2003), 80. In the camps Stakhanovite inmates received special privileges, extra food, and more clothing.

6. They overtook Demchenko by gathering 539 and 531 tsentners respectively. See *Krest'ianskaia gazeta*, 6 November 1935, 3; *Krest'ianka*, no. 13 (May 1936): 10–11; For the story of Feodora Lopatina, who became a 600er, see *Kolkhoznitsa*, no. 5 (May 1936): 7. The press regularly printed open letters to Mariia Demchenko from those committing themselves to emulating her and to meeting fresh targets. See Anna Gaponenko's open letter in *Kolkhoznitsa*, no. 10 (October 1936): 21.

7. *Krest'ianskaia gazeta*, 14 October 1936, 1.

8. *Krest'ianskaia gazeta*, 22 October 1935, 2.

9. *Sovkhoznaia gazeta*, 3 December 1935, 4; *Sovkhoznaia gazeta*, 8 April 1936, 3; *Krest'ianka*, no. 1 (January 1937): 6–7; A. Kuznetsov, "Geroini kolkhoznogo zhivotnovodstva," *Sotsialisticheskaia Rekonstruktsiia Sel'skogo Khoziaistva*, no. 3, (March 1936): 149. See also *Kolkhoznitsa*, no. 1 (January 1936): 18.

10. For discussions of Fedor Kolesov's achievements, see M. Zubkov, "Chelovek bol'shoi dushi," in *Stakhanovtsy polei: k piatidesiatiletiiu stakhanovskogo dvizheniia* (Moscow: Agropromizdat, 1985), 45–54. On Konstantin Borin see Iu. Kovyrialov, "Sovetskaia vlast' vyrastila," in *Stakhanovtsy polei*, 19–29. For discussion of Aleksandr Os'kin and his brothers, see M. Portnov, "Na trekh 'kitakh'," in *Stakhanovtsy polei*, 30–44. For coverage of Petr Gusev's Komsomol tractor brigade, consult *Krest'ianskaia gazeta*, 6 October 1935, 4. For Pasha Angelina's own story, see P. Angelina, *Liudi Kolkhoznykh Polei* (Moscow and Leningrad: Gosudarstvennoe Izdatel'stvo Detskoi Literatury, 1952). For Dar'ia Garmash's life, refer to Natal'ia Pentiukhova, "Dar'ia Garmash: o samom dorogom," *V Budniakh Velikikh Stroek*, ed. Stishova, 172–82.

11. *Krest'ianskaia gazeta*, 24 October 1935, 3.

12. *Sovkhoznaia gazeta*, 26 October 1935, 1; Azovo-Chernomorskii kraevoi komitet soiuza rabochikh svinovodcheskikh sovkhozov SSSR, *Stakhanovtsy-svinari*

o svoem opyte (Rostov: Kraikom soiuza rabochikh svinosovkhozov, 1936), 37–51; G. Mokshantsev, *"Agrotekhnicheskii opyt stakhanovtsev khlopkovodstva," Sotsialis-ticheskaia Rekonstruktsiia Sel'skogo Khoziaistva*, no. 2 (1936), 165; Iurii Il'inskii, "Iunaia stakhanovka," in *V Budniakh Velikikh Stroek*, ed. Stishova, 181; *Krest'ian-skaia gazeta*, 14 December 1935, 3; *Krest'ianskaia gazeta*, 22 September 1936, 1. See also Ia Pelve, G. Skliarov, and I. Meleshkevich, "Opyt stakhanovstev l'novodstva— vsem l'novodnym kolkhozam," *Sotsialisticheskaia Rekonstruktsiia Sel'skogo Khozi-aistva*, no. 9 (September 1938): 56–64.

13. *Krest'ianskaia gazeta*, 26 November 1935, 1; *Krest'ianskaia gazeta*, 16 Octo-ber 1936, 2; *Stakhanovtsy Ovtsesovkhozov o svoei rabote* (Rostov: Izdanie TsK soiuza rabochikh ovtsevodcheskikh sovkhozov SSSR, 1936), 7–18.

14. R. W. Davies, *The Socialist Offensive: The Collectivization of Soviet Agricul-ture, 1929–1930* (London: Macmillan, 1980) and his *The Soviet Collective Farm, 1929–1930* (London: Macmillan, 1980); Moshe Lewin, *Russian Peasants and Soviet Power: A Study in Collectivization* (London: George Allen and Unwin, 1968); Robert Conquest, *Harvest of Sorrow: Soviet Collectivization and the Terror-Famine* (Lon-don: Hutchinson, 1986); Lynne Viola, *The Best Sons of the Fatherland: Workers in the Vanguard of Soviet Collectivization* (New York: Oxford University Press, 1987) and her *Peasant Rebels Under Stalin: Collectivization and the Culture of Peasant Resis-tance* (New York: Oxford University Press, 1996).

15. Jerry Hough and Merle Fainsod, *How the Soviet Union Is Governed* (Cam-bridge, MA: Harvard University Press, 1982), 147.

16. Edwin Bacon, *The Gulag at War: Stalin's Forced Labour System in the Light of the Archives* (London: Macmillan, 1996); J. Arch Getty and Roberta Manning, eds., *Stalinist Terror: New Perspectives* (New York and Cambridge: Cambridge University Press, 1993); Stephen Kotkin, *Magnetic Mountain: Stalinism as a Civilization* (Berkeley and Los Angeles: University of California Press, 1995); Peter H. Solomon Jr., *Soviet Criminal Justice Under Stalin* (Cambridge: Cambridge University Press, 1996); Sarah Davies, *Popular Opinion in Stalin's Russia: Terror, Propaganda and Dissent, 1934–1941* (Cambridge: Cambridge University Press, 1997); Sheila Fitz-patrick, *Everyday Stalinism: Ordinary Life in Extraordinary Times: Soviet Russia in the 1930s* (New York: Oxford University Press, 1999); Jochen Hellbeck, "Fashioning the Stalinist Soul: The Diary of Stepan Podlubnyi (1931–1939)," *Jahrbücher für Geschichte Osteuropas*, 44, Heft 3 (1996): 344–73. Jochen Hellbeck, "Working, Struggling, Becoming: Stalin-Era Autobiographical Texts," *The Russian Review* 60, no. 3 (July 2001): 34–59; Igal Halfin, *Terror in My Soul: Communist Autobiographies on Trial* (Cambridge, MA: Harvard University Press, 2003); Veronique Garros, Na-talia Korenevskaya, and Thomas Lahusen, eds., *Intimacy and Terror: Soviet Diaries of the 1930s* (New York: The New Press, 1995); Sheila Fitzpatrick, ed., *Stalinism: New Directions* (London and New York: Routledge, 2000); Amir Weiner, "Nature, Nurture, and Memory in a Socialist Utopia: Delineating the Soviet Socio-Ethnic Body in the Age of Socialism," *The American Historical Review*, 104 no. 4 (October 1999), 1114–55. Juliane Fürst, "Prisoners of the Soviet Self?: Political Youth Opposition in Late Stalinism," *Europe-Asia Studies* 54, no. 3 (May 2002), 353–76. Among the many outpourings in Russian are: L. Viola, T. Macdonald, S. V. Zhuravlev, and A. N.

Mel'nik, *Riazanskaia Derevnia v 1929–1930gg: Khronika Golovokruzheniia* (Moscow and Toronto: Rosspen, 1998); A. K. Sokolov, ed., *Obshchestvo i Vlast' 1930-e gody* (Moscow: Rosspen, 1998); Elena Osokina, *Za Fasadom "Stalinskogo Izobiliia"* (Moscow: Rosspen, 1998).

17. Sheila Fitzpatrick, *Stalin's Peasants: Resistance and Survival in the Russian Village after Collectivization* (New York: Oxford University Press, 1994), 8–13.

18. Eric Hobsbawm, "Peasants and Politics," *Journal of Peasant Studies* 1, no. 1 (1973), 3–22; James C. Scott, *Weapons of the Weak: Everyday Forms of Peasant Resistance* (New Haven and London: Yale University Press, 1985); David Moon, *The Russian Peasantry 1600–1930: The World Peasants Made* (London: Longman, 1999), 269–80. Moon usefully distinguishes four main forms of protest: revolt, flight, "disturbances," and everyday resistance. On the last he observes that it was "the hardest to detect, the most limited, the least confrontational, the most difficult to prevent and the one in which peasants' objectives were the lowest." Simultaneously it was "probably the most successful." Moon, *Russian Peasantry*, 269. The methodological dilemma is that the most successful attempts "escape detection."

19. "Weapons of the weak" is a term used by James C. Scott to consider everyday forms of peasant resistance that he sees as the "prosaic but constant struggle between peasantry and those who seek to extract labour, food, taxes, rents and interest from them." He argues that peasant rebellions are rare and that "low-profile techniques" of this subordinate class merit attention. See his *Weapons of the Weak*, xv–xix.

20. Fitzpatrick, *Stalin's Peasants*, 10.

21. Alexander Baykov, *The Development of the Soviet Economic System: An Essay on the Experience of Planning in the USSR* (Cambridge: Cambridge University Press, 1947); Alec Nove, *An Economic History of the USSR* (Harmondsworth: Penguin, 1969); Joseph Berliner, *Factory and Manager in the USSR* (Cambridge, MA: Harvard University Press, 1957); Solomon M. Schwartz, *Labor in the Soviet Union* (London: The Cresset Press, 1953); Leonid E. Hubbard, *Soviet Labor and Industry* (London: Macmillan, 1942); Francesco Benvenuti, "Stakhanovism and Stalinism, 1934–1938," *Soviet Industrialisation Project Series*, no. 30, CREES discussion paper; Donald Filtzer, *Soviet Workers and Stalinist Industrialisation: the Formation of Modern Soviet Production Relations, 1928–1941* (London: Pluto, 1986).

22. R. W. Davies and Oleg Khlevnyuk, "Stakhanovism and the Soviet Economy," *Europe-Asia Studies* 54, no. 6 (September, 2002): 867–903. They point out that relatively modest levels of investment in 1933 and 1934, substantially lower than in the First Five-Year Plan, troubled the People's Commissariats. After much pressure, a change in policy took place and the investment plan for 1936 was increased along with the expectation that labor and capital productivity would increase. Leaders were then looking for huge increases in production without further increases in investment.

23. Filtzer, *Soviet Workers*; Vladimir Andrle, *A Social History of Twentieth-Century Russia* (London: Edward Arnold, 1994), 158; Lewis Siegelbaum, *Stakhanovism and the Politics of Productivity* (Cambridge: Cambridge University Press, 1988).

24. Siegelbaum, *Stakhanovism.*

25. Viola, *Peasant Rebels*, preface; Fitzpatrick, *Stalin's Peasants*, 4. For a summary of the origins and nature of serfdom and the literature on it, consult David

Moon, "Reassessing Russian Serfdom," *European History Quarterly* 26, no. 4 (October 1996): 483–526. For fuller treatment, consult the classic J. Blum, *Lord and Peasant in Russia from the Ninth to the Nineteenth Century* (Princeton, NJ: Princeton University Press, 1961).

26. See Mark B. Tauger, "Modernisation in Agriculture," paper delivered at the Conference on Modernization and Russian Society in the Twentieth Century, University of Birmingham, 17–18 October 2003; and his "Soviet Peasants and Collectivization, 1930–1939: Resistance and Adaptation," *Journal of Peasant Studies* 31, nos. 3 and 4 (April and July 2004): 427–56.

27. Roberta T. Manning, "Women in the Soviet Countryside on the Eve of World War II, 1935–1940," in *Russian Peasant Women*, eds. Beatrice Farnsworth and Lynne Viola (New York: Oxford University Press, 1996), 228.

28. Fitzpatrick, *Stalin's Peasants*, 142.

29. Genadii Andreev Khomiakov, *Bitter Waters: Life and Work in Stalin's Russia*, trans. Ann E. Healy (Bolder, CO: Westview, 1977), 41.

30. George. L. Yaney, *The Urge to Mobilize: Agrarian Reform in Russia, 1861–1930* (Urbana: University of Illinois Press, 1982). Yaney discusses how the Stolypin Reform attempted to convert subsistence agriculture into commercial farming, replace patriarchal structures, and redivide the peasants' land. He argues that there was no coherent idea about what officials in the countryside should do to enact it. David Moon summarizes how although the land reforms allowed peasants to leave the commune and to enclose land separately, only a minority in fact left and many peasants tried to stop others from leaving, amid conflict and some disorder. See David Moon, *The Russian Peasantry 1600–1930: The World Peasants Made* (London: Longman, 1999), 350–51.

31. I do not assume that when resistance occurred it was a manifestation of liberal individualism attempting to express itself, as Anna Krylova has accused some of portraying it. See her "The Tenacious Liberal Subject in Soviet Studies," *Kritika* 1, no. 1 (Winter 2000), 119–45. Nor do I assume that collective values existed out of a normative preference for egalitarianism. Rather collectivism as a pattern fit practical necessity, dating back to the village commune. Dorothy Atkinson has stressed, "the concept of equality was cast in material, economic terms." See her "Egalitarianism and the Commune," in *Land Commune and Peasant Community in Russia,* ed. Roger Bartlett (Basingstoke and London: Macmillan, 1990), 7–19. Consult, too, Boris Mironov, "The Russian Peasant Commune after the Reforms of the 1860s," in *The World of the Russian Peasant: Post-Emancipation Culture and Society*, eds. Ben Eklof and Stephen Frank (London: Unwin Hyman, 1990), 7–43; and Judith Pallot, ed., *Transforming Peasants: Society, State and Peasantry, 1861–1930* (Basingstoke and London: Macmillan, 1998).

32. Isaiah Berlin, "Two Concepts of Liberty," in *Political Philosophy,* ed. Anthony Quinton (Oxford: Oxford University Press, 1968), 141–52.

Chapter One

Historical Context

The contours of rural Stakhanovism are better grasped if set in the context of the policies, processes, and outcomes that preceded them. The historical context includes urban famines of 1917–1921, famine in Ukraine in 1928–1929, requisitioning, variable harvests due to environmental factors, collectivization, famine again in 1932–1933, Five-Year Plans, grand mobilizations, Stalin's cult of personality, purges or "cleansings," and political repression. By the onset of Stakhanovism in late 1935, the problems for the regime to tackle in the countryside were still huge, despite rapid economic growth in industry since 1934 and a more stable rural situation.[1] The recent rural past had witnessed dire crisis in agriculture and some resentment, hostility, and weariness among the peasantry. There is controversy among historians about how much rural support there was for collectivization, with arguments ranging from little to none, on to "a determined minority" showing backing, through to the recent contention that resistance has been hugely exaggerated and "was not the most common response."[2] It is tricky to establish precisely the representativeness of support, acceptance, and resistance. Nonetheless, against this broad backdrop, there were serious challenges in rural conditions for those who aspired to be rural Stakhanovites. This chapter briefly considers the main features of the contexts of agriculture, industry, politics, and society.

AGRICULTURAL BACKGROUND

S. G. Wheatcroft and R. W. Davies have discussed how agriculture was in crisis in 1916–1921 and 1930–1933. The famine of 1932–1933 was complex and due to several mutually reinforcing problems, of which collectivization was one.[3] Collectivization began in 1929, a year after the large state farm (*sovetskoe khoziaistvo*, or *sovkhoz*) was set up in eastern regions. Collectivization's full force was unleashed in 1930, although the beginning of a new direction in agrarian policy had earlier been decided at the 15th Party Congress in 1927. According to Davies, Wheatcroft, and others, Stalin had advocated emergency measures in order to address the problem of inadequate grain purchases. Peasants were not selling enough grain to the state, partly because there were fewer consumer goods to purchase with the money earned and partly because the state set low grain prices. David Moon has observed that throughout the 1920s the Soviet government had difficulties meeting its needs for agricultural produce. With no incentives for the peasant to sell grain to the state, the higher prices of the black market were more attractive.[4] In this context, Stalin gave support to the "Ural-Siberian method" according to which local officials seized grain and shut down markets. Triggering much rural unrest, villages were required to meet fixed-price quotas. The hoarding of grain was put down to "kulak sabotage," although as James Hughes has observed, this was "economically rational and logical" given changes in market conditions and prices.[5] In late 1929 Stalin advocated the collectivization of agriculture and called for the liquidation of the kulaks as a class.[6]

A kulak was officially a "rich peasant," as distinct from a "middle peasant" (*seredniak*) and a "poor peasant" (*bedniak*). A secret Central Committee resolution divided the kulaks into three groupings: "counter-revolutionaries" to have all property confiscated and to be prosecuted, then exiled or executed; "exploiters" who were "economically strong" kulaks, guilty of "pitiless exploitation of their neighbors," to be deported but permitted some possessions; and those kulaks who could remain on their land but not join collective farms, thereby subject to partial dekulakization.[7] The first bitter irony of dekulakization was that the regime was disposing of those hardworking peasants who were considered to be the most efficient farmers. The second irony later was that many of the Stakhanovite "lessons" that the regime urged collectivized peasants to emulate were among the work practices so well performed by the liquidated kulak "enemies." Thus a case can be made that the purpose of rural Stakhanovites was to replace the "idea" of kulaks as prosperous and productive peasants, but in a more politically correct guise.[8]

In November 1929, the Central Committee approved collectivization and called for 25,000 urban workers, who became known as the 25,000ers (*dvadtsatipiatitysiachniki*), to launch the campaign. Lynne Viola has argued that the 25,000ers' main purpose was to represent the interests of Moscow "against a rural officialdom perceived to be incompetent, socially alien and politically suspect."[9] The volunteering 25,000ers were meant to bring consciousness to the campaign and to assume leadership roles on collective farms, thereby transferring "proletarian experience" to rural areas.[10] The problems they faced, however, were often intractable, and they were far away from the support of urban militancy and enthusiasm for revolutionary change. The campaign was transformed from "crusade" to a "state of siege" as repression became necessary. The 25,000ers were not the only agents of the state promoting collectivization. Other mobilizations from the towns included members of the party and Komsomol, workers, and students. Key local actors included representatives from district and rural soviets, the local party, and the OGPU (*Ob'edinённoe gosudartsvennoe politicheskoe upravlenie*), or secret police.[11]

In short, collectivization brought a radical transformation of the countryside through a pooling of land, animals, equipment, and labor, often coercive. Dekulakization was one aspect of this process, what Moshe Lewin has described as "a drama of epic proportions," entailing the expropriation of the property, even clothing and boots of rich peasants and their harrowing deportation eastward on "death trains."[12] The victims were not exclusively kulaks since the label was arbitrarily and tragically bestowed. The process was brutal and embarrassingly messy, including a "gold rush" to grab confiscated property, share-outs, settlings of old scores, and waves of suicides among more prosperous peasants.[13] The seized property of the kulaks was meant to go toward starting up the new collective farms, poor peasants thereby benefiting immediately by membership.

The picture on the ground was further complicated by what Moon dubs "self-dekulakization." Some peasants "deliberately impoverished themselves" in order to avoid being branded as kulaks. In these cases, peasants calculated that self-dekulakization "was preferable to the horrors of official policy."[14] These peasants seriously dissembled while others fled their villages, making for towns or moving eastward. Tens of thousands also petitioned the central authorities.[15] Some of the peasant violence was meted out against those who joined the collective farm voluntarily.

Local officials were not given detailed plans on how to go about collectivizing their areas. Fitzpatrick has argued that the lack of adequate instructions was a deliberate strategy "to get local cadres pushing for the absolute maximum." They knew it was better for their own careers "to go too far in collectivizing than not to go far enough" (*"luchshe peregnut', chem nedognut'"*).[16] Their intimidations, threats, and harsh coercion provoked fierce resistance in some areas, including *bab'i bunty* or women's riots, resulting in the militarization of some villages.[17] "Rebellion gripped the countryside," according to Viola, and some 13,000 riots occurred in the 1930s, involving over two million peasants.[18] In an attempt to distance himself from the violence, in

March 1930 Stalin wrote the now famous article titled "Dizzy with Success," which criticized the excesses of what had become a highly brutal process. As a consequence, peasants left the collective farms in large numbers, only to be forced back onto them.[19] Whereas only 3.9 percent of the peasantry was collectivized in 1929, the figure reached 65 percent in 1933 and 93 percent by 1938. The figures are presented in Table 1.1.[20]

The state now promoted two main sorts of farm: collective farms, or *kolkhozy*, and state farms or *sovkhozy*. The main difference between them was that the former were nominally cooperatives and the latter were under the command administrative system, organized on the same principle as factories. This meant that sovkhoz workers, or *sovkhozniki*, were paid wages by the state. By contrast, *kolkhozniki* in a given year received a number of labor days (*trudodni*) calculated according to the task they performed and linked to the output of their own farm. Those working on state farms were called "workers" rather than peasants and were part of the state system of trade unions that collective farmers were not. Between 1929 and 1938, the number of collective farms increased from 57,000 to 242,400.[21] There were fewer state farms, rising from 1,538 in 1929 to 3,961 in 1938.[22]

The machine tractor station, known as the MTS, was also established at this time. It was set up to house all farm machinery and to perform mechanized farm work, in particular tractor driving and combine harvesting, for collective farms. The MTS was meant to ensure that grain would be harvested and delivered to the state, thereby dealing with the problem of grain procurements. The MTS had its own political department, or *politotdel*, to which urban workers and members of the OGPU were sent. At a party plenum in 1933, Lazar' Kaganovich, then a Central Committee Party Secretary, observed, "the head of the MTS political department is simultaneously the deputy director of the MTS for political work."[23] More bluntly, Fitzpatrick has described the *politotdel* as "a new control institution in the countryside."[24] It was in the *politotdel*'s brief to ensure that spring sowing took place and to rid collective farms and local parties of undesirable elements.[25] Machine tractor stations grew in number from 158 in 1930 to 2,916 in 1933 and to 5,617 in 1937.[26]

According to the dominant perspective in the literature, a key reason cited alongside collectivization for the crisis in agriculture was the government's high procurement policies in a broader context of declining agricultural production. Peasants not only resented collectivization, but were angered by the brutality of the system of *zagotovki* or grain procurements. Moshe Lewin has depicted the process of extracting grain from the peasants as a "permanent state of warfare against them" and for peasants "a symbol of arbitrariness and injustice."[27] A spiral of evasion and repression was integral to *zagotovki*. Peasants tried to keep back grain so the regime adopted more repressive tactics and "in many places *zagotoviteli* went berserk," stripping villages of all grain, even grain legitimately earned, thereby condemning peasants to starvation.[28] In 1933, forced grain procurements became "compulsory state duty."[29] Vladimir Andrle has commented that since 1928 grain requisitioning was "relentless," and left "no reserves in the rural stores." Moreover when harvests worsened, "the state's demands did not relax."[30] Industrializing towns had to be fed and grain needed to be exported in order to earn foreign capital, even if this meant death in the countryside.

Decrees of July and August 1932 specified tough grain procurement targets, for Ukraine and the North Caucasus in particular, which included legal sanctions for the confiscation of peasants' grain. Hoarders, whether starving or not, were automatically "enemies of the people," liable to be shot or imprisoned for ten years. Historians have catalogued a range of brutal consequences.[31] Desperate people with swollen limbs ate bread made from nettles, roots, bark, dogs, mice, earthworms, and also horse manure because it contained grains of wheat. There were instances of suicide, murder, and cannibalism. Wherever grain and potatoes piled up, left to rot, the starving were denied access, shot if they attempted to steal.[32] In short, the countryside starved in the name of feeding the towns and boosting industrialization.

In defiance of collectivization and requisitioning, peasants sowed reluctantly and slaughtered their animals rather than share them. Peasants on collective farms pilfered, embezzled, and neglected the maintenance of machinery, all of which were dubbed by the regime as examples of "lack of discipline." Revisiting Russia after collectivization, Maurice Hindus noted how the "kolkhoz" had become "the most storm-stirring word." Older peasants, in particular, "could shout, fume, curse, but they could not dodge the challenge the kolkhoz had thrust on them."[33] Mikhail Sholokhov in *Virgin Soil Upturned* offers a more glossy, socialist realist description of events. Of the slaughter of animals, he reports that the following rumors circulated: "Kill, it's not ours now!" "Kill, they'll take it for the meat collection tax if you don't." "Kill, for you won't taste meat in the collective farm."[34] There was much confusion among officials and peasants about what collectivization really meant and wild rumors held that it heralded the Antichrist, Apocalypse, a return to serfdom, a sharing of women, and foreign invasion.[35]

Against those above who argue that resistance to collectivization was a common response with serious consequences for agriculture, Mark Tauger has suggested that their sources are misleading, unrepresentative, and overlook "*kolkhoz* patriotism." Whilst recognizing the upheaval and violence of collectivization, he suggests that only about 4 percent of the adult rural population protested and that many agreed to join once their misconceptions were dispelled and rumors shown to be unfounded. Tauger also maintains that collectivization as a policy was not designed to exploit agriculture for industrialization nor was it a response to the "grain crisis" of 1927–1929 in which peasants withheld grain from markets. Rather, in his view, Stalin was keen to prevent famines and to minimize the impact of droughts and crop failures by modernizing agriculture to produce more food just as the U.S. secretary of agriculture had been keen to modernize in the 1920s.[36]

Even allowing for this recent challenge to dominant perspectives, which many may contest, one can still hold that the consequences of collectivization and requisitioning were serious and several. First, some of the peasantry, and one cannot give a precise percentage, was angry and/or demoralized, reacting violently or with evasion, passive resistance, and sabotage. Second, the re-luctance to sow and harvest meant in the short-term inadequate grain and fod-der, contributing to famine and lack of animal feed. The number of animals had declined through slaughter and now, too, through starvation. Third, the fall in the number of horses negatively affected traction power and the ability to harvest, a fall which came on top of earlier losses of millions of horses for the Tsarist, Red, and White armies.[37] This situation was compounded by the inadequate availability of tractors in the early 1930s; consequently acres of grain went unharvested in the autumn of 1932. The winter of 1932–1933 was one of cruel famine. Fourth, animal losses meant reductions in manure that, in turn, affected the quality of the soil. It is against this tumultuous back-ground that an understanding of rural Stakhanovism must be set.

THE LEGACY OF COLLECTIVIZATION

In the decade after collectivization, according to Sheila Fitzpatrick, "the dom-inant mood among peasants seemed to be a mixture of resentment, malice, and lethargy."[38] Reaching a similar conclusion, very differently put, is a clas-sic of Soviet historical scholarship. Amid his necessary paragraphs on the achievements of collectivization, M. A.Vyltsan more soberly concluded, "more than one-fifth of collective farmers of working ability participated only 'symbolically.'"[39] In 1937, according to Vyltsan, there were as many as 4,658,000 collective farmers not earning even one "work day" (*trudoden'*) a year and 8,528,000 clocking up between 1 and 50 workdays. This latter group therefore worked for less than one month a year. Around 50 workdays amounted to one-and-a-half months' work. Vyltsan does not argue that col-lectivization caused this pattern. Rather, he linked "weak work discipline" to "inadequate material interest" in the kolkhoz economy and to a desire to do better through individual economic efforts.[40] Implicitly, in this language of Soviet-speak that could not talk openly of failures, loyalty to the collective farm was wanting.

Table 1.2. Percentages of "Workdays" Per Year Across Groupings of Collective Farms

	Collective Farms					
Year	*Up to 50*	*51–100*	*101–200*	*201–300*	*301–400*	*Above 400*	*Total*
1936	22.3%	18.3	26.5	17.4	9.8	5.7	100.00
1937	21.2	15.6	25.0	18.4	11.3	8.5	100.00

Source: Adapted from M. A. Vyltsan, *Zavershaiushchii etap sozdaniia kolkhoznogo stroia* (Moscow: Izdatel'stvo Nauka, 1978), 101.

Table 1.2 shows how only 8.5 percent of collective farm peasantry in 1937 earned over 400 workdays a year. The range of workdays varied, with a quarter of the peasantry acquiring between 101 and 200 a year. Thus across collective farm peasantry there were varied work patterns.

Peasants' efforts, moreover, were also directed toward their private plots. By 1938, private plots constituted 3 percent of farmed land, but had over half the cattle.[41] Whatever peasants grew here, they could sell in collective farmers' markets and thereby boost their meager earnings. The meaning of work on the private plot was significantly different for peasants than the meaning of work for the collective. Self-interest fueled enthusiasm for the former to a degree that it may not have reached for the latter.

It would be incorrect, however, to imply that all peasants were indifferent to work on the farm or that no one benefited. Some peasants definitely did support collectivization and championed Soviet power in the countryside. Moon also notes that a few women welcomed collectivization as a means of escaping the "patriarchal authority of their husbands and fathers" and some younger Red Army veterans sought to leave behind the older generation's hold on them.[42] Moreover, there were variations in the pattern of reaction across the huge landmass.[43] Certainly, poor peasants, once on collective farms, also benefited from the land confiscated from rich peasants. So whilst some middle and rich peasants may have had axes to grind against the regime, the same cannot be said of poor peasants and some middle peasants. The patterns of their lives, nonetheless, had been disrupted, too. Collectivization redefined rural communities, wrenched key decisions away from peasants, and meant a transformation of aspects of rural worlds.

INDUSTRY AND FIVE-YEAR PLANS

The nature of the Five-Year Plans is also relevant to our understanding of the context of Stakhanovism. The New Economic Policy that replaced War Communism in 1921 restored limited market relations between town and countryside. Amid conflict, NEP was abandoned in 1928 in favor of the *pi-atiletka* or Five-Year Plan, touted as the means to catch up with capitalist economies and to outpace them. At a time of war, the importance of autarky and the boosting of heavy industry were accentuated. In a burst of excited revolutionary fervor, competing proposals were put forward for fantastic upwardly spiraling production targets. The frenzied slogan to "fulfill the five-year plan in four years" was part of the whirlpool of excitement. In December 1932, the First Five-Year Plan was declared met. In fact, the wildly ambitious targets had not been reached, although huge advances had been made, albeit with social strain and upheaval, and overload on transport systems and on rapidly growing cities.[44] New and inexperienced industrial labor streamed from rural areas, siphoning men from farms. The Politburo held the view that successful industrial growth needed a collectivized agriculture that would guarantee grain procurements.[45] Thus the two huge projects of industrial and agricultural transformation were linked.

Advances in the countryside, particularly mechanization, also depended upon industrial output. The number of tractors on the MTS went up from 7,100 in 1930 to 356,800 in 1937 and combine harvesters increased from 10,400 in 1933 to 96,300 in 1937. Table 1.3 presents fuller details, including strength in thousand horsepower and the number of trucks.[46] State farms had their own tractors and these rose from 9,700 in 1929 to 85,000 in 1938. Table 1.4 elaborates on the number of state farms, the average yearly number of workers on them, and the number of tractors at the end of 1929, 1933, and 1938.[47] The encouragement of the peasantry, male and female, to take to tractor driving and to produce heroic results was part of this huge mechanization drive. So mechanization and Stakhanovism became linked.

Formally, the Second Five-Year Plan ran from 1933 to 1937, although its third draft was not ratified until January 1934 at the Seventeenth Party Congress. Emphasis fell on mastering technique, improving quality, championing specialists, and consolidating gains already made. In his speech to the congress Stalin attacked "levelling."[48] Hard work was to be rewarded by wage increases. The process of building socialism in one country now explicitly condoned differential pay and hierarchy. In this context, Stakhanovism was born, itself contributing to increases in expected work norms. Divisions arose among workers and peasants, despite propaganda to end "antagonistic" classes. Peasants were now also permitted to keep their own livestock.

R. W. Davies and Oleg Khlevnyuk have suggested that industrial Stakhanovism should also be understood in the context of changed investment levels. In 1934, the People's Commissariats became troubled by lower investment levels in the Second Five-Year Plan in comparison with the First. They pushed for higher levels of production and there was indeed some success, but not enough to meet overall plan targets. A "sharp change in policy" in 1935, after much pressure, resulted in Stalin adopting a much larger investment plan for 1936, opposed by Viacheslav Molotov, then Chairman of the Council of People's Commissars (Sovnarkom), and by Gosplan. Davies and Khlevnyuk hold that this in turn "reinforced the expectation that labor and capital productivity would sharply increase."[49] They interpret Stakhanov's feat as "certainly inspired by the general atmosphere of encouraging the intensification of labor" and cite evidence to indicate that it was not arranged in advance by Stalin and the Politburo in the classic "from above" scenario.[50]

What became known as the "three good years" of 1934 to 1936 were followed by difficulties in 1937. Investment was redirected to defense due to concern about possible war. A hard winter in 1937–1938 caused fuel shortages which negatively affected industrial production, transportation, and distribution. Wreckers were blamed again and this fed into the growing momentum of purges.[51] The Third Five-Year Plan, meant to run from 1938 to 1942, in drafting and execution was "dominated by the lengthening shadows of war."[52] Like the Second plan, it was formally adopted late, this time at the Eighteenth Party Congress in March 1939. Stress fell on industry and defense with further fantastic increases in production.

Whereas Stephen Kotkin views Stalin's projects as the building of a genuine utopia, Leon Trotsky declared that the revolution was now indeed "betrayed" and Nicholas Timasheff held that a "Great Retreat" had begun.[53] With the advent of the Second Five-Year Plan in particular, conservatism and tradition were seen to triumph at the expense of revolutionary effervescence and "cultural revolution."[54] A tightening of divorce laws and a ban on abortion in 1935 and 1936 were consistent with Trotsky's and Timasheff's interpretations.[55]

The introduction of pay differentials and rewards for Stakhanovites' increased output were perceived by critics as consistent with the new "retreat." Among the rewards were presents of bicycles, record players, wristwatches, better accommodation (very selectively provided), invitations to conferences and congresses attended by top leaders, and fame through newspaper publicity. Films of the period glorified industrial and rural shock work and Stakhanovism, portraying labor heroes and heroines as keen to enter socialist competitions, as selfless, honest, kind, and hardworking people, often engaged in weary battles with obstructive managements or backward coworkers and peasants.[56] The loud message was that for their efforts in increasing food production, Stakhanovites merited reward and personal happiness.

Roy Medvedev has observed that hierarchies and inequalities were not new in the 1930s, having been established in the 1920s.[57] Differences in kind, however, can be identified as well as differences in degree. Taken together, the features of the 1930s make the decade sufficiently distinct in nature from that of the 1920s. It is not the place here to rehearse the various shades of argument revolving around whether Stalinism was Bolshevism writ large or a different phenomenon with its own distinguishing features.[58] Suffice to note for our purposes that rural Stakhanovism was embedded in a political setting that now indicated that egalitarianism in wages was undesirable, reward for hard work was acceptable, and that specialists should be respected, not vilified. The system promoted heroes and heroines of production, and gave positive reinforcement for consumerism despite prevailing shortages. Julie Hessler has shown how during the years 1935–1938, "asceticism gave way to cultured consumerism" in which aspirations for consumption became "a new public value" sanctioned by Stalin through his promises of "material benefits."[59] Jukka Gronow has documented how in this period Soviet champagne was introduced amid fanfare, vintage wines and cognac went into production, the chocolate industry enjoyed a rebirth, and Soviet kitsch appeared.[60] In this context, Stakhanovites were pitched as "ideal Soviet consumers."[61]

An official homogeneity in a state of "the whole people," to whom state property now allegedly "belonged," accompanied these trends and was written into the 1936 constitution.[62] Although a "dictatorship of the proletariat" was working toward a "socialist state of workers and peasants," exploiters of the past were no longer disenfranchised and a "uniform citizenship" was declared.[63]

POLITICAL CONTEXT

Fanfare and commitment to a bright future was a crucial dimension of Stalinism. Current "battles" and "struggles" were the "achievements" which cumulatively built toward the final crescendo of communism. Ideology instructed that hard work, endurance, discipline, and direction would guarantee a more moral and superior society in which needs would be met. Citizens were "fighters" for this glittery noble goal. They came together as collectives, involved in parades, campaigns, rallies, and mass events. Citizens were mobilized on particular days to commemorate the anniversary of the Revolution or May Day or organized to participate in socialist competitions in order to increase output. Selected citizens were invited to take part in rallies or conferences attended by top leaders. For Kotkin this was not a retreat from revolution, but rather a crucial part of the building of a new socialist society, a forward-looking civilization. New symbols and language were integral to this genuine utopia, this "progressive modernity," which was able to foster wonder and surprise.[64] For Igal Halfin the new communist person was "equipped with a brand-new identity" which was the "key to the Communist emancipatory project."[65] The self was malleable and those who strove to be party members experienced the Stalinist system by being mobilized and by working on themselves, attempting to sculpt their own souls or subjectivities, as Jochen Hellbeck has described, to show appropriate consciousness.[66] Integral to the eschatology of the system were notions of what was "good" and "evil," "pure" and "impure." Hard-working Stakhanovites were among the good and the pure.

An important part of this ongoing revolution was the Stalinist cult of personality into which Stakhanovism fed. Stakhanovites made work pledges to Stalin, praised Stalin, and thanked him for making life "better and merrier."[67] Censors carefully watched the nature of reporting on Stakhanovism and what Stakhanovites said in public arenas. New narratives developed with Stalin as the "center of public obligation and loyalty," what Jeffrey Brooks has called a "moral economy" of the gift in which the state "was presumed" to dispense the necessary goods and services for which citizens were "tremendously beholden" and "obligated to provide their labor in return."[68] Those who maligned, baited, threatened, or harmed Stakhanovites failed to express these narratives and should, in theory, have been investigated by the party, procuracy, and secret police. These culprits included "enemies of the people" working to undermine the Soviet state and to insult Stalin. A bleak component of this system in motion was the purging of those deemed to undermine the glorious project. From the regime's perspective, however, this amounted to a cleansing of the impure.

Shock work and Stakhanovism were encouraged at a time when the purges had already begun and also been further accelerated after the murder in December 1934 of Sergei Kirov, first secretary of the Leningrad party committee. Moreover, they were about to worsen with the onset of the "Great Purge" of 1936–1938.[69] Although their impact was less in the countryside than the towns due to lower party membership and weaker policing, a broader "culture of condemnation" nevertheless prevailed and its language could be harnessed by Stakhanovites wishing to complain about farm leaders' alleged crimes and inefficiencies, part of a sanctioned attack on inept management. Peasants also moaned about daily life on their farm, about bath-houses that needed repair or squalid housing. Peasants on both collective and state farms complained to the press, party, procuracy, or trade union about various aspects of rural life. This was part of a much broader process, integral to the

Soviet state, which encouraged letters of complaint as a form of participation in the system, practiced by millions.

As the oppressiveness and arbitrary nature of the Stalinist political system increased, so the predictable routine of politics declined. For instance, the almost yearly regularity of party congresses seen in the 1920s was broken. The Seventeenth Party Congress was held in 1934, the Eighteenth in 1939, at which rural Stakhanovism was praised in some detail, and the Nineteenth did not convene until 1952. Invasion by the Nazis in June 1941 and four years of "Great Patriotic War" were responsible for part of the interruption in routine. But Stalin's growing cult of personality mirrored the fact that he towered above the party. Any democratic mechanisms that remained were seriously diluted in an atmosphere of fear, informing, and punishment, perpetuated by the secret police.[70] Most rural areas, however, were distant from the epicenter in Moscow of terror and purges, less affected than cities by the frightening night-time "knock at the door," and characterized by lower levels of penetration by the party and law enforcement authorities. Nonetheless, district party committees endured a higher turnover of party secretaries than would otherwise have been the case.[71]

CONCLUSION

Immense upheavals in agriculture and industry amid growing political repression and purges frame rural Stakhanovism. Migration flows from countryside to town to provide factories with labor power were integral to these processes of change and affected social structures. Outflows from villages, which accelerated during wartime, meant that young males in particular were leaving, as had been the case during conscription to the Tsarist Army, the First World War, and Civil War.

Against this historical backdrop of grain procurements, collectivization, animal losses, droughts, poor harvests, and famine, the encouragement of rural shock work and Stakhanovism can be interpreted as an attempt by the regime to foster enthusiasm and greater unity of purpose in order to spur production at a time of effervescent expectations for increased productivity. Appropriate work practices and values for using new machinery had to be instilled and the ethic of hard work developed again in those who had remained demoralized. Any residual fury, alienation, indifference, and neglect had to be replaced by commitment, energy, buoyant enthusiasm, and careful attention to sowing and harvesting practices. Animals had to be cared for, ensuring their reproduction and survival after birth. Rural Stakhanovism was meant to bring about a massive improvement in productivity, lead to more animals and no more famines. In fact, the poor harvest of 1936 and hard winter of 1936–1937 underscored the fact that problems were not over, even if less dire. Bread shortages persisted in the countryside. In early 1937, Stalin blamed wreckers and saboteurs, thereby triggering further purges.[72]

The task of accelerating the peasantry's commitment to maximum productivity was not straightforward. It was not simply a case of restoring past loyalties, but rather of building new ones to the collective and to the state. In effect, this meant transferring loyalty from the household as an economic unit to the state. This required a new perspective on what work meant and for whom it was performed. Peasants did know how to work, but the meaning of the endeavor now carried a new significance for them. How much effort peasants thought that work now merited was linked to how they interpreted its meaning.

Herein lies the relevance of peasants' interests, defined as making the best of their own survival, and also of the importance of the idealistic and grandiose visions of Stalinism, of building a huge communist project. What is relevant here to the broad question of context is that mobilization of the people was an integral part of Stalinism. Whether it was sending the 25,000ers into the countryside to oversee collectivization, finding volunteers and prisoners to build Magnitogorsk from scratch and to construct the White Sea canal, or urging the Stakhanovite movement to spread, sociopolitical mobilizations served grand purposes which welded the people together to serve Stalin, socialism, and distant goals. Sparks of interest in society and captivated keenness, moreover, could ignite a movement. Overall, grand mobilizations can be seen as part of what Daniel Bell has viewed as the necessary value-systems of societies, the moral glue which gives meanings, reference points, and purposes.[73] Those who became "Sovietized," or who tried hard to be, or who pretended to be for various reasons — be it out of self-interest, genuine belief, conformity, or self-protection — constituted ready participants in mobilizations.

Just as industry possessed its keen Stakhanovites, so too in agriculture there arose a minority of enthusiastic Stalinist subjects who were ready and committed to exceed targets and to mold themselves into good shock workers and Stakhanovites, to varying degrees. In this context, the regime tried to encourage, harness, steer, and shape rural Stakhanovism's momentum on the ground. Leaders had their own narratives and administrative orders through which these attempts were orchestrated. Quite what was said, when, and how is found in party archives.

SUPPLEMENTAL TABLES FOR CHAPTER 1

Table 1.1. Number of Collective Farms, 1929–1938

	1929	1933	1938
Number of collective farms (in thousands)	57.0	224.6	242.4
Number of collective farmers (in thousands)	1,000.7	15,258.5	18,842.9
% of peasantry collectivized	39.0	65.6	93.5
% of sown land collectivized	4.9	83.1	99.3

Source: Tsentral'noe upravlenie narodnokhoziaistvennogo ucheta gosplana pri SNK SSSR, *Sotsialisticheskoe stroitel'stvo soiuza SSSR (1933–1938): Statisticheskii sbornik* (Moscow and Leningrad: Gosplanizdat, 1939), 85.

Table 1.3. Growth of the MTS, Tractors and Combines, 1930–1937

	1930	1933	1937*
Number of MTS	158	2,916	5,617
Tractors (in thousands)	7.1	123.2	356.8
Strength (in thousand horsepower)	86.8	1,758.1	6,511.6
Combine harvesters (in thousands)	none	10.4	96.3
Trucks (in thousands)	none	12.3	56.0

*1937 data for 1 August, except number of MTS

Source: 20 let Sovetskoi vlasti: statisticheckii sbornik (Moscow: Partizdat TsK VKP [b], 1937), 48.

Table 1.4. Growth of State Farms and Tractors, 1929–1938

	1929	1933	1938	1938 as % of 1933
Number of state farms (end of year)	1,536	4,208	3,961	94.1%
Average yearly number of workers	416.4	2,422.2	1,517.7	62.7%
Number of tractors (in thousands at end of year)	9.7	83.2	85.0	102.2

Source: Tsentral'noe upravlenie narodnokhoziaistvennogo ucheta gosplana pri SNK SSSR, *Sotsialisticheskoe stroitel'stvo soiuza SSSR (1933–1938): Statisticheskii sbornik* (Moscow and Leningrad, Gosplanizdat, 1939), 87.

NOTES

1. For discussion of the wider economic context of Stakhanovism, see R. W. Davies and Oleg Khlevnyuk, "Stakhanovism and the Soviet Economy," *Europe-Asia Studies* 54, no. 6 (September 2002): 867–903. See, too, O. V. Khlevnyuk, *Stalin i Ordzhonikidze: Konflikty v Politburo v 30-e gody* (Moscow: Rossiia Molodaia, 1993), 55–66.

2. For a range of interpretations see Robert Conquest, *Harvest of Sorrow: Soviet Collectivization and the Terror-Famine* (Cambridge: Cambridge University Press, 1982); Sheila Fitzpatrick, *Stalin's Peasants: Resistance and Survival in the Russian Village after Collectivization* (New York: Oxford University Press, 1994); Lynne Viola, *Peasant Rebels under Stalin: Collectivization and the Culture of Peasant Resistance* (New York: Oxford University Press, 1996); and Mark Tauger, "Soviet Peasants and Collectivization, 1930–1939: Resistance and Adaptation," *Journal of Peasant Studies* 31, nos. 3 and 4 (April and July 2004): 427–56.

3. See S. G. Wheatcroft, "The Soviet Economic Crisis of 1932: The Crisis in Agriculture," paper presented at the annual conference of NASEES, March 23–25, 1985; S. G. Wheatcroft and R. W. Davies, "Agriculture," in *The Economic Transformation of the Soviet Union, 1913–1945*, eds. R. W. Davies, Mark Harrison, and S. G. Wheatcroft (Cambridge: Cambridge University Press, 1994), 106–30.

4. David Moon, *The Russian Peasantry 1600–1930: The World Peasants Made* (London: Longman, 1999), 358.

5. James Hughes, *Stalinism in a Russian Province: A Study of Collectivization and Dekulakization in Siberia* (Basingstoke and London: Macmillan, 1996), 7.

6. For fuller details, consult: Moshe Lewin, *Russian Peasants and Soviet Power: A Study in Collectivisation* (London: George Allen and Unwin, 1968); R. W. Davies, *The Socialist Offensive: The Collectivisation of Agriculture, 1929–1930* (London: Macmillan, 1980) and also his *The Soviet Collective Farm, 1929–1930* (London: Macmillan, 1980). For a general introduction, see Chris Ward, *Stalin's Russia* (London: Edward Arnold, 1993), 39–72. Whether or not kulaks should be permitted to join collective farms was debated and controversial. See Lewin, *Russian Peasants*, 485.

7. Lewin, *Russian Peasants*, 496–97; Davies, *The Socialist Offensive*, 234–36.

8. I use "idea" here since conversations with Iain Blanchard of the University of Edinburgh have, in part, persuaded me that "kulak" was not only a Leninist construct but also a term about which undemonstrated assumptions may have been made. Blanchard argues that claims about the higher productivity of kulaks in comparison with other peasants are questionable and lack verification.

9. Lynne Viola, *The Best Sons of the Fatherland: Workers in the Vanguard of Soviet Collectivization* (New York: Oxford University Press, 1987), 3.

10. Viola, *The Best Sons*, 161.

11. Fitzpatrick, *Stalin's Peasants,* 50–59.

12. Lewin, *Russian Peasants*, 505–06.

13. Lewin, *Russian Peasants*, 501–05.

14. Moon, *The Russian Peasantry,* 359.

15. Moon, *The Russian Peasantry*. For a range of responses to collectivization by peasants, see James Hughes, *Stalinism in a Russian Province*, 160–66.

16. Fitzpatrick, *Stalin's Peasants*, 49.

17. Lynne Viola, *"Bab'i Bunty and Peasant Women's Protest During Collectivization,"* in *Russian Peasant Women*, eds. Beatrice Farnsworth and Lynne Viola (New York: Oxford University Press, 1992), 189–205.

18. Viola, *Peasant Rebels Under Stalin*, 4.

19. See *Pravda*, 2 March 1930 and 10 February 1930.

20. See Table 1.1.

21. *Sotsialisticheskoe stroitel'stvo soiuza*, 85.

22. *Sotsialisticheskoe stroitel'stvo soiuza*, 87. By 1939, state farms accounted for 51.1 million hectares of Soviet agricultural land, compared with 370.8 million hectares devoted to collective farms and individual peasant farms. See I. Laptev, *Sovetskoe Krest'ianstvo* (Moscow: Gosudarstvennoe izdatel'stvo kolkhoznoi i sovkhoznoi literatury, 1939), 123.

23. For Kaganovich's report on *"Politotdel pri MTS,"* see Rossiiskii Gosudarstvennyi Arkhiv Sotsial'no-Politicheskoi Istorii (RGASPI), fond 81, opis' 3, delo 23, list 99. Other comments by Kaganovich on the role of the *politotdely* are in RGASPI, f. 81, op. 3, d. 24 (1934–1935) and d. 77 (1932–1933). Vyltsan notes that it was decided in 1933 that "the MTS frequently does not have a political face" and that "theft and embezzlement of collective property required action." More than 17,000 party workers were dispatched to work in the *politotdely* of the MTS and 45 percent of all leaders of the *politotdely* had higher party or special education. See M. A. Vyltsan, *Zavershaiushchii etap sozdaniia kolkhoznogo stroia* (Moscow: Izdatel'stvo Nauka, 1978), 75–76.

24. Fitzpatrick, *Stalin's Peasants*, 76.

25. On 31 May 1943, the Politburo decided to "liquidate" the *politotdely* on state farms and on the MTS on the grounds that their "positive role" was in the past and now duplicated by farm and MTS directors. See RGASPI, f. 17, op. 3, d. 1047, l. 73.

26. *20 Let Sovetskoi Vlasti: Statisticheskii Sbornik* (Moscow: Partizdat TsK VKP[b], 1937), 48.

27. Moshe Lewin, *The Making of the Soviet System: Essays in the Social History of Inter War Russia* (London: Methuen, 1985), 143.

28. Lewin, *The Making of the Soviet System,* 155.

29. Lewin, *The Making of the Soviet System,* 145.

30. Vladimir Andrle, *A Social History of Twentieth-Century Russia* (London: Edward Arnold, 1994), 158.

31. See, for instance, Robert Conquest, *Harvest of Sorrow: Soviet Collectivization and the Terror-Famine* (Cambridge: Cambridge University Press, 1982), 22.

32. Conquest, *Harvest of Sorrow*, 230–58.

33. Maurice Hindus, *Red Bread: Collectivization in a Russian Village* (Bloomington: Indiana University Press, 1988), 210.

34. Mikhail Sholokhov, *Virgin Soil Upturned* (London: Putnam, 1935), 157.

35. Viola, *"Bab'i Bunty and Peasant Women's Protest During Collectivization,"* 193–96.

36. Tauger, "Soviet Peasants and Collectivization" and his "Modernisation in Soviet Agriculture." In the latter, Tauger also makes the point that the issue of peasants losing their "independence" through collectivization can be usefully compared with similar responses from small farmers in the U.S. His thesis is that Soviet government officials wrestled with "similar and often the same, ideas and problems as US specialists." Lynne Viola has argued that "a minority" of peasants supported collectivization and I. V. Pavlova has more recently suggested that the peasantry was not socially united against it. See Viola, *The Best Sons* and I. V. Pavlova, *Mekhanizm Vlasti i Stroitel'stvo Stalinskogo Sotsializma* (Novosibirsk: 2001), 85.

37. Moon, *The Russian Peasantry,* 358.

38. Fitzpatrick, *Stalin's Peasants*, 14.

39. M. A. Vyltsan, *Zavershaiushchii etap sozdaniia kolkhoznogo stroia* (Moscow: Izdatel'stvo Nauka, 1978), 101.

40. Vyltsan, *Zavershaiushchii etap,* 101. These data need to be considered bearing in mind a point made by Mark Tauger. In drought years, fields of crops could be ruined, requiring no harvesting, and therefore bring no labor days. Since patterns could vary across the vast landmass, it makes it hard to interpret yearly summaries. Furthermore, mechanization required fewer laborers, leaving some without work. See Tauger, "Soviet Peasants and Collectivization."

41. John Channon with Rob Hudson, *The Penguin Historical Atlas of Russia* (Harmondsworth: Penguin, 1995), 109; Elena A. Osikina, "Economic Disobedience under Stalin," in Lynne Viola, ed., *Contending with Stalinism: Soviet Power and Popular Resistance in the 1930s* (Ithaca and London: Cornell University Press, 2002), 170–200.

42. Moon, *The Russian Peasantry*, 360.

43. See Hughes, *Stalinism in a Russian Province.*

44. For greater detail, see Edward Hallett Carr and R. W. Davies, *Foundations of a Planned Economy, 1926–1929*, Vols.1 and 2 (London: Macmillan, 1969), especially Volume 2, 787–924; R. W. Davies, *Soviet Economic Development from Lenin to Khrushchev* (Cambridge: Cambridge University Press, 1998); Alec Nove, *An Economic History of the USSR* (Harmondsworth: Penguin, 1969).

45. Lewin, *Russian Peasants,* 518–19. James R. Millar has argued that collectivization was "an unmitigated economic policy disaster" and that agricultural output increased only marginally in the 1930s. See his *The Soviet Economic Experiment*, edited and introduced by Susan J. Linz (Urbana and Chicago: University of Illinois Press, 1990), 58.

46. See Table 1.3.

47. See Table 1.4.

48. I. V. Stalin, *Sochineniia*, Vol. XIII (Moscow, 1951), 340–60.

49. Davies and Khlevnyuk, "Stakhanovism," 897.

50. Davies and Khlevnyuk, "Stakhanovism," 878. They hold that if any top leader was active at the outset, it is most likely to have been Ordzhonikidze.

51. For a handy summary, see Ward, *Stalin's Russia*, 97.

52. Maurice Dobb, *Soviet Economic Development Since 1917* (London: Routledge and Kegan Paul, 1948), 291.

53. Stephen Kotkin, *Magnetic Mountain: Stalinism as Civilization* (Berkeley: University of California Press, 1995); Leon Trotsky, *The Revolution Betrayed: What Is the Soviet Union and Where Is It Going?* (New York: Pathfinder, 1972); Nicholas Timasheff, *The Great Retreat: The Growth and Decline of Communism in Russia* (New York: Dutton, 1946).

54. Sheila Fitzpatrick, ed., *Cultural Revolution in Russia, 1928–1931* (Bloomington: Indiana University Press, 1978).

55. Wendy Goldman, *Women, State and Revolution: Soviet Family Policy and Social Life, 1917–1936* (Cambridge: Cambridge University Press, 1993); Gail Warshofsky Lapidus, *Women in the Soviet Union: Equality, Development and Social Change* (Berkeley: University of California Press, 1978), 95–112; Mary Buckley, *Women and*

Ideology in the Soviet Union (Hemel Hempstead: Harvester/Wheatsheaf, 1989), 156–58; Barbara Alpern Engel, *Women in Russia, 1700–2000* (Cambridge: Cambridge University Press, 2004), 166–85.

56. For discussion of the place of cinema in popular culture see Richard Stites, *Russian Popular Culture* (Cambridge: Cambridge University Press, 1992).

57. Roy Medvedev, *Let History Judge: The Origins and Consequences of Stalinism* (London: Spokesman Books, 1976), 538–41.

58. There is a huge literature on this topic. The central arguments are rehearsed in Robert Tucker, ed., *Stalinism: Essays in Historical Interpretation* (New York: W. W. Norton, 1997). For a commentary on the "state of the field" see E. A. Rees, "Stalinism: The Primacy of Politics" in *Politics, Society and Stalinism in the USSR*, ed. John Channon (Basingstoke and London: Macmillan, 1998), 35–67.

59. Julie Hessler, "Cultured Trade: The Stalinist Turn Towards Consumerism," in *Stalinism: New Directions*, ed. Sheila Fitzpatrick (London and New York: Routledge, 2000), 182–209.

60. Jukka Gronow, *Caviar with Champagne: Common Luxury and the Ideals of the Good Life in Stalin's Russia* (Oxford and New York: Berg, 2003), 6.

61. Gronow, *Caviar*, 133.

62. S. E. Finer, ed., *Five Constitutions* (Harmondsworth: Penguin, 1979), 119. It was not until the 1977 Constitution that Article 1 declared the USSR to be "a socialist state of the whole people." See Finer, *Five,* 149.

63. Finer, *Five*, 123.

64. Kotkin, *Magnetic Mountain*.

65. Igal Halfin, *Terror in My Soul: Communist Autobiographies on Trial* (Cambridge, MA: Harvard University Press, 2003), 8.

66. Jochen Hellbeck, "Fashioning the Stalinist Soul: The Diary of Stepan Podlubnyi (1931–1939)," *Jahrbücher für Geschichte Osteuropas* 44, Heft 3 (1996): 344–73; and his "Speaking Out: Languages of Affirmation and Dissent in Stalinist Russia," *Kritika: Explorations in Russian and Eurasian History* 1, no. 1 (Winter 2000): 71–96.

67. The famous slogan "Life has become better, life has become merrier" was declared by Stalin in November 1935 at the First All-Union Conference of Stakhanovites. See *VseSoiuznoe Soveshchanie Rabochikh i Rabotnits-Stakhanovtsev, 14–17 Noiabria 1935: Stenograficheskii otchët* (Moscow: Partizdat TsK VKP [b], 1935), 355–69. Discussion of Stalin's speech and of reactions to it is found in Sarah Davies, *Popular Opinion in Stalin's Russia: Terror, Propaganda and Dissent, 1934–1941* (Cambridge: Cambridge University Press, 1997), 34. Stalin referred again to this slogan in December 1935 at a meeting of drivers of combine harvesters. See *"Rech' Tovarishcha Stalina na soveshchanii peredovykh kombainerov i kombainerok 1-go Dekabria 1935 goda," Bol'shevik*, no. 23–24, 15 December, 2.

68. Jeffrey Brooks, *Thank You, Comrade Stalin: Soviet Public Culture from Revolution to Cold War* (Princeton, NJ: Princeton University Press, 2000), xv and 83–105. See also David L. Hoffmann, *Stalinist Values: The Cultural Norms of Soviet Modernity, 1917–1941* (Ithaca, NY: Cornell University Press, 2003).

69. For recent discussions refer to: J. Arch Getty and Roberta T. Manning, *Stalinist Terror: New Perspectives* (New York and Cambridge: Cambridge University Press,

1993); Sheila Fitzpatrick, *Stalin's Peasants*, 296–312; Terry Martin, "The Origins of Soviet Ethnic Cleansing," *The Journal of Modern History* 70, no. 4 (1998), 813–61; James R. Harris, "The Purging of Local Cliques in the Urals Region, 1936–1937," in *Stalinism: New Directions,* ed. Fitzpatrick, 262–85; Paul Hagenloh, "'Socially Harmful Elements' and the Great Terror," in *Stalinism: New Directions*, ed. Fitzpatrick, 286–308; Barry McLoughlin and Kevin McDermott, *Stalin's Terror: High Politics and Mass Repression in the Soviet Union* (Basingstoke and London: Palgrave Macmillan, 2002); Michael Ellman, "The 1937–1938 Soviet Provincial Show Trials Revisited," *Europe-Asia Studies* 55, no. 8 (December 2003): 1305–21; Sheila Fitzpatrick, "A Response to Michael Ellman," *Europe-Asia Studies* 54, no. 3 (May 2002), 473–76; Michael Ellman, "Soviet Repression Statistics: Some Comments," *Europe-Asia Studies*, 54, no. 7, (November 2002): 1151–72.

70. For summaries of the Stalinist political system refer to: Jerry Hough and Merle Fainsod, *How the Soviet Union Is Governed* (Cambridge, MA: Harvard University Press, 1982), 147–91 and 449–79; Martin McCauley, *Stalin and Stalinism* (Harlow, Essex: Longman, 1983).

71. Robert T. Manning, "The Great Purges in a Rural District: *Belyi Raion* Revisited," in *Stalinist Terror: New Perspectives,* eds. J. Arch Getty and Roberta T. Manning (Cambridge: Cambridge University Press, 1993), 168–97.

72. Sarah Davies, *Popular Opinion in Russia*, 36. For further discussion of Stakhanovism and the purges, see chapter 7 below.

73. Daniel Bell, "Ideology and Soviet Politics," *Slavic Review* 24 (December 1965): 591–603.

Chapter Two

Rural Stakhanovism on Official Agendas

This movement began spontaneously, practically uncontrolled, from below, without any pressure from administrators.

—Stalin, November 1935[1]

Komsomol organizations on collective farms must be initiators of socialist competition and of Stakhanovite labor in all spheres of kolkhoz production.

—*Postanovlenie* of the Komsomol Central Committee, September 1938[2]

In one-party states, particularly those with official and comprehensive ideologies such as Marxism-Leninism, leaders develop official versions of events and developments. These accounts or scripts describe and construct dimensions of reality, fashion their contours, and indicate their relevance to the present and future. Official interpretations are relayed to the people through articles in the press, speeches at congresses and conferences, and in official slogans. Leaders also consider amongst themselves the meaning of a new development such as rural Stakhanovism. It becomes a topic on the agendas of Politburo meetings, of plenary sessions of the party and Komsomol central committees, of meetings within party departments and government commissariats, and also at party and Komsomol congresses.

This chapter presents the official story of how rural Stakhanovism arose, as it was delivered to the Soviet people through the press, and explores how the topic appeared on official agendas of party, Komsomol, and state institutions at the apex of the system.[3] The aim is to discuss what was said about it, by whom, and with what significance. A reading of scripts generated by the apex of the system reveals how leaders approached rural Stakhanovism, what it meant to them and what their priorities and concerns were. It also sheds light on the political roles played by different institutions in the Stalinist system and how they attempted to steer, oversee, and control the transformation of the countryside.

THE OFFICIAL STORY

According to the official story, Stakhanovism began spontaneously in the mines of the Donbas, inspired by the feats of Stakhanov and his emulators. Front page reporting in *Pravda* informed readers on 9 September 1935, "Comrade Diukanov hewed in six hours of work 115 tonnes of coal, Comrade Stakhanov 102 tonnes."[4] Two days later, *Pravda* announced that Stakhanov "for the first time" in one shift dug 175 tonnes of coal, thereby outstripping Diukanov.[5] Momentum built and on 13 September *Pravda* blazoned that "Stakhanovite methods of work are widening in the Donbas,"crescendoing on 14 September with the news that "Stakhanovite methods" had spread to machine workers.[6] *Pravda* praised the fact that "Coal cutters are joining the Stakhanovite movement."[7] For the first time it applied the label "movement." No mention of direction by the party was made in these early reports.

Readers of the rural press received a similar picture, but later. *Krest'ianskaia gazeta* (Peasant newspaper) reported the first successes of Stakhanov and Diukanov on 6 October 1935 under the heading "Stakhanov and Stakhanovites." This was not front-page news, but relegated to page four. The article revealed that in the Donbas there was a "strong Stakhanovite movement embracing thousands of people." Moreover, "the wonderful initiative of the best people of the Donbas had also been taken up by collective farmers and state farm workers. The Stakhanovite fields are growing."[8] Journalists put emphasis on the "initiative" of workers, which quickly inspired the emulation of peasants. The picture was one of the town leading countryside, the proletariat fittingly ahead of the peasantry and spurring it on. Now the impetus officially came from keen workers and peasants. What mattered at this stage, according to *Krest'ianskaia gazeta*, was that "they must be managed, they must be led, they must be matched!"[9] Here was the "invitation" for the party and Komsomol to step in and play appropriate guiding roles.

A further prod to rural Stakhanovism came in mid-October when Stakhanov issued a call to peasants to follow in his footsteps. He challenged tractor and combine drivers who were attending an oblast congress in Odessa to emulate "the socialist work methods of advanced people of the Donbas."[10] In reply, tractor driver Chabenko pledged to do so. The pattern of urban workers at the forefront of change urging peasants to follow their lead was in keeping with the dominant script that proletarians spearheaded revolutionary transformations and inspired peasants to follow their enlightened examples.

INTERACTIONS BETWEEN WORKERS, PEASANTS, AND PARTY PRIORITIES

Some Sovietologists would contest the idea that in the 1930s a movement began on the ground without a cue that was passed down the party hierarchy instructing those at the local level to behave in a particular way. Backing from the *partkom* (party committee) and liaison with the trade union were usually necessary for most activities in factories, although to a lesser extent on farms given a relatively weak party presence in many rural areas and also due to the absence of trade unions from collective farms. Certainly when "initiative" did develop spontaneously, it needed party approval to sustain itself. Stakhanovism could not have endured for long without the party's sanction and ongoing backing.

It is not inconceivable, however, that enthusiastic workers, already encouraged since the end of the 1920s to aspire to the status of "shock worker" (*udarnik*) themselves wanted to attain "maximum productivity." The regime had already organized conferences around shock work (*udarnichestvo*) since the late 1920s, such as the First All-Union Congress of Shock Work Brigades in December 1929, the First All-Union Congress of Kolkhoz Shock Workers of Advanced Collective Farms in February 1933 and the Second All-Union Congress of Kolkhoz Shock Workers in February 1935.[11] Lewis Siegelbaum has noted how in 1927 shock work began when particularly keen and isolated groups of workers set out to over-fulfill assignments.[12] Exceptional local initiatives did occur, subsequently harnessed by the system if appropriate to its goals. R. W. Davies and Oleg Khlevnyuk have recently reached this conclusion, too.[13]

By the mid-1930s, it was widely known that shock work was approved of and something to emulate, so those faithful to the regime were merely doing its bidding by trying to work even harder than ever before. As Jochen Hellbeck and Igal Halfin have suggested, some subjects did try to work on themselves too, to sculpt themselves into better Stalinists, aware that their own personal transformation into something purer meant endeavor.[14] This could apply to their work patterns just as much as to their subjective outlooks. Indeed, the two were interrelated. Heroic Stakhanovite efforts, however, could not have long continued or expanded without party approval. In town and countryside, reciprocal backing between workers and peasants on the one hand and party on the other was required for the movement to gain momentum.

Thus the party could not orchestrate Stakhanovism without willing, diligent, and also compliant workers and peasants. Convincing cases have already been made that the movement in industry was complex, prompting varied responses among both workers and managements.[15] The same appears graphically the case in the countryside where, arguably, the movement was more multifaceted, affected by a wider range of variables. Most farms also lacked the large economies of scale that characterized industry and transport.

THE ONE-PARTY STATE

In the USSR, decrees, decisions, and orders or commands flowed down the party hierarchy from the General Secretary, Politburo, and Central Committee. On rural issues, these were often based upon information gathered by the Central Committee party departments within the party secretariat, such as the Department of Agriculture, or in liaison with the relevant commissariats, later called ministries, such as the Commissariat of Agriculture and the Commissariat of State Farms. Information came up the system as well as went down it. Sometimes "decisions" were in the name of the Central Committee alone and sometimes they were made jointly with Sovnarkom (*Soviet Narodnykh Kommisarov*), the Council of People's Commissars—which constituted the apex of the system of government. Decisions within the party system flowed from the All-Union Central Committee to republican central committees and down to party organizations at krai (territory), oblast (region), city, and raion (district) levels. Administrative orders were also sent from people's commissariats (found at All-Union and sometimes republican levels), directly to directors of state farms, directors of machine tractor stations, and heads of *politotdely*. Those situated at republic, regional, and local levels, such as district party secretaries, collective farm chairpersons, state farm directors, and MTS directors reacted to these directives in their workplace and also sent information back up the hierarchy.

POLITBURO MEETINGS AND
CENTRAL COMMITTEE PLENARY SESSIONS

Archives reveal numerous and varied decisions about Stakhanovism made at the very top political decision-making level in the Politburo. This underscores how the movement became a high priority and how its outcomes were of great concern to leaders. They perceived it as a vital dynamo for the mobilization of the countryside, as a key mechanism for solving a range of rural problems. Even quite minute details were considered at this high level. Although it was characteristic of the one-party state to have a "top heavy" decision-making process, that Stakhanovism featured with a visible prominence in the Politburo protocols reflects its importance.

Decisions ranged from giving approval for local Stakhanovite rallies, to deciding how many tons of paper were needed for the publication of speeches given at Stakhanovite conferences, to calling for legal action against those who victimized Stakhanovites. Discussions also considered how Stakhanovism could best be presented and in Central Committee plenary sessions focused on Stakhanovism's meaning.[16] Selected examples illustrate the tone and substance of decisions and debates.

Often details are brief, but clear. Under the heading "On the rally of Stakhanovites in agriculture in Kuibyshev oblast," the text reads "Permit the Kuibyshev obkom VKP (b) to call on the 6 January an oblast rally of Stakhanovites in agriculture."[17] The oblast had submitted a request for the rally to go ahead, the Politburo now granted it. Similar examples are cited concerning permission for conferences of "advanced" collective farmers in Buriat Mongolia, Krasnoiarsk krai, and Arkhangel'.[18] Very precise details down to the number of people permitted to attend the conferences were included in the telegrams sent out by the Politburo. The general pattern was approval for the event, its timing and numbers. Even if not all oblasts and districts requested permission for rallies to go ahead—clearly far more rallies took place than there is evidence on file of permission given—many did, indicating a pattern.

The Politburo also named Central Committee members who should be dispatched to participate in rallies. This not only reflected official support but also an interest to find out what was happening outside Moscow. Mikhail Kalinin, for example, already on the Politburo, was sent to a congress of shock workers in agriculture and in animal husbandry in Gor'kii krai in 1936 and also to an oblast rally of flax growers in Iaroslavl'.[19] Semen Budennyi was dispatched to one in animal husbandry in Belorussia, at the request of the Belorussian Central Committee.[20]

As well as granting permission for rallies and conferences, the Politburo also prevented them. In 1936 the Politburo witheld consent for a conference of Stakhanovites in the far north and for a gathering of advanced peasants in potatoes, vegetables, and grapes.[21] These particular refusals were recorded but not explained, indicating the finality and the power of the Politburo over distant events.[22] Rejections by the Politburo could have been because the targets were unrealistic in local conditions at that time of year or because the Politburo

wanted to stress the importance of following procedures and referring upward
in the hierarchy for guidance. In keeping with the latter, the Politburo reprimanded some party committees lower down the hierarchy for supporting enthusiastic Stakhanovite calls for production challenges that had been made at
conferences without prior approval from a higher level.[23] Too much spontaneity could get out of hand. Certainly archives indicate that on many occasions
initiative indeed came from the local level. In response, a clear message left
the Politburo that formally it needed approval to happen.

A clearer case occurred when both the Politburo and Central Committee
castigated Moscow oblast after bubbling Stakhanovites had called for a
month of Stakhanovite records in 1938. The Moscow party committee was
scolded for behaving out of line and for not seeking approval in advance.
According to those at the apex of the system, the very idea of a
Stakhanovite month in January was seriously flawed due to "specific difficulties of a seasonal nature."[24] People's Commissariats were instructed to
inform *obkomy* and *kraikomy* that this should not go ahead and a
Stakhanovite month for Moscow oblast would be switched from January to
March.[25] Prior approvals from the apex in cases like this were not just about
power at the top insisting on its preeminence, but part of a process of ensuring sensible decisions.

Regular approval was also given at Politburo level for the awarding of decorations and medals to Stakhanovites at conferences. Rewarding Stakhanovites
was integral to the party's encouragement of the movement and this routine
priority was highly visible at the apex of the system. It usually took the form
of confirmation in a *postanovlenie* (decision or resolution) coming from the
Central Executive Committee (*Tsentral'nyi Ispolnitel'nyi Komitet*). Accordingly, in November 1935, the Politburo approved such a decision for awards to
over thirty "500ers" on collective farms, with Mariia Demchenko and Marina
Gnatenko at the top of the list.[26]

Approval for decorations persisted throughout the 1930s, although it came
in waves: late 1935, early 1936, and early 1939.[27] These were three periods
when special emphasis was put on Stakhanovism. Late 1935 indicated approval and reward for the first great Stakhanovite feats. Early 1936 was the
time of the "big push" for Stakhanovism at the beginning of what was proclaimed "Stakhanovite year." And a renewed flurry of decorations in 1939
was part of the gloomy warning that the blackness of war was on the horizon
and overwhelmingly huge efforts were now required. The Politburo awarded
decorations in the 1940s and later, too, but explicit references to "shock workers" and "Stakhanovites" were dropped in favor of the broader "*peredoviki*"
or "advanced workers." Although the latter term had been regularly used
by the Politburo in the 1930s, too, frequently subsuming *udarniki* and

stakhanovtsy, now it became the only term applied.[28] Thus "Stakhanovite" dropped out of usage from Politburo protocols.

Even decisions about the publication of the proceedings of Stakhanovites' conferences and congresses were taken at Politburo level. In November 1935, the Politburo approved publication of 500,000 copies of the text of the First All-Union Conference of Stakhanovites, naming four editors to oversee the project.[29] In this manner, the Politburo decided what would be published about Stakhanovism and how much coverage it would receive, thereby shaping the content of the official story of the Stakhanovite movement.

Sometimes very detailed guidelines were given by the Politburo to the press on how to report a given conference. In December 1935, the Politburo decided that *Pravda, Izvestiia, Sotsialisticheskoe zemledelie* (Socialist Agriculture) and *Sovkhoznaia gazeta* (State Farm paper) would publish the text of speeches delivered to a gathering of tractor drivers, together with participants' photographs. Other newspapers were to print the official TASS press release. *Pravda* and *Izvestiia* were permitted to send along their own reporters as well. The Politburo named Comrades Tal' and Iakovlev as overseers of the coverage and specified that the party publishing house, *Politizdat,* would print 300,000 copies of the proceedings, together with photographs of the speakers.[30] In another instance, the Politburo sanctioned *Krest'ianskaia gazeta* to produce a special publication in 1936 of peasants' letters with a view to exerting "influence on readers" on given themes.[31]

The Politburo also reflected upon how exactly certain Stakhanovite activities should be portrayed. In early 1936, there appears to have been some excitement about the apparent misuse of the word *konkurs* (competition) in the reporting of socialist competition. This was a *sorevnovanie,* not a *konkurs.* The Politburo instructed that not only had Lenin used the term *sorevnovanie,* but *konkurs* connoted an individual activity, such as competing for designing the best statue or building or writing the best song or book. By contrast, socialist competitions characteristic of the Stakhanovite movement referred to "communist methods of building socialism" performed "by the maximum activity of the working masses," not individuals.[32] The Politburo declared that all newspapers had to be informed of this difference and that the Central Executive Committee of the USSR, People's Commissariats, and trade unions had to cease their "dangerous and anti-Bolshevik" use of *konkurs* and also *konkurs-sorevnovanie.*[33] Only *sorevnovanie* would do.

While the above examples were largely routine decisions or focused reflections, there were occasions when the topic of Stakhanovism generated substantial reports, promoting debate and discussion at the highest level. The first clear instance of this occurred in December 1935 in preparation for the forthcoming Central Committee Plenum at which the broader significance of

Stakhanovism was discussed.[34] A reading of Politburo materials in conjunction with those of the Plenum itself indicates the extent to which top leaders themselves were grappling with what to make of Stakhanovism. Isidor Liubimov, for instance, Commissar of Light Industry, noted "that many of us did not immediately understand the great significance this movement had," until it spread to hundreds of workers, then to thousands. By 20 October 1935, there were allegedly 14,000 Stakhanovites. Liubimov talked about the "mood among backward workers against the Stakhanovite movement" and argued for the need to make workers more interested in working hard, specifically by introducing pay incentives.[35] Stakhanovism, he felt, should be encouraged to spread to all sectors of the economy.[36]

Within three months of the movement's appearance debate among top party leaders embraced the topics of opposition, incentives, and expansion. Resolutions coming out of the Plenum regretted that some administrators had not understood the "meaning" of Stakhanovism and were merely "on the tail" of the movement.[37] The Plenum declared it crucial "to break remaining resistance" and "to help in every way" those so far unable to lead the movement, to put themselves at its head.[38] In sum, the December Plenum stressed that the movement had to be led and should spread. It did not, however, refer to rural Stakhanovism. Stress fell on coal, ore, oil, metallurgy, chemicals, fish, wood, and railways.

Fuller consideration of rural Stakhanovism within the Central Committee came in 1936. Close scrutiny of the press nonetheless shows top leaders at the end of 1935 already forecasting rural Stakhanovism's success. Alongside *Pravda*'s coverage of the December Plenum was an article reporting Kalinin's speech on cotton to a meeting of the Presidium of the Central Executive Committee. Kalinin announced that he had no doubts that Stakhanovism in agriculture would become just as widespread as in industry. He pointed out that although 8 tsentners of cotton per hectare were considered average, some collective farmers were gathering from 20 to 50 tsentners and this was "not the limit." Iunusov Faizula, Kalinin praised, had peaked at 57 tsentners.[39]

Subsequent speeches from political leaders echoed Kalinin's message. Addressing the Central Committee Plenum of June 1936, Mikhail Chernov, People's Commissar of Agriculture, declared that conferences of "advanced" peasants and leaders held in the autumn and winter had shown that there were "genuine talents" in the countryside. Socialist competitions were spreading and tens of thousands of collective farmers were committed to harvesting 50 tsentners of wheat, 500 tsentners of sugar beet, and 30 tsentners of cotton. In sum, the "struggle" for a good harvest was a genuine "people's struggle."[40] Moreover, the spread of Stakhanovism in 1935 among tractor drivers had meant that less of the harvest was lost and illustrated that better attention had to be paid to machinery.[41] Chernov went on to list production successes. Pasha Kovardak had pledged to harvest 4,900 hectares per year on her ChTZ tractor and after the spring sowing campaign had already covered 1,500 hectares. Likewise, Volishin had promised to work 2,000 hectares a year and had already covered 700 hectares in spring sowing. Chernov told Central Committee members about similar success stories in cotton and sugar beet.[42] At the same Plenum, M. Kalmanovich, People's Commissar of Grain and Animal State Farms, spoke on the harvest and grain requisitioning. Like Chernov, he singled out individual farms and Stakhanovites for praise, citing details of their production feats.[43]

Rural shock work and Stakhanovism, then, were very visibly on the agendas of the Central Committee from 1936. While not every speech by Chernov on agriculture included discussion of Stakhanovites, such as his suggestions to a Plenum in June 1937 on how to improve the work of the MTS, the topic nonetheless regularly appeared.[44] By 1938, the idea was firmly put to the Central Committee that Stakhanovite feats brought a range of improvements in the countryside. At the January 1938 Plenum, for example, R. Eikhe, from November 1937 the new People's Commissar of Agriculture (after the Politburo had "freed" Chernov of his "duties," as the official version put it, but had actually shot him),[45] declared that "decisive successes" in agriculture in 1938 would be made "on the basis of socialist competitions and the Stakhanovite movement." He emphasized the ongoing "struggle" for:

> high quality indicators in all agricultural work (tractor repair, the selection of high quality seed, deep plowing, sowing in a brief period, careful tending of the soil, harvesting without losses) for an increase in labor productivity, further mastery of handling machinery, and the techniques of agronomy for caring for the soil and in sowing.[46]

Eikhe's points all reflected the official emphasis in 1938 on learning lessons from Stakhanovites in every aspect of the agricultural process. Eikhe's main message delivered at Central Committee Plenary meetings was that rural Stakhanovism was growing and together with socialist competitions and production pledges it would result in better ways of working and in higher productivity.

What stands out in official discourse among leaders is that rural Stakhanovism was increasingly portrayed as the means to solving the disrepair of machinery, shallow plowing, neglect of the soil, and a range of other rural problems. More broadly, rural Stakhanovism was a motor for making collective farms and state farms work. This amounts to a tacit admission that the reorganization of farming had not hitherto been successful and was in need of a unifying force which committed peasants to the state. In this sense, rural Stakhanovism was a tool for the transfer of loyalty to the collective and to the state. Although it was also a possible tool for the development of local cohesion after the divisiveness of "class war" in the countryside that had characterized collectivization, its very nature backfired here since rewards for Stakhanovites and the increased output targets associated with the movement created further animosities among peasants. Nonetheless, leaders at the apex cast Stakhanovism as panacea for the woes of Soviet agriculture and implicitly, through an expected increase in productivity, as healer for the sores and divisions of collectivization, as a great movement which mobilized the peasantry around magnificent production feats, Stalinist glory, and a gleaming future.

"DECISIONS" FROM GOVERNMENT AND PARTY

Another source of the direction of Stakhanovism was the government or party *postanovlenie*. This can be translated as decision or resolution, but effectively it amounted to an enactment. Sovnarkom (*Soviet narodnykh komissarov*), or the Council of People's Commissars, generally in conjunction with the Central Committee of the party (but not always), issued various *postanovleniia* on agriculture that referred specifically to harnessing rural Stakhanovism.[47] The word "Stakhanovism," however, did not usually appear in the title of a decision but was frequently tucked at the end of a series of instructions. In early 1936, for example, Sovnarkom and the Central Committee issued "On contracting for the sugar beet harvest of 1936." After confirming the plan, the *postanovlenie* concluded with a brief mention of the success of the 500ers, followed by:

> Sovnarkom SSSR and TsK VKP (b) oblige party and soviet organizations, MTS directors, kolkhoz chairs of sugar beet districts, to head the developing mass movement of 500ers, having facilitated wide application of 500ers work methods.[48]

This was signed by Viacheslav Molotov, as Chair of Sovnarkom, and by Stalin as party secretary. Here is clear evidence that the local party, soviet, and farm leaders were encouraged by the regime to direct the 500ers. A similar decision, "On contracting for the cotton harvest of 1936," referred favorably to the "30ers" in cotton, and issued a similar call.[49] Likewise, these messages were repeated in 1937 in connection with the state plan for spring sowing.[50] Successful sowing was explicitly linked by leaders to promoting Stakhanovism.

Thereafter mention of rural Stakhanovism was erratic. There was nothing about it in the agricultural plan for 1938 or in various plans "On contracting for . . ." in 1938.[51] But then rural Stakhanovism reappeared in a *postanovlenie* of Sovnarkom "On gathering the harvest in 1938." It called for a "higher level of organization of kolkhoz construction," for "further growth of socialist competition," and specifically for soviet and land organs (*zemel'nye organy*) "to head the Stakhanovite movement in agriculture."[52] Land organs here referred to the local land department, or *raizo (raionnyi zemel'nyi otdel)*. Since land organs were heavily criticized at the time for their inefficiency, it is not surprising that a decision pressed them to improve. Other factors also came into play. In 1938 there were concerns that the Stakhanovite movement was weakening in the countryside, evidenced by fewer Stakhanovites. The Great Purge was also in full swing and Narkomzem, which oversaw the land departments, was a serious target.

References to rural Stakhanovism continued in 1939. A *postanovlenie* of January referred to the need to pass on the experience of Stakhanovites familiar with winter crops.[53] The text of the Third Five-Year Plan covering 1938 to 1942 also called for the "development of socialist competition and of the Stakhanovite movement" in both industry and in agriculture with "strong labor discipline."[54] This was done in the name of the Eighteenth Party Congress which was to be held in 1939. The Third Plan explicitly required involvement of party, soviet, and trade union organizations in the promotion of Stakhanovism.[55]

Multiple sources, then, show that the party and government wanted to back, build, and increase rural Stakhanovism's momentum in the interest of a more efficient and productive agriculture. More targeted instructions concerning the implementation of these policies are seen in *prikazy*, or orders.

ORDERS (*PRIKAZY*) FROM ABOVE

From 1936 on, a steady spate of *prikazy* on rural Stakhanovism were issued.[56] A typical example is *prikaz* number six, dated 15 January 1936, titled "On the organization of Stakhanovite work methods and of the Stakhanovite movement on grain state farms," which was sent to all such farms from the People's Commissariat of State Farms at All-Union level.[57] It selected three particular farms for criticism, scolding the head of the political department on the Seventeenth Party Congress grain state farm, Comrade Vasil'ev, for not repairing machinery, for a breakdown in mass party work, and for "inactivity in developing the Stakhanovite movement."[58] Other heads of *politotdely* were also reprimanded for not promoting Stakhanovism. All farms were then ordered to implement decisions of the Central Committee Plenum of December 1935, which were to help the Stakhanovite movement to spread and to support shock workers.

The *prikaz* went on in some detail, outlining the necessary course of action. It instructed all heads of political departments to develop special programs of "political" work that included discussions of Stakhanovite records and to convene production meetings of Stakhanovites. They were told to attach teachers to Stakhanovites in order to raise their technical and educational levels. The pay of Stakhanovites was to be checked, as was their accommodation. Political departments were to ensure that Stakhanovites enjoyed a higher "cultural" level.[59] The central goal, however, was to popularize Stakhanovism and to pass on Stakhanovite work experiences to others. The final part of the *prikaz* ordered the organization of Stakhanovite days, five-days and ten-days, and the "careful facilitation of a transition to a higher mass form of the Stakhanovite movement."[60] An attachment to order number six followed on 16 January. This was a detailed "information letter" (*informatsionnoe pis'mo*) titled "On the organization of Stakhanovite methods of work and of the Stakhanovite movement in repairs." It observed that grain state farms were witnessing "the first sprouts of the Stakhanovite movement."[61] However, there were hundreds and thousands of state farm workers qualified to join the ranks of Stakhanovites. Farms were ordered to provide the necessary conditions for their workers to become Stakhanovites.

Prikazy were especially critical when a *politotdel* did not know who the shock workers were and when it classified "Stakhanovites" wrongly. *Prikaz* number 34 listed numerous faults on the Volzhnaia Kommuna pig farm in Kuibyshev krai which included these. All blame fell on Comrade Men'shikov, head of the *politotdel*, for his lack of organizational skills and his inability to lead. K. Soms, head of the Political Department of the People's Commissariat who signed the prikaz ordered him "to eliminate all shortcomings in the work of the *politotdel* and party organizations concerning the development of the Stakhanovite movement" and warned that "in the event of no improvement in work and of failure to eliminate shortcomings, strong measures of party punishment will be taken against him."[62] *Prikazy* aimed to encourage Stakhanovism by scolding and by threatening those who showed no interest in it.

"Discrediting Stakhanovism" was another charge. The *politotdel* on the Stavropol grain farm was reprimanded for this and for not organizing even one Stakhanovite day.[63] The farm was ordered to organize special Stakhanovite five-days. Copies of the *prikaz* were sent to all heads of grain *politotdely*, so everyone knew which farms were isolated for criticism, what constituted wrongful behavior, and precisely which patterns should be followed.

Prikazy insisted that Stakhanovism needed to be led. Heads of *politotdely* on dairy farms were instructed to stand "at the head of the Stakhanovite movement and be its genuine organizer." They were told to arrange widespread socialist competitions among Stakhanovites in close liaison with the trade unions and to work out concrete work pledges on how much should be milked from cows in advance.[64] Other *prikazy* in late 1936 regretted that the number of shock workers and Stakhanovites appeared to be dropping.[65]

By contrast, some *prikazy* exuded praise. *Prikaz* number 72 of 8 June 1936 commended a farm director and head of the *politotdel* on a farm in Sverdlovsk oblast. Here "huge work" had been carried out in promoting Stakhanovism. The whole farm was involved in competitions, everyone making work pledges. Daily, everyone knew work results. Moreover, "exceptional warmth" surrounded the care and attention of *znatnye liudi* (distinguished people) and Stakhanovites. Their flats were pleasant and they enjoyed vacations in sanatoria. With wide circulation, such a *prikaz* served to inform heads of *politotdely* of how they should be working and made clear what would merit praise from those above.[66] A similar style was adopted when successful farms were singled out, giving details of productivity and explaining why it was so good.[67] Another style of *prikaz* began by praising achievements, then itemizing weaknesses.[68]

Orders also went from the All-Union Commissariat directly to heads of *politotdely* on farms concerning the role of the Komsomol in promoting Stakhanovism. In order number 13, dated 28 January 1936, "On carrying out a raid of the light cavalry on questions of the Stakhanovite movement," Komsomol members were ordered to conduct a storming activity.[69] The aim was to demolish obstacles to Stakhanovism posed by its opponents on farms. The Komsomol was also reprimanded for performing such raids too slowly and inadequately.[70]

Prikazy, then, were various in form but united in message. The *politotdely* in particular, in liaison with the Komsomol and party and trade unions, were ordered to ensure that Stakhanovism spread and to check any falls in Stakhanovite numbers. Through *prikazy* those in commissariats at All-Union and republican levels attempted to exert leverage on those in positions of authority at local levels. They were met, however, with responses ranging from attempted implementation to noncompliance. In instances of the latter, attitudes or the impossibility of the task in local conditions or a combination of both lay behind inaction. The power of the *prikaz* to influence rural life was variable.

THE EIGHTEENTH PARTY CONGRESS

Whereas *prikazy* targeted specific groups of rural leaders, party congresses made explicit to larger audiences in a public forum what party policies, priorities, and preferences were, to be covered in the press afterward. By the later years of the Soviet state, in the 1970s and 1980s, party congresses were huge affairs which mobilized thousands of party members from all over the Union and instructed them in party agendas. In the early 1920s they met, on average, yearly and were policy-making bodies. Under Stalin they became infrequent as power became more arbitrary and was more heavily concentrated in the leader's hands. Given the spacing of congresses after the Seventeenth Party Congress in 1934, only the Eighteenth Party Congress in 1939 could conceivably have referred to Stakhanovism.

At this congress Central Committee Secretary Andrei Andreev delivered the main speech on agriculture. After criticizing "enemies of the people" in the countryside for making animals ill, killing them, destroying machinery, and sowing too shallowly, he proceeded to regret poor harvests in 1938 in Saratov, Stalingrad, Moscow, and other oblasts due to a dry summer and echoed Stalin's call for 8 million poods of grain in 1939, or 13 tsentners per hectare.[71] Once these obligatory opening themes had been addressed, Andreev went on to devote considerable time to "advanced" peasants, reporting their production feats and selecting individual work teams for praise. Among many others he named "the famous advanced collective farmers" Efremov and Chumanov in Altai krai for harvesting from between 213 and 372 poods per hectare in 1936. This, he commented, "was completely unexpected by the local agronomists."[72] Andreev proudly announced, "in the following year these and many other links in Beloglazovskii district attained an unprecedented harvest—427 to 457 poods per hectare. Comrade Chumanov in 1938 got 512 poods from a hectare."[73] Praise was due not only to the peasants themselves but also to the local party secretary in Beloglazovskii district for taking initiative. Andreev observed, "this shows that our district party committees in any district can do it, if they want, and are able to do it."[74]

There were three didactic messages in this information. First, ordinary hardworking peasants could produce good results; second, agronomists had to pay attention to new work methods; and third, local party organizations needed to take special initiative to promote Stakhanovism. Andreev hammered across that local parties had to be decisive, but regrettably many were not.

There was, moreover, serious reason for initiative to be taken. Andreev underscored to the congress that the difference between the average harvest of 56 poods per hectare and Chumanov's feat of 512 poods was huge. Likewise, the difference between the average cotton harvest of 12.9 tsentners and the best result of 151 tsentners was significant. In flax, too, the lesson was identical. The average of 2.7 tsentners paled against records of 21 tsentners. In other sectors, such as sugar beet, this pattern repeated itself.[75] Were, then, high records "accidental," asked Andreev rhetorically? This truly Soviet question received a predictable reply:

> These people, comrades, are the most ordinary. They came from families of the middle peasantry, from *batrachka* and from the poor peasantry. And just as Comrade Stalin spoke of Stakhanovites, these people are simple and modest without pretentions of being in the limelight as All-Union figures.[76]

Stakhanovites, Andreev insisted, "loved their work." The secrets of their success stemmed from diligence and work methods and were as follows:

> First, advanced workers in agriculture adopt a combination of techniques of agronomy, reciprocally coordinated, not severing one method from another. Secondly, their methods amount to a struggle for the common good through snow retention and early autumn plowing, plowing up of fallow, harrowing of sowing (not only winter, but also spring) for the removal of crust after rain.[77]

Thirdly, Stakhanovites battled with weeds and paid attention to the soil; fourthly, they facilitated early sowing; and lastly, they thought about where to plant seed, its quality, how to use manure, and the relevance of soil composition and climate.[78]

In sum, Andreev's message to the congress on shock work and Stakhanovism was that higher productivity in the fields was possible and was already being attained by "tens of thousands" of ordinary peasants who were prepared to change their work methods.[79] Andreev's words echoed what Kalinin had said in December 1935 but developed the points with much greater detail.

Andreev's speech was based upon a wide range of thoroughly prepared documents, now held in party archives. Not only had he, or his speechwriters, studied the detailed application of agronomy, but he had also read extensively about the biographies and work practices of Stakhanovites in different sectors of the economy, including the above mentioned Efremov.[80] The documents include details of the reaction of local party committees to Stakhanovism. Evidently, Secretary Gusev of the Altai kraikom had taken three years to respond to Efremov's first feats of production. The land department had similarly failed to pass on Efremov's lessons to others and Narkomzem had been silent, too.[81] Among these lessons was that "without exception" all *Efremovtsy* practiced snow retention and used manure, despite the lack of encouragement that they had encountered.[82]

Andreev insisted at the Eighteenth Party Congress that local parties should back such "ordinary" peasants. He posited that any honest and hardworking peasant could become a Stakhanovite and that, as also suggested at Central Committee Plenary sessions in 1936 and 1938, Stakhanovites' above-average productivity addressed a range of problems of Soviet agriculture.

THE KOMSOMOL

The All-Union Leninist Communist Union of Youth, or Komsomol (VLKSM—*Vse-soiuznyi Leninskii Kommunisticheskii Soiuz Molodezhi*), like the party, was exhorted to encourage rural Stakhanovism. The Komsomol was the youth group of the party for those aged 14 to 32.

There were two sorts of instructions or messages sent to local Komsomol organizations: the *postanovlenie* issued by the Central Committee of the VLKSM, very much repeating the pattern of "decisions" in the party machine; and the content of speeches delivered to congresses, such as the Tenth Congress of the Komsomol held in April 1936.

In September 1936, a Plenum of the VLKSM Central Committee called directly upon Komsomol organizations to draw its members and young people "into the Stakhanovite movement and to improve their technical training."[83] The Plenum announced that "Komsomol organizations play a leading role in the Stakhanovite movement."[84] Similarly, in September 1938, a *postanovlenie*, "On improving the work of the Komsomol in the countryside," declared, "Komsomol organizations must not stand to one side of socio-political work of the village."[85] It instructed them to "be initiators of socialist competition and of Stakhanovite labor in all spheres of kolkhoz production" and "to the utmost to help each Komsomol member, young male and female collective farmers, to become shock workers and Stakhanovites of agriculture."[86]

In contrast to this general call, sometimes a decision concerned particular oblasts, such as Tula and Kuibyshev in 1939.[87] Here Komsomol organizations and local land departments were told to "head the mass movement among young people" and to guide socialist competitions.[88] The order even specified the precise number of first, second, and third prizes. Similar exhortations were made at Komsomol congresses.

As at the Eighteenth Party Congress, it was Andreev who delivered a speech at the Tenth Congress of the VLKSM that included a section titled "The Stakhanovite movement and the Komsomol." Concerning the sabotage of Stakhanovism, Andreev urged that: "The Komsomol must in every way help the party to crush this sabotage and resistance and to develop the Stakhanovite movement still further."[89] Andreev put special emphasis on the "espe-cially decisive role" of the Komsomol in the countryside in developing Stakhanovite agriculture and in meeting Comrade Stalin's task of "achieving in three to four years an increase in the production of bread to 7–8 milliard poods."[90] The narrative was that enough bread depended upon Stakhanovism. Yet the movement, Andreev pointed out, was a new one and needed energy for it to spread: "We must recognize that the Stakhanovite movement on the collective farms is still only beginning but the basis is there for a quick and wide development."[91]

Andreev trumpeted that the results of Pasha Angelina and Mariia Dem-chenko had already pulled the countryside out of backwardness and the po-tential was enormous. But he warned that:

> The Stakhanovite movement in agriculture will not go on its own. This demands great organizational work. And the Komsomol will play a special role in this. The role of young people in agriculture is more significant than in industry.[92]

Older generations in rural areas, he argued, were more accustomed to the tra-ditions of individual labor, whilst the young were more "progressive," so the Komsomol, in particular, had a vital part to play in rural areas.[93] Underpin-ning this plea was concern that loyalties to the collective should be cemented. Thus the mobilization of the Komsomol was essential to the glorious project of reshaping the countryside, redefining the meaning of work, and fashioning Stakhanovite souls. As a reward for their efforts, Stakhanovites themselves were also mobilized beyond the farm to rallies, conferences, and congresses.

CONGRESSES AND CONFERENCES MOBILIZE PEASANTS "FROM ABOVE"

Part of the part played by rural shock workers and Stakhanovites involved their mobilization beyond the farm to attend grand events. Here they were re-warded for their efforts in production and were told what the regime's poli-cies and priorities were. A crucial element in these mobilizing events was that peasants rubbed shoulders with an array of top leaders, even if at a distance. In speeches, leaders instructed them in the significance of their work and their status for farm, productivity, party, and Stalin.[94] Peasants were thus "in-volved" in the proceedings, enjoying the opportunity to participate and "be-long" in the system, getting something back from it. These events saw inter-actions of top decision makers with the labor power who fulfilled their plans. They needed each other for their scripts to work.

There were various important congresses and conferences, held in the capital and also in the republics, which celebrated shock work and Stakhanovism, particularly in 1935 and 1936. These gatherings generally glorified production feats and urged peasants to work even harder, either to become Stakhanovites or to improve upon their Stakhanovite records. Prominent events included the First and Second Congresses of Kolkhoz Shock Workers in 1933 and 1935 and the First All-Union Conference of Stakhanovites in 1935, as well as the Conference of "500ers" in sugar beet production in November 1935, the Conference of Advanced Male and Female Combine Harvester Drivers in December 1935, the gathering of advanced collective farmers of Tadzhikistan and Turkmenistan in December 1935, the Conference of Best Workers in Animal Husbandry in Novosibirsk in February 1936, the All-Union Conference of Advanced Workers in Animal Husbandry with the leaders of party and government in December 1936, and the Third Conference of Advanced Workers in Animal Husbandry of Kazakhstan in January 1939.[95] Sometimes conferences took place at oblast and raion levels too, such as the Smolny Conference of Stakhanovite Flax Growers in Leningrad oblast in February 1939 and the Conference of Advanced Workers in Agriculture in Iampol'skii raion of Vinnitsa oblast in February 1939.[96]

These grand events were characterized by cues and exhortations. At the Second All-Union Congress of Kolkhoz Shock Workers, Chernov praised rural shock workers and urged them to spread their techniques:

> Your duty, the duty of advanced and distinguished people of collective farms, kolkhoz shock workers, includes not only working as shock workers yourselves, but also raising the whole collective farm mass to your pace and quality of work.[97]

Scripts frequently referred to shock workers and Stakhanovites as "advanced" (*peredovye*) and "distinguished" (*znatnye*). Both had "duties" to increase their own output and to encourage others to do likewise. At the same Congress, Nikolai Ezhov, then Chairperson of the Party Control Commission and one year later People's Commissar of Internal Affairs, echoed Chernov with "our task must be to raise the whole mass of collective farmers to the level of advanced shock workers."[98]

Narratives on the meaning of Stakhanovite labor were common. At the First All-Union Conference of Stakhanovites, Stalin's famous speech argued that Stakhanovism was a special movement, representing a "new stage" of socialist competition, preparing the conditions for transition from socialism to communism.[99] Stakhanovites were "new people" and "special people" able to discard old ideas about technology. They were "cultured," able to harness technology, and free of conservative ideas. Moreover, Stakhanovites were examples of "precision and accuracy in work, able to value the time factor, learning to consider time not only in minutes but in seconds."[100]

A repeated message was that Stakhanovism as a special movement was also destined to spread. Although, Stalin noted, "Today there are still few Stakhanovites, who cannot doubt that tomorrow there will be ten times more?"[101] Politburo member Anastas Mikoian also indicated the openness of the movement, stating, "Today we cannot fully and precisely say what the Stakhanovite movement, which is growing daily, will give."[102] Linking it directly to the purges, Mikoian observed that once its enemies were conquered, and once managements had undergone a "*perestroika*" (restructuring) from the top down, and as soon as leaders were able to "head" the movement, then successes in production were certain.[103]

Stalin also emphasized that Stakhanovism had developed "from below" and that Stakhanovites often toiled "in spite of the will of the administration" in workplaces and "even in struggle" with those in it.[104] Leaders pitched Stakhanovism at its outset as a movement against backward factory managements, and used Stakhanovism as a weapon in the regime's own purges of factory directors. Stalin also acknowledged that there were workers who opposed Stakhanovism. Although Stalin's words at this event applied to industry, his points were generalizable to agriculture and subsequently applied to it.

At the same conference, Commissar of Heavy Industry, Grigorii Ordzhonikidze, affectionately known as Sergo, suggested that Stakhanovites were, in fact, following Stalin's famous words of May 1935 that "cadres decide everything" and were working in the spirit of Stalin's observation that technology and people "can and must give wonders."[105] The implication was that even if Stakhanovism had developed "from below," it was entirely consistent with the regime's priorities and Stalin's guidance. Like Stalin, Molotov argued that Stakhanovism had grown from deep among the rank and file of ordinary workers. Molotov signaled that no longer were there merely individual Stakhanovites or separate groups of Stakhanovites but a "genuine torrent of strong force" with "many thousands of Stakhanovites."[106]

The overall narrative from the First All-Union Conference of Stakhanovites was that the movement came from the grass roots, was growing, was ripe for leadership from enlightened managements, and was consistent with the regime's priorities, but was suffering shortsighted opposition from workers and administrators. Its future was highly promising but open ended.

Although common messages were delivered at most conferences, the emphasis of what leaders imparted shifted according to context. At a gathering with shock workers from the sugar beet fields, Stalin paid special attention to the role of rural women—particularly apt since the vast majority of 500ers present were women. Stalin praised that:

> We heard the speeches of women, not ordinary ones I would say—women heroines of labor. Only heroines of labor could have achieved their successes. We did not have such women before. I am fifty-six years old, I have seen things, I have seen sufficient working men and women. But such women I have never met. They are completely new people.[107]

The script reminded those present that not only were shock workers and Stakhanovites "new people," but female heroines were emancipated, unlike in the tsarist past. Stalin singled out Mariia Demchenko for special praise, decorating her and her brigade with medals.[108]

Particularly relevant to the Conference of Advanced Male and Female Combine Drivers, held in December 1935, were reflections on grain. Here Stalin noted that in 1935 the country would harvest more than 5.5 milliard poods of grain. He stressed that demands, however, were increasing and productivity had to rise. Asking how much grain might be needed in three or four years, Stalin pointed out "We'll need no less than 7–8 milliard poods of grain."[109] Such a colossal increase in demand was explained by industrial growth, technological possibilities, urbanization, and higher living standards. Quoting now famous words, Stalin added, "Everyone now says that the material position of workers has considerably improved, that life has become better, more cheerful." As a consequence, Stalin argued, "people are reproducing faster than in the old days" and "the death rate is lower and the birth rate higher."[110]

In short, life was moving at a rapid pace and improving. Shock workers and Stakhanovites had to guarantee an appropriate momentum in production since much hung on it. Stalin also urged drivers of combine harvesters to minimize the loss of grain,[111] imparting, "the great significance of combine harvesters is that they keep loss at an insignificant minimum."[112] Given that previous years had seen grain losses of between 20 and 25 percent, and given that combine drivers were the key to reducing such losses, Stalin called for an increase in the number of male and female combine drivers "not by the day, but by the hour."[113]

Different in emphasis again was one of the central messages to the Conference of Advanced Collective Farmers of Tadzhikistan and Turkmenistan in December 1935. After discussing the cotton crop, Stalin insisted: "But there is, Comrades, one thing more valued than cotton—it is the friendship of the peoples of our country." That the conference was taking place was evidence that "the friendship among peoples of our great country is strengthening."[114]

Stalin's script was consistent with official policy on the "friendship of peoples" and suggested that the Russian people were no longer subjugators as under repressive tsarism with its capitalist goals. Contrasts were drawn between the "dark" past and dynamic production feats.

Congresses and conferences delivered multiple messages, some truer than others. Although repeated signals about production were at the core, other arguments pivoted around them. And if peasants did not grasp the meaning of Stakhanovism from congresses, they were didactically instructed in it twice yearly in official slogans.

OFFICIAL SLOGANS: MAY DAY AND 7 NOVEMBER

The content and sequence of slogans to celebrate May Day and the Anniversary of the 1917 Revolution can be used as quick indicators of priorities of official ideology in given years.[115]

Predictably, the first May Day slogans on rural Stakhanovism appeared in 1936, and also the most. Out of a total of thirty-six slogans published in *Pravda*, twelve referred to Stakhanovism, one to the 500ers in sugar beet and another to *znatnye liudi*, or "distinguished people," of the collective farms. Praise was given to Stakhanovism in the Red Army, in heavy industry and in light industry generally, and more specifically in transport, coal, and oil. Directed at agriculture, slogan 37 declared "First of May greeting to the 500ers in sugar beet fields!" and slogan 38 praised "Glory to male and female Stakhanovites of the cotton fields! We will give the country 40 million poods of cotton."[116] Slogan 39 brought "Glory to the distinguished (*znatnye*) people of the kolkhoz countryside—male and female tractor drivers, male and female combine drivers, brigade leaders, link leaders, male and female kolkhoz chairpersons!"[117] As the Stakhanovite movement had just begun, it was greeted with enthusiasm in all sectors of the economy and in the army. Relatively low down on the list, however, Stakhanovism was behind other official priorities and rural Stakhanovism was lower than industrial, the countryside ever behind the town.

For the duration of the 1930s and into 1941, shock work and Stakhanovism were lauded in slogans. The burst of excitement of May 1936, however, was not repeated. Just three slogans on Stakhanovites, shock workers, and "distinguished people" celebrated the anniversary of the revolution in 1936.[118] Thereafter in 1938, 1939, 1940, and 1941, either two or three slogans in May and November referred to them.[119] This pattern reflected a loud launch in the spring of 1936 and the movement's ebb in the early 1940s with the advent of war and new priorities.

Within this broad pattern, slogans with messages specific to a given year, or time of year, are evident. In May 1937, slogan 20 emphasized the huge size of a "multi-million army" of shock workers in industry at a time when the size was of concern. The party wanted higher numbers, but Stakhanovites were experiencing opposition and in some areas dropping in numbers. Slogan 24 greeted Stakhanovites of the fields for fulfilling the spring sowing plan at a time when good sowing was a priority, as it did in 1938.[120] More broadly, slogan 23 in 1938 exhorted, "Achieve fulfilment and overfulfilment of the economic plan for 1938—the first year of the third five year plan! Develop wider the mighty Stakhanovite movement!"[121] These slogans linked the glorification of Stakhanovism to seasonally desirable productive feats and to the start of the Third Five-Year Plan.

The emphasis on size continued up to 1939. Slogan 21 for May Day glorified the fact that "the Stakhanovite movement is growing and strengthening" and categorized it as "one of the most remarkable results of the Second Five-Year Plan!"[122] This mirrored official priorities from 1937 to 1939 for the movement's expansion. Although it was proclaimed huge, there was serious concern that it was not large enough.

In 1940 there were no separate slogans for industry and agriculture and what was said was similar in May and November, bringing broad greetings to Stakhanovites in industry, transport, and agriculture.[123] This message was repeated for May Day of 1941, but slogans for the anniversary of the revolution in that year were silent about Stakhanovism.[124] Similarly, in 1942 both shock workers and Stakhanovites dropped out of official holiday slogans.[125] Now at war, the USSR had other priorities for its people. Although heroic work was still encouraged, it was defined in terms of serving the front and destroying the enemy.[126] Local initiatives did spawn "wartime Stakhanovites" but their prominence was low.[127]

Thus holiday slogans on rural Stakhanovism began in May 1936 and petered out after May 1941, reflecting the movement's rise and fall and official hopes for it. While many citizens may have paid little attention to the slogans, those intent upon becoming good communists will have known how to read their meanings. Along with posters, slogans constituted a vital part of the transmission belt of official scripts and suggestions from political apex to Soviet ground.

CONCLUSION

From 1935 through to 1941, multiple narratives about rural shock work and Stakhanovism could be found at various sites at the apex of the political system where they served to transmit to party members and interested citizens its meanings. These ranged from simple slogans published in *Pravda* to ponderous reflections by Andreev at Party and Komsomol Congresses after poring over reports on technical details held in the Central Committee Department of Agriculture. Rural Stakhanovism was an important issue on political agendas as leaders increasingly viewed it as the key to higher productivity in the countryside. Leaders saw Stakhanovites as an elite grouping, not least because they were generally fewer in number than shock workers and since ordinary peasants usually outnumbered both of these categories of hardworking peasants. Official reasoning went that without Stakhanovites, exhortations to increase productivity would go unmet.

The press in the one-party state played a crucial role in attempts to direct rural Stakhanovism. Journalists served the regime by defining what Stakhanovism was for its readers and by suggesting how peasants could become Stakhanovites. Their constructed images of Stakhanovism were an integral part of the movement's development and demise.

NOTES

1. *Pervoe Vsesoiuznoe Soveshchanie Rabochikh i Rabotnits-Stakhanovtsev, 14–17 Noiabria 1935: Stenograficheskii otchët* (Moscow: Partizdat TsK VKP [b], 1935), 361.
2. RGASPI, fond 17, opis' 3, delo 994, list 35.
3. Sources for this chapter include all those listed in appendix I under RGASPI as well as party and Komsomol congresses, special conference gatherings of Stakhanovites with political leaders, and annual slogans to commemorate May Day and the Bolshevik Revolution.
4. *Pravda*, 9 September 1935, 1.
5. *Pravda*, 11 September 1935, 1.
6. *Pravda*, 13 September 1935, 1.
7. *Pravda*, 14 September 1935, 2.
8. *Krest'ianskaia gazeta*, 6 October 1935, 4.
9. *Krest'ianskaia gazeta*, 6 October 1935, 4.
10. *Krest'ianskaia gazeta*, 14 October 1935, 2.
11. *Pervyi Vsesoiuznyi S"ezd Udarnykh Brigad (k tridtsatiletiiu s"ezda): Sbornik dokumentov i materialov* (Moscow: Izdatel'stvo VTsSPS Profizdat, 1959); *Pervyi Vsesoiuznyi S"ezd Kolkhoznikov-Udarnikov Peredovykh Kolkhozov, 15–19 Fevralia 1933 g: Stenograficheskii otchët* (Moscow and Leningrad: 1933); *Vtoroi Vsesoiuznyi S"ezd Kolkhoznikov-Udarnikov, 11–17 Fevralia 1935 g: Stenograficheskii otchët* (Moscow: Sel'khozgiz, 1935).
12. According to Lewis Siegelbaum, the term *udarnichestvo* had originated during the Civil War "to denote the performance of particularly arduous or urgent tasks." It then developed a new meaning in 1927 as workers were dedicated to over-fulfilling

assignments. It was not linked solely to output, however, and could mean a commitment to abstaining from alcohol or from being absent less frequently. See Lewis H. Siegelbaum, *Stakhanovism and the Politics of Productivity in the USSR, 1935–1941* (Cambridge: Cambridge University Press, 1988), 40.

13. R. W. Davies and Oleg Khlevnyuk, "Stakhanovism and the Soviet Economy," *Europe-Asia Studies* 54, no. 6 (September 2002): 867–903.

14. Jochen Hellbeck, "Fashioning the Stalinist Soul: The Diary of Stepan Podlubnyi (1931–1939), *Jahrbücher für Geschichte Osteuropas* 44, Heft 3 (1996): 344–73.

15. Siegelbaum, *Stakhanovism.*

16. See, for instance, RGASPI, f. 17, op. 3, d. 973, ll. 4, 6, 7, and 9. See also f. 17, op. 3, d. 994, l. 12 giving permission to a factory to hold a meeting of Stakhanovites.

17. RGASPI, f. 17, op. 3, d. 994, l. 35.

18. Very precise details down to conference numbers were included in the telegram sent by the Politburo. On permission for the party in Western Siberia to organize a conference in July 1936 of "advanced" collective farmers in Buriat Mongolia, see RGASPI, f. 17, op. 3, d. 977, l. 9. According to the same pattern, in April 1938 the Politburo sent a telegram which declared: "Permit the party committee of Krasnoiarsk krai to call in the first half of April a krai conference of collective farm chairpersons and rural Stakhanovites, of 700 to 800 people." Approval was given for the event, its timing, and the number of participants. See RGASPI, f. 17, op. 3, f. 998, l. 15. The same applied to a Stakhanovite conference in Arkhangel'. Here the obkom was given approval for a gathering of 250 people on 29 June. See RGASPI, f. 17, op. 3, d. 1000, l. 7. See, too, f. 17, op. 3, d. 997, l. and f. 17, op. 3, f. 998, l. 15.

19. RGASPI, f. 17, op. 3, d. 975, l. 8; f. 17, op .3, d. 978, l. 51. Also in October 1935, the Politburo announced that D. Sulimov should be sent for eight days to the Bashkir ASSR to take part in a rally of Stakhanovites. See RGASPI, f. 17, op. 3, d. 972, l. 36.

20. RGASPI, f. 17, op. 3, d. 975, l. 52. Occasionally, too, the Politburo advised another organization to send a member to be present at a particular gathering. Accordingly, in 1936, the Politburo told Narkomzem to send a representative to an animal husbandry congress in Kazakhstan. See RGASPI, f. 17, op. 3, d. 980, l. 58.

21. RGASPI, f. 17, op. 3, d. 979, l. 45.

22. RGASPI, f. 17, op. 3, d. 374, l. 3.

23. RGASPI, f. 17, op. 3, d. 994, l. 79. The Politburo also agreed to many initiatives. For instance, in early 1936 in somewhat subdued language it informed that it would "not object to the suggestion of VTsSPS to make 11 January 1936 shock worker day." This referred to *Vsesoiuznyi tsentral'nyi sovet professional'nykh soiuzov*, or the All-Union Central Council of Trade Unions. See RGASPI, f. 17, op. 3, d. 974, l. 3.

24. RGASPI, f. 17, op. 3, d. 994, l. 79.

25. RGASPI, f. 17, op. 3, d. 994, l. 79.

26. RGASPI, f. 17, op. 3, d. 972, l. 67 and ll. 159–61. Similarly, in December 1935, the Politburo awarded medals to "advanced" male and female drivers of combine harvesters. See RGASPI, f. 17, op. 3, d. 973, l. 30 and ll. 64–73. Sometimes approval was given to a *postanovlenie* that decorated collective farmers in particular republics, such as in Uzbekistan, Turkmenistan, Tadzhikistan, Kazakhstan, and Kara-Kalpakskaia ASSR in December 1935, or in Armenia in January 1936, or which

awarded presents of trucks to "advanced" collective farms in Uzbekistan and Kaza-khstan. See RGASPI. f. 17, op. 3, d. 974, l. 14; l. 13; f. 17, op. 3, d. 974, l. 29; f. 17, op. 3. d. 974, l. 57. More frequently, however, specific sectors were named. In Feb-ruary 1936, for instance, approval was given to decorating "advanced" peasants in an-imal husbandry and in March to those in flax and hemp. Refer to RGASPI, f. 17, op. 3, d. 975, l. 24; f. 17, op. 3, l. 976, l. 20.

27. For examples of decorations in 1939 to advanced peasants in Ukraine, Moscow oblast, Uzbekistan, Kazakhstan, Rostov oblast, Belorussia, Turkmenia, and Leningrad and Voronezh oblasts, see RGASPI, f. 17, op. 3, d. 1006, ll. 11, 23, 27, 20, and 64; f. 17, op. 3, d. 1016, l. 35; and f. 17, op. 3, d. 1008, l. 44 and l. 51.

28. See, for instance, awards to rural *peredoviki* in 1940, 1941, and 1942: RGASPI, f. 17, op. 3, d. 1020, l. 49; f. 17, op. 3, d. 1029, l. 21; f. 17, op. 3, d. 1030, l. 13; f. 17, op. 3, d. 1033, l. 32; f. 17, op. 3, d. 1044, l. 26.

29. RGASPI, f. 17, op. 3, d. 972, l. 77.

30. RGASPI, f. 17, op. 3, d. 974, l. 15.

31. RGASPI, f. 17, op. 3, d. 976, l. 4.

32. RGASPI, f. 17, op. 3, d. 975, l. 47.

33. RGASPI, ll. 47–48.

34. RGASPI, f. 17, op. 3, d. 973.

35. RGASPI, f. 17, op. 2, d. 549, ll. 2–22.

36. RGASPI, f. 17, op. 2, d. 549, l. 2.

37. RGASPI, f. 17, op. 2, d. 548, l. 19.

38. RGASPI, f. 17, op. 2, d. 548, l. 19.

39. *Pravda*, 27 December 1935, 3.

40. RGASPI, f. 17, op. 2, d. 563, l. 8.

41. RGASPI, f. 17, op. 2, d. 563, l. 15.

42. RGASPI, f. 17, op. 2, d. 563, ll. 15–41.

43. RGASPI, f. 17, op. 3, d. 565, ll. 1–6.

44. RGASPI, f. 17, op. 2, d. 623, l. 23.

45. This decision was taken on 20 October 1937. See RGASPI, f. 17, op. 3, d. 993, l. 8.

46. RGASPI, f. 17, op. 2, d. 635, l. 99.

47. Many a decision coming out of the Central Executive Committee also referred to rural Stakhanovism, but usually concerned the awarding of Orders of Lenin and Orders of the Red Banner.

48. *Krest'ianskaia gazeta*, 24 February 1936, 8. For other examples of decisions coming out of the People's Commissariat of Agriculture, consult RGAE, f. 7486, op. 1, d. 884. Details of socialist competitions among women's tractor brigades are found on l.105.

49. *Krest'ianskaia gazeta*, 1 March 1936, 2.

50. A *postanovlenie* from Sovnarkom "On the state plan for spring sowing in 1937" called upon the People's Commissariat of Agriculture (*Narkomzem)*, the Peo-ple's Commissariat of State farms (*Narkomsovkhozov)*, the People's Commissariat of the Food Industry (*Narkompishcheprom*), local soviet organizations, directors of state farms and machine tractor stations, and kolkhoz chairs to fulfill the sowing plan. This

was to be on the basis of "further development of the Stakhanovite movement on collective and state farms." See *Krest'ianskaia gazeta*, 4 February 1937, 1.

51. *Krest'ianskaia gazeta,* 28 January 1938, 1, and 24 March 1938, 1 and 2.

52. *Krest'ianskaia gazeta*, 24 July 1938, 1 and 4. For reiteration of the point that the land departments should improve their work, see Ivan Benediktov, People's Commissar of Agriculture, in *Krest'ianskaia gazeta*, 28 December 1938, 3.

53. This was "On broadening winter sowing and measures for increasing harvesting in Eastern districts of the USSR." See *Krest'ianskaia gazeta*, 6 January 1939, 1.

54. See *Krest'ianskaia gazeta*, 30 January 1939, 4.

55. By the early 1940s, mention of Stakhanovism was generally absent from *postanovleniia* concerning productivity, although "wartime Stakhanovites" were mentioned. For discussion of disagreements at the apex of the system concerning wartime Stakhanovism in plowing see Mary Buckley, "The Nagornovskoe Dvizhenie: A Stakhanovite Movement in Ploughing That Was Not" in *Edinburgh Essays on Russia*, ed. Elspeth Reid (Nottingham: Astra Press, 2000), 39–47.

56. This draws on *prikazy* issued by the People's Commissariat of State Farms to heads of *politotdely* (political departments) on farms, which are held in RGASPI, and on *prikazy* issued by the Commissariat of State Farms of the RSFSR, stored in TsGA RSFSR. The former *prikazy* were signed either by K. Soms, head of the political department of the People's Commissariat, or by Zaitsev, his deputy, and the latter by Commissar Iurkin.

57. RGASPI, f. 349, op. 1. d. 239, ll. 38–39. This *opis'* is in the process of being reorganized and current *dela* and *listy* may soon be altered, rendering these references partially inaccurate. Materials, however, can easily be found through the dates and *prikaz* numbers given here. Note that this *opis'* is not currently advertised in the reading room and one has to make a special request for it. The materials used to be part of f. 349, op. 11, *Politicheskoe Upravlenie Narkomata Sovkhozov SSSR, 1933–1943g.*

58. RGASPI, f. 349, op. 1, d. 239, l. 38ob.

59. RGASPI, f. 349, op. 1, d. 239, l. 39.

60. RGASPI, f. 349, op. 1, d. 239, l. 39.

61. RGASPI, f. 349, op. 2, d. 239, l. 40.

62. RGASPI, f. 349, op. 1. d. 239, l. 157.

63. RGASPI, f. 349, op. 1, d. 239, l. 166.

64. Order number 40, RGASPI, f. 349, op. 1, d. 239, l80ob.

65. Order number 98 of 10 October to a sheep farm in Saratov krai noted that Stakhanovites were "significantly falling" in number and pressed for an improvement in work with them. See RGASPI, f. 349, op. 1, d. 240, l. 106.

66. RGASPI, f. 349, op. 1, d. 239, l. 106.

67. Commissar Iurkin, for example, on 29 October 1936, praised Chulki Sokolovo, a farm in Moscow oblast, for harvesting on average 1,250 tsentners of sugar beet per hectare, for animal feed. Four state farmers were named for their exceptional results. Iurkin explained that this excellent harvest was due to "the correct organization of labor, Stakhanovite work methods, the application of agronomy and new norms of manure." See TsGA RSFSR, f. 317, op. 4, d. 1, l. 1. This is *prikaz* number one. Iurkin

awarded the state farm director 1,000 rubles and the agronomist 500 rubles. A further 2,400 rubles was to be distributed among Stakhanovites and shock workers. Working with the state farm director, academics were told to produce a report on the farm's work methods. Iurkin declared that other state farm directors and agronomists were to send their best field workers to Chulki Sokolovo to study the farm's experience. The *prikaz* ended on the note that all state farms in four oblasts would send workers to follow courses.

68. Order number 22 of 14 February 1936 sent to pig farms started with "Political departments have achieved several successes in developing Stakhanovism." Changing tone, it castigated *politotdely* on two targeted farms for not doing this and blamed communists, Komsomol, and the trade union for unsatisfactory performance. See RGASPI, f. 349, op. 1, d. 239, ll. 106–08.

69. RGASPI, f. 349, op. 1, d. 239, ll. 72–72ob.

70. RGASPI, f. 349, op. 1, d. 239, ll. 72–72ob. Several related orders followed. Order number 20 itemized shortcomings in Komsomol work and order number 24 scolded Komsomols for carrying out the All-Union Raid of the Light Cavalry "with great lateness." See RGASPI, f. 349, op. 1. d. 239, ll. 100–100ob and ll. 112–13. On some farms the Komsomol did not start preparations until ten days after receiving information about the decision of the Central Committee of the Komsomol to promote the idea. Others did nothing until specifically urged from the People's Commissariat. The *prikazy* also stressed that prompt action was needed. See RGASPI, ll. 112–13. Other *prikazy* scolded party and Komsomol members on farms for not striving to be Stakhanovites themselves. *Prikaz* number 61 to a sheep farm noted that the *politotdel* was failing to promote Stakhanovism and that communists seemed oblivious of their avant-garde role in leading it. Moreover, "from among communists and komsomol members on the state farm there is not one Stakhanovite." Refer to RGASPI, f. 349, op. 1, d. 240, ll. 247–48. For examples of *prikazy* coming out of the People's Commissariat of Agriculture, consult RGAE, f. 7486, op. 1. See, for instance, d. 887.

71. *Pravda*, 14 March 1939, 3.

72. *Pravda*, 14 March 1939, 3.

73. *Pravda*, 14 March 1939, 3.

74. *Pravda*, 14 March 1939, 3.

75. *Pravda*, 14 March 1939, 3.

76. *Pravda*, 14 March 1939, 3.

77. *Pravda*, 14 March 1939, 4.

78. *Pravda*, 14 March 1939, 4.

79. *Pravda*, 14 March 1939, 4.

80. RGASPI, f. 477, op. 1, d. 64, ll. 1–20.

81. RGASPI, f. 477, op. 1, d. 64, l. 21.

82. RGASPI, f. 477, op. 1, d. 64, ll. 22–23.

83. TsKhDMO, f. 1, op. 2, d. 125, l. 8.

84. TsKhDMO, f. 1, op. 2, d. 121, l. 19.

85. *Tovarishch Komsomol: Dokumenty s"ezdov, konferentsii i TsK VLKSM, 1918–1968*, Tom 1, 1918–1941, p. 577.

86. *Tovarishch Komsomol: Dokumenty s"ezdov, konferentsii i TsK VLKSM, 1918–1968*, Tom 1, 1918–1941, p. 577.

87. In April 1939, a *postanovlenie* from the Central Committee of the Komsomol in conjunction with *Narkomzem* and *Narkomsovkhozov*, "On socialist competition named after the Third Stalinist Five-Year Plan for the further development of agriculture and animal husbandry," singled out Tula and Kuibyshev oblasts.

88. TsKhDMO, *Perechen': Kopii Postanovlenii Biuro TsK VLKSM po rabote sredi sel'skoi molodezhi za 1932–1939 gody*, 192.

89. *Krest'ianskaia gazeta*, 22 April 1936, 3.

90. *Krest'ianskaia gazeta*, 22 April 1936, 3.

91. *Krest'ianskaia gazeta*, 22 April 1936, 3.

92. *Krest'ianskaia gazeta*, 22 April 1936, 3.

93. *Krest'ianskaia gazeta*, 22 April 1936, 3.

94. At the Second All-Union Congress of Collective Farm Shock Workers, the new rules of agricultural cartels were explained by Iakov Iakovlev, head of the agriculture department of the Central Committee.

95. See footnote 11 above. In addition, consult "Priem kolkhoznits-udarnits sveklovichnykh polei," *Sotsialisticheskaia Rekonstruktsiia Sel'skogo Khoziaistva*, Part 5 (November 1935): 17; *Krest'ianskaia gazeta*, 26 November 1935, 2; "Rech Tovarishcha Stalina na soveshchanii peredovykh kombainerov i kombainerok 1-go Dekabria 1935 goda," *Bolshevik*, no. 23–24 (15 December 1935): 1–6; *Krest'ianskaia gazeta*, 6 December 1935, 1; "'Rech' Tovarishcha Stalina na soveshchanii peredovykh kolkhoznikov i kolkhoznits Tadzhikistana i Turkmenistana," *Bolshevik*, no. 23–24 (15 December 1935): 7–8; *Bolshevik*, no. 1 (1 January 1936): 36–40; *Krest'ianskaia gazeta*, 24 February 1936, 8; *Krest'ianskaia gazeta*, 16 December 1936, 2; *Krest'ianskaia gazeta*, 4 January 1939, 3.

96. *Krest'ianskaia gazeta*, 16 February 1939, 1; and 5 February 1939, 7.

97. *Vtoroi Vsesoiuznyi S'ezd Kolkhoznikov-Udarnikov*, op. cit., 231.

98. *Krest'ianskaia gazeta*, 14 November 1935, 2.

99. I. V. Stalin, "Znachenie Stakhanovskogo Dvizheniia," in *Pervoe Vsesoiuznoe soveshchanie rabochikh i rabotnits-stakhanovtsev, 14–17 Noiabria 1935: stenograficheskii otchët*, 357–61. This was followed by Stalin's "Korni stakhanovskogo dvizheniia," 361–65.

100. *Pervoe Vsesoiuznoe soveshchanie rabochikh i rabotnits-stakhanovtsev*, 360.

101. *Pervoe Vsesoiuznoe soveshchanie rabochikh i rabotnits-stakhanovtsev*, 360.

102. *Pervoe Vsesoiuznoe soveshchanie rabochikh i rabotnits-stakhanovtsev*, 161.

103. *Pervoe Vsesoiuznoe soveshchanie rabochikh i rabotnits-stakhanovtsev*, 161.

104. *Pervoe Vsesoiuznoe soveshchanie rabochikh i rabotnits-stakhanovtsev*, 8.

105. *Pervoe Vsesoiuznoe soveshchanie rabochikh i rabotnits-stakhanovtsev*, 8.

106. *Pervoe Vsesoiuznoe soveshchanie rabochikh i rabotnits-stakhanovtsev*, 261.

107. "Priem kolkhoznits-udarnits sveklovichnykh polei," *Sotsialisticheskaia Rekonstruktsiia Sel'skogo Khoziaistva*, Part 5 (November 1935): 17.

108. Mariia Demchenko was awarded the Order of Lenin and members of her brigade received the Order of Labor.

109. "'Rech' Tovarishcha Stalina na soveshchanii peredovykh kombainerov i kombainerok 1-go Dekabria 1935 goda," *Bolshevik*, no. 23–24 (15 December 1935), 2.

110. "'Rech' Tovarishcha Stalina na soveshchanii peredovykh kombainerov," 3.

111. "'Rech' Tovarishcha Stalina na soveshchanii peredovykh kombainerov," 5–6.

112. "'Rech' Tovarishcha Stalina na soveshchanii peredovykh kombainerov," 6.

113. "'Rech' Tovarishcha Stalina na soveshchanii peredovykh kombainerov," 6.

114. "'Rech' Tovarishcha Stalina na soveshchanii peredovykh kombainerov," 7.

115. Not surprisingly, the slogans to celebrate the eighteenth anniversary of the revolution, which were issued in October 1935, did not include one on Stakhanovism. Although the movement had begun, the drawing up of slogans, planned in advance, predated it. Stalin's famous "cadres decide everything" which was later linked to the Stakhanovite movement was slogan number 26.

116. *Pravda*, 22 April 1936, 1. See, too, *Krest'ianskaia gazeta*, 24 April 1936, 1.

117. *Pravda*, 22 April 1936, 1.

118. *Pravda*, 29 October 1936, 1.

119. *Pravda*, 20 April 1938, 1; *Pravda*, 3 November 1938, 1; *Pravda*, 26 April 1939, 1; *Pravda*, November 1939, 1; *Pravda*, 26 April 1940, 1; *Pravda*, 4 November 1940, 1; *Pravda*, 29 April 1941, 1; *Pravda*, 31 October 1941, 1.

120. *Pravda*, 26 April 1937, 1; *Krest'ianskaia gazeta*, 20 April 1938, 1; *Pravda*, 3 November 1938, 1.

121. *Pravda*, 20 April 1938, 1.

122. *Pravda*, 26 April 1939, 1.

123. *Pravda*, 26 April 1940, 1; *Pravda*, 4 November 1940, 1.

124. *Pravda*, 29 April 1941, 1; *Pravda*, 31 October 1941, 1.

125. *Pravda*, 25 April 1942, 1; *Pravda*, 28 October 1942, 1.

126. See, for instance, *Pravda*, 28 October 1942, 1, slogan number 44.

127. For discussion of the young Valentin Nargornyi who, in 1942 in Krasnoiarsk krai instigated a wartime Stakhanovite movement in plowing which ultimately received enthusiastic backing from party secretary in the krai and at the apex of the system from the Central Committee Department of Agriculture but condemnation from the Central Committee Department of Agitation and Propaganda, see Mary Buckley, "The *Nagornovskoe Dvizhenie*: A Stakhanovite Movement in Ploughing That was Not." pp. 39–47 in *Edinburgh Essays on Russia*, edited by Elspeth Reid, Nottingham: Astra Press, 2000.

Chapter Three

Official Images of Rural Shock Work and Stakhanovism

Mariia Demchenko in the kolkhoz field did the same as Aleksei Stakhanov in the Donbas mine.

— Pravda[1]

Iosif Vissarionovich Stalin laughs with us, converses with us, shares with us his thoughts on how to work on the collective farm and on how we can live better.

— Mariia Demchenko[2]

Integral to the mobilization of the peasantry into shock work and Stakhanovism was the construction of images in the press and movies about what Stakhanovism was and what it meant for peasants, rural life, socialism, party, and Stalin. The fashioning of Stakhanovites coincided with the sculpting of "new communist persons" and the two became intertwined. Mariia Demchenko was the peasant most frequently compared to Aleksei Stakhanov as his rural equivalent and together they became icons of the "new woman" and "new man," inspirers of heroines and heroes in the fields. Mobilization into Stakhanovism also fostered a redefinition of gender relations as communism stood for the emancipation of women, their participation in social production, and more generally for equality of the sexes. Propaganda insisted that both women and men could be Stakhanovites and that as "advanced" people they shared certain special qualities that others ought to emulate.

In the one-party state, journalists, propagandists, and film directors conveyed appropriate messages to Soviet citizens about what rural shock workers and Stakhanovites were like, in keeping with policy priorities coming out of the apex of the party and government. They reported production successes and explained good results by describing, quoting, and praising Stakhanovites. Thus the press, memoirs, and movies projected images of Stakhanovites' personalities and attitudes toward work, thereby constructing the politically correct features of Stakhanovism. At a time of "socialist realism" when life was often shown in propaganda, art, plays, and cinema as it "should" be rather than it actually was, press, art gallery, stage, and screen all carried glossy messages and positive smiling suggestions, many of which appeared exaggerated or fictive, in sharp contrast to a blacker reality of purges and repression. This quality, however, was integral to Stalinist mobilization and to stories of its heroic Stakhanovite agents. Its upbeat tempo and jubilance also became elements in Stakhanovites' own scripts in public settings.

The images presented in the national and rural press helped to define the contours that framed Stakhanovism. Narratives in *Pravda*, *Krest'ianskaia gazeta*, and *Sovkhoznaia gazeta* fashioned what Stakhanovism represented by generating categories, labels, and evaluations. The newspaper images of Stakhanovism were like filters or prisms through which peasants could look at Stakhanovism and interpret its meanings with ready pointers or handy benchmarks.

The loud messages of progress, more technology, bigger harvest, more food, better life, and success that accompanied Stakhanovism had an impact on citizens' consciousness about the world in which they lived, however cynical they were about it and however many jokes they chose to tell at the system's expense.

IMAGES OF SHOCK WORKERS AND STAKHANOVITES

Images of shock workers and Stakhanovites as new communist persons conveyed enthusiasm, hard work, strict discipline, superiority, selflessness, strength of character, resilience against resistance, ability to override emotional disappointment, eventual happiness, and a morally correct approach to work. The press and movies portrayed these personality traits as vital keys to new output records in the fields and also depicted Stakhanovites as members of the technical intelligentsia with voracious appetites for learning and as committed to bettering themselves. Their behavior was exemplary and "revolutionary," full of "lessons" for other peasants, and inspired by Stalin, to whom Stakhanovites readily gave thanks. The press also blazoned rural Stakhanovism as a movement that was energetically spreading. References to resistance paled in comparision with the number of shining success stories. The press repeatedly lauded Mariia Demchenko for exhibiting all the characteristics listed above and for being dedicated to building a "new life."[3] *Pravda* instructed readers that her work showed that "there are really no boundaries or limits to the increase in labor productivity in our socialist country."[4]

ENTHUSIASM, DISCIPLINE, AND DILIGENCE

According to *Krest'ianskaia gazeta*, Stakhanovites were keen to work, often brimming over with so much enthusiasm that they rushed into the fields with excitement at the beginning of the day. Klavdiia Epikhina from Kaluzhskii raion of Moscow oblast, the newspaper suggested, generally hurried into the fields where she and her friends did not feel the cold. Their enthusiasm to start work was boundless. As a brigade leader, Epikhina even scolded her mother for turning up late to work and noted this down on the blackboard, but did not fine her. When asked about the incident, Epikhina replied, "to have done otherwise was not possible. Discipline in the brigade is the priority."[5] Diligence was another key to Epikhina's success. She strove to know everything about different potato strains, advocating that the fourteen-year-old *"lorkh* was one of the tastiest."[6] Thus Epikhina was a good example of a "new communist person" in the making.

Due to their enthusiasm for work, propaganda suggested that older Stakhanovites did not feel their age. When the sixty-three-year-old Ganna Koshevaia returned to her farm from a meeting in Moscow concerned with an All-Union competition in sugar beet, she did not feel at all tired. Everyone wanted to hear what had happened to her, so the story went, even those in neighboring districts.[7] Not deterred by her advanced years, Koshevaia then pledged to exceed her record of 630 tsentners per hectare and become a 700er.[8] Propaganda insisted that peasants did not have to be young to become "new" persons and that old and young alike could change their work patterns, as shown in Figure 3.1. In fact, the effort required for Stakhanovism was more appealing to the young and the regime was indeed concerned about hardened attitudes among the elderly.

Above all, love of work and elation about it were the official hallmarks of Stakhanovism. These were expressed in memoirs as well as in the press. Tractor driver Dar'ia Garmash put it like this:

Here, on the first day of plowing, I keenly felt the depth of my love for my chosen profession. I celebrated my triumph, rejoiced at the fulfilment of my dreams, experienced what that happiness is to be occupied with one's favourite work. "There is no force," I thought, "that could tear me away from the fields."[9]

Pasha Angelina, Mariia Demchenko, and many others expressed similar elation at being in the fields.[10] Rural Stakhanovism was not just about

Figure 3.1.   K. Klinkovskaia's tractor brigade from Riazan oblast that took part in the 1937 All-Union Socialist Competition of Women's Tractor Brigades. Source: Adapted from Krest'ianka, no. 9, March 1938, p. 1.

work but was linked to emotion, passion, dreams, and love of the land, soil, and animals.

SUPERIORITY AND SELFLESSNESS IN THE INTELLIGENTSIA

Just as shock workers were greeted at conferences with "You, the best of the best," before praising their "selfless struggle for a good harvest, a high quality of flax and a rise in livestock farming," so this notion of "the best" carried on into Stakhanovism.[11] Distinct from shock workers, however, Stakhanovites were accorded the status of members of the technical intelligentsia. This was because they mastered technology and were keen to learn from agricultural specialists and livestock experts. As *Krest'ianskaia gazeta* put it, "Stakhanovites are an inexhaustible reserve of cadres for the Soviet intelligentsia in general and of the technical intelligentsia in particular."[12]

The press informed readers that this superiority derived not only from good work and enthusiasm but from general character and outlook on life. Narratives told how Stakhanovites were keen to learn both about their speciality and more generally about literature and world politics. *Krest'ianskaia gazeta* quoted Mariia Demchenko saying: "We shall study arithmetic, geography, biology; we will listen to lectures on agronomy. We decided to read not only agricultural books, but literary ones too."[13] More specifically geared to her Stakhanovite tasks, *Krest'ianskaia gazeta* illustrated how Demchenko was taking advice from the agronomist Dudnikov. In her farm's "field cultivation circle" they were studying the soil and different plants. The newspaper gave coverage to Demchenko's call to other farms to study field cultivation in winter since "study facilitates our struggle for a big harvest."[14] Explicitly, bigger harvests through booming records were the main aims of Stakhanovism.

Thus articles focused on Stakhanovites devouring books, mastering agronomy, digesting Chekhov, and becoming *"kul'turnyi"* or "cultured." Vadim Volkov has noted the popularity of the concept of *kul'turnost'* in the Soviet civilizing process, particularly from 1935 to 1938, and its several facets. Accompanying the Second Five-Year Plan and fresh emphases on consumer goods and "the right to a prosperous (*zazhitochnaia*) life," advocacy of *kul'-turnost'* called for "extensive changes in everyday behavior, manners and tastes" which meant politeness, cleanliness, tidy homes, better clothes, more consumer goods, and a striving to read literature and to become more educated.[15] The press described how Stakhanovites went on to study at agricultural academies, a clear sign of *kul'turnost'*, all the time modest about their potential and making references to the "duty" and "responsibility" before them.

BIGGER RECORDS,
BIGGER HARVESTS, LESSONS FOR OTHERS

The press heavily couched success in terms of records, escalating output, and new achievements. Typical headlines included: "How I got 1,054 tsentners of sugar beet from a hectare"; "Gather the sugar beet in a Stakhanovite way"; "The new records of Vladimir Zuev!"; "We'll give 55 tsentners of cotton per hectare!"; "To new Stakhanovite victories!"; "Five thousand litres of milk from every cow"; and "Let the powerful Stakhanovite movement spread."[16]

Articles generally illustrated these records through citing individual cases, such as how Evdokiia Piliukh in 256 days milked 4,256 litres from her cow named "Canada" or how Almaz Alieva in Azerbaidzhan gathered 443 kilos of American cotton a day using both hands.[17] The press stressed the importance of studying successful techniques and noted that through imitating what Alieva had done, Iagut Askerova picked 401 kilos.[18] Narratives held that Stakhanovites were both achievers and teachers. Many a headline like "The great school of Stakhanovite experience" dwelled on how Stakhanovite "lessons" inspired others.[19]

Special fanfare surrounded big records. As soon as Khristina Baidich and Ekaterina Androshchuk gathered over 1,000 tsentners of sugar beet per hectare, outstripping Mariia Demchenko, the press carried the story of how their kolkhoz chair in Vinnitsa oblast proudly announced it publicly.[20] By the end of 1936 *Krest'ianskaia gazeta* was claiming "there are already batallions of 500ers" and now "a movement of 1,000ers."[21] Scripts frequently used the language of fighters and armies embroiled in struggles and battles, adopting "new" methods that resulted in triumphs and victories.

Success was often pitched as resulting from "pioneering techniques." Accordingly, *Sovkhoznaia gazeta* reported how Vladimir Zuev's achievements stemmed from dividing his 110 pigs into 6 groups and by following new feeding techniques.[22] Numerous headlines exhorted peasants "To work like Zuev,"[23] proclaiming a "Stakhanovite-Zuev movement."[24] *Sovkhoznaia gazeta* delivered the message that as a result of new techniques, "hundreds and thousands of workers" showed "high records" were attainable on state farms.[25] The press also signaled that there was no limit to successes. If peasants followed the "lessons" which shock workers, Stakhanovites, and advanced agronomy imparted, then plenty would follow. Articles on sowing argued that "the harvest has no limits" and that agronomists were there to serve Stakhanovites and to explain how to work better.[26]

The press created an atmosphere of buoyant momentum. With each new year, articles stressed that the tempo of success would continue to escalate. At the beginning of 1937 *Krest'ianskaia gazeta* reported that 1936 had been rich with Stakhanovite experience and that 1937, as the second Stakhanovite year, would bring a mass Stakhanovite movement, mass records, wide competition, and a year of no backward collective farms.[27] Likewise, 1938 began with numerous references to "the plan of struggle for a big harvest" ahead[28] followed in 1939 with insistence that "1939 will be a year of further ascent of the whole economy," "of further growth of the Stakhanovite movement," and "a year of unseen records and heroic feats."[29] The press consistently fashioned rural Stakhanovism as increasing only in exponential curves, spiraling ever upward. This was typically under the appropriate headline "Forward under the banner of the party of Lenin and Stalin!"[30]

STAKHANOVITE DAYS, FIVE-DAYS, TEN-DAYS, MONTHS, AND YEAR

Attention to output records was heightened by focus on special Stakhanovite days (usually 24 hours), five-days, ten-days, months, and on 1936 as Stakha-

Figure 3.2.   Stakhanovite tractor drivers G. Rykhtiuk and T. Kolytsia from Vinnitsa oblast, Ukraine. Source: *Adapted from* Krest'ianka, *no. 12, June 1939, p. 23.*

novite year. Both *Sovkhoznaia gazeta* and *Krest'ianskaia gazeta* regularly carried headlines such as "Stakhanovite days, five-days and ten-days," imparting information and extolling the necessity of such efforts.[31] The press explained to peasants that special Stakhanovite days required that everyone on the farm, not a minority, work heroically.[32] Smiling Stakhanovites, as in Figure 3.2, were regularly selected for special praise.

Krest'ianskaia gazeta applauded the "exceptional success" of a Stakhanovite day on 11 January 1936 on the "Bolshevik" collective farm.[33] An instructive article followed, giving readers advice on how to organize a Stakhanovite day.[34] Aiming to instill a general mobilization around

Stakhanovite days, *Krest'ianskaia gazeta* campaigned around the suggestion that 11 February should become an All-Union Stakhanovite day in honor of the anniversary of the Second All-Union Congress of Kolkhoz Shock Workers. The party secretary of the Western oblast immediately supported this, urging everyone "to prepare well, to map out in advance and make known new work objectives and to arrange people."[35] "Success" was inextricably tied to "preparation." Further support followed with 230 Komsomol members in the Northern Caucasus writing an open letter backing the idea and pledging to conduct a "a charge of the light brigade" to help Stakhanovism and to denounce sabotage.[36] *Krest'ianskaia gazeta* constructed a picture of "unanimous and ardent support," claiming to receive "daily hundreds of letters and telegrams" in favor of Stakhanovite day on 11 February.[37] Under the heading "From Stakhanovite days to Stakhanovite year," *Krest'ianskaia gazeta* went on to proclaim, "1936 must be Stakhanovite year! Thus decided workers, thus decided collective farmers!"[38] The chorus of approval continued with letters from shock workers and with articles on "The whole district prepares itself."[39]

Stakhanovite days often amounted to intensive work around the clock for 24 hours. How this was conducted varied across farms. On the Sverdlov state farm in Belorussia, pigs weighing from 40 to 60 kilos were fattened on 1,500 to 1,600 grams of food additive and cleaning went on around the clock.[40] One participant reported, "we made the territory of our farm cleaner than it has ever been."[41] On other farms special Stakhanovite days were seen as opportunities to change work patterns. In Pochinkovskii raion of Gor'kii krai, shock-work milkmaids began looking after more cows. Ol'ga Malova usually cared for 10 cows and assumed responsibility for 15, promising to take on more.[42] The press also printed official recommendations ranging from clearing snow and preparing seed to collecting manure.[43]

Sometimes the press stayed with the example of a particular farm, tracing its progress from Stakhanovite days to Stakhanovite months. Again reporting on the Sverdlov pig farm, *Sovkhoznaia gazeta* stressed the importance of advance preparation for successful Stakhanovite months. Here the farm's livestock expert had a special room in the farm's club where he advised peasants. The pig breeders also liaised with the bookkeeper to work out the cost of feed and the cost of a tsentner of pork. This affected how much they fed their animals. Their slogan became "The *Sverdlovtsy* will give 1,100 tsentners of meat!"[44]

Just as *Krest'ianskaia gazeta* orchestrated 11 February 1936 as a Stakhanovite day, similarly *Sovkhoznaia gazeta* publicized the call from the Aleksandrovo dairy farm in Moscow oblast to make December 1937 a

Stakhanovite month. The goals of the "monthers"(*mesiachniki*) included "the liquidation of sabotage and the over-fulfilment of state plans for butter, meat and wool."[45]

Sovkhoznaia gazeta tended to be more didactic than *Krest'ianskaia gazeta*, the paper generating a different atmosphere with its simpler Russian and more instructive style. It made it plain to directors of state farms that they must "create all the conditions for the development of the Stakhanovite movement," and "completely finish the transportation of feed." Above all, they should ensure that workers knew "their productive tasks each day" and arrange for the results of each worker's plan to "be considered daily."[46] In this manner, rural newspapers played crucial roles in instigating, coordinating, and propagandizing.

Stakhanovite days and months were characterized by new production pledges. In Riazan oblast, Stakhanovites announced that in 1938 they would milk not less than 3,100 litres from each cow and also ensure that all offspring lived.[47] Milkmaids in Leningrad oblast aimed even higher with the cry "We shall fight for 5000 litres of milk from each cow."[48] Those repairing tractors in Riazan oblast promised to complete outstanding work by 1 January and field workers declared they would finish sorting and checking the seed.[49] *Sovkhoznaia gazeta* blazoned these pledges as exemplary practice. Then following the example of state farms, collective farms in Moscow oblast organized a Stakhanovite month for January 1938 around the slogan "A Stalinist month of Stakhanovite records."[50]

SOCIALIST COMPETITION

Out of production pledges came socialist competitions, especially after 1937. *Krest'ianskaia gazeta* publicized that collective farmers were devoting "all their passion and energy" to competitions which would broaden Stakhanovism.[51] The message here was that the "struggle" for success through competitions demanded both physical and emotional energy and that once "hearing of" an All-Union competition, peasants would want to join in. Once so inspired, farms would enjoy commitments to higher targets, such as 10,000 litres of milk per year.[52]

One farm would issue a challenge to another to compete, thereby fueling higher productivity in the effort to win. Socialist competitions amounted to new rounds of target setting. *Sovkhoznaia gazeta* declared the news that "socialist competition is growing" and that the best farms were pledging more grain, milk, meat, and wool.[53] Frequently peasants called for help in the organization of competitions. Combine drivers in Donets oblast, for example, challenged the Komsomol to organize pre-October Stakhanovite competitions on grain state farms.[54] The Komsomol was also involved in setting targets for women's tractor competitions.[55] Once fresh records were set, the results were blazoned across the press with photographs of the best tractor drivers, milkmaids, and pig breeders on individual farms.[56]

Famous names were given special headlines. Pasha Angelina initiated a competition among women tractor drivers, explicitly linked to Stalin's call for 7 to 8 milliard poods of grain. More than 1,000 brigades took part, involving 10,000 tractor drivers. A special meeting was held in Moscow in February 1937 to relay the results at which the fifty-three best brigades and 113 best tractor drivers were given medals. New heroines of the tractor were named, such as Pasha Ledovskaia from Moscow oblast and M. Timasheva from Voronezh oblast.[57] Coverage of this big event splashed into subsequent newspaper editions with headlines such as "Wonderful results of a wonderful competition." Here, women tractor drivers from the northern Caucasus wrote in to tell of their increasing records. The key to their success was that "we looked after our machines with love, thoroughly organized technical maintenance, but the main thing, we worked honestly."[58] The loud message was that successful competition involved preparation, care for machines, and hard work.

This coverage of Pasha Angelina also conveyed that "new" women were being mobilized through competitions and could achieve fantastic results. Socialist competitions were therefore motors of the redefinition of gender relations, too, itself part of the grand Stalinist project. Pasha Angelina was a Stakhanovite who worked hard, shone with success, and inspired others. Now she called upon thousands of women to compete with each other, taking on a directing role. Of course, the party backed this, but Angelina was co-opted by it to take a leadership position and in the process developed herself. The party needed such women and gave them patronage.

Sometimes socialist competitions were named after other events, such as the Eighteenth Party Congress, or explicitly linked to the agricultural cycle, be it spring sowing or autumn harvesting.[59] Whatever the occasion, however, the message was generally the same: "The main thing is competition."[60] Amid the details of record outputs that followed, the press painted a picture of competition fever spreading across the fields. This was especially evident at the end of each year and at the beginning of the next, in the run-up to harvesting and sowing. In January 1937 *Sovkhoznaia gazeta* boomed out "a new wave of state farm socialist competition is swelling."[61] Enthusiasm for competition was reported to be so great that housewives were joining their husbands.[62]

STAKHANOVISM IS SPREADING, UNSTOPPABLE AND REVOLUTIONARY

One regular fanfare surrounding Stakhanovism was that it was spreading throughout the countryside at a great pace. After one year, the press congratulated that Stakhanovites "are not alone. There are lots of them, thousands and thousands," bringing in harvests "unseen until now."[63] Articles on the movement's rural growth usually referred to "thousands" or "hundreds and thousands."[64] Accompanying headlines called for further growth with "Widen the ranks of Stakhanovites!" and "Multiply the number of Stakhanovites!"[65]

On the second anniversary of Stakhanov's feats in industry, *Sovkhoznaia gazeta* made the point that "the All-people's Stakhanovite movement is widely developed in socialist agriculture too. It has given rise to thousands of advanced workers of the countryside: Mariia Demchenko, Pasha Angelina and others." The general message was that "each new year in agriculture has brought tens of thousands of new Stakhanovites."[66] Holidays were also used to champion Stakhanovism with announcements that it was "like a powerful flood" which was "pouring across the country."[67] Such imagery implied that Stakhanovism was unstoppable, advancing at speed over whatever stood in its way.

History books and the press often went into minute detail about numbers by singling out a district or republic to illustrate the upward curve of progress and its penetration into all sectors, even into women's workshops in the hills of Dagestan.[68] After praising these increases in Stakhanovite numbers, the press began to call for the promotion of Stakhanovites to leadership posts on farms, subsequently highlighting and congratulating any such instances of elevation.[69] Meeting the third anniversary of Stakhanovism in 1938, *Krest'ianskaia gazeta* proclaimed that Stakhanovism was truly "revolutionary" and "preparing the conditions for the transition from capitalism to socialism."[70] Its Leninist credentials were unquestioned. In this manner, propaganda ceaselessly proclaimed the movement was successful, of growing strength in all sectors, and proceeding apace across the Soviet landmass even into remote parts. Part of this success was attributed to the triumph over technology.

TRIUMPH OVER TECHNOLOGY

The new Soviet person was someone prepared to change her self and to strive to alter and improve the world around her. This was consistent with Karl Marx's and Friedrich Engels's historical materialism, according to which human beings could change their own nature and potential by working on nature and transforming it.[71] This is what distinguished persons from animals. In so doing, socioeconomic systems would alter the way in which citizens lived. Machines and technology played huge roles in men's and women's transmogrification of their environments.

In the USSR, machines and technology were icons of progress. In the 1920s and 1930s, there was a cult of the machine, epitomized in the countryside by the tractor. Its arrival made a huge impact, symbolizing advanced mastery of the land, much more rapid progress, and an enormous contribution to transforming the countryside and building a new civilization. The tractor was a mighty machine billed as meriting respect and honor. Pasha Angelina's father revered the tractor in the following way: "I myself have read in *Pravda*, little daughter, that in the fields of the Kuban tractors have appeared built by the hands of workers in our factories. Strong, intelligent machines."[72] Here the tractor is personified as intelligent and strong, suggesting that it will bring rationality to the more backward countryside, helped by the laboring efforts of more advanced urban workers.

One persistent image was of the ability of peasants to use these heavy machines and of the joy at doing so for the first time. This was part of a serious attempt to challenge the stereotype that peasants, particularly women, would be unable to cope. The tractor was there not just to transform the countryside's productivity but also to help redefine the way peasants lived, part of which was the emancipation of women and their taking on of new roles. In keeping with this goal, E. Usova told readers of *Krasnaia Sibiriachka*: "And here I am at the wheel of a tractor—the first time in my life that I steer a complicated machine. The engine works wonderfully. Its booming, roaring noises carry a long way around the neighborhood."[73]

The message was that women could handle heavy machinery and delight at its mechanisms and power. The first time aboard would give thrill and success rather than fear and failure. Booms and roars also signaled progress and massive potential. New women and men on tractors would guarantee bigger harvests, greater efficiency, record-breaking records, and plentiful food. That both women and men exuded excitement at driving tractors gave the message that equal opportunities were officially there, even if reality suggested otherwise.

The link between machines and Stakhanovism was stronger in heavy industry since in agriculture all sectors were undermechanized. Milking was done by hand and the horse, rather than the tractor, had been the most common way of plowing. With the advent of the tractor, however, triumph over technology was now factored into the image of the rural Stakhanovite. Above all, the tractor symbolized the socialist realist future and was perceived as the salvation of the fields.

TRIUMPH OVER OPPOSITION THROUGH RESILIENCE

A related image is that because new men and women were determined to make the harvest successful, whenever setbacks occurred, they were resolute. If misfortunes befell them unexpectedly, such as bad weather, even if temporarily upset, they quickly responded in innovative ways. Or if anyone stood in their path or challenged their "duty," they nobly dismissed criticism, overrode obstacles, and persisted down their determined path. Biographies and the press painted Stakhanovites as creatures of firm resolve, holding unshakable goals and generally possessing the ability to override emotional disappointment.

When, for instance, an unexpected frost threatened Mariia Demchenko's pledge to Stalin to pick 500 tsentners of sugar beet per hectare, at first she was anxious. Allegedly she said: "You know, I simply did not know what to do. I had given my word to Comrade Stalin, and suddenly such a misfortune. Well, tell me please, when I made my pledge, could I have expected such a frost?"[74] Staring at her field, Demchenko wondered what to do. Then, it occurred to her, "Perhaps smoke?"[75] Helped by a worker from the district party committee and the secretary of the Komsomol, she lit fires. Thus protected, 60 percent of her sugar beet endured. Then in August came drought. Without rain, Demchenko's crop would have withered. Although the nearest river was two kilometers away, with her team she carried buckets and barrels of water. And supportive as only Stakhanovites could be, Marina Gnatenko, against whom Demchenko entered into socialist competitions, also helped.[76] Sisterly Stakhanovites thus also aided those in difficulty to overcome the hardship. In return, Demchenko later ensured that moths did not destroy Gnatenko's crop.[77] The importance of the crop was a determining notion that shaped Demchenko's actions and in Hellbeck's sense shaped her soul. It molded her attitudes and pursuits and fine-tuned her being.

The press depicted Stakhanovites as undaunted by setbacks and as ready to fight back if wronged. They would do this by bringing issues to meetings on the farm, by writing to the local party, or by sending letters of complaint to *Krest'ianskaia gazeta* and *Sovkhoznaia gazeta*. The image projected here was that Stakhanovites always acted in order to obtain results. It cited the example of Melan'ia Slesarenko, who did not let the fact that peasants jeered at her deter her from Stakhanovite work.[78] Similarly, Ol'ga Peunkova was worn down by lack of support on the farm and in the district where no one took seriously the attacks on her record-giving cows. Taking action, she wrote to *Krest'ianskaia gazeta*, who exposed the story.[79] If by their own efforts alone, Stakhanovites could not triumph due to local opposition, then *Krest'ianskaia gazeta* as a "folk hero" would investigate the case to ensure that justice was done. The newspaper liaised with the local party and procuracy on such matters, fulfilling a political role.

As well as suffering negative reactions to Stakhanovism, female Stakhanovites often had to combat hostility to changing gender roles, elaborated further later. Worthy of note here is that books and newspapers showed how women like Pasha Angelina and Dar'ia Garmash refused to let opposition to their dreams defeat them. Their personality traits of perseverance and resilience ensured that they became tractor drivers, despite opposition from boyfriends or fathers to their taking on "men's work." In a biography of Garmash, her fiancé Nikolai becomes the stereotype of a handsome, broad-shouldered, strong, but backward looking, narrow-minded chauvinistic peasant, and the tractor symbolizes progress, liberation, and a fulfillment of dreams. The choice between Nikolai who objects to Dar'ia's ambition to drive a tractor and the tractor is clearcut for a determined woman of Stakhanovite potential, despite temporary romantic tragedy.[80] According to Soviet propaganda, Stakhanovites stuck to their course whatever attempts were made to undermine them. In fact, this was not always the case.

PARTY LEADERSHIP

A recurrent theme was that new communist men and women enjoyed inevitable success as a consequence of enlightened party guidance. The press hammered across the message that when the party and Komsomol became involved with the Stakhanovite movement "there are excellent examples of work, greater successes and hundreds of Stakhanovites come to light."[81] Thus the press fashioned the party as an official icon in the mobilization of Stakhanovism. There was also a subtext in this picture, since not all local parties did lead the Stakhanovite movement and this was a very loud cue informing them that they should.

The press and biographies made clear that it was the exemplary party committees who watched over and supported shock workers and Stakhanovites. Demchenko's biography held that:

> Workers of the district party committee considered the fulfilment of Mariia's promise a matter of their honor. They took an interest in Demchenko's work. They telephoned nearly every day to the collective farm administration and more often began to visit the farm.[82]

It informed readers that in the cases of Mariia Demchenko and Marina Gnatenko, the district party committee and the Komsomol committee "carefully followed their work, helped them, instructed both Stakhanovites."[83]

When the sudden frost threatened Demchenko's crop, a party worker was quickly on the scene to help.[84]

Members of the political department also figured in Stakhanovites' autobiographical stories as staunch defenders of individual Stakhanovites. When everyone in Pasha Angelina's family opposed her aspirations to become a tractor driver, it was Ivan Kurov in the *politotdel* of the MTS who bolstered her downtrodden spirits.[85] It was also the political department that ensured that Angelina was finally assigned to a tractor once her training was complete and was taken out of the storehouse where she had been wrongly put, ignoring her abilities.[86] It was the political department yet again who came to her aid when women of *Krasnyi Pakhar* collective farm tried to block her women's tractor brigade from entering the fields.[87] Dar'ia Garmash similarly found encouragement and inspiration when she needed it coming from the enlightened Gurov in the *politotdel.*[88]

HAPPINESS THROUGH STAKHANOVISM IN CONTRAST TO THE DARK PAST

Consistent with socialist realism, new Soviet men and women were happy, smiling, and jubilant about the future under socialism, then communism. Officially constructed images of happiness were prolific. Short one-page biographies were particularly common with titles such as "I want to tell about my happiness," as were poems such as "Happy sisters."[89] The hallmark of these were how awful the past had been and how illuminating and joyous the present.

The story of E. Nikolaeva from the "Forward to Socialism" collective farm in the Western oblast is typical. For a woman decorated with an Order of Lenin for her excellent work and also having met Stalin, life sharply contrasted with past miseries. She told *Krest'ianskaia gazeta* how "A year ago I was an illiterate common milkmaid."[90] The message was that opportunities in the USSR were huge and the rewards immense. Likewise, the successful Mariia Petrova, driver of a combine harvester, was born in 1915 into a poor family. She had enjoyed only three years of schooling and began work at twelve years of age. Not until her family moved onto a collective farm in 1929 did her "new life" begin. After having worked for three years in the children's nursery, Petrova trained to repair tractors and then in 1925 to drive a combine harvester. From a poor illiterate peasant girl, she found herself in 1936 at the All-Union Conference of Combine Drivers in the Kremlin. Here she proudly promised Stalin to work 700 hectares in 1936 and, in fact, mowed 1,251. As a reward, Petrova earned a place in Moscow at the All-Union Academy of Socialist Agriculture.[91]

Figure 3.3.   Shairbiuiu Tezikbaeva in the sugar beet fields of Kirgizia in Soviet Central Asia. She became a Deputy of the Supreme Soviet of the USSR. Source: *Adapted from* Krest'ianka, *no. 17, September 1939, p. 8.*

The "happiness message" was also linked to the theme of the "friendship of peoples." Inhabitants of Central Asia, in particular, as shown in Figure 3.3, were in the spotlight since their "more backward" and "dark" lives were transformed under Soviet power. Wide coverage was given to the story of Mamlakat Nakhangova, a young Pioneer record-breaker in the cotton fields. She was born into a poor family where life was "hard." Whenever Mamlakat became ill, her mother prayed to Allah.[92] But from the moment when Mamlakat took the initiative to suggest to her school friends "Let's help our parents to pick the cotton," her life altered.[93] Not only did she appear at district and All-Union conferences and receive medals, but she was named to the Soviet Anti-Fascist Committee and even visited England and America.[94]

The early life of Saty Tokombaev in Kirgizia was the most unstable of these tales. According to his biographers:

He was born in 1911 in the hamlet Shalba, son of a poor peasant by social origin. His father had only one horse. In 1916 at the time of the Kirghiz uprising his family fled to China. His father died in 1917. After his father's death, comrade Tokombaev found himself the dependent of his uncle, also a poor peasant.[95]

After having returned from China, Tokombaev joined the kolkhoz in 1930 and became its chair in 1934. The excellent grain harvest in 1936, which averaged 23 tsentners per hectare, was due to his organizational skills, putting him in Stakhanovite ranks.[96] From a poor unstable migrant life, Tokombaev enjoyed the fruits of a successful kolkhoz which he ran.

The root of the above Stakhanovites' happiness, however, was not only their record-breaking achievements, but Stalin's leadership. He was the kind father figure who, through the party of Lenin and Stalin, promoted joy throughout the land.

THANKS TO STALIN

Stakhanovism was explicitly linked to the fulfillment of Stalin's wishes. *Krest'ianskaia gazeta* depicted the movement as playing "a decisive role" in realizing "Stalinist slogans" whether for the yearly production of 7 to 8 milliard poods of bread or for more sugar beet.[97] Whatever Stalin's exhortations were for productivity in a given year, in a given sector, then Stakhanovites were there to meet them.

The cult of Stalin was integral to narratives on Stakhanovism and it was politically inappropriate for shock workers and Stakhanovites to deliver speeches or to write autobiographies without greeting Stalin, making a pledge to Stalin, informing Stalin of recent output feats, or without thanking him for his inspiration. Discourse pivoted around Stalin. The emphases and forms may have varied, but the great charismatic leader was always acknowledged. Jeffrey Brooks has argued that this amounted to a theatrical "performance that continued without a break, encompassed all aspects of public life and was the only show in town." Everyone from super-citizens to ordinary people had to declare in public that "they owed their lives and all the goods and services" to Stalin and to the Soviet state in the "moral economy of the gift."[98]

Klavdiia Epikhina, for example, made a pledge to Nikita Khrushchev, then party leader of Moscow oblast, that she would pick 500 tsentners of potatoes per hectare. She subsequently wrote to Stalin with her results of 718 tsentners gathered for each hectare and of 810 picked on her record-giving plot.[99] The press covered this story and published her concluding thanks to Stalin: "Thank you dear beloved Iosif Vissarionovich for opening the eyes of us peasants and for leading us to a happy and joyful life."[100] Numerous such letters were commonly printed.[101]

Large congresses were occasions at which shock workers and Stakhanovites were obliged to praise Stalin. At the Second Congress of Kolkhoz Shock Workers, Pasha Angelina ended her speech with the inevitable "Glory to the great leader of the entire proletariat, Comrade Stalin!"[102] And Karp Bogdanov from Voronezh oblast declared "Glory to the great communist party of bolsheviks and its leader—the great expert of socialist construction—Comrade Stalin!"[103] Certain buzzwords repeated themselves in such adulations: "glory," "great," "bolshevik," "leader," and "expert." These were part of what Wittgenstein would dub the "language game" of the personality cult.[104]

In addition to these routine, compulsory, somewhat rote acknowledgments to Stalin, peasants sometimes highlighted his fatherly, friendly attitude toward them. Mariia Demchenko put it this way:

> Here we sit together with Stalin. I chatted to him and to other leaders (Applause). I talked to him just like to my father or mother. He is a pleasant person to us, as are all the leaders. Iosif Vissarionovich Stalin laughs with us, converses with us, shares with us his thoughts on how to work on the collective farm and on how we can live better.[105]

Here Stalin is portrayed as personable, wise, and as finding time for those less elevated than himself in order to explain how to live improved lives. Above all, his humanity is emphasized and his readiness to get close to his subjects. Figure 3.4 shows Stalin next to Mariia Demchenko, at her side to guide, support, inspire, and lead.

Autobiographies and newspaper accounts often recalled with affection intimate chats with Stalin. As a delegate to the Eighteenth All-Union Congress of Soviets, Khristina Baidich met Stalin. She subsequently told agricultural students:

> I was favored with the honor of talking to Comrade Stalin. It is already the second time. I cannot describe the joy enveloping us all when Stalin presented his report. Holding our breath, we listened to the wonderful story of how our Bolshevik party and our beloved Stalin fought for a happy and joyous life for us.[106]

To talk to Stalin was billed as a privilege that resulted only in joy.

Another message was that Stalin could convey matters to peasants simply and clearly so that they could understand. When the tractor driver Pasha Kovardak was addressing a plenum of a local rural soviet in Azovo-Chernomore

Figure 3.4. Stalin and Mariia Demchenko on 11 April 1936 on the Presidium of the Tenth Komsomol Congress. Source: Adapted from Kolkhoznitsa, no. 3–4, April 1936, p. 3.

krai she was asked from the floor how Stalin spoke. She replied: "He speaks simply, not like many of our orators, who don't so much talk about the business as shout and gesticulate (laughter, applause)."[107] Kovardak went on:

> Comrade Stalin's report was very clear and simple, giving every delegate a sharp understanding of what a great affair drew us to the congress, of what enormous significance our constitution has, of what great strength there is in every article of the constitution.[108]

Stalin thus facilitated everyone's grasp of big questions. He was "teacher" as well as leader.

Whatever Stalin said, Stakhanovites reiterated in public arenas, whether about output, May Day, the new 1936 Stalin Constitution, or the show trials of 1938. An important part of Stakhanovites' image was that they served Stalin, were kindly encouraged by him and overwhelmingly indebted to him.

MOVIES

Films deserve examination since they were important sources of entertainment throughout Soviet history and one medium through which "socialist realism" was projected. The cinema of the 1930s and 1940s cannot be dismissed as dull, even though much was not permitted by the censors. Musical comedies such as *Veselye Rebiata* (The Happy Lads), one of Stalin's favorites, and *Volga Volga* were hilarious and fun, painting a light-hearted world untouched by arrest, purge, and death sentence. Films were part of popular culture, what Richard Stites has wonderfully described as "a ceaseless bubbling up of stories and tales."[109] Films of shock workers and Stakhanovites were part of this effervescence and they beamed dynamic stories about the lives of new women and men in action.

Directors portrayed peasants in particular ways, transmitting suggestions to audiences about their characters and the value of their work. Films showed rural shock workers and Stakhanovites above all as good, decent, and kind people, who were likable. Consistent with images from the press, they were also energetic, hardworking, keen to try new work techniques, and were worthy of emulation. They served Soviet socialism, took care in their work, were attentive to their machines and animals and, if they were brigade leaders, they inspired peasants who worked with them. Inevitably such movies incorporated love stories in order to create broad appeal. Here the message was that shock workers and Stakhanovites deserved to fall in love only with similarly keen workers and not with those whose productive skills were inferior and who could not bring personal happiness to the worthy. Competition fever was part of the story.

In *Bogataia Nevesta* (The Rich Bride), a love story revolves around the harvest. Marinka, the young woman with the most workdays *(trudodni)* due to heroic efforts, is obviously a good catch in marriage for her fine earnings. The hardworking tractor driver, Pavlo, loves her but his courting is temporarily undermined by Kovyn'ko, the naughty adventurist bookkeeper, who indeed fancies Marinka's money and leads her to believe that this is the reason for Pavlo's attentions. The night before the harvest begins, kissing couples are sent to their separate beds with the cry "harvest!" and "it's time to get some sleep." In the pep talk before work begins, the harvest is described as a "battle" and as a "tactical assault." Tractor drivers are urged to drive in third gear for the best results and every brigade is encouraged in socialist competition to win a red flag. Dynamism is suggested as trucks, carts, and horses then speed to work. Predictably, the hard workers perform splendidly during the socialist competition, not deterred by looming black clouds and rain. Excellent brigades then receive their red flags. Marinka's brigade leader, proud at achievements, announces "We will never give up this flag to anyone." And finally, of course, Marinka and Pavlo grasp the scoundrel Kovyn'ko's deceit, and deserving only each other, marry.

Films blazoned that tractors meant progress and that good workers were keen to learn how to use them. In *Traktoristy* (Tractor drivers) there are dramatic scenes of Mar'iana Bazhan's women's brigade efficiently combing the fields, with sun umbrellas on their tractors to shield them, creating dynamic images of technology in movement. In a farm meeting, Mar'iana is praised as a "bright example" and in the press she receives front-page acclaim. The handsome mechanic, Klim, is also a fine fellow newly arrived on the farm, adept at repairing tractors with skill and flair and prepared to point out to slackers how they are abusing their machines. The inevitable romance that develops between Mar'iana and Klim revolves around his respect for her success on the tractor and her esteem for his strength and skill at repairing them. Indeed, before Klim even met Mar'iana, when he was returning from military service on the train, he read of her feats in the newspaper and declared to his pals, "I'll go to her." Thereafter they drank to her health. Once on the farm, he salutes her with respect in a playful exchange and calls her "comrade brigade leader," at which she salutes him back with "comrade mechanic." The film portrays both as energetic, honest, kind, hardworking, keen to apply the fruits of technology for the good of all, and to treat machines sensibly as members of the "technical intelligentsia." Once again the implicit link is made between success at work and happiness. The new woman is also in a leading role and celebrated for her success as a tractor driver and as a brigade leader.

The image of tractors and combine harvesters advancing across fields is a powerful one. The opening scenes of Pyr'ev's *Kubanskie Kazaki* (Cossacks of the Kuban) show rows and rows of combines cutting the harvest. The didactic message is that technology masters nature to humankind's advantage. Corn blows dramatically in the wind as red flags flap on combines and on trucks, women march military style with pitchforks, peasants work faster and faster, and the background music becomes more frantic. Grain flows along conveyor belts and trucks adorned with the slogan "bread for the motherland" transport the grain speedily away down the road. In *Bogataia Nevesta*, too, scenes of gathering the harvest conflate speed and success.

Films also stressed the importance of special care of animals and new techniques. In *Svinarka i Pastukh* (The Female Pig Rearer and the Herdsman), Glasha Novikova, who is a kind, modest, popular, and pretty pig-rearer, devotes attention to the birth of piglets and saves the lives of those who stop breathing. She is shown devising special feeding techniques for the newly born and ensuring that older pigs have sufficient feed. Rewarded for her diligence, as shock workers should be, she is sent to represent her farm at an agricultural exhibition in distant Moscow. This is an honor and privilege which excites her and which she takes seriously, as she writes down copious notes from the exhibits on display in order to learn from them. Here she meets Musaid, the exotic shepherd from Dagestan. Quickly fond of each other, the audience sees the "friendship of peoples" ignite at the personal level between different nationalities. As exemplary workers they are destined for each other, despite living miles apart, despite the fact that Glasha cannot read the love letters sent to her in a strange language, and notwithstanding the attempts of another who loves Glasha to prevent their union.

Films, like the press, served a crucial propaganda role, by transmitting messages and fashioning images. They were, however, more alive due to their visual impact and probably more enjoyable for their lighthearted entertainment.

CONCLUSION

Almost daily after August 1935, bold images of what shock workers and Stakhanovites were like, and of what they could become, filled the rural press and became prominent on cinema screens. Journalists interpreted their activities for peasants and gave didactic lessons on how to behave on Stakhanovite days and months, thereby participating in the process which tried to educate peasants in what to think and do. Stakhanovites received pointers on what their "self" should be like and how it linked to high output, to party, socialism, and Stalin. Heroic tales accentuated certain politically desirable Stakhanovite traits and icons such as Mariia Demchenko and Pasha Angelina were held up for emulation and praise.

The way in which Stakhanovites were propagandized in the press, memoirs, and film had to meet the approval of strict censors. Editors, in particular, played a highly political role in selecting material for publication. They were, in fact, self-censors, screening material to ensure it was free of "mistakes" or incorrect emphases. Thus their relationship with journalists reporting from the fields was a politically sensitive one. The editorial archive of *Krest'ianskaia gazeta* gives us a rare insight into what editors said to journalists, into how they reacted to fresh material, and on what grounds they rejected it.

NOTES

1. *Pravda,* 25 October 1935, 3.
2. *Vtoroi Vsesoiuznyi S"ezd Kolkhoznikov-Udarnikov: stenograficheskii otchët* (Moscow: Sel'khozgiz, 1935), 144.
3. *Pravda,* 25 October 1935, 3.
4. *Pravda,* 25 October 1935, 3
5. *Krest'ianskaia gazeta,* 16 October 1936, 2.
6. *Krest'ianskaia gazeta,* 16 October 1936, 2.
7. *Krest'ianskaia gazeta,* 8 December 1935, 1.
8. *Krest'ianskaia gazeta,* 8 December 1935, 1.

9. Dar'ia Garmash, "O samom dorogom," in *V budniakh Velikikh stroek: zhen-shchiny-kommunisti geroini pervykh piatiletok*, ed. L. I. Shishova (Moscow: Politiz-dat, 1986), 183.

10. Praskovya Angelina, *My Answer to an American Questionnaire* (Moscow: For-eign Languages Publishing House, 1949), 11–12; I. Vershinin, ed. *Mariia Safronovna Demchenko* (Moscow: Gosudarstvennoe izdatel'stvo politicheskoi literatury, 1938), 5.

11. *Krest'ianka v zapadnoi oblasti*, June 1936, inside cover. This was a greeting from the editor of *Krest'ianka v zapadnoi oblasti* (Peasant Woman in the Western oblast) to an oblast conference of advanced female collective farmers.

12. *Krest'ianskaia gazeta*, 14 November 1938, 1.

13. *Krest'ianskaia gazeta*, 8 December 1935, 3.

14. *Krest'ianskaia gazeta*, 8 December 1935, 3.

15. Vadim Volkov, "The Concept of *Kul'turnost'*: Notes on the Stalinist Civilizing Process," in *Stalinism: New Directions*, ed. Sheila Fitzpatrick (London and New York: Routledge, 2000), 216. See, too, Mary Buckley on *kul'turnost'* in the move-ment of wives in "The Untold Story of *Obshchestvennitsa* in the 1930s," *Europe-Asia Studies* 48, no. 4 (July, 1996): 569–86; and Buckley, "The Soviet Female Activist Down on the Farm," *Social History* 26, no. 3 (October 2001): 282–98.

16. See, for example, *Krest'ianskaia gazeta*, 14 October 1936, 1; *Krest'ianskaia gazeta*, 30 December 1938, 3; *Krest'ianskaia gazeta*, 14 November 1938, 1; *Sovkhoz-naia gazeta*, 20 July 1936, 1; *Sovkhoznaia gazeta*, 8 January 1937, 1; *Sovkhoznaia gazeta*, 1 December 1937, 1.

17. *Krest'ianskaia gazeta*, 22 September 1936, 3.

18. *Krest'ianskaia gazeta*, 12 October 1936, 3.

19. *Sovkhoznaia gazeta*, 18 June 1937, 1. These "lessons" are discussed more fully in chapter 5.

20. *Sovkhoznaia gazeta*, 14 October 1936, 1.

21. *Krest'ianskaia gazeta*, 28 December 1936, 1.

22. *Sovkhoznaia gazeta*, 26 October 1935, 1.

23. *Sovkhoznaia gazeta*, 28 October 1935, 1.

24. *Sovkhoznaia gazeta*, 8 January 1936, 1.

25. *Sovkhoznaia gazeta*, 20 July 1936, 1.

26. *Krest'ianskaia gazeta*, 10 January 1939, 3.

27. *Krest'ianskaia gazeta*, 8 February 1937, 1.

28. *Krest'ianskaia gazeta*, 30 January 1938, 1.

29. *Krest'ianskaia gazeta*, 1 January 1939, 1.

30. *Krest'ianskaia gazeta*, 1 January 1939, 1.

31. *Sovkhoznaia gazeta*, 28 January 1936, 1.

32. *Krest'ianskaia gazeta*, 8 January 1936, 1.

33. *Krest'ianskaia gazeta*, 20 January 1936, 1.

34. *Krest'ianskaia gazeta*, 20 January 1936, 2.

35. *Krest'ianskaia gazeta*, 4 February 1936, 1. The campaign appeared orches-trated.

36. *Krest'ianskaia gazeta*, 6 February 1936, 1.

37. *Krest'ianskaia gazeta*, 8 February 1936, 1.

38. *Krest'ianskaia gazeta*, 8 February 1936, 1.

39. *Krest'ianskaia gazeta*, 10 February 1936, 1.

40. *Sovkhoznaia gazeta*, 6 January 1936, 1.

41. *Sovkhoznaia gazeta*, 6 January 1936, 1.

42. *Krest'ianskaia gazeta*, 10 January 1936, 4.

43. *Krest'ianskaia gazeta*, 10 January 1936, 1.

44. *Sovkhoznaia gazeta*, 22 January 1936, 3.

45. *Sovkhoznaia gazeta*, 28 November 1937, 1. More specifically, the month had to be marked by "growth in labor productivity and an increase in milk yields, in animal feed and over-fulfilment of repair norms for agricultural machinery." Thereafter followed headlines such as "Today begins Stakhanovite month," "We'll work even better, more productively," and "Stakhanovite month on state farms." See *Sovkhoznaia gazeta*, 1 December 1937, 4; *Sovkhoznaia gazeta*, 10 December 1937, 4; *Sovkhoznaia gazeta*, 14 December 1937, 3.

46. *Sovkhoznaia gazeta*, 28 November 1937, 1.

47. *Sovkhoznaia gazeta*, 10 December 1937, 4.

48. *Sovkhoznaia gazeta*, 18 December, 3.

49. *Sovkhoznaia gazeta*, 10 December, 4.

50. *Krest'ianskaia gazeta*, 18 December 1937, 8.

51. *Krest'ianskaia gazeta*, 30 December 1938, 3.

52. *Krest'ianskaia gazeta*, 20 January 1936, 3.

53. *Sovkhoznaia gazeta*, 12 January 1937, 1.

54. *Krest'ianskaia gazeta*, 12 October 1935, p. 1.

55. See TsKhDMO, f. 1, op. 23, d. 1185, ll. 14–33; TsKhDMO, f. 1, op. 3, d. 158. ll. 104–06; TsKhDMO, f. 1, op. 23, d. 1357, ll. 7–90; TsKhDMO, f. 1, op. 23, d. 1261, ll. 17–39.

56. *Krest'ianskaia gazeta*, 12 February 1936, 3. Regular announcements were made of ceremonies to award Stakhanovites medals after successful competitions.

57. *Krest'ianskaia gazeta*, 10 February 1937, 8.

58. *Krest'ianskaia gazeta*, 12 February 1937, 1.

59. *Krest'ianskaia gazeta*, 12 February 1937, 1.

60. *Krest'ianskaia gazeta*, 10 January 1938, 2.

61. *Sovkhoznaia gazeta*, 12 January 1937, 1.

62. *Sovkhoznaia gazeta*, 8 October 1937, 1.

63. *Krest'ianskaia gazeta*, 12 October 1936, 1.

64. *Sovkhoznaia gazeta*, 16 August 1937, 1; *Sovkhoznaia gazeta*, 20 July 1936, 1.

65. *Sovkhoznaia gazeta*, 28 December 1937, 1–2.

66. *Sovkhoznaia gazeta*, 30 August 1937, 2.

67. *Krest'ianskaia gazeta*, 1 May 1936, 1.

68. R. M. Gasanov, *Stakhanovskoe Dvizhenie v Dagestane* (Makhachkala: Dagestanskoe knizhnoe izdatel'stvo, 1975), 5. Gasanov points out that in November 1935 there were 280 Stakhanovites in Dagestan, increasing to 494 in December and over 1,300 by January 1936.

69. *Sovkhoznaia gazeta*, 2 December 1937, 1, and 10 December 1937, 4.

70. *Krest'ianskaia gazeta*, 30 August 1938, 1.

71. Karl Marx and Friedrich Engels, *The German Ideology* (New York: International Publishers, 1969).

72. Pasha Angelina, *Liudi Kolkhoznykh Polei* (Moscow and Leningrad: Gosudarstvennoe izdatel'stvo detskoi literatury, 1952), 9.

73. *Krasnaia Sibiriachka*, no. 3–4 (February 1939): 17.

74. I. Vershinin, ed., *Mariia Safronovna Demchenko* (Moscow: Gosudarstvennoe izdatel'stvo politicheskoi literatury, 1938), 11.

75. Vershinin, ed., *Mariia Safronovna Demchenko*, 12.

76. Vershinin, ed., *Mariia Safronovna Demchenko*, 14.

77. Vershinin, ed., *Mariia Safronovna Demchenko*, 15.

78. *Krest'ianskaia gazeta*, 16 April 1936, 2.

79. *Krest'ianskaia gazeta*, 28 March 1936, 4.

80. Dar'ia Garmash, "O samom dorogom," 181–82.

81. *Krest'ianskaia gazeta*, 4 February 1936, 1.

82. Vershinin, ed., *Mariia Safronovna Demchenko*, 10.

83. Vershinin, ed., *Mariia Safronovna Demchenko*, 16.

84. Vershinin, ed., *Mariia Safronovna Demchenko*, 12.

85. Angelina, *Liudi Kolkhoznykh Polei*, 23.

86. Angelina, *Liudi Kolkhoznykh Polei*, 29.

87. Angelina, *Liudi Kolkhoznykh Polei*, 34.

88. Dar'ia Garmash, "O samom dorogom," 178–80.

89. *Kolkhoznitsa*, no. 3–4, April 1936, 11; *Krasnaia Sibiriachka*, no. 3–4, February 1939, 7.

90. *Krest'ianskaia gazeta*, 28 December 1936, 4.

91. *Sotsial'isticheskaia Rekonstruktsiia Sel'skogo Khoziaistva*, no. 3 (March 1938): 205. For special emphasis on revolutionary changes in women's lives, see *Kolkhoznitsa*, no. 3–4 (April 1936), 11.

92. Iurii Il'inskii, "Iunaia stakhanovka," in *V budniakh velikikh stroek*, ed. L. Stishova, 54.

93. Il'inskii, "Iunaia stakhanovka," 55.

94. Il'inskii, "Iunaia stakhanovka," 64.

95. I. V. Liashenko and B. F. Kniazevskii, *Stakhanovtsy zernovykh kul'tur Kirgizii* (Frunze: Kirgizgosizdat, 1937), 25.

96. Liashenko and Kniazevskii, *Stakhanovtsy zernovykh kul'tur*, 25.

97. *Krest'ianskaia gazeta*, 14 November 1938, 1. A pood is 36 pounds.

98. Jeffrey Brooks, *Thank You, Comrade Stalin: Soviet Public Culture from Revolution to Cold War* (Princeton, NJ: Princeton University Press, 2001), 82–105.

99. *Krest'ianskaia gazeta*, 10 October 1936, 1.

100. *Krest'ianskaia gazeta*, 10 October 1936, 1.

101. See, for instance, *Krest'ianskaia gazeta*, 24 October 1936, 1. This published S. Nikulina's letter to Stalin, informing him that she had met her pledge of twelve tsentners of flax per hectare.

102. *Vtoroi Vsesoiuznyi S"ezd Kolkhoznikov-Udarnikov: stenograficheskii otchët* (Moscow: Sel'khozgiz, 1935), 102.

103. *Vtoroi Vsesoiuznyi S"ezd Kolkhoznikov-Udarnikov*, 143.

104. Ludwig Wittgenstein, *Philosophical Investigations*, trans. G. E. M. Anscombe (New York: Macmillan, 1968).

105. *Vtoroi Vsesoiuznyi S"ezd Kolkhoznikov-Udarnikov,* 144.

106. *Krest'ianskaia gazeta*, 14 December 1936, 2.

107. *Krest'ianskaia gazeta*, 14 December 1936, 3.

108. *Krest'ianskaia gazeta*, 14 December 1936, 3.

109. Richard Stites, *Russian Popular Culture* (Cambridge: Cambridge University Press, 1992), 1.

Chapter Four

The Press as Constructor of Images

> The task of the press is to propagandize the experience of the best Stakhanovites and to pass it on to the backward peasants.
>
> —Editor at *Krest'ianskaia gazeta* to a rural correspondent in Ukraine[1]

Behind-the-scenes pressures were put on journalists to construct politically appropriate stories about Stakhanovism. Newspaper editors and instructors encouraged *sel'kory* (*sel'skie korrespondenty*), or rural correspondents, to frame their reports in particular ways, giving critical feedback if they did not.[2] In an authoritarian one-party state it was vital for the press to deliver correct messages and to honor party lines. Editors had highly sensitive "political" roles to play in orchestrating their team of rural correspondents and had to make them acutely aware how information should be selected and how commentaries should be packaged. In this respect, editors were agents of the state constructing the dimensions of rural reality. The articles and reports that they approved and solicited were there, as Matthew E. Lenoe has observed, to shape the public identity of Soviet subjects.[3] Moreover, part of this framing involved attempts to mobilize peasants and to influence their grasp of what that meant for themselves and for socialism.

At a time when literacy levels were improving but the campaign to "liquidate illiteracy" was still pressing in the countryside, editors also educated rural correspondents in how to write well and in how to construct a good story. In 1926, 51 percent of the rural population between nine and forty-nine years of age was literate. By 1939 this had risen to 84 percent. There was, however, a significant gender difference. In 1926, 67 percent of rural men and only 35 percent of women were literate, rising in 1939 to 91 percent and 77 percent respectively.[4] And "literate" did not necessary mean able to write flowing prose. In this context, instruction in how to write and to present material was firstly educational and secondly fitted under the general umbrella of bringing *kul'turnost'* to the countryside with the promise of self-improvement and some upward mobility.

In the politically charged relationship between editor and journalist, the former represented the state's interests by being censor, ideologue, propagandist, educator, and overseer of surveillance. The information gathered for stories also served as intelligence gathering and was a way of informing the authorities what was happening in rural areas. Among the *sel'kory* were keen and loyal watchers of rural events who noted achievements and docked failures, problems, and errors. As vigilant observers, they had information of interest to the secret police, with whom editors at *Krest'ianskaia gazeta* liaised. In the 1920s this newspaper had regularly forwarded intelligence reports to the Central Committee. It has been suggested elsewhere that after 1930 its information on popular moods was needed less, either because repression was so strong or because the main job of rural correspondents was now to *organize* public views rather than to register them.[5] In the 1930s, however, *Krest'ianskaia gazeta* was definitely of service to the secret police and procuracy in its uncovering of sabotage of Stakhanovism.

Editors themselves also needed instructions about how reporting should proceed. Not only did the Politburo issue precise instructions to different newspapers on how to cover specific Stakhanovite conferences, but editors had to keep abreast of official statements on the nature of the press.[6] Editors sometimes visited leaders, such as Mikhail Kalinin, President of the Supreme Soviet, for informal discussions as well. Accordingly, this chapter focuses on relationships between editors at *Krest'ianskaia gazeta* and *sel'kory* and examines the instructions and advice editors received from their political superiors. It reveals the demands made on journalists and editors in reporting, constructing, and encouraging Stakhanovism and the pressures, priorities, and official emphases with which they worked.

EDITORS LIAISE WITH *SEL'KORY*

Krest'ianskaia gazeta's Department of Rural Correspondents was the hub of liaison with rural correspondents. It looked for new cadres, had close ties with existing *sel'kory*, and also guided the work of Circles of Friends of the Newspaper (*Kruzhki Druzei Gazety*).[7]

Editors required ready on-the-spot coverage of events in the countryside but were not guaranteed a buoyant supply of educated peasants to aid them. Rural correspondents were valuable to editors and the latter took pains to help them develop their writing skills. Archives indicate that editors showed great patience with peasants who sent in poorly written reports, going to great lengths to explain errors. Moreover, *sel'kory* frequently endured hostility from other peasants and their murder was not unknown. As a consequence, many *sel'kory* felt exposed and vulnerable, some wishing to write under pseudonyms. Instructor Polovinkin took Comrade Tarasov from Orël oblast to task for this:

> In your letter you use the pseudonym "Tikhanov." Why? Why do you fear to write openly? Our revolutionary legal system strictly punishes the persecution of *sel'kory*. It is necessary to unmask any kind of abuse bravely and openly, as in battle.[8]

The issue of whether or not to adopt pseudonyms was a heated one among rural correspondents which, in 1935, they debated in their journal *Sel'kor*.[9] The main anxieties concerned the possibility of attacks and whether or not they would be thrown off their farms. One peasant noted that even on the wall newspapers on farms, everything was written anonymously, otherwise nothing would have been written at all.[10] Another added that if good work had been written about, then the author would sign the comments, but if a criticism had been made, a pseudonym was inevitable for fear of reprisal from farm leaders or from other peasants.[11] The general message trumpeted by the journal *Sel'kor*, however, was that *sel'kory* should be open and fearless because "under the defense of the party and Soviet power, rural correspondents can work openly."[12]

Acting as conveyor belts of information from locality to center, *sel'kory* were often perceived in villages as representatives of the system, as investigators who exposed peasants' misdemeanors against the state, or as collaborators with the Soviet regime, resented for uncovering wrongdoing and for meddling in local affairs. Simultaneously, *sel'kory* were champions of peasants suffering harm and injustice or defenders of those who were victims of a settling of old scores or of those who self-interestedly set out to manipulate the state for their own ends.[13] *Sel'kory* were consequently reviled and vilified by their targets and praised by those whose interests they defended. It was in this context of low literacy levels and suspicion of *sel'kory* that editors liaised with their reporters.

HOW TO BECOME A RURAL CORRESPONDENT

Keen peasants wrote in a wide range of styles to *Krest'ianskaia gazeta* offering to become *sel'kory*. Some sent rather naïve letters in childlike handwriting while others made terse requests.[14] Editorial responses were typically encouraging:

> You write that you want to become a *sel'kor.* That is very good. A *sel'kor* is an active, class conscious collective farmer, the best public-spirited person *(ob-shchestvennik)*, the best production worker.[15]

Editors usually praised the peasant a little, stressed the huge responsibility of becoming a *sel'kor,* indicated its immense social value, and sometimes set the first assignment. Editors insisted that good *sel'kory* were "advanced" people, even Stakhanovites. Accordingly, Poliakov wrote to Comrade Matvienko in Zhitomir oblast, "To be a *sel'kor* is a great and honorable duty, to be an advanced person in the village, the best Stakhanovite, shock worker, active public spirited person."[16] Poliakov praised him for warranting "with honor the name of *sel'kor*" which meant he would be "an example in the village."[17] As such, the *sel'kor* was performing a highly responsible duty to the community, to the state, and to socialism. Rural correspondents were "new" men (evidence suggests most were male), helping to transform the countryside and themselves. Like Stakhanovites they were motors of change, specifically geared to developing the consciousness of peasants and their understanding of Soviet power.

Editors asked *sel'kory* to fill in detailed questionnaires about themselves and to send in stories on a regular basis.[18] Those who were tardy in reporting received gentle reprimands.[19] Editors also urged *sel'kory* to attend lectures in their local area. Sometimes experienced correspondents gathered twenty or so *sel'kory* together and went over topics such as Russian language and geography. Here the newspaper took on the function of giving basic schooling. Editors also asked correspondents for information about their conversations with the collective farms' press offices, evidently checking on their work in order to establish whether and how they helped in basic study skills.[20] By the press office this might be interpreted as spying and informing, but for editors it was gathering data about the countryside and more generally promoting education, *kul'turnost',* and serving the advances of socialism.

The numerous rejection letters that have been preserved in the archive illustrate the sorts of pictures of rural Stakhanovism that editors wished *sel'kory* to create and the changes they wished to forge. They also provide us with a window on the texture and styles of interactions between editors and reporters and on the newspaper's agendas and priorities.

STATISTICS, NOT REAL PEOPLE AND NO WORK METHODS

Editors demanded reporting that told vivid stories, named real people, and explained how better output could be attained. A typical letter was sent by instructor Golikov to comrade V. F. Groshev concerning his reporting on the harvest in which he reprimanded, "you report only statistics, not showing specific people." Golikov showed how to shape the points with "it would have been good if you had described why one link achieved a bigger harvest than another; if you had narrated in detail the work methods of particular Stakhanovites."[21] The main point for Groshev was that "figures without facts are not interesting for readers."[22]

Failure to talk about socialist competitions or to name Stakhanovites also triggered soft rebukes. A kindly letter to another *sel'kor* ran that "Your farm is of great interest to us, but in reporting about it, you did not give one example, nor name one Stakhanovite in animal husbandry."[23] Editors specifically requested "more about your Stakhanovites" and details of the competition "for the right to participate in the All-Union Agricultural Exhibition."[24]

Empty reporting came under special fire. Kirichok in Chernigov oblast was criticized for his dull treatment of a tractor competition that omitted how special records were attained.[25] Information was needed in order to instruct, educate, enlighten, mobilize, and inspire peasants to work in particular ways and to alter their lives. Reporting was meant to be a mechanism of social change, not a recipe for bored readers. Poliakov softened the blow of rejection with "we would like to know you better. Write us a short biography. Indicate where you work and as what."[26] The personal touch was evident in many letters, serving two functions: to make the *sel'kor* feel at ease and flattered; and provide information about reporters for editors and personal files.

Often editors were extremely precise about what was missing from articles. Instructor Polovinkin told Comrade Khrustalev that you "said nothing about how the MTS prepares for spring work, how they are repairing the tractors, what pledges they are making and how they think they can fulfil them."[27] Polovinkin made clear that coverage of "lessons" for peasants was paramount. Editors repeatedly reiterated that they did not want *sel'kory* to skim over successful work methods since peasants who worked badly or slowly needed instruction. What mattered were tips on how to attain a better harvest or how to get more milk from a cow.[28] Gorbachev advised Rylov that his reporting would be much more interesting if he concentrated on brigade number 15 where Comrade Kirienko worked and if he elaborated upon why such high output was attained by his particular tractor.[29] In this manner editors told how to recast reporting, even down to the detail of which brigades to follow.[30]

UNCLEAR FOCUS AND POOR ELABORATION

Editors were keen that the main point of an article be clear and not confused. One correspondent was asked if his article was about whether Ivanova's Stakhanovite team was prevented from working or that she had been baited. These were separate themes in need of distinction. For example, if the baiting of Ivanova were the main focus, then

> Taken separately, you could develop it more fully and show the role of the brigade leader in baiting a Stakhanovite, the role of the kolkhoz chairperson and the head of the district land department (*raizo*) in this business. They know about the baiting, but take no measures. Does this happen due to political blindness or for other reasons? Each of your reports must have a clear main idea. It must be developed in the report.[31]

These very basic instructions illustrate the extent to which editors had to educate their *sel'kory* and demonstrate the process of schooling peasants in how to think, analyze, and intepret the meaning of "baiting," "political blindness," and appropriate "measures." Training was in place which was much wider than how to write, extending into how to understand rural life through a particular political prism. This *sel'kor* was also told to avoid insertions that made reporting cumbersome or erroneous, and if necessary, to consult a literary worker (*literaturnyi rabotnik*), who would be available to help.[32]

Also essential in reporting was detailed coverage of what editors called "huge questions." How Stakhanovites studied was a top-priority issue and should not have been dealt with "literally in a few words."[33] One *sel'kor* was told, "you wrote very little about how the study itself is organized, who teaches, what program is followed [and] the experience of advanced Stakhanovites in agriculture."[34] Similarly, details about the library were wanting: "you only say that the library has so many books and that *kolkhoznik* Prosteniuk read so many books." Poliakov inquired, "why don't you show the library *aktiv*, talk about its needs, its requests, what it reads and what demands are made on the library."[35] The spread of *kul'turnost'* through Stakhanovites' studies and the use of libraries were favored editorial themes.

Editors regretted, however, that a common problem was that *sel'kory* created confusing pictures by beginning with three themes and then tackling none. Instructor Aver'ianov wrote very kindly to one peasant:

Krest'ianskaia gazeta receives a huge number of letters and naturally there is no chance of placing them all. Only the most interesting are published, and not all of those. In your correspondence the main deficiency is that you immediately take several themes and state them in two or three words. This is not adequate for our paper.[36]

Aver'ianov enclosed a brochure on how to write articles and suggested that "if anything is unclear, write to us."[37] In providing booklets on how to write, the newspaper yet again acted as a school for journalists. Through such mailings, editors hoped to foster clarity, sharp focus, and logical development of a given theme, thereby fashioning the state's reporters.

OUT-OF-DATE MATERIALS AND FAILURE TO SHOW NEW PROSPERITY AND CHANGE

Other articles were rejected because they conveyed out-of-date information. Poliakov turned down a piece on the best Stakhanovite brigades in Krolevets raion, Chernigov oblast, because dated facts "have lost their value." He advised the *sel'kor* to concentrate on the work of separate brigades and how they had prepared for the spring sowing so that 1939 would see an even greater harvest.[38] Didactic messages about what "should" result "if only" certain patterns were followed were needed.

Editors also dismissed reports that did not cite outstanding production feats. An article by Comrade Khram in Krasnodar Krai was turned down because "the cotton picking norms of individual *kolkhozniki* that you report are not high. We have masses of letters stating that the best Stakhanovites pick 80–100 kilos of cotton a day, even 150 kilos."[39] Khram did not seem to know that dozens of collective farmers in his district had picked 120 kilos a day. As Stakhanovite records became larger, rural correpondents had to keep apace. What had been a "feat" in the autumn of 1935 was officially commonplace by 1938 and to be outstripped.

A consistent theme in newspaper reporting throughout the entire history of the Soviet state was that of progress under socialism. Therefore articles that dwelled upon the failures of the past without portraying the advances of the present were deficient. P. Semichev of the Socialist Cultural Department told Comrade Krasniak that he needed to describe how "genuine culture" came to the village of Antonovka. Not giving one example of a reading hut, cinema, or library "your letter cannot satisfy the demands of our readers."[40] The growth of *kul'turnost'* had to be linked to progress in general and to broadening prosperity.

Semichev tried to instigate better reporting on "cultural construction" and "cultural mass work." He requested coverage of the work of reading huts, clubs, and red circles with attention to help given by district education departments. Semichev also asked for articles on "enthusiasts" in cultural work, rich with detail. This extended to examples of building bath-houses, stadiums, electric stations, roads, and water mains. Not to be excluded were cases of "patriotism and heroic achievements of *kolkhozniki*" and work in defense and in sanitation.[41] *Kul'turnost'* was very broadly conceived.

After Stalin had declared that life was getting better, the theme of building a more prosperous life was extremely popular. Pis'man wrote to V. M. Stoian in Borispol' district in Kiev oblast with very specific recommendations about what needed to be said on prosperity:

> Write in more detail. If you are talking about the prosperity of your collective farm, then show those *kolkhozniki* who achieved what, thanks to which measures; show that instead of 800 grammes of bread in 1935, they received 4 kilos in 1937. Write so that the picture of the collective farmers' struggle for prosperity and success is vivid.[42]

Editors emphasized that "struggle" was a necessary verb. Linked to prosperity, income and the value of collective farmers' "work days" were other favored themes. Poliakov explained to Comrade Ivan Artiukh that:

> You should have taken one of the most advanced collective farms and shown it fully. Tell what income comes from which branches, how different brigades and teams worked. What was the income last year, what was the main difference this year from last, what was the value of the kolkhoz work day (*trudoden'*), how much it is higher than last year's.[43]

Like other instructors in the Department of *Sel'kory* and Letters, Poliakov stressed the importance of comparisons with previous years to highlight improvement. He also required that stories of economic growth be accompanied by examples of positive developments in culture, changes in consciousness and psychology. Poliakov informed *sel'kory* that: "their culture grows, an entirely new world outlook develops, psychology is changed" and went on to advise reporters to:

> focus in detail on one or two collective farm families, talk about their budget, compare this budget with the one they had before the revolution. You need to write profoundly, in a well thought-out way.[44]

More generally, editors often called for specific treatment of the big theme of "advances" made under Soviet socialism. Poliakov asked for more articles about changes under Soviet power, new relations between young and old people, parents and children, and men and women. He called for study of kolkhoz families "in which these changes are most sharply visible" thereby finding "concrete facts and examples, illustrating changes in daily life."[45] Offering a more open brief, Poliakov ended with "Also write about other questions which are worrying you and all *kolkhozniki*."[46] Thus Poliakov gave space to journalists, too, to select their own topics and to take initiative.

Improvements in daily life, growing prosperity, and widening *kul'turnost'* were key socialist realist themes in rural reporting, a necessary backdrop against which images of Stakhanovism were set and advances which Stakhanovism both reflected and caused. Stakhanovism itself was an official motor of rural progress and transformation and had to be portrayed in this way, whether or not this happened to be the case in reality.

IMPATIENCE WITH *SEL'KORY*

Whilst most rejection letters in the archives were polite and constructive, one or two showed signs of weary impatience. Lengthy correspondence between Poliakov and Comrade Magl'ovannyi in Chigirin raion of Kiev oblast fell into this category. Poliakov began one letter with the tired point that inadequacies in Magl'ovannyi's material had already been pointed out in previous letters. Poliakov went on, "But you have still not shed these mistakes. They are repeated in practically every letter."[47] Poliakov nonetheless ran over the *sel'kor*'s writing problems for him yet again.[48] Magl'ovannyi was warned that he "must henceforth avoid stock phrases, seriously and with greater depth work on your material." Finally, however, came the kind words: "We think you will take into account your mistakes. Do not be offended by our remarks. We will not set a task; you know what to write about. With greetings."[49] Reprimand and kindness were the hallmarks of editors' treatment of weaker reports. The style was firm and indulgent.

In another letter Poliakov scolded Magl'ovannyi for briefly conveying how many tsentners of millet were gathered but:

> did not even tell the size of the sown area, or which particular agro-technical measures were used. And from the letter it is also not clear what their positions were—brigade leaders or team members. Next time you must take these circumstances into consideration.[50]

Poliakov spelled out the acceptable formulae for portraying rural Stakhanovism and specified that the next assignment should cover how the harvest was progressing, paying attention to "how much is expected, how much has been gathered, whether there has been wastage. Show the best brigades and teams achieving a good harvest. Cite more facts and examples and analyze them."[51] Successful harvesting and minimal wastage were politically pressing themes which had to receive coverage and editors persisted in their demands for them. Due to insufficient numbers of high-quality *sel'kory* and the fear some of them wrote under, editors and instructors addressed poor journalism with patience.

SPECIFIC REQUESTS FROM EDITORS

As well as reacting to articles sent to them, editors sometimes specified in advance exactly what reporters should consider. Anniversaries of the Stakhanovite movement were particularly special. Zharikov from the paper's Agricultural Department wrote to *sel'kor* Burdeinyi as follows:

> On the 31 August the country will mark the third anniversary of the Stakhanovite movement. We recommend that you familiarize yourself with Comrade Stalin's speech about the Stakhanovite movement and with Lenin's articles "on socialist competition." Having acquainted yourself, think up a theme for the paper.[52]

Having given Burdeinyi the chance to "think up," Zharikov then did it for him and zoomed in on a good angle. He pointed out that Burdeinyi's district in Vinnitsa oblast had excellent records in sugar beet. Given this, "these new Stakhanovites must be made famous in all the land. The topic is serious and interesting. You should work basically on that."[53] Then even more pointedly, Zharikov ordered,

> We ask you to organize a letter from your best Stakhanovites concerning the object-lessons with which they will mark the anniversary of the Stakhanovite movement, how they prepare for this day.[54]

This is among the strongest evidence on file showing that letters from Stakhanovites were often "organized" by *sel'kory* and orchestrated ahead of time by editors. Thus newspapers instigated forms of Stakhanovite mobilization beyond productive feats using *sel'kory* as their agitators.

Vinokurov in the Agricultural Department asked another *sel'kor* to concentrate on how the experience of the best Stakhanovites in 1938 would be used by the farm administration in the following year. In particular, he should focus on how the best teams picked more than 40 tsentners of maize per hectare and how the agronomist helped. More generally, what role did agronomy play? These were pressing questions for 1939.[55] As the regime's priorities and emphases shifted, so reporting had to reflect them.

Quite specific details were also requested in connection with sowing or harvesting. Instructor Polovinkin asked for reporting on "how the storage of grain is being organized, where it will be put and how cleaning of the grain is being conducted."[56] These were vital practices to ensure minimal loss. Another *sel'kor* was asked for details of "discussions of socialist competition" with attention to "what help is shown to neighboring kolkhozy."[57] A repeated yearly favorite was the pre-October competitions and new production victories planned for anniversaries of the October Revolution.[58]

The press also tried to create a sense of buildup to the Eighteenth Party Congress of March 1939. In early February, V. Abramovich of the Department of *Sel'kory* and Letters wrote to a correspondent in Ukraine linking the Congress to "a new and wide wave of socialist competitions."[59] Abramovich drew the journalist's attention to the All-Ukraine Conference of Stakhanovites in Animal Husbandry and then wrote:

> We request that you, Vasilii Ivanovich, flesh out your letter. Write to us if your collective farm is involved in the pre-Congress competition. What work pledges have the *kolkhozniki* made in connection with the opening of the Eighteenth Party Congress?[60]

Stakhanovites were encouraged by editors to mobilize around key political events like party congresses and to impart to others how they experienced this process, instilling it with personal meaning and wider significance.

Even the drier government *postanovlenie* was sometimes honored. One request asked for an article on whether the district fulfilled party and government decisions of 19 April 1938 concerning "the incorrect distribution of income on collective farms."[61] Thus articles on Stakhanovism were to be linked to anniversaries, congresses, and government "decisions," as well as to the agricultural cycle. Whatever was on the political agenda, there was a Stakhanovite angle on it which both mobilized Stakhanovites and gave a value to the everyday functioning of rural life expressed in terms of official language.

EDITORS RECEIVE ADVICE "FROM ABOVE"

Just as editors conveyed to *sel'kory* what it was appropriate to write about, so top political leaders gave editors guidance. Liaison took place in several ways: editors were given instructions at special meetings, such as on the Day of the Press; editors actively sought leaders' advice; editors asked political leaders to contribute to an edition of the paper; and editors visited leaders for

face-to-face consultation. There were also telephone calls between leaders
and editors, although these are not part of the historical record.

Editors received specific instructions on Press Day. At a gathering on 5 May
1936, B. Tal' delivered a speech which included a special section on "the press
and the Stakhanovite movement."[62] Tal' argued, "the new tasks of the press
are connected with the phenomenon which brightly characterizes 1936 with
the Stakhanovite movement."[63] What mattered above all was that the press
was not dragging behind this movement but actively involved in its spread. He
noted that "not all papers" were active enough. Although most had mastered
the "easy task" of showing the achievements of individual Stakhanovites,
"many of our papers have not yet been able to climb higher than description
of separate records of separate Stakhanovites." What was needed from the
press was more active participation in the struggle for Stakhanovite five-days
and ten-days, even more for the Stakhanovite month.[64]

Tal' demanded that the press make a "profound and serious study of production," discuss technical matters, and rage against those who hindered or
sabotaged Stakhanovism. The press had to encourage the dynamo of Stakhanovism. Tal' explained that editors, however, should not muddle up "competition" (konkurs) among individuals with "socialist competition" (sotsialisticheskoe sorevnovanie) which helped others to improve, as had been an issue of
Politburo concern.[65] Tal' urged editors to keep a main goal in mind: "the organization and development of socialist competition."[66] Thus the regime made
clear to its editors and correspondents how it wanted the Stakhanovite movement to be approached and pressed ahead. In short, the press had to rouse the
countryside into action.

Kalinin was regularly approached by the press. In 1939, N. Anisimov, editor of Sotsialisticheskoe Zemledelie, wrote to Kalinin asking for advice about
how to pitch the paper's ten-year anniversary. Anisimov requested that
Kalinin send his "desires for the immediate tasks of our newspaper" and wondered about the questions upon which the editors "should concentrate attention in the near future."[67] Themselves in a politically vulnerable position, editors wished to avoid making errors and falling afoul of leaders. Consulting
with those above about good themes and relevant content was one way of attempting self-protection.

Editors also frequently involved leaders directly in what was published.
This could take the form of asking leaders to write an article on a particular
political topic that was timely or to respond to readers' letters. In 1939, editors at Krest'ianskaia gazeta approached Kalinin about answering five questions from readers to appear in one edition of the paper.[68] Sent later the questions were: What does it mean that the foundations of socialism have been
built? How can socialism in one country be built when we are surrounded by

capitalist ones? What expresses the transition from socialism to communism? How can we liquidate the difference between town and countryside? What is the dictatorship of the proletariat? Drawing Kalinin into answering questions provided a link between peasant and leader and also enabled the newspaper to give "correct" responses to ideological issues.

Another letter to Kalinin asked him to answer peasants' questions about the constitution. Some of these were very smart: The constitution says the land is free, so why do peasants pay tax? Concerning article 33, what signifies a two-chamber system here and in other countries? And how can there be power to the working class under conditions of equality if the number of peasants is low and workers are fewer?[69] Kalinin would then select which questions were worthy of attention. He would also be given a feel of attitudes in the countryside about the new constitution. Newspapers passed on these "opinion barometers" as feedback on the regime's policies and effectively acted as intelligence gatherers. As an indication of editors' concerns about defining and pitching "news" correctly, numerous papers requested Kalinin's participation, including *Pravda, Molodaia Gvardiia, Komsomol'skaia Pravda, Krasnyi Arkhiv*, and *Iskusstvo*. If documents among Kalinin's papers are just a selection of the letters received, then every month he was inundated with requests.[70]

Editorial boards were concerned to please leaders in order not to provoke criticism and to acquire their guidance as a form of protection, as illustrated by a visit to Kalinin from editor Anisimov and other staff of *Sotsialisticheskoe Zemledelie* in June 1938. Kalinin opened their meeting with: "What do you want from me? It seems, simply, that you want to talk. Tell me what worries you."[71] Kalinin was sensitive to the fact that editors did indeed worry and that they needed direction, tips, and reassurance. In the context of the Great Purge, editors like everyone in prominent posts experienced fear and arbitrary arrest and were unsettled by show trials and death penalties. They had to be careful about what their papers said.

The record of Kalinin's conversation with Anisimov and his staff reveals a great deal about what the socialist state expected from its press. After admitting that he had not followed *Sotsialisticheskoe Zemledelie* recently, Kalinin nonetheless observed, "you print few leading articles on the economy and politics. Such articles could, in fact, be published once a week."[72] He went on to advise Anisimov to be quiet about exhibitions and to write about the harvest instead.[73] This was apposite given that the opening of the Agricultural Exhibition kept being postponed. Kalinin effectively instructed Anisimov to be silent about something which was not happening which should have been. Unfettered investigative reporting was explicitly not the order of the day.

Kalinin then dwelled at length on the difference between metaphysical scribbling (*metafizicheskie bumazhki*) as "the worst sort of reporting" and "alive reporting" (*zhivaia korrespondentsiia*).[74] According to Kalinin, the former could be written sitting in an office without contact with the real world and would "give nothing." Good reporting, by contrast, was about "a particular place where tractors were poorly prepared." Here the journalist writes "why they were not properly ready" because "something was missing" or because "that is how workers worked" or "they did not go to work on time." Reasons and analysis were crucial so that readers felt that reporters had stood for a week alongside the tractor; then, reporting would be "alive and interesting."[75] Kalinin took care to warn that reporting should not proceed in the manner of Soviet Control (*Sovetskii kontrol'*) whose job was to seek only the negative:

> You reporters, you must show all sides of a question. Along with the bad, show the good. You know on every very bad MTS we will find a couple of people who are fighting for work. You must learn to write in a bolshevik way (*po-bol'-shevistski*).[76]

Reporting *po-bolshevistski* meant that negative and positive sides to stories had to be shown. Portrayal of collectivization, as an illustration, required coverage of both destructive and conscious processes (*razrushitel'nye i soznatel'nye protsessy*).[77]

Editors and *sel'kory* thus had to forge themselves to work in a politicized Bolshevik way that affected how they approached their topics and what they did with them. A dynamic process of interaction with the material was required in which reporters as "new" people worked on themselves first in order to bring enlightened perspectives to bear. This interactive process demanded that a leading article was not something that necessarily had to be written in Moscow since wide consultation and rewriting were necessary too. Kalinin recommended that: "you discuss it with the peasants around you, talk about it with the kolkhoz chairperson, with various local people about what to include, what to toss out. From that will result a good leading article."[78] Journalism was about listening and debate, albeit from a conscious position, and not distant theorizing.

The context of the purges explicitly entered Kalinin's advice when he pointed out discussions with local people were also vital in areas where Socialist Revolutionaries were still fomenting counterrevolution among peasants and intellectuals, as in Saratov oblast. Kalinin urged correspondents not to be shy:

> You are a journalist, a public spirited person, a communist. You are not a representative of the NKVD and can very freely talk politics with them. I, you say,

will not lead you to repression, but politically I assess you thus. Perhaps the NKVD will come to you later.[79]

Kalinin urged correspondents not be afraid to say directly, "Villains, you here are against Soviet power, are conducting counterrevolution."[80]

It is illuminating that Kalinin brings in the NKVD and counterrevolution in this way. He is effectively saying that *sel'kory* perform surveillance work, the details of which can be passed on to the secret police if necessary. He stresses that rural correspondents are not themselves part of the secret police and so it is fine to talk with peasants and to gather information from them, indicating that no threat can come from *sel'kory*. But then, should the NKVD hear of incidents in the countryside that need attention, the *sel'kor* is duty-bound for the good of the social community to pass details on. Indeed, by implication, the *sel'kor* and newspaper will inform the NKVD when deemed necessary. This links to the aforementioned resentment of *sel'kory* among peasants and to rural correspondents seeking protection through pseudonyms. Those who sabotaged Stakhanovism were among those in whom the NKVD had an interest and rural newspapers played a huge political role in passing on information and in generally liaising with the local party and secret police. In this sense, *sel'kory* were the ears and the eyes of the NKVD and this role was part of working *po-bolshevistski*.

Working in a Bolshevik way required both body and soul. Kalinin declared of good reporting, "into it your blood flows." He suggested that result was a picture, not a photograph, in which a fraction of the writer is embedded. This fraction included feelings about what perturbed and caused anxiety. It reflected "communist feeling" and contrasted with distant reporting of an observer, like an American, who could punctiliously describe what he saw in a notebook but miss the depth.[81] Soviet reporting amounted to an interaction between the Bolshevik soul and reality.

Kalinin also stressed the importance of writing honestly, avoiding scholasticism, not using stock formulae, and being goal-oriented rather than all over the place.[82] He praised particular pivotal themes such as the weakening of the procuracy of its struggle with illegality—which "has to be shown." Here was a very explicit cue to engage with the purges and be vigilant about those who performed work badly.[83] A negligent procuracy had to be called to account. As part of the broadening of *kul'turnost'*, Kalinin also advised editors and correspondents to study hard, write concisely, and to read Goncharov, Turgenev, and Chekhov.

Quite how much reassurance editors reaped from Kalinin cannot be gauged. Before they left, he reminded them that journalists carried authority and so mistakes would not be forgiven. He made it quite clear that they were being watched, which most likely guaranteed a "terror in their souls."[84]

CONCLUSION

Scrutiny of correspondence in the *Krest'ianskaia gazeta* archive graphically illustrates how images of Stakhanovites and messages about them were frequently crafted by editors who predetermined particular emphases, didactic meanings, and exhortations to action. Although *sel'kory* "worked with" realities surrounding them on the farm, the lenses through which they selected and interpreted events could be nudged, prompted, or requested by editors. If the rural correspondent's treatment of "reality" did not match what was required, then it was rejected with guidance for reconstruction and improvement. Although *sel'kory* were also permitted to take initiative in what they produced, they were reprimanded if they fell afoul of official frames.

In turn, editors were briefed on the sort of reporting they should encourage and were scolded when the regime's priorities were not advanced. Although both *Krest'ianskaia gazeta* and *Sovkhoznaia gazeta* orchestrated Stakhanovite days, it was clear from Tal''s speech that not all newspapers were so devoted to agit-prop. Moreover, Tal''s remarks were also a cue for rural newspapers since their calls for special Stakhanovite work periods came, in the main, after his speech. In this way, leaders in Central Committee departments could shape the direction that reporting took. Vigilant editors, for job security, would follow these cues.

In sum, the process of reporting on rural Stakhanovism was highly politicized, as was media coverage of all issues in the Soviet state. Leaders wanted editors to promote certain lines on Stakhanovism and to fashion ideas about its significance. It was hoped that politically correct attitudes, beliefs, and behavior among the peasantry could thereby be inculcated and molded. This was part of the process of building the "new life" of which rural Stakhanovism was a tiny part.

NOTES

1. RGAE, f. 396, op. 11, d. 153, l. 176. This was written by Gorbachev in the Agriculture Department of *Krest'ianskaia gazeta* to *sel'kor* V. Rylov in Ukraine. Many editors and instructors usually signed letters using their last name only, occasionally giving an initial, too.

2. The editorial archive of *Krest'ianskaia gazeta* is held in RGAE, f. 396, op. 10 and op. 11. This archive for the 1930s covers correspondence between editors and *sel'kory* written in 1938 and 1939 only. Archivists say they do not know what happened to materials of 1930–1937. Documents of the 1920s, however, are also available. The files for 1938 and 1939 hold copies of rejection letters to *sel'kory*, but usually unaccompanied by the original submission. For further details about the newspaper, see appendix II. For a history of the newspaper and discussion of letters

written in 1938, consult Sheila Fitzpatrick, "Readers' letters to *Krest'ianskaia gazeta*, 1938," *Russian History* 24, nos. 1–2 (Spring–Summer 1997): 149–70; and her "From *Krest'ianskaia gazeta*'s Files: Life Story of a Peasant Striver,"*Russian History* 24, nos. 1–2 (Spring–Summer 1997): 215–37. Examination of the role of *sel'kory* can be found in Steven R. Coe, "Peasants, the State and the Languages of NEP: The Rural Correspondents Movement in the Soviet Union, 1924–1928" (Ph.D dissertation, University of Michigan, 1993). For the dilemmas faced by the state in meetings its need to create a "new intelligentsia" of would-be writers, consult Michael S. Gorham, "Tongue-tied Writers: The *rabsel'kor* Movement and the Voice of the 'New Intelligentsia' in Early Soviet Russia," *The Russian Review* 55, no. 3 (July 1966): 412–29. For general discussion of the role of the early Soviet press, see Jeffrey Brooks, "Public and Private Values in the Soviet Press, 1921–1928," *Slavic Review* 48, no. 1 (Spring 1989): 16–35; and Peter Kenez, *The Birth of the Propaganda State* (Cambridge: Cambridge University Press, 1985).

3. Matthew E. Lenoe, "Letter Writing and the State: Reader Correspondence with Newspapers as a Source for Early Russian History," *Cahiers du Monde Russe* 40, no. 1–2 (January–June, 1999): 167. Lenoe categorizes the functions of letter writing as: surveillance; education; control of the state apparatus; and adjusting the state's distribution of values. For discussion of categories of letters of denunciation, see Sheila Fitzpatrick, "Petitions and Denunciations in Russian and Soviet History," *Russian History* 24, Nos 1–2 (Spring–Summer 1997): 1–9; her "Signals from Below: Soviet Letters of Denunciation of the 1930s," *The Journal of Modern History* 68, no. 4 (December 1996): 831–66; and her "Supplicants and Citizens: Public Letter Writing in Soviet Russia in the 1930s," *Slavic Review* 55, no. 1 (Spring 1996): 78–105.

4. Tsentral'noe Statisticheskoe Upravlenie, *Narodnoe Khoziaistvo SSSR 1922–1972: iubileinyi statisticheskyi ezhegodnik* (Moscow: Statistika, 1974), 35.

5. Matthew Lenoe notes that in the 1920s, *Krest'ianskaia gazeta* was the only newspaper regularly to send intelligence reports to the Central Committee executive apparatus. In his estimation the paper changed, however, from "the peasant megaphone" and a "barometer" of peasant mood in the 1920s, to a shaper of the countryside in the 1930s. See Lenoe, "Letter Writing and the State," 152–54.

6. RGASPI, f. 17, op. 3, d. 974, l. 15; f. 17, op. 3, d. 976, l. 4; f. 17, op. 3, d. 975, ll. 47–48; f. 78, op. 1, d. 728.

7. By 1925, there were 5,000 *sel'kory*, of whom 3,843 were in the RSFFR, around 400 in Ukraine, more than 150 in Belorussia, and the remainder from elsewhere. By 1926, there were 1,450 *kruzhki*. See See E. B. Derusova, " '*Predislovie*' k f. 396, *Redaktsiia 'Krest'ianskaia gazeta*'" (Moscow 1990) which is at the beginning of RGAE, f. 396 op. 10 and 11.

8. RGAE, f. 396, op. 11, d. 41, l. 179.

9. *Sel'kor*, no. 1 (January 1935): 39–42.

10. *Sel'kor*, no. 1 (January 1935): 41.

11. *Sel'kor*, no. 1 (January 1935): 42.

12. *Sel'kor*, no. 1 (January 1935): 39.

13. Sheila Fitzpatrick underscores the extent to which *sel'kory* were resented. She also observes that officials were aware that "peasants were using mutual denunciation

as a tool to pursue village feuds." See Fitzpatrick, 'Signals from Below," and her *Stalin's Peasants: Resistance and Survival in the Russian Village after Collectiviza-tion* (New York and Oxford: Oxford University Press, 1994), 237.

14. Ivan Lezur from Chernigov oblast sent a rather sweet and naïve letter express-ing his wish to cover local events. He wrote in a large childlike hand, "Dear editorial staff, send me an answer about what I must write . . . May I write about complaints, about school and about all the countryside?" Lezur had carefully made the envelope himself that matched the paper on which he had written. See RGAE, f. 396, op. 10, d. 153, l. 55. A quite different, very brief, letter came from V. Rylov, a Komsomol member in Ukraine, who declared, "I want to be a correspondent for *Krest'ianskaia gazeta*. I work as secretary of the editorial staff on the local paper 'Lenin's Way.'" See RGAE, f. 396, op. 10, d. 153, l. 178.

15. RGAE, f. 396, op. 10, d. 153, l. 55.

16. RGAE, f. 396, op. 11, d. 17, l. 48.

17. RGAE, f. 396, op. 11, d. 17, l. 48.

18. New *sel'kory* were generally asked to fill in a questionnaire giving biographi-cal details, including address for telegrams, whether or not they were party members, their branch of work, the name of their local wall newspaper and its editor. Other questions asked how they were raising their literacy level, what they read, and whether they participated in correspondence classes for *sel'kory*.

19. These were usually along the lines of "it is desirable that you, Comrade Tsim-bal, wrote to us more often." See RGAE, f. 396, op. 11, d. 17, l. 115.

20. There were accusations that "local leaders do not give this question sufficient attention." See RGAE, f. 396, op. 11, d. 17, l. 115. Although *sel'kory* needed instruc-tion, they often lacked the opportunity to receive it on the spot so the newspaper was keen to know how the kolkhoz press office helped *sel'kory*. One *sel'kor* received the following request for information:

> Tell what this kolkhoz office of the press gives to kolkhozniki, to *sel'kory*, how it helps their growth, how it improves the work of the kolkhoz wall newspaper, the work of the brigade wall newspaper. You must focus especially on the readings and conversations which you have in your press office.

See RGAE, f. 396, op. 10, d. 153, l. 72. Although this letter from *Krest'ianskaia gazeta* was a reaction to a piece that the *sel'kor* had submitted for publication, editors themselves had a special interest in the information sought.

21. RGAE, f. 396, op. 10, d. 27, l. 209. Groshev was in Rabotkin raion, Gork'ii oblast.

22. RGAE, f. 396, op. 10, d. 27, l. 209. A similar letter to Comrade Derkach in Kazakh ASSR reprimanded that "you scarcely point to vivid facts from Stakhanovites' work or their lives; you give few colourful examples, which we must suggest are not rare in your district." See RGAE, f. 396, op. 10, d. 38, l. 308.

23. RGAE, f. 396, op. 10, d. 38, l. 277.

24. RGAE, f. 396, op. 10, d. 38, l. 277.

25. Poliakov observed, "you list only facts. But you do not report how the tractor drivers attain overfulfilment of norms, you do not pass on their experience." See

RGAE, f. 396, op. 10, d. 153, l. 76. In the letters on file to this correspondent, his name is spelled in different ways: Kirichok; Kirichak; and Kiriuchok. Variations in spelling were common, as were grammatical errors.

26. RGAE, f. 396, op. 10, d. 153, l. 76.

27. RGAE, f. 396, op. 11, d. 41, l. 254. Sometimes reports were turned down because *sel'kory* did not write about what they claimed to be covering. One rejection sent to a reporter in Belorussia noted that although the piece was titled "Stakhanovite work methods," in fact "You absolutely do not recount Stakhanovite work methods, but write only that *kolkhozniki* overfulfill work norms." He was asked to write more about work methods and labor organization during the harvest. See RGAE, f. 396, op. 10, d. 9, l. 20; and f. 396, op. 10, d. 153, l. 176.

28. RGAE, f. 396, op. 10, d. 153, l. 176.

29. RGAE, f. 396, op. 10, d. 153, l. 176.

30. Numerous articles were rejected for not describing work methods. See also, RGAE, f. 396, op. 10, d. 9, ll. 37, 89, 95, 97, and 99. Others were praised for isolating negative aspects of the harvest but were requested to pay attention, too, to "positive sides of work." Consult f. 396, op. 10, d. 48, l. 203. Other letters were rejected for failing to show how agitators worked, who they were, or even what their names were. See f. 396, op. 10, d. 38, l. 310.

31. RGAE, f. 396, op. 10, d. 70, l. 27.

32. RGAE, f. 396, op. 10, d. 70, l. 27.

33. RGAE, f. 396, op. 11, d. 17, l. 51.

34. RGAE, f. 396, op. 11, d. 17, l. 51.

35. RGAE, f. 396, op. 11, d. 17, l. 51.

36. RGAE, f. 396, op. 11, d. 41, l. 151. Gentle advice followed to the effect that "it would be better to take one theme, but to elaborate it in detail."

37. RGAE, f. 396, op. 11, d. 41, l. 151.

38. RGAE, f. 396, op. 10, d. 153, l. 166.

39. RGAE, f. 396, op. 10, d. 70, l. 29.

40. RGAE, f. 396, op. 10, d. 153, l. 86.

41. RGAE, f. 396, op. 10, d. 153, l. 84. As well as enumerating the topics he desired, Semichev also painted the ideological context for *sel'kory*. He declared that along with the growth of material well-being, "the cultural demands of *kolkhozniki* are increasing." This meant "collective farmers are making greater demands on the work of clubs, reading huts and red corners." However, "unfortunately, cultural-mass work is the most backward." The paper needed articles on "radical improvement in cultural mass work," and so the *sel'kor* should "constantly write to us about cultural construction and cultural mass work." See RGAE, f. 396, op. 10, d. 153, l. 84. Thus Semichev gave loud pointers to *sel'kory*. They should look for cases of peasant demand and problems of backwardness in the provision of cultural facilities. Semichev's letter is an excellent example of the "creation" of news by editors.

42. RGAE, f. 396, op. 10, d. 48, l. 80.

43. RGAE, f. 396, op. 10, d. 48, l. 83.

44. RGAE, f. 396, op. 10, d. 48, l. 83.

45. RGAE, f. 396, op. 11, d. 17, l. 58.

46. RGAE, f. 396, op. 11, d. 17, l. 58.
47. RGAE, f. 396, op. 10, d. 48, l. 89.
48. RGAE, f. 396, op. 10, d. 48, l. 89.
49. RGAE, f. 396, op. 10, d. 48, l. 89.
50. RGAE, f. 396, op. 10, d. 48, l. 91.
51. RGAE, f. 396, op. 10, d. 48, l. 91. Magl'ovannyi also failed to impress Poliakov with his attempt to describe entry into the party of brigade leaders on Voroshilov collective farm. Poliakov argued that "the question of Komsomol members being accepted into the party is very serious and timely" and that Magl'ovannyi should "show the best, most advanced young people joining the ranks of the party of Lenin and Stalin." Poliakov took Magl'ovannyi to task for not "coping" with the subject since he said "nothing of party work." Moreover, "you do not talk about those who joined and what authority they hold among *kolkhozniki* or how they work on the kolkhoz. Are they initiators or pioneers of socialist work methods?" See RGAE, f. 396, op. 10, d. 48, l. 95. Poliakov, point by point, indicated how improvements could be made. Generally then, the endings of rejection letters were quite polite and upbeat with constructive suggestions for better reporting. The shortage of literate peasants who were willing to become *sel'kory* contributed to the newspaper's tactful patience with the willing ones. Poliakov enclosed a copy of *Krest'ianskaia gazeta*'s brochure titled "How to write notes" in order to help Magl'ovannyi. The friendly ending of "We await your letters. With greetings" was repeated. Poliakov always took pains not to provoke resentment and sometimes stated, "We hope that you will not be offended and will continue to write as before." See RGAE, f. 396, op. 11, d. 17, l. 36; and RGAE, f. 396, op. 10, d. 70, l. 27. Although editors usually took pains to explain why an article was rejected, occasionaly curt rejections were sent with no reason given. Comrade Duritskii was coldly informed by Novikov, "We received your supplementary report on flax Stakhanovites in Cherniakovskii raion, Zhitomir oblast. Unfortunately we cannot use them." See RGAE, f. 396, op. 11, d. 17, l. 170.
52. RGAE, f. 396, op. 11, d. 4, l. 120.
53. RGAE, f. 396, op. 11, d. 4, l. 120.
54. RGAE, f. 396, op. 11, d. 4, l. 120.
55. RGAE, f. 396, op. 10, d. 92, l. 293.
56. RGAE, f. 396, op. 11, d. 41, l. 179.
57. RGAE, f. 396, op. 10, d. 48, l. 85.
58. RGAE, f. 396, op. 10, d. 70, ll. 27 and 29.
59. RGAE, f. 396, op. 11, d. 19, l. 6.
60. RGAE, f. 396, op. 11, d. 19, l. 6.
61. RGAE, f. 396, op. 10, d. 70, l. 27.
62. B. M. Tal', "O zadachakh bol'shevistskoi pechati," *Sel'kor,* 10 May 1936, 3–5.
63. Tal', "O zadachakh bol'shevistskoi pechati," 3.
64. Tal', "O zadachakh bol'shevistskoi pechati," 4.
65. For discussion about differences between *konkurs* and *sorevnovanie* at Politburo level, refer back to chapter 2 and the section "Politburo meetings and Central Committee Plenary sessions."
66. Tal', "O zadachakh bol'shevistskoi pechati," 4–5.

67. RGASPI, f. 78, op. 1, d. 750, l. 11.

68. RGASPI, f. 78, op. 1, d. 750, l. 19.

69. RGASPI, f. 78, op. 1, d. 649, ll. 64–68.

70. RGASPI, f. 78, op. 1, d. 750.

71. RGASPI, f. 78, op. 1, d. 728, l. 1.

72. RGASPI, f. 78, op. 1, d. 728, l. 1.

73. RGASPI, f. 78, op. 1, d. 728, ll. 2–3. One can trace discussions about the All-Union Agricultural Exhibition and its ongoing postponement in the Politburo protocols. See, for instance, RGASPI, f. 17, op. 3, d. 974, l. 324 and f. 17, op. 3, d. 976, ll. 94–95. Comments on the final opening in 1939 are found at RGASPI, f. 17, op. 3, d. 1007, l. 6 and f. 17, op. 3, d. 1012, l. 35. Finally, it was decided to extend the exhibition. See RGASPI, f. 17, op. 3, d. 1015, l. 17.

74. RGASPI, f. 17, op. 3, d. 1015, l. 3.

75. RGASPI, f. 17, op. 3, d. 1015, l. 3.

76. RGASPI, f. 17, op. 3, d. 1015, l. 4.

77. RGASPI, f. 17, op. 3, d. 1015, l. 24.

78. RGASPI, f. 17, op. 3, d. 1015, l. 4.

79. RGASPI, f. 17, op. 3, d. 1015, l. 32.

80. RGASPI, f. 17, op. 3, d. 1015, l. 32.

81. RGASPI, f. 17, op. 3, d. 1015, ll. 17–18.

82. RGASPI, f. 17, op. 3, d. 1015, ll. 4–15.

83. RGASPI, f. 17, op. 3, d. 1015, l. 24.

84. RGASPI, f. 17, op. 3, d. 1015, l. 14. See Igal Halfin, *Terror in My Soul: Communist Autobiographies on Trial* (Cambridge, MA: Harvard University Press, 2003).

Chapter Five

Specialist Lessons of Stakhanovism

Dudnik told Mariia Safronovna in detail about the soil on her plot and what sugar beet required from the land. Sugar beet like deep soil.[1]

Harvest is a seasonal affair and she does not like to wait. Gather in time and you win—do it late and you lose.[2]

—Stalin

As "advanced" peasants, rural Stakhanovites were told that they had a duty to encourage slack workers to perform better and to educate erring farm leaders in how to help Stakhanovites. So as well as excelling in their own fields, Stakhanovites had a duty to share information on better performance in order to boost food production. Their speeches and autobiographies were printed in the press, in anthologies, and in specialist journals. Numerous short books were also published in the late 1930s devoted almost entirely to Stakhanovite "lessons," invariably with titles which began "Stakhanovite experience in . . ." (*Stakhanovskii opyt v . . .*)[3] The recommendations inside were often highly detailed, technical and dry reading about one sector of the economy. They played an indispensable part in educating the countryside in how to work and in providing data for discussions among specialists. These handbooks amounted to "training manuals" in which Stakhanovites served as exemplars or conduits of technical and expert practices and as mouthpieces of handy tips.

WHY LESSONS AT ALL?

Why, one must ask, was so much effort devoted to publicizing *uroki* or lessons? The word "*urok*" was most prominent in narratives on Stakhanovism,

115

but to what extent did peasants need them? Would not peasants already have known about the need for thorough preparation for sowing and harvesting? Was this not obvious to those living in a predominantly rural society? Would not peasants know that the quality of the soil affected what was grown on it? Was it not elementary that weeds needed to be picked and not get out of control? Surely it was not a revelation to those working with animals that cows varied, as did pigs and sheep, some requiring more feed than others or a different sort of attention? Did not milkmaids know that they needed to take special care of their hands since cracks, blisters, and sores told them that? And even in cases of learning how to use new machinery, would not the sensible agricultural worker know that a tractor had to be kept in good condition in order to function properly? Surely, even if most peasants may have been ignorant about how to maintain a combine harvester, would they not have already acquired other seasonal lessons, passed down from generation to generation? Many semiliterate peasants would not have devoured these manuals, but their content was meant to filter down to them via the press and farm agronomists.

From Stalin's perspective, many rural practices were backward and in need of scientific input for improvement. Hence the urgency for research institutes to study how Stakhanovites boosted production. Those peasants who were disaffected on new farms also needed to be instructed about what they may already have known (as well as what they did not) since they were refusing to apply that knowledge. The countryside by late 1935 may have been more "normalized" than in was in 1931, now "cowed" into submission rather than rebellious, but peasant loyalty to their farms had still to be built. Alongside more committed peasants were those with alienated attitudes to the system who did not necessarily apply known lessons enthusiastically. Peasants, generally, may have ceased to oppose the system openly through riots or the slaughter of animals, but negligence and unwillingness to overfulfill norms were calmer forms of expressing demoralization.[4]

Many successful farmers, moreover, had been exiled through dekulakization. Whilst there is debate among economic historians about how backward the Russian peasantry was and also some skepticism about how productive the kulak really was, one view holds that there was a need for modernization and that "old peasant habits and attitudes and methods of work were inevitably carried over in the new economic form."[5] Moreover, given that the countryside at the beginning of the 1930s had experienced grim famine, grain shortages, and huge loss of animal life, peasants had to be exhorted to harvest in time, to ensure that livestock survived and reproduced, and generally to produce more to feed the town for the success of industrialization. Related to the slaughter of animals and consequent loss of manure, lessons concerning how best to fertilize the land were crucial. These factors combined help to account for the fervor surrounding the campaign to learn from Stakhanovites. In short, the resourcefulness and energy of erstwhile prosperous peasants had to be instilled in all peasants and commitment to the collective and to the state, beyond the family unit, had to be built.

The transmission belt of information did not flow only from Stakhanovite to non-Stakhanovite. Stakhanovite work methods were studied in meticulous detail by agronomists in the All-Union Scientific Institute of the Agricultural Economy and their findings are stored in the Russian State Archive of the Economy (*Rossiiskii gosudarstvennyi arkhiv Ekonomiki*, or RGAE).[6] Researchers from the institute interviewed Stakhanovites about their daily and seasonal routines and Stakhanovites responded to questionnaires about how they lived and worked in different months of the year.[7]

Those who worked with machines revealed to the institute what they did with them before, during, and after work. The institute's researchers were keen to know which spare parts were available to them and above all "how the care of Stakhanovites for their machines differs from the care given by other collective farmers."[8] Those who worked with horses were asked how they organized their night pasture, who gave the horses water to drink in the morning before work and how often the horses were fed during the day, and when they were allowed a break.[9] Likewise, types of animal feed and periods of feed were tabulated for different animals.[10] Milkmaids reported on how much they milked over time and the institute drew up detailed comparative tables.[11] Milkmaids also indicated how many times a day they milked and when. One practice in the Northern oblast, to milk six times a day beginning at 2 am and finishing at 10 pm was criticized by the institute on the grounds that many short milkings "disturb cows' peace."[12]

Data were collected not just on what Stakhanovites did but also on what they thought about various problems. Stakhanovite shepherd Comrade Gerenshchenko, for instance, gave various reasons for the death of lambs at birth.[13] The institute drew on such firsthand observations before making its own recommendations. The institute also asked Stakhanovites about relations with farm leaders. Its researchers were interested to know how Stakhanovites were helped and hindered and what improvements could be made on farms and on machine tractor stations. Members of the institute also appraised the ways in which farm leaders and directors of machine tractor stations "directed" the Stakhanovite movement.

Specialist committees within people's commissariats, or *glavki* (*glavnye komitety*), also took a special interest in Stakhanovite methods. *Glavki* are best understood as central directorates controlling a particular sector. Narkomzem's *glavki,* for instance, pondered the effect of manure on sugar beet harvests, the impact of socialist competitions, the improvements of mechanized sowing, the role of agronomists, and different Stakhanovite work methods across republics, krais, and oblasts.[14] A special committee on horses examined their reproduction and survival rates and made suggestions on how to achieve "the quickest growth" in their numbers and "maximum survival rates."[15] The committee concerned with sugar beet organized numerous gatherings on work methods, generating piles of reports.[16] Study of how manure was used was so important that it also merited a specialist institute. In 1931 the All-Union Institute of Manure, Agrotechnology and Soil Science (*Vsesoiuznyi Institut Udobrenii, Agrotekhniki i Agropochvovdeniia*, or VIUAA) was established by *Narkomzem* specifically "for the study of the correct application of manure."[17]

So Stakhanovite performance was studied in minute detail by specialists in institutes and in Narkomzem for transmission to other peasants, to farm leaders, to each other, and to politicians who wanted to know what was "possible." Thus an academic bureaucracy that studied Stakhanovism accompanied the movement with a view to learning from it, propagating its best results, and aiding its spread. In the process, a mountain of information was collected about Stakhanovite "lessons" for working practices and for farm relations, much of which was published in handbooks and in the specialist journal *Socialist Recontruction of Agriculture* (*Sotsial'isticheskaia Rekonstruktsiia Sel'skogo Khoziaistva*). Some of these data on farm relations were also of interest to the procuracy and secret police due to their relevance to the purges and to attacks on inept farm managements for not facilitating improved working techniques.

In the early 1930s Stalin and Molotov had bewailed mismanagement of the farms, inefficiency, and a failure of chairpersons and directors to cope with their tasks.[18] So the "lessons" of Stakhanovites were timely and had to be reiterated for peasant and manager alike. Obstruction from management to working in a Stakhanovite way, however, stemmed not simply from opposition to it. Reasons included innate conservatism, hesitation about working differently, fear of dislocation, difficulties in obtaining scarce inputs, or wariness about upsetting non-Stakhanovites, who after all constituted the majority of peasants. The issue of facilitating peasants to "work differently" was a complex one.

The Second Five-Year Plan, as Alec Nove summed it up, championed "consolidation," increased productivity and yields, learning, efficiency, improved quality, technique, and a pulling up of the lagging consumer goods industries.[19] Where technique brought increased speed, however, it did not automatically follow that quality was better, that overall output was increased, or that norms were sensible.[20] Faster tractor driving or faster milking did not always mean increased output or a better product; rather, they could mean sweated labor. Fields might be shallowly plowed and the amount of milk obtained might be greater per hour than overall. In contrast to exhortations to speed up, other lessons concentrated on thoughtful planning and preparation for harvesting, care of the soil, affection for animals, and attention to one's own health. These lessons, arguably, were not reducible to the charge of promoting sweated labor, even though they may have been helpful prerequisites. Whilst one element of Stakhanovism did involve working faster, other aspects suggest that considerations in the countryside were much broader than speed alone. Getting peasants to work again with some commitment and urging them to pay attention to soil, pests, seed, spare parts, waste, and cleanliness were necessary, too.

The most common lessons from industrial Stakhanovites to all factory workers concerned how to effect an efficient division of labor, how best to position one's machines, how most quickly to walk around them, how to coordinate work across machines, and how best to keep them in good running order.[21] In agriculture, the lessons were much more varied. As well as giving advice on how to maintain tractors in good condition, Stakhanovites instructed in how to sow better, how efficiently to gather the harvest, how to build a caring relationship with cows, pigs, and sheep, how best to massage the udder for productive results, how to manure the land, and how to tackle different kinds of weed and pest. Rural Stakhanovites not only gave highly detailed advice on every aspect of their work, they also linked it to the seasonal nature of agricultural work. Rural "lessons" dovetailed with the party's concerns about preparedness for the spring sowing, for the autumn harvest, and for the onset of winter. Indeed, Soviet party leaders used Stakhanovites' voices to get across the seasonal messages that they wanted peasants to hear. The party urged peasants to learn from Stakhanovites, to emulate their work methods, to adopt their attitudes, and to follow their superior lead as members of the rural technical intelligentsia.

LESSONS ON MACHINERY

Often quoted with fanfare were Molotov's words to the effect that Stakhanovites should know their machines well and make use of the technical possibilities that they offered.[22] Figure 5.1 shows *Traktorist-Kombainer* illustrating for its readers the importance of running in a tractor after repair to test it. Certainly the first lesson for tractor and combine drivers was to keep their machines in good running order so that unnecessary repairs could be

Figure 5.1. "Running in of a repaired tractor." Source: *Adapted from* Traktorist-Kombainer, *no. 5, 15 March 1937, p. 5.*

avoided. A handbook held up Pasha Kovardak, shown in Figures 5.2 and 5.3, as a shining example:

> On the ChTZ tractor she had worked 5143 hectares. It is amazing that after this the tractor needed only average repairs. Such a result stems from strict adherence to the rules of technical care for the machine. Comrade Kovardak says "it is better take an hour from one's spare time and give the required attention to the machine."[23]

Kovardak was also approvingly quoted to the effect that "it is easier to prevent trouble than to deal with it later."[24] The lesson here was that it could seem that "the tractor does not need to be repaired, it is working well, but we still check it according to schedule without delay."[25] Note, however, that Kovardak checked her machine in her spare time, not her working hours, showing a degree of commitment many would have withheld, lending credence to the argument that Stakhanovism could indeed constitute sweated labor.

Going one step further than Kovardak by learning how to dismantle, check, change parts, and reassemble his combine harvester, Comrade Stepanov from Palkinsk MTS in Leningrad oblast was cited in the same handbook for his

Figure 5.2. Pasha Kovardak, Stakhanovite tractor driver from the Kanelovsk MTS in Azovo-Chernomore Krai. Source: Adapted from Krest'ianka, no. 12, 1936.

Figure 5.3. A photograph of Pasha Kovardak. Source: Traktorist-Kombainer, no. 3, 15 February 1937, p. 5.

technical knowledge and ability to regulate dummy runs after repair.[26] Repeated messages were that personal care and attention were essential for the good running of a machine whilst neglect and indifference could only mean poor machinery and a worse harvest. Pasha Angelina is shown in Figure 5.4 devoting special attention to ensuring a good repair job and no time-wasting.

Films popularized these messages to huge audiences. In *Traktoristy*, the hero Klim is an excellent mechanic who readily points out how a particular tractor is in rotten condition. After listening to its engine, Klim announces that he detects problems in the first and third cylinders and poor regulation. He concludes, "There has never been any care for this poor machine." The driver, who happened to be in love with Mar'iana, too, was shamed by Klim in front of other men on the farm. The message is that Stakhanovites are proud to look after their machines whereas sloppy peasants should be embarrassed. A subtext of *Traktoristy* is that a negligent tractor driver does not deserve a hard-working female brigade leader's heart. Poor workers were socially inferior to Stakhanovites and not to be respected.

Far more technical "lessons" were given on the desirable speed of tractors. The All-Union Scientific Research Institute reported comparative results across different types of tractor performing different operations and concluded that the best results came from working in third gear, citing the successes of Stakhanovite Konstantin Borin.[27] Specialists advocated third gear

Figure 5.4. Pasha Angelina on the MTS. "How best to minimize time repairing machines." Source: *P. Angelina,* Liudi Kolkhoznykh Polei *(Moscow and Leningrad: Gosudarstvennoe Izdatel'stvo Detskoi Literatury, 1952).*

over second and argued that at this speed no breakdowns occurred. Accordingly, as an icon of the fields, Borin adopted the slogan "Gather the harvest in third gear" along with "lubricate the chains more often."[28] In keeping with this, the film *Bogataia Nevesta* attempted to popularize the lesson, showing a scene with a pep talk before harvesting in which tractor drivers are urged to proceed in third gear.

Attention in handbooks and the press to how many hectares Stakhanovites harvested put an emphasis on speed-up. How much land was covered may, or may not, however, have affected the quality of the work performed. Handbooks put out by People's Commissariats also drew attention to the negative consequences of speedy work, reminding that the quality of the grain was vital and that loss should be avoided. They emphasized that grain losses could stem from bad cutting practices.[29] Some combines in their haste to achieve high output cut with the header too high, thereby leaving some grain uncut in the fields. And some farms failed to do a third mowing, which again left grain behind. The book propagated that Stakhanovites did not make such errors, drawing attention to the necessity for care and quality. Certainly a large area covered per hour was not synonymous with either good mowing or high total output.

LESSONS FOR SOWING AND HARVESTING

Lessons on machinery were often linked to lessons for sowing and harvesting. A specialist book on sugar beet noted that many chairpersons of collective farms were at first apprehensive about tractors and prejudiced that they "would sow beet badly."[30] Results, however, allayed their fears showing "the best sowing and pre-sowing work," the likes of which not even the most experienced and elderly had ever seen.[31] The book instructed that sowing took six days from 9 to 15 April. Every day the tractors sowed 20 to 25 hectares and on the collective farm called "Five-Year Plan," Stakhanovite Natasha Popova on her tractor had managed 30 to 35 hectares of beet. The loud lesson from the first use of tractors for sowing was that "High tractor technology worked on sugar beet fields gave wonderful results."[32] A related lesson was that "science and practice have shown that an earlier period of sowing beet always gives a bigger harvest than a late sowing."[33]

Articles repeatedly stressed that "sowing is early and quite compressed" and that peasants had to get started with enthusiasm and work intensively at the right time. In specialist journals, agronomists compared the sowing dates of different Stakhanovites in sugar beet, as seen in Table 5.1. Exemplary Stakhanovites were shown moving up their sowing dates in order to attain a better harvest. Being in the extreme north-east of the sugar beet zone in Russia, however, Dadykina and Rebrova sowed later than Baidich and Koshevaia in Ukraine since weather conditions did not permit an early April sowing.[34] By contrast, the press scolded farms that sowed badly with headlines such as "State farms met the spring of 1937 poorly prepared."[35] The repeated message was that the quality of work was the key to success and that

Table 5.1.   Sowing Periods of Sugar Beet

Stakhanovites	1935	1936
Baidich	15–18 April	2–3 April
Koshevaia	10 April	9–10 April
Dadykina	12 May	29–30 April
Rebrova	13 April	1–2 April

Source: M. Dolgopolov, "Stakhanovskaia agrotekhnika v sveklovodstve," Sotsialisticheskaia Rekonstruktsiia Sel'skogo Khoziaistva, no. 3 (March 1937): 76.

"People no longer think only about how to plow, harrow and sow more, but about how to do field work better."[36]

Every year the press carried articles before spring and autumn on how best to prepare for sowing and harvesting. Headlines such as "To meet Stakhanovite sowing" and "Greetings to Stakhanovites of the socialist fields, we will fulfill the plan for spring sowing in a Bolshevik manner" were typical.[37] Comrade Stepanov of Leningrad oblast was held up as a sound planner: "Long before the beginning of the harvest, N. S. Stepanov studies the plots to be worked by his combine, marks with stakes the ruts, ravines, stumps and other obstacles. Then he establishes the route."[38] Drivers were encouraged to think ahead, to familiarize themselves with the terrain to be worked, and to consider the most efficient route. Egor Galunchikov from Cheliabinsk stressed the importance of round-the-clock work, advocating "full use of the working day" and "evening work under electric light," during which there was "a movement for increasing speed with the header at full capacity."[39] He told how "We get up early, usually at 5:30. At six we already start work and are mowing. Many combine drivers categorically refuse to mow before 9 am. They say that the wheat is damp."[40] Galunchikov insisted that this excuse meant a loss of good working time. His own drivers made maximum use of the day, even taking lunch at staggered intervals so that work did not stop. When it got dark at 6 pm, lights went on. Being cooler, tractors then worked better. He narrated how before going to bed at night a brief "production meeting" (proizvodsvtennoe soveshchanie) was held at which they aired good points about their work that day as well as problems. Galunchikov revealed, "we talk about each worker. I draw attention to the initiative each has taken during work time."[41] What mattered was that people were correctly arranged in the fields and that they had "precise knowledge" of their duties

Such intensive work from light into darkness, almost nonstop, can be viewed as a storming of the fields, in which effort is almost nonstop. The emphasis on "increasing speed" conveys a notion of dynamism, but does not necessarily result in bigger harvests and no losses. Night work can also be interpreted as another example of sweated labor. Some handbooks did issue cautions about it:

> Night harvesting must not be at the expense of the day. If in the morning and afternoon the weather is good, then it is necessary to work during the day, and rest at night. If the morning is wet and work is not done during the day, but towards evening the grain dries out and the night looks like being dry, it is necessary to use working time completely.[42]

Thus three Stakhanovites might work during the day in a team while two rest. This source advocated a flexible division of harvesting.

Geographical location and climate meant that the advantages of night work in some areas were emphasized. A problem on farms in the Urals and Siberia was that heavy dew and fog did not permit work to begin before eight or even ten o'clock. The lesson here was that "at night, up until one or two, there is dry weather, permitting excellent harvesting of grain. Motors work wonderfully and grain is easy to gather."[43] This had to be understood since harvest time was two months later than in the south and daylight was five to six hours shorter. The crucial dates were from 1 to 20 September. From Ufa to Magnitogorsk and to Omsk, dawn broke at 5 am with the sun coming up at 6:25 am and setting in the evening at 6:30 pm. By 7:20 pm it was completely dark.[44]

Other immensely detailed lessons on harvesting were also included in sections of handbooks on "Work plan," "apportionment of fields," "organization of work," "quality of the harvest," and "getting used to the combine harvester." Several diagrams showed how best to divide up work in the fields and the direction in which to work. Other illustrations highlighted parts of combine harvesters and explained how to look after them.[45] Handbooks labored the point that "the peculiarities of different fields" had to be considered such as shape and size:

> If the field is square, then it is necessary to divide it into not less than two halves. To mow a square field in a circle is not advantageous. The nearer to the centre the machine, then the unit will more frequently and steeply keep turning. This must be avoided.[46]

Moreover, "experience shows" that the width of the strips was best when between 360 and 600 meters.[47] Propaganda attempted to reinforce these general lessons. Figure 5.5 shows Pasha Angelina taking an interest in a member of her brigade, checking her work, instructing her, and encouraging her forward.

Another lesson was that every minute was dear to Stakhanovites, and Stalin was quoted to this effect.[48] Again, this was particularly relevant to farms in

Figure 5.5.   *Pasha Angelina as brigade leader.* Source: *P. Angelina,* Liudi Kolkhoznykh Polei *(Moscow and Leningrad: Gosudarstvennoe Izdatel'stvo Detskoi Literatury, 1952).*

Siberia where harvest time was short and where late harvesting meant bread lost to the rain. Understanding this, Stakhanovites "try to mow as quickly as possible and better."[49] Once again, however, speed-up may not have meant better, as was so often assumed.

Many other technical lessons for good harvesting were imparted such as how best to clean machinery and how often to grease it. The general picture was that sowing and harvesting required many lessons. Work discipline, planning, and awareness of the land were central ones. These efforts to catalogue and impart "scientific" ways of working underscore the seriousness with which the Soviet state approached the gargantuan task of transforming the countryside. Administrators attempted to collect and relay as much expertise as possible in what became a huge bureaucratic onslaught of data. Many peasants, however, will have been oblivious to most of it, reached mainly by the rural press's exhortations.

LESSONS ON LAND: SOIL, MANURE, SEED, AND WEEDS

Education through handbooks put huge emphasis on the importance of learning from agronomists. They instructed that the first lessons about land were to understand the soil and the needs of the crop on it. Agronomist Grigorii Dudnik taught Mariia Demchenko that the root of the sugar beet required deep soil, at least one and a half meters. His central lesson was that anything could grow anywhere provided the condition of the soil was understood and treated appropriately.[50] The press propagated related messages by citing successful flax growers in Kirov krai who announced at a socialist competition, "we must know well the soil on our plot, what the soil lacks, and how much manure to add, and what kind."[51] *Krest'ianskaia gazeta* added that local agronomists could offer relevant advice. Specialists were especially keen to encourage farm leaders and peasants to heed what agronomists had to say and to listen to experts. Stakhanovite Dadykina from Kursk oblast was used as a mouthpiece for the lesson that "poor, weed-infested" land demanded hard work and that "it is possible to work well with bad land."[52] Manure, however, had to be used carefully. As a conduit for sensible advice, the potato grower Anna Masonova observed, "manure must be applied with intelligence."[53] She explained that the practice of applying the same amount of manure, whatever the soil, had to stop because manure had to vary according to the soil and the crop. Through Stakhanovites talking, specialists got across the lesson that science and knowledge instructed to good ends and the wise should follow agronomists' advice.

Texts gave immense detail on types of manure. One handbook told how: "Mariia Demchenko widely used local fertilizers (ashes, humus, chicken droppings, and others)."[54] It narrated how when Demchenko began collecting chicken droppings "many were perplexed" and noted that she gathered it "like gold." Championing the advice of agronomists, "Mariia patiently explained to the collective farmers why she was doing it: excrement is the most valued manure for sugar beet."[55] Due to a serious scarcity of manure, peasants like Demchenko used whatever they could find. The slaughter of horses had meant a serious fall in the amount of manure and there was little artificial fertilizer because output was low, although the production of mineral fertilizer was planned to increase. In 1936 it was announced that according to the Second Five-Year Plan, by the end of 1937 there should be 8,290,000 tons. This was eight times higher than the figure for 1932.[56]

An accompanying lesson was that different fertilizers varied in strength with varying effects on the soil, which had to be learned. Handbooks also insisted that manure was necessary for record harvests. The 500ers, Dadykina and Kirichenko, were conduits for the lesson that mineral fertilizer should be "widely applied" and that even though fields had been manured the previous year, it was essential to repeat this.[57] Demchenko was a frequent mouthpiece on the necessity of advance preparation. In 1937 she announced that her new record of 1,012 tsentners per hectare would be exceeded in 1938 and that this had required her Komsomol team to begin preparing the manure in the summer of 1937. Accordingly, they "gathered ashes, dung, acquired mineral fertilizer in time and kept them in a dry place. In the autumn plowing they transported 25 tonnes of manure per hectare."[58] The correct storage of manure was important as was a generous amount. Famous Stakhanovites, however, were privileged in receiving more fertilizer than others. Nonetheless, the message for peasants was that yearly attention to manure contributed to more plentiful harvests. Their dilemma was how best to obtain it.

Specialists dwelled at length upon the relative merits of different types of manure for different soils and crops, compiling comparative statistics across Stakhanovites. Table 5.2 shows how inventive Stakhanovites had to be in their sources of manure. Of interest to specialists was not only what fertilizer was used, but on what date every year it was dug into the soil and

Table 5.2.   Stakhanovites' Use of Fertilizer in Sugar Beet (in Tsentners Per Hectare)

	Baidich	Koshevaia	Dadykina	Rebrova	Filipenko
Dung	200	200	330	800	100
Superphosphate	5	4	8.5	2.75	7
Phosphate salt	—	0.85	—	—	—
Chlorine (sylvinite)	—	—	6	—	—
Salt pepper (leina)	—	—	—	0.6	—
Ammonia nitrate	0.8	0.85	2.15	—	—
Ashes	7	6	5	9	2
Bird droppings	—	—	—	9	—
Feces (pure)	25	—	14	42	—
Composted feces	—	—	—	—	100
Dung wash	60	—	3	10	—
Peat compost	45	—	—	50	—
Defecatory sludge	30	—	—	—	—

Source: M. Dolgopolov, "Stakhanovskaia agrotekhnika v sveklovodstve," Sotsialisticheskaia Rekonstruktsiia Sel'skogo Khoziaistva, no. 3 (March 1937): 78.

how amounts varied across the seasons.[59] Numerous tables also imparted this information.

A third lesson from agronomists concerned "a good selection of seed." Evdokiia Iufegeva and her flax growing team in Kirov krai explained how vital it was. They had been sowing "Al'fa" seed but they knew that the 0–120 was better, so they switched.[60] Stakhanovites emphasized the need to familiarize themselves with seed and potato strains. Studying the seed germination process was also advised. Stakhanovite Rebrova illustrated the benefits of sorting the seed in sieves and then "selecting the best and largest seeds for sowing."[61] Stakhanovites also passed on the agronomists' advice that a "good pre-sowing breaking up of the soil" was vital, as was a "correct covering of the seed."[62] When it came to cabbages, handbooks instructed that the distance between them was desirably 65 centimeters, with 70 centimeters between rows, which would give 22,000 cabbages per hectare.[63]

Snow retention was another essential practice that began to be applied in the "advanced" sugarbeet fields mainly in 1936. A specialist article described how Khristina Baidich laid the branches of trees on the ground to get the required result.[64] Technical assessment concluded, "Thanks to snow retention, the soil on Stakhanovites' plots in the spring period, notwithstanding the lack of rain, had a considerable amount of moisture."[65] Handbooks pitched snow retention as "a necessary agronomical method in a complex of measures facilitating a good harvest."[66] They demonstrated that on four collective farms in the drought year of 1938, snow retention had increased the harvest "by 2.8 to 5 tsentners per hectare."[67]

Another vital lesson was that "weeds threaten the harvest" and were seen as such a serious threat that conferences were held on how to combat them. Newspaper headlines "Against weeds!" informed that the Third All-Union Conference on Weeds had taken place in Leningrad in December 1934.[68] The press informed that in Dnepropetrovsk heavy rain in May 1937 had caused a rapid growth of weeds, which were outstripping everything else and as a consequence, a thick carpet of "the green enemy" threatened the harvest.[69] Shock workers and Stakhanovites delivered the lesson that peasants should ensure that their plots were free of them.[70] Didactic headlines such as "annihilate weeds" called for vigilance, condemning weeds as "malicious enemies of the harvest."[71]

Stakhanovites alone, however, could not eradicate weeds, since they could spread from surrounding fields worked by negligent non-Stakhanovites.[72] Agronomists also warned that weeds were a breeding ground for pests, especially moths, who also had to be combated. The lesson was that quick action was essential. A widely cited example of this was that moths appeared on Marina Gnatenko's crop; Mariia Demchenko immediately helped her to get rid of them.[73]

LESSONS ON ANIMALS

Specialists in animal husbandry cited successful Stakhanovite examples in order to relay lessons about the distinct needs of each animal. Pig breeder Tat'iana Daeva announced how her "most important task" was to be "kind and attentive to the animal, to relate emotionally." From this, she suggested, "it will be clear what to do."[74] She maintained that cleanliness was paramount and advised others to wash their pigs, massage them, and touch their teats so that the pigs got used to that feeling which would help them quietly to lie down when piglets took nourishment.[75]

The journal *Sotsialisticheskaia Rekonstruktsiia Sel'skogo Khoziaistva* argued that "devotion and love" for their cows were priorities for successful milkmaids Persiantseva and Nartova who, through their understanding of the animals, milked between 140 and 160 liters an hour while other milkmaids managed only 60–70 liters.[76] More milk also resulted when these milkmaids changed the order of their tasks to milking first, followed by succulent feed, then hay, and finally watering.[77] The specialist lesson there was that the sequence in which milking was done was crucial. It should be pointed out, however, that although they stressed measurement by the hour, this may not have meant higher productivity overall.

Elizaveta Kuz'menkova took this theme one step further, pointing out that it was not enough to understand a cow's "character, habits and appetite." The "difficulty" was that "cows are different, yet we feed them the same. On our farm we even feed milch cows and dry cows the same."[78] This was further exacerbated by the fact that milk was measured from a group of cows, not each one individually, "therefore milkmaids do not know exactly how much milk each cow gives. And not knowing that, it is hard to work for a high milk yield."[79] In this way Stakhanovite milkmaids could use specialist observations to criticize practices on their farms. Their own successes gave legitimate credence to their remarks. Stakhanovites also served as mouthpieces of specialists' preferred practices in attempts to shake up the way in which farm leaders directed work.

Stakhanovite milkmaids from Leningrad oblast did, however, feed differently. They passed on their lesson that "we study each cow separately and feed according to weight in individual rations." When udders were dry it was important to "feed plentifully" and when a cow was pregnant "we are not afraid to deviate from the usual norms of livestock experts."[80] Integral to this message was a clear twist. It implied that Stakhanovites who are close to their animals might know better how to feed them than distant experts with general solutions. Although Stakhanovites were meant to learn from specialists, there was also a feedback loop that went the other way, indicating a process of mutual education.

The extra time required to calculate individual food portions for each animal, prepare them, and administer with care was not discussed or moaned about. Milkmaids might describe how they added salt to feed if a cow ate little silage, or how they changed the consistency of the feed depending upon whether it suited the cow to have it thick or more liquid, and even vary the temperature of the water that each cow drank, but no one complained that this was an excessive work load.[81] It is unquestionable, however, that such attentiveness would have meant an extremely long working day.[82]

Another crucial lesson was how to prevent the death of calves, which was common. In early 1938, according to Stakhanovite Anna Konstantinova, 30 percent of the newly born on her farm had not survived. She insisted that it was elementary "to care for the calf long before its birth."[83] If pregnant cows were on half rations and did not receive succulent feed or food concentrates, then calves would suffer. Articles in *Kolkhoznitsa* reiterated this and also stressed that attention had to be paid to animal survival after birth, with hygiene as particularly essential as the newly born had to be wiped carefully with a clean cloth and mucus removed from nose and mouth. Only a sterilized knife, moreover, should cut the umbilical cord.[84] Anna Konstantinova blamed All-Union and republican level People's Commissariats for not relaying Stakhanovites' experience in this area, criticizing that "so far, apart from the people's commissariats of the Russian and Belorussian republics, who in this connection took the first steps," other republican commissariats had taken "little initiative" to advertise how Stakhanovites worked.[85] Here is an example of a Stakhanovite voice being co-opted to deliver a political message scripted by others.

The cinema blazoned the lesson of the importance of individual attention to animals. The film *Svinarka i Pastukh* (the Female Pig Rearer and the Herdsman) showed the heroine Glasha agonize over the birth of piglets when in turn they stopped breathing. Special care from Glasha ensured that they were revived and lived. Glasha also took pride in installing a new system of feeding bottles for the piglets. Her care, devotion, innovation, and enthusiasm, the film suggested, were the appropriate characteristics for success.

"Care of the horse" merited special attention given their importance in fieldwork and in providing manure. A central lesson was that "Stakhanovites never permit the overload and overwork of horses."[86] One insisted that at the start of a shift, horses should go at their own pace, otherwise they could tire quickly and bolt. Only after three hours was it prudent to press them to go faster. Rest, too, was essential and ten-minute breaks after 50 to 70 minutes' work were beneficial.[87] In this case, the opposite of speed-up was urged. The slaughter of animals and the consequent loss of draft animal power made the horses that survived extremely valuable.[88]

As well as caring for their animals, Stakhanovites were meant to look after their own health. This "lesson" on personal hygiene was less prominent in the press, but occasionally *Krest'ianskaia gazeta* relayed that "the experienced milkmaid has healthy hands" but some suffer badly from painful rheumatism. Others endured blisters or abscesses under the nails. The message was that "it is easy to avoid these illnesses." Tips included "milk at an even pace" so that hands "do not tire," take "warm little hand baths" before and after the morning and evening milking sessions at a temperature of between 35 to 37 degrees, and massage the hands.[89]

CONCLUSION

Stakhanovites, agronomists, and specialists in animal husbandry broadcast the multiple lessons that constituted a huge training program in how to farm in more modern ways. Stakhanovites were often mouthpieces for specialists, although on occasion they used their status to challenge expert practices with which they disagreed. Their success also made them legitimate critics of farm leaders who were reluctant to innovate or initiate change.

Whereas non-Stakhanovites needed to take Stakhanovite lessons on board in order to improve their work patterns, so directors of machine tractor stations, collective farm chairpersons, and state farm directors had to be reminded that party priorities required them to take specialists' advice on board. This was not necessarily easy. Not only were their education levels generally low, but their turnover in leadership positions on farms was high. Stephan Merl estimates that during the 1930s roughly 50 percent of collective farm chairpersons "were removed from office every year," most after just a few months.[90] Many were scapegoats in the purges or removed for simple incompetence, while others, in fact, enjoyed promotion to other farms, or simply chose to leave.

Innovation, furthermore, was especially hard since conditions on some farms were indeed harsh, with shortages of spare parts and fuel and insufficient animal feed and manure as recurring problems, despite increased investment. Providing Stakhanovites and aspiring Stakhanovites with the prerequisites for success was not always possible or easy. Those who ran farms had simultaneously to overcome different sorts of material and attitudinal problems when they themselves often subscribed to the attitudes that needed to be changed. Reminders of what they should be doing provided ready pointers. But some peasants refused to be influenced by lessons, slogans, and exhortations, preferring to resist Stakhanovism and even punish Stakhanovites; and farm leaders themselves displayed various reactions to Stakhanovism. Complex patterns of enthusiasm, accommodation, reaction, and resistance resulted.

NOTES

1. "Mariia Demchenko," *Kolkhoznik*, no. 1 (1936): 59. This is a short story about Mariia Demchenko and her agronomist.

2. Quoted in Narodnyi kommissariat zernovykh i zhivotnovodcheskikh sovkhozov SSSR, *Stakhanovskii opyt uborka urozhaia v zernosovkhozakh Povolzh'ia i Sibiri* (Moscow: 1939), 11.

3. See, for instance, the typical articles: Ia Peive, G. Skliarov, and I. Meleshkevich, "Opyt stakhanovtsev l'novodstva — vsem l'novodnym kolkhozam," *Sotsialisticheskaia Rekonstruktsiia Sel'skogo Khoziaistva*, no. 9 (September 1938): 56–64; S. Kosaurov, "Opyt bor'by stakhanovtsev kolkhoznogo svinovodstva za rasshirennoe vosproizvodstvo," *Sotsialisticheskaia Rekonstruktsiia Sel'skogo Khoziaistva*, no. 4 (April 1937): 93–109; G. Mokshantsev, "Agrotekhnicheskii opyt stakhanovtsev khlopkovodstva," *Sotsialisticheskaia Rekonstruktsiia Sel'skogo Khoziaistva*, no. 2 (1936): 163–177; "Opyt stakhanovskoi raboty Azovskoi MTS," *Sotsialisticheskaia Rekonstruktsiia Sel'skogo Khoziaistva*, no. 11 (November 1938): 88–94.

4. Refer to footnote 18 of the introduction.

5. Maurice Dobb, *Soviet Economic Development Since 1917* (London: Routledge and Kegan Paul, 1978), 278.

6. This institute was set up in 1930 and existed until 1938. Consult RGAE, f. 260, op. 1.

7. Through questionnaires filled out by Stakhanovites, the institute gathered data on age, education level, courses taken, attendance at Party school, newspaper subscriptions, second jobs, and party membership. See RGAE, f. 260, op. 1, d. 690, l. 1.

8. RGAE, f. 260. op. 1, d. 690, l. 2.

9. RGAE, f. 260. op. 1, d. 690, l. 2.

10. RGAE, f. 260, op. 1, d. 823, l. 19–29.

11. RGAE, f. 260, op. 1, d. 823, ll. 5–14.

12. RGAE, f. 260, op. 1, d. 823, l.50.

13. Ibid., f. 260, op. 1, d. 855, l. 2.

14. See, for example, RGAE, f. 9495, op. 1, d. 146, ll. 4, 32, 38, 39; RGAE, f. 9495, op. 1, d. 158, ll. 1–13, ll. 29–34, and ll. 106–10; RGAE, f. 9495, op. 1, d. 102, ll. 19–20.

15. RGAE, f. 9481, op. 1, d. 765, ll. 5–6, ll. 20–29, and ll. 65–68.

16. These are stored in RGAE. See f. 9495, op. 1.

17. *Traktorist-Kombainer*, no. 2 (1936): 13–14.

18. Dobb, *Soviet Economic Development Since 1917*, 251.

19. Alec Nove, *An Economic History of the USSR* (Harmondsworth, Middlesex: Penguin, 1969), 220–37.

20. I am grateful to Bob Davies for alerting me to the different meanings of "quality" in a Soviet context. It might refer to more sophisticated work using machinery. It might mean that the quality of the product has improved. It could also mean that the cost per unit of output had fallen (where *kachestvennye pokazateli* are cost indicators).

21. The magazine *Stakhanovets* carried such lessons in every edition.

22. B. Shapiro, "Opyt stakhanovtsev kolkhoznykh brigad," *Sotsialisticheskaia Rekonstruktsiia Sel'skogo Khoziaistva*, no. 4 (April 1937): 150.

23. *Stakhanovskii opyt—v kolkhozy dal'nego vostoka* (Khabarovsk: Dal'nevostochnoe gosudarstvennoe izdatel'stvo, 1940), 48.

24. *Stakhanovskii opyt—v kolkhozy dal'nego vostoka*, 48.

25. *Stakhanovskii opyt—v kolkhozy dal'nego vostoka*, 48.

26. *Stakhanovskii opyt—v kolkhozy dal'nego vostoka*, 45.

27. In third gear on his "Stalinets" combine, Borin gathered 93 hectares of cereals and in the harvesting of sunflowers his maximum daily was 113 hectares. See P. Lapaev, "Primenenie tret'ei skorosti stakhanovtsami-traktorikstami i kombainerami," *Sotsialisticheskaia Rekonstruktsiia Sel'skogo Khoziaistva*, no. 2 (February 1937): 141–45.

28. *Stakhanovtsy polei: k piatidesiatiletiiu stakhanovskogo dvizheniia*, 24.

29. *Stakhanovskii opyt uborka urozhaia v zernosovkhozakh Povolzh'ia i Sibiri*, 16.

30. I. A. Ivin and P. P. Masalov, *Na Bor'bu za rekordnyi urozhai sakhsvekly: opyt piatisotnits-ordenonosok Dadykinoi i Kirichenkoi* (Kursk: Kurskaia Pravda, 1936), 13.

31. Ivin and Masalov, *Na Bor'bu*, 13.

32. Ivin and Masalov, *Na Bor'bu*, 13.

33. Ivin and Masalov, *Na Bor'bu*, 13.

34. M. Dolgopolov, "Stakhanovskaia agrotekhnika v sveklovodstve," *Sotsialisticheskaia Rekonstruktsiia Sel'skogo Khoziaistva*, no. 3 (March 1937): 76. It also gave the elementary message that sowing "is an important operation in all Stakhanovite teams." Instructive tables on sowing periods, such as Table 5.1, were common: See Table 5.1.

35. *Sovkhoznaia gazeta*, 18 April 1937, 1.

36. *Sovkhoznaia gazeta*, 18 April 1937, 1.

37. *Sovkhoznaia gazeta*, 4 February 1937; *Sovkhoznaia gazeta*, 14 March 1936; *Sovkhoznaia gazeta*, 28 April 1937, 1; *Krest'ianskaia gazeta*, 10 August 1937; *Sovkhoznaia gazeta*, 8 August 1937.

38. *Stakhanovskii opyt—v kolkhozy dal'nego vostoka*, 45.

39. *Sovkhoznaia gazeta*, 26 September 1938, 2.

40. *Sovkhoznaia gazeta*, 26 September 1938, 2.

41. *Sovkhoznaia gazeta*, 26 September 1938, 2.

42. *Stakhanovskii opyt uborka urozhaia v zernosovkhozakh Povolzh'ia i Sibiri*, 15.

43. *Stakhanovskii opyt uborka urozhaia v zernosovkhozakh Povolzh'ia i Sibiri*, 13.

44. *Stakhanovskii opyt uborka urozhaia v zernosovkhozakh Povolzh'ia i Sibiri*, 13.

45. *Stakhanovskii opyt uborka urozhaia v zernosovkhozakh Povolzh'ia i Sibiri*, 4–16.

46. *Stakhanovskii opyt uborka urozhaia v zernosovkhozakh Povolzh'ia i Sibiri*, 6–7.

47. *Stakhanovskii opyt uborka urozhaia v zernosovkhozakh Povolzh'ia i Sibiri*, 6–7.

48. *Stakhanovskii opyt uborka urozhaia v zernosovkhozakh Povolzh'ia i Sibiri*, 11.

49. *Stakhanovskii opyt uborka urozhaia v zernosovkhozakh Povolzh'ia i Sibiri*, 11.

50. "Mariia Demchenko," *Kolkhoznik*, no. 1 (1936): 59.

51. *Krest'ianskaia gazeta*, 14 December 1935, 3.

52. "Priem kolkhoznits-udarnikov," *Sotsialisticheskaia Rekonstruktsiia Sel'skogo Khoziaistva*, II, part 5 (November 1935): 17.

53. *Krest'ianskaia gazeta*, 22 November 1935, 1.

54. *Stakhanovskii opyt—v kolkhozy dal'nego vostoka*, 29

55. I. Vershinin, ed., *Mariia Safronovna Demchenko* (Moscow: Gosudarstvennoe izdatel'stvo politicheskoi literatury, 1938), 10.

56. *Traktorist-Kombainer*, no. 2 (1936), 13.

57. Ivin and Masalov, *Na Bor'bu.*

58. *Stakhanovskii opyt—v kolkhozy dal'nego vostoka*, 31.

59. Dolgopolov, "Stakhanovskaia agrotekhnika v sveklovodstve," 84–7.

60. *Krest'ianskaia gazeta*, 14 December 1935, 3.

61. Dolgopolov, "Stakhanovskaia agrotekhnika v sveklovodstve," 76.

62. Dolgopolov, "Stakhanovskaia agrotekhnika v sveklovodstve," 76.

63. *Stakhanovskii opyt—v kolkhozy dal'nego vostoka*, 34.

64. Dolgopolov, "Stakhanovskaia agrotekhnika v sveklovodstve," 74.

65. Dolgopolov, "Stakhanovskaia agrotekhnika v sveklovodstve," 75.

66. *Stakhanovskii opyt—v kolkhozy dal'nego vostoka*, 40.

67. *Stakhanovskii opyt—v kolkhozy dal'nego vostoka*, 40.

68. *Sovkhoznaia gazeta*, 23 February 1935.

69. *Sovkhoznaia gazeta*, 8 May 1937, 1.

70. The example for all to follow was that "during cultivation Stakhanovites extremely carefully picked all the weeds from their plots." See Dolgopolov, "Stakhanovskaia agrotekhnika v sveklovodstve," 75.

71. *Krest'ianskaia gazeta*, 18 May 1935, 1.

72. Dolgopolov, "Stakhanovskaia agrotekhnika v sveklovodstve," 90.

73. Vershinin, *Mariia Safronovna Demchenko*, 15.

74. *Stakhanovtsy-svinari o svoem opyte*, (Rostov: Kraikom soiuza svinosovkhozov, 1936), 39.

75. *Stakhanovtsy-svinari o svoem opyte*, 41. Zuev was also regularly cited for lessons in pig breeding. See *Sovkhoznaia gazeta*, 20 July 1936, 1; and *Sovkhoznaia gazeta*, 8 January 1936, 1.

76. A. Kuznetsov, "Geroini kolkhoznogo zhivotnovodstva," *Sotsialistichskaia Rekonstruktsiia Sel'skogo Khoziaistva*, no. 3 (March 1936): 149–51.

77. Kuznetsov, "Geroini kolkhoznogo zhivotnovodstva," 153. Several articles cited Tereshkova's lessons in milking as an inspiration to others. See *Sovkhoznaia gazeta*, 16 March 1936, 3.

78. *Sovkhoznaia gazeta*, 8 January 1936, 3.

79. *Sovkhoznaia gazeta*, 8 January 1936, 3.

80. In the case of Luna they had decided to increase her feed more than one and a half times. As a result Luna bore a healthy strong bullock weighing forty-eight kilograms and began to give up to forty-one liters of milk every twenty-four hours instead of her earlier sixteen liters.

81. *Krest'ianskaia gazeta*, 16 December 1936, 2. Similar messages on cleanliness and feed were given at the All-Union Conference of Advanced Workers in Animal Husbandry in December 1936. See *Krest'ianskaia gazeta*, 16 December 1936, 2.

82. Attention to sufficient quantities of feed was often highly detailed. Milkmaids in Siberia wrote, "On our farm number three, every milch cow is allotted twenty-two tsentners of hay, four and a half tsentners of food concentrate, seven tsentners of straw and two of silage. Milkmaids are supplied with buckets, milk measuring vessels and pans." See *Krasnaia Sibiriachka*, no. 3–4 (1936): 15. On farms that lacked food concentrate, however, such a recipe would not be possible.

83. *Sovkhoznaia gazeta*, 4 April 1938, 1.

84. *Kolkhoznitsa*, no. 1–2 (March 1936): 21.

85. *Sovkhoznaia gazeta*, 4 April 1938, 1.

86. B. Shapiro, "Opyt stakhanovtsev kolkhoznykh brigad," 153.

87. Shapiro, "Opyt stakhanovtsev," 53. Other lessons relevant to animals can be found in: I. Shaposhchnikov, "Stakhanovtsy kolkhoznogo zhivotnovodstva," *Sotsialisticheskaia Rekonstruktsiia Sel'skogo Khoziaistva*, no. 4 (April 1937): 163–69; S. Danilov, "Stakhanovtsy v bor'be za razvitie nashego ovtsevodstva," *Sotsialisticheskaia Rekonstruktsiia Sel'skogo Khoziaistva*, no. 4 (April 1937), 111–30.

88. A Stakhanovite movement in plowing in wartime was halted by the Central Committee Department of Agitation and Propaganda on the grounds that it wore out the horses. See Mary Buckley, "The *Nagornovskoe Dvizhenie*—A Stakhanovite Movement in Ploughing That Was Not," in *Edinburgh Essays on Russia,* ed. Elspeth Reid (Nottingham: Astra Press, 2000), 39–48.

89. *Krest'ianskaia gazeta*, 14 August 1935, 3.

90. Stephan Merl, "Social Mobility in the Countryside," in *Social Dimensions of Soviet Industrialization*, eds. William G. Rosenberg and Lewis H. Siegelbaum (Bloomington: Indiana University Press, 1993), 50.

Chapter Six

Resistance on the Farm

The loafer Stepan Ishchenko pushed Domka Litvin into the pit of manure.[1]

Don't dare move. If you do, we'll pull your hair out and kick you out of here![2]

— Angry women to Pasha Angelina's women's tractor brigade

Most peasants did not heed the multiple Stakhanovite "lessons" and become Stakhanovites themselves. Although the fierce opposition of the early 1930s to Soviet policies in the countryside had abated, some peasants, individually or in groups, continued to defy official recommendations on how they should behave. They greeted Stakhanovism with various forms of resistance, ranging from malicious gossip about Stakhanovites to their murder. Procuracy archives, *Krest'ianskaia gazeta*, and Stakhanovites' memoirs provide the richest illustrations, supplemented by details in the archives of state farm trade unions and in *Sovkhoznaia gazeta.*

In the field of peasant studies, the methodological problems of discussing rural opposition or resistance to policies have been well aired. Important questions can be raised, such as whether acts must be communal rather than individual to be classified as resistance or how best to dissect subtle mixes of outward compliance and tentative resistance. For the purpose of this chapter, resistance is defined as acts of individuals or groups that belittle, demean, insult, threaten, harm, maim, or kill. Some definitions include "intentionally."[3] Whilst one expects that such acts are indeed intentional, establishing the precise nature of intent seventy years later is hazardous. Thus in my definition the thorny question of intention remains open. One cannot establish beyond a reasonable doubt whether a peasant slandered or beat a Stakhanovite just because the latter was a Stakhanovite rather than because the assailant was drunk and would have picked on anyone at hand, had long disliked the Stakhanovite anyway, or was settling an old score now disguised as anger against Stakhanovism. Whilst recognizing that some attacks on Stakhanovites may have been independent of hostility to the movement per se, I nonetheless assume that many hostile acts were directed against Stakhanovism and its perceived role in Soviet society.[4] Neither can one definitively conclude how representative dislike of Stakhanovism was or the extent to which resistance varied across farms. One can, however, usefully categorize different forms of resistance along a continuum.

The material presented below suggests that the reasons for abusing Stakhanovites were probably several and included: anger that all peasants would be expected to work harder, too; resentment at the higher wages and perks received by Stakhanovites; reaction against the social injustice that Stakhanovites should have preferential help in the allocation of animal feed, manure, fuel for tractors, and other scarce inputs; cultural values which militated against behaving differently from the "collective"; and a more generalized and dissipated lingering hostility toward Soviet power in the years immediately after collectivization which identified Stakhanovites as upholders of the system and as colluding with communist leaders. Taken together these various reasons made Stakhanovites ready targets since they embodied much that appeared to be "wrong," threatening, and "unjust" to other weary peasants.

CATEGORIES OF RESISTANCE

Russian primary sources use various words when describing what I consider to be resistance. These include *travlia* (baiting, persecution or badgering), *oskorblenie* (insult), *sistematicheskie nasmeshki* (systematic mocking), *izdevatel'stvo* (humiliation), *protivodeistvie* (opposition), *soprotivlenie* (resistance), *ozhestochennoe soprotivlenie* (fierce resistance), *sabotazh* (sabotage), *prepiatstvie* (obstacle), *deskriditirovanie stakhanovskie metody rabot* (discredited Stakhanovite work methods), and *ugrozy* (threats). The continuum of undermining behavior spanned as follows: condemnations and rumors behind Stakhanovites' backs; direct belittling, humiliation, and baiting; victimization at work by those in authority; acts of sabotage against Stakhanovites' machines, animals, land, and homes; threats of physical violence; and actual violence.

Taken together, the sources provide graphic details. For the purpose of illustration here, I have selected stories that are either representative of an apparent pattern (of which there are numerous examples from which to select) or tales that are especially vivid.

GOSSIP AND RESENTMENT

A clear example of gossip is provided by remarks about Mariia Demchenko after her participation in 1935 in the Second Congress of Kolkhoz Shock Workers. It was at this Congress that she made her pledge to Stalin to pick 500 tsentners of sugar beet per hectare. On the Comintern collective farm where she worked in Petrovsk district, Kiev oblast, allegedly it was said behind her back:

> Just think! Mariika, daughter of Safronov, a most ordinary peasant girl, just like the rest of us, and what has she undertaken! Only the second year that she is working as a team leader and she already wants to outstrip everyone.[5]

Strong cultural resistance to being different nurtured such opinions. There was resentment at anyone wanting to be "better," which was perceived as putting themselves above the others and inappropriately breaking out of the collective. Traditional values required conservative conformity to prevailing social norms and values, not a ruffling of them. Four out of eight peasants in Demchenko's team felt offended because "it seem[ed] to them that they had worked together, they had not worked badly, but the honor and the presents went to Mariika."[6] These four young women left Demchenko's team, not all wishing to speak to her anymore. Here peasants felt slighted because they had been overlooked in the allocation of rewards. The perks and status received by Demchenko were the object of envy and resentment, resulting in a festering sense of social injustice. Others allegedly gossiped about Demchenko's abilities. These were *kolkhozniki* sympathetic to Mariia but who "did not believe in her strength."[7] There was thus suspicion that Demchenko was not really as good as had been claimed. That women could achieve very much went against the grain of the widespread prejudice that they were inferior to men.

Pasha Angelina recounted similar local antagonism. In her autobiography she claimed:

> I nursed my Fordson as a mother nurses her child; I did not mind how much time I spent on it. But in spite of all my efforts I could see that people, even my friends, had no confidence in me. And we also had avowed enemies. Somebody was energetically spreading nasty rumors about me. Instigated by the priest, pious old women used to spit on seeing "shameless Pasha" in an overall sitting at the tractor wheel.[8]

Women in overalls who took on "men's work" were discredited as inept and shameful. Apparently when she fell off her tractor during a thunderstorm, "at once there was talk in the village about God having punished Pasha."[9] The male tractor drivers had a simpler explanation: "she's a woman, what else can you expect of her."[10] Even Pasha's friends did not think she should be driving a tractor and believed that she had managed it only because she was very bright. They declared: "Pasha succeeded because she is an exceptionally bright girl, but after all, the tractor is no place for a woman."[11]

Rather different "incorrect rumors" circulated about the Stakhanovite tractor driver Frantsev who, since arriving on his farm in 1932, had always been a good worker and became a Stakhanovite in his speedy repair of tractors. In 1936, the malicious Petrov put it about that Frantsev had deserted from the Red Army during the Civil War and had taken to banditry.[12] By discrediting someone's past, peasants could attempt to tarnish a Stakhanovite's current image. This was especially the case in a political system in which citizens were accountable for their political behavior in the past and frequently judged according to social origins. Peasants could thus manipulate the rules of the system to their advantage by trying to discredit their target according to the regime's value system. In this case, however, socialist justice was meted out to the errant Petrov, who received a sentence of three years' imprisonment under Article 73 of the Criminal Code.[13]

A more generalized rumor began in 1936 in Belotserkovskii raion in Ukraine after the death of a 500er from a collective farm. Sources do not indicate how she died, but her death was subsequently talked about as though it was an omen. Mariia Chernenko, whom procuracy archives dub a "kulak," gossiped that: "The 500ers have started to die; the 500ers will not, after all, give 500 tsentners of sugar beet; everyone is pegging out."[14] Such a rumor fed on village prejudices and superstitions, implying that anyone who tried to become a 500er ran the risk of dying. In this manner, superstition justified the peasants' reluctance to exert themselves.

Rumors themselves, then, came in different forms. They could discredit a particular individual for alleged behavior or cast aspersions on Stakhanovites in general, making use of social slander, politically correct behavior, and superstition.

BELITTLING, HUMILIATION, AND BAITING

Sources cite numerous instances of baiting and belittling after a peasant had received medals, presents, and perks or had made a fresh public commitment to increase output to a new high. Procuracy archives, in particular, draw special attention to instances of verbal abuse from other peasants that demoralized Stakhanovites and prevented them from working.

In Kanevskii district of Kiev oblast, for example, the 500er Kosar' had at the beginning of January 1936 made a pledge to gather more sugar beet. While she was collecting some dung to help her meet the new target, one "Pustovoit stood not far from Kosar', unceasingly cursed, jeered and taunted her" reducing her "to such a condition that she stopped work and ran away crying."[15] Likewise, newly arrived on the "Red Lake" collective farm in Sirotinskii raion, Belorussia, Elena Gardovkina was put out by Shchelkunova's Stakhanovite methods. Through humiliating and scolding Shchelkunova, Gardovkina reduced the Stakhanovite to the point where she went up to the collective farm chairman in tears and said: "Take my work days and divide them among the kolkhoz women. And don't call me a Stakhanovite because they won't let me live because of it."[16] Some belittled Stakhanovites whose lives were made a misery preferred to give up their status rather than endure ongoing hostility. In exceedingly unpleasant circumstances, the emotional cost-benefit analysis militated against soldiering on. Gardovkina had attempted to disrupt work by declaring to the kolkhoz women: "Let the shock worker Shchelkunova work, but we women will not go to work tomorrow." Gardovkina was then imprisoned for two years.[17]

Peasants sometimes wrote to *Krest'ianskaia gazeta* about the abuses that they endured, especially if they had made complaints elsewhere and received no satisfaction. The newspaper reported the case of Ol'ga Peunkova, who was the best Stakhanovite milkmaid on her farm. After she had received a medal for her work, she declared, "I immediately felt that somebody incited the *kolkhozniki* against me." The Chair of the kolkhoz, Shishkov, "belittled Peunkova in petty fault-finding ways and in an underhand manner set *kolkhozniki* on her."[18] Although Peunkova wrote "to everyone in the district" asking for help, she received no responses and things "became worse and worse."[19] Lethargy in the local party could have been reinforced by the fact that moderate male officials themselves felt threatened by dynamic female Stakhanovites and were thus loath to help them.

Those who were the first to be named "Stakhanovite" on farms were especially vulnerable. When this title was bestowed on Melan'ia Slesarenko in Urazovskii raion, Kursk oblast, other *kolkhozniki* responded by making her life difficult. Two, for example, blocked her path one day, saying "You'll go no further. You want to be ahead, but you'll find you'll be the last."[20] They refused to let Slesarenko pass and jeered at her.

The awarding of medals provoked similar behavior. Stakhanovite pig tender Fillipova in Soligalichskii raion of Iaroslavl' oblast had her Order of Lenin snatched away from her. The farm's accountant came to hate her and squandered money that was meant to be spent on the construction of a pig house. Others on the farm were lazy and did not bother to feed the pigs that went hungry for twenty-four hours at a time. When Fillipova complained, the response to her was: "Drop it. In any case, they won't give you a second medal."[21] Unpleasant jeering and ways of undermining appear to have been relatively common.

Refusal to acknowledge invitations by the party to attend celebrations and special gatherings off the farm was another way of belittling Stakhanovites. When Slesarenko was called to Kursk by the raikom to join in the October festivities, her kolkhoz chair rudely retorted, "Since the district is sending you, let it provide a horse." He did not provide transport to the station, as was customary.[22] When Slesarenko returned from Kursk, she asked the Chair to call a meeting so that she could tell *kolkhozniki* about her trip. He mocked, "how do you like that! What a cultured speaker you have become."[23] He refused her request.

Failure to show recognition to Stakhanovites was also a way of demoralizing them. On International Women's Day, Stakhanovite Ruzhentsova in Kholm-Zhirkovsk raion of the Western oblast, was forgotten about on her farm and no one mentioned her as was customary on farms where Stakhanovites were praised.[24] At the end of 1937, *Krest'ianskaia gazeta* announced that in a series of districts *piatisotennitsy* "are being ignored, their achievements disregarded." In Krasnopol'skii raion of Khar'kov oblast the success of 500ers was so deprecated, "they already no longer thought of themselves as Stakhanovites."[25] According to 500er Zelenskaia, workers in the district held the now-widespread view that "500 tsentners of sugar beet per hectare was not an achievement."[26] The lesson to be drawn, according to *Krest'ianskaia gazeta*, was that now "here and there interest is taken only in special records, forgetting about the mass Stakhanovite movement."[27] The message was that everyone needed encouragement through praise.

By 1939 the criticisms of those who ignored Stakhanovites were sharper. Some authorities were bitingly exposed for not even being able to identify their Stakhanovites, reflecting the movement's ebb. In Leningrad oblast, one raikom and other district organizations were accused of "entirely not knowing the best Stakhanovites in the district or the women activists" and of "not conducting any work with them."[28]

Sometimes those aspiring to Stakhanovite status were persecuted for ostensibly different reasons. Dar'ia Pastukhova had spotted that the sister of the farm's *partorg* stole products from the children's crèche, where she was in charge. Everyone knew about this, but unlike Pastukhova, they were all silent. At two kolkhoz general meetings, Pastukhova publicly exposed the thefts. The *partorg* subsequently came to her and said: "Listen, live with us in peace, that will be better." Then ensued "base baiting." She was accused of sorcery (*v znakharstve*), fined ten rubles, and then her monthly pension was cut in half which she received for the murder of her husband, a Red partisan, by the Whites. She subsequently discovered that the castor oil plant and maize which her team had nurtured was on show at a local exhibition, but not attributed to her efforts.[29]

Forms of belittling, then, were several. Their main results appear to have included demoralization, readiness to give up Stakhanovite status for a quieter life, or readiness to fight against the perpetrators, insistent to remain a Stakhanovite. Thus Stakhanovites' responses to humiliation varied. Some backed off and others remained resolute. Accounting for these variations is difficult and must be linked to factors of personality, family support, ambience on the farm, the attitude of the kolkhoz chair or sovkhoz director, and the role played by the *politotdel* on the MTS.

VICTIMIZATION AT WORK BY THOSE IN AUTHORITY

As well as being subjected to various forms of slighting and taunting from other peasants, Stakhanovites were sometimes hindered in their attempts to work well or prevented from working at all from those in positions of authority. In these cases, no encouragement was given either from the brigade leader, kolkhoz chair, sovkhoz director, or director of the Machine Tractor Station. Appeals to district organizations for help produced mixed results.

Melan'ia Slesarenko, for example, was told by her brigade leader, "dig, don't dig, we won't count digging among your work days." The kolkhoz chair supported this.[30] Similarly, Elena Veretilova, a Stakhanovite in the tobacco fields in Crimea, did not receive any support from the kolkhoz leadership. Rather, they victimized her as initiator of a Stakhanovite team and interfered with her work. The agronomist Komsomol member, Kernoz, and a member of the auditing commission, Peronko, openly opposed Veretilova and set her norms beyond her strength. Thus "the Stakhanovite was put in such a position that she was obliged to quit her work."[31] *Krest'ianskaia gazeta* described how she had been an ideal worker in inspiring others. During the harvesting of tobacco, Veretilova had broken away from her team, taking a separate strip of land. She worked extremely efficiently with the result that "other *kolkhozniki* looking at her increased the productivity of their work."[32] Here resistance to Stakhanovism arose as soon as it was clear that a group of workers was producing at a faster pace than others.

The same reason provoked hostility to Dar'ia Pastukhova, a team leader in Azovo-Chernomore krai who had pledged 825 tsentners of sugar beet per hectare. She carefully prepared the manure toward this end. Opposition to her goal resulted in her team being dispersed. Frequently kolkhoz chairs split up productive teams. Pastukhova was also evicted from her hut and forced to leave the kolkhoz.[33]

Despite being the best Stakhanovite on the Iskra collective farm in Kamenskii raion of Cheliabinsk oblast, Anastasiia Ulanova suffered a similar fate. Ulanova reported that:

> When I pledged to gather 50 tsentners of grain per hectare and 500 tsentners of potatoes, they promised help. But now the director of Kolchedanskii MTS and the kolkhoz management for some reason decided to disband my team. They sent the kolkhozniki in my team to do other work—one as a cook, another as a transporter of fuel. After long work and preparations for a record harvest, my team was dissolved.[34]

Throughout 1937, *Krest'ianskaia gazeta* regularly made the observation that Stakhanovite teams were inadvisably being broken up.

Reasons behind attempts from those in authority to prevent Stakhanovites from stepping up the tempo of work could be several. First, whatever the regime's political priorities, giving preferential treatment to Stakhanovites on the farm must have been a difficult task since farm leaders knew that other peasants resented this. Second, in cases where animal feed or manure was insufficient there were the questions of whether it was fair, or even possible, to give Stakhanovites proportionally more than others. Third, if the Stakhanovites were female, gender prejudices among farm leaders and district party officials may have worked against supporting them. Fourth, not all farm chairpersons and directors may have supported the idea of Stakhanovism. Like other peasant critics, perhaps they did not. Fifth, it has, moreover, to be asked whether like industrial Stakhanovism, rural Stakhanovism was often disruptive of other aspects of agricultural work.

VILLAINS WHO SABOTAGED

Krest'ianskaia gazeta portrayed "enemies of the Stakhanovite movement" as progressing in stages. After the belittling and humiliation of Stakhanovites and various acts that deterred or prevented them from working "in a Stakhanovite way" came acts of sabotage. These were conducted against Stakhanovites' machines, their animals, their land, their homes and possessions, and their own bodies.

Machines

Although, in theory, Machine Tractor Stations were meant to facilitate work on the kolkhozy, in practice this was not always the case. After a Komsomol brigade of tractor drivers in Starobel'skii okrug in Ukraine attained Stakhanovite status, the deputy director of the MTS refused to give the brigade fuel. Upset by this, the Stakhanovites went to the director of the MTS, who told them, "now all shock work brigades will be without fuel." Instead, fuel would go in the first place to "those who have low output. It will be done this way in order to raise them to the level of advanced workers."[35] Resilience of the cultural idea that no one should receive more than others, and of the notion that a leveling of all was appropriate, may have been behind this. Moreover, in the event of a scarcity of inputs, giving proportionally more fuel to Stakhanovites in order to aid them in fulfilling their higher norms, may automatically have disadvantaged others.

The brigade leader Romanenko and his eight tractor drivers, however, complained to *Krest'ianskaia gazeta* that this was "sheer mockery."[36] What *Krest'ianskaia gazeta* does not comment upon is whether sufficient fuel was available. The supply of feed, seed, and fuel were serious problems on some farms, however, which Stakhanovism exacerbated for non-Stakhanovites.

Animals

Krest'ianskaia gazeta reported two incidents against the cows of Stakhanovite milkmaid Ol'ga Peunkova. One cow suddenly died and examination showed two steel needles lodged in her heart. A veterinary surgeon concluded that the needles had been put in the feed three or four weeks earlier when Peunkova had been away in Moscow at a meeting of advanced workers in animal husbandry. The kolkhoz chair seemed to back the persecution of Peunkova.[37] Ten days later, *Krest'ianskaia gazeta* reported that Peunkova's best cow "Melekha" had also died because of a needle in her feed. Only then did raikom secretary, the chair of the district soviet executive committee, and investigators come to the farm. They all concurred that it was "a simple accident" and left. The experience upset Peunkova, who fell ill and took to her bed, but nobody nursed her. Only at the insistence of a visiting representative from *Krest'ianskaia gazeta* was she found a place in a hospital.[38] Journalists frequently cast the newspaper in the role of "folk hero," championing the cause of the worthy versus the "folk devils" who ill-treated them. Prior to these incidents, Peunkova had declared her intent in 1936 to milk 5,500 liters of milk from record-giving cows.[39] Once again, open commitment to attaining a higher record had provoked local hostility.

Milder acts against animals included not giving them enough feed. The milkmaid Galina Shaiorova in Bogorodsk district, Gor'kii krai, pledged to milk, on average, 4,500 liters of milk from each cow. The kolkhoz chair, however, did not give her enough feed to accomplish this goal and the raikom secretary did nothing to intervene.[40] The problem here may have been a much larger one than *Krest'ianskaia gazeta* reported since lack of sufficient feed was a serious problem on many farms. Low inputs meant that animals often did go hungry. And other peasants perceived giving proportionally more feed to Stakhanovites as iniquitous.

Land

Stakhanovites' attempts to care for the land that they worked were often sabotaged. Melan'ia Slesarenko, for example, put a snow screen on her field to protect it, but at night someone smashed it. On the ashes she had collected, someone poured water and caused her manure to freeze. An unknown person or persons scattered soot on the snow and threw around the collected dung.[41] During the day, Slesarenko took manure to the field and at night sledges took it away.

The politics of dung could be serious. Garpyna Kobanets was the best *piatisotennitsa* in Bershadsk raion, Vinnitsa oblast, who one day found her plot of land littered with undecomposed manure. This amounted to vandalism of the land but it provoked little sympathy among local peasantry and "no one helped her to clean the land. She did it herself."[42] Stakhanovites were often isolated in their efforts to excel and left alone to deal with upsetting situations.

Whereas *kolkhozniki* opposed to Stakhanovites messed up their land in various ways, discouraging kolkhoz leaders took their carefully tended land away from them. Disregard for the painstaking work preparations of Anna Romaniuk is one such example. On the sugar beet plot of her Komsomol brigade in Cherno-Ostrovskii raion, Vinnitsa oblast, Romaniuk "took full responsibility for the manure, picked the weeds, closely watched the quality of the plowing." Yet when spring came, this land was taken away from Romaniuk and she was given barren land covered in "tall weeds."[43] *Krest'ianskaia gazeta* commented dryly that this made it hard for Stakhanovites to have a good sugar beet harvest.[44]

Whereas the press provided details of individual cases, party archives tend to provide more sterile lists of the number of cases in a particular district sent to the local procuracy, but without elaboration of what exactly had been done to the land. The Smolensk archive notes that from May to November 1937, Sychevskii district had informed the procuracy of 19 cases in which Stakhanovites had in some way been abused. Two of these concerned damage to Stakhanovites' flax crops.[45]

Homes and Possessions

Another way of getting at Stakhanovites was by entering, damaging, or destroying their homes, and ruining their possessions. Such attacks were highly personal.

On the Frunze state farm in Ivanovo oblast, one livestock worker, Stepanov, entered milkmaid Krutikova's home and illegally searched it, the next day claiming that she had stolen bran and milk.[46] In Sychevskii raion in Smolensk oblast evidence reveals several cases of Stakhanovites' windows being smashed.[47] Procuracy archives also provide numerous references to Stakhanovites' smashed windows in the countryside and in cities.[48] Such petty vandalism against Stakhanovites appears to have been one of the more routine acts against them.

Sources suggest that smashed windows were sometimes one part of a bigger attack on different parts of a home. For example, in January 1936 in Bogoslavskii raion, Ukraine, Vasilii Dubin and Klim Razakhovskii:

> went into the hut of 700er Mar'iany Dubina, who at the time was at a district rally of 500ers, smashed a window, pulled down the flu, spread the ashes about, mixed them with husks and threw them onto the stove and the bench.[49]

They received five-year sentences and the Chair of the kolkhoz was also tried for knowing of the attack and not notifying the appropriate authorities for two weeks.[50]

Sometimes an attack resulted in total destruction of the home. *Krest'ianskaia gazeta* reported that Melan'ia Slesarenko had her house set alight and reduced to ashes. This act was committed by the embittered Belichenko after he had lost his job as kolkhoz chair. This finally came about after the investigation of district and oblast procuracies into his bad treatment of Slesarenko. Belichenko was especially keen to get revenge since his earlier attempt to pin his theft of a horse on Slesarenko's father had failed. He also burned down the barn.[51]

Before Pasha Angelina became a tractor driver, her family's house was burned down because they were supporters of the collective farm.[52] Destruction by fire was a common way of expressing hostility in rural life, which has persisted. Under Gorbachev and also after the disintegration of the USSR, city dwellers bought an increasing number of rural homes and locals sometimes burned them down.[53] Incomers were reluctant then to build in wood and started construction in stone. Roberta T. Manning has also made the point that attacks on homes, fields, and animals were incidents which:

> commonly occurred in Russian villages, both before and after the 1917 Revolution, and apparently served as the means by which the village community and its members expressed feelings of jealousy or resentment toward the good fortune of others and sought to control the behavior of deviant villages.[54]

The fact that many forms of resistance were traditional suggests that they represented an older culture battling against new kolkhoz and sovkhoz work patterns and values. Not only did peasants resent Stakhanovism, but they articulated this in ways that peasants had traditionally vented a culture of resentment and a lack of generosity to those who possessed more than themselves. The sour did not seek to improve themselves and to haul themselves up to a standard which would bring them prizes, too, but instead aimed to drag the achievers down. They acted as serious rate limiting factors in rural transformations.

Resentment at Stakhanovites' presents and higher salaries also prompted violence against their newly acquired possessions. On the "New Life" collective farm in Mekhovskii raion, Belorussia, Stakhanovites working with flax were rewarded by the farm, by the rural soviet, and by the raiispolkom. According to procuracy files, they then spent their bonus on new clothes. Other peasants on the farm tried to humiliate them and made various threats. When the threats led nowhere, at an evening gathering of young people, "they poured sulphuric acid on the Stakhanovites' clothes." The culprits were sentenced to four and five years' imprisonment.[55]

Threats of Physical Violence

Threats of physical violence came from men and women alike. References to them are most readily found in autobiographies and in procuracy archives.

When Pasha Angelina's women's tractor team drove toward the fields from the MTS for the first time there was immediate resistance. A crowd of angry women barred their way, shouting, "Turn back!" Integral to this opposition was hostility to changing gender roles. The women, however, then threatened violence. According to Angelina, they warned: "'Don't dare move. If you do, we'll pull your hair out and kick you out of here!' We knew that if we did move there would be a scrap."[56] Angelina defused the situation by running back to Staro-Beshevo to seek help before continuing into the fields.

Sometimes threats were made to Stakhanovites' parents, especially if the Stakhanovites were young pioneers or Komsomol members. In Tadzhikistan, men from the *chaikhana* (all men's tea shop) visited Mamlakat Nakhangova's father. Allegedly, they said: "You're a fine fellow, Nakhang. Everyone respects you. But your daughter, excuse us, puts us all in a ridiculous position." Another interjected: "It makes us look like saboteurs. They could think that we pick little cotton on purpose, that we drag out the harvest." A third asked, "what sort of men are we if a little school girl works better than we do?"[57] Consistent with patriarchal tradition, fathers were expected to control and influence offspring, especially daughters. It was therefore culturally appropriate to attempt to change Mamlakat's behavior through her father. Collective values meant that the actions of one family member concerned the entire family. This was even more so in Central Asia.

Often threats of violence were preceded by insults and harassment. For example, in Dymerskii raion of Kiev oblast, Kuz'ma Pavlenko chased after the Stakhanovite Praskov'ia Muliar and:

> at every step jeered at her and threatened to pin her up with a pitchfork. In the end, in February, he threw an anonymous letter at her with the suggestion that she renege on her given work pledge, otherwise there would be violent reprisals.[58]

It seems that many threats of violence were made for two main reasons: first, out of objection to Stakhanovites working harder and thereby raising work expectations; and second, out of opposition to changing gender roles. When it was women who threatened to work well and to raise work standards, traditional gender hierarchies were threatened. This was particularly so when women broke into new fields of tractor and combine driving, thought to be highly inappropriate for women, especially since they could now earn as much as men, or more.

Acts of Physical Violence

Violence against Stakhanovites came in various degrees, ranging from skirmishes to severe beatings and murder. Yet again it was often public pledges on the part of eager workers to attain Stakhanovite records that provoked acts of violence.

Kolkhoz worker Boboshko in Kiev oblast, for example, promised to pick more sugar beet. One day drunken Fedor Iur came to tell her in December 1935 that she would achieve nothing. Then six days later he returned and:

> began to laugh at Boboshko, then grabbed her by the breast and threw her onto the bench. Next Iur picked her up, sat her on the bench and began to shove her in the side, saying: "here are your 350 tsentners per hectare and here is your Stakhanovite movement."[59]

Iur was given a two-year sentence.[60]

In Zhitormirskii raion, Kiev oblast, Domka Litvin was the best shock worker of the "New Life" collective farm. One day in the fields she was "spreading fertilizer evenly and from the pit, not far away, she fetched a bucket of manure for compost. Arriving at this time, the loafer Stepan Ishchenko pushed Domka Litvin into the pit of manure."[61] Although Ishchenko could have done this for amusement or merely because he disliked Litvin, the procuracy report considered it part of a general pattern of attacks on hardworkers.

Similarly, when a group of female Stakhanovites, led by the 500er Polutskaia, rose early in the morning to go into the fields, "Rat'ko, standing not far off, all the time cursed them" in foul language. When Polutskaia defended her team and demanded that he go away and not prevent them from working, "Rat'ko replied by hitting her twice."[62]

In their reports on "resistance against Stakhanovism," the procuracy sometimes gave lists of violent acts without much elaboration of the broader circumstances. For instance, in Zlatopol'skii raion of Kiev oblast, a drunken kolkhoz brigade leader "hit the 500er Melan'ia Kalina and the *kolkhoznitsa* Elena Gavrik." He was given three months' hard labor.[63] In Chernobaevskii raion, Kiev oblast, a drunken *kolkhoznik* "wrecked a general meeting" and "beat up a 500er." The culprit was imprisoned for three years.[64] In Zhashkovskii district, Kiev oblast, male *kolkhozniki* arrived in a hut where female 500ers were gathered and "caused a brawl, broke furniture in the hut, beat the 500ers and prevented them from going to work."[65] This case had yet to go to court at the time of the procuracy report.

These examples and many more highlight the behavior of drunken male peasants toward female 500ers. Precise motivations are unknown. We might wonder whether the men were embittered and slighted lovers? Had they always disliked these women? Were they settling an old score? Did they regularly beat up any women when drunk? Whatever the complications, we cannot dismiss as insignificant the fact that the women were 500ers. Drunken violence was certainly a regular feature of Russian rural life. And the fact that female 500ers were repeated victims suggests both disapproval of 500er status and disgust that women were aspiring to it. Most cases cited in procuracy archives are of female victims. This could be because in certain sectors most 500ers were women due to the predominance of female labor. It could also be because men beat women 500ers more readily than male 500ers, perhaps assuming that retaliation would be milder or that the beatings against women were socially appropriate.

Particularly tense fights took place within families where there were disagreements about Stakhanovism. One procuracy report noted that as the Stakhanovite movement grew:

there arose arguments within families, in connection with the participation of individual members in the Stakhanovite movement. Arguments broke out between husband and wife, father and daughter, brother and sister, ending in various ways and in fights.[66]

Unfortunately, precise details are again missing. It is suggestive, however, that no mention is made of fights between father and son, mother and daughter, among brothers, or among sisters. It is likely that, as with the examples of 500ers above, women were the conventional targets of male violence. Without clear information, however, this can only be conjecture.

Occasionally newspaper and journal reports gave reasons for the violence. The message from *Krasnaia Sibiriachka* was that class enemies who opposed collectivization tried to bait, torment, and persecute excellent workers:

> On the kolkhoz named after Dimitrov in Marushinskii district enemies of collectivizaton unmercifully beat Akulina Andreichenko, a delegate of the Second All-Union Congress of Kolkhoz Shock Workers. Enemies of the people did not like the fact that komsomol member Andreichenko worked in a Stakhanovite manner.[67]

The official link was always between enemies of the people and resistance to Stakhanovism and never between mere dislike that output records would have to increase and resistance.[68] Opponents were, by official definition, "enemies" rather than lazy and their punishment under Article 58 of the Criminal Code was an indication from above that their resistance was political and counter-revolutionary.

Sometimes threats of violence remained at the level of threat, not developing into violent action. This was the case when women blocked Pasha Angelina's path to the fields. In the end the jeering women permitted her tractors to proceed to work under the protective eye of Ivan Kurov from the *politotdel*. Although Pasha Angelina was spared the actualization of the women's threats against her, three young men attacked her in a separate incident. As she told it:

> One day, as I was cycling to the fields, I heard the rattling of a heavy cart behind me. I swerved off the road, but the cart turned to the right. I felt that I was being hunted and that in another moment something frightful would happen. Two enormous horses hurled themselves upon me, the heavy cart rolled over my body and then dashed off. . . . I lay bleeding in a trampled furrow for several hours. I was picked up in an unconscious condition and taken to the hospital.[69]

Opponents of Stakhanovism were sometimes out to kill, indicating the depth of their venom.

On other occasions, threats were fulfilled. Mamlakat Nakhangova was attacked two days after her father had been warned to take control of his daughter. Nakhangova was returning from the fields when, "they severely beat her."[70] For three weeks she was unable to get up. But as soon as she did, she returned to the fields where she developed a following among the pioneers, who subsequently worked with her. But undeterred, her critics then "beat her a second time. They beat her within an inch of her life."[71] Angry and embittered peasants could mete out especially harsh violence when they felt threatened by those working for the transformation of rural patterns as they knew them.

The worst acts committed by "enemies" were physical beatings of Stakhanovites and even murder. The reporting of attempted murders and murders, however, was rare in the press. The one case of murder covered in 1936 in available editions of *Krest'ianskaia gazeta* was of a schoolteacher who was returning from the Eighth All-Union Congress of Soviets, not of a Stakhanovite.[72] The Smolensk archive, however, notes in 1937 a case of murder of a Stakhanovite in Sychevskii raion, giving no details other than it was carried out by a kulak on "Fighter" collective farm.[73]

Evidence of the attempted murder of Stakhanovites and also suicide is most readily found in procuracy archives. Here one sees more instances in towns and in heavy industry than in the countryside, but this reflects the greater number of documents on towns.[74] A graphic illustration from the countryside concerns tractor driver Petin from Krotovskii MTS in Kuibyshev district. Having been decorated with a medal, Petin "was badly beaten" about the head by a group of five "loafers." Petin was about to be sliced to death with a knife when a passing peasant seized the weapon from his attacker.[75]

Very occasionally trade union archives cite instances of violent opposition to Stakhanovism on state farms. On the "Red Molochar" farm in Donetsk oblast, for example, a brigade leader, the "son of a kulak," is reported to have killed a milkmaid, also denouncing her as a thief.[76] The trade union report regrets that the union only learned of this one month later and that in many areas trade union organs did not "unmask" class enemies in time. As a result the enemy could "discredit" Stakhanovism and "sometimes killing shock workers, discredit socialist work methods." [77] Although details are not given, the report does refer to shock workers in the plural being killed.

In sum, one detects in the press and in trade union archives a hesitancy to report the murder of rural shock workers and Stakhanovites. Procuracy archives, however, confirm that murders took place, even if many details are absent. Since most of the murders appear to have been committed by other peasants, rather than by those in positions of authority, and since much propaganda surrounding Stakhanovism was directed at incompetent management rather than at obstructive peasants (the peasants, after all, were meant to be welcoming the movement with dynamic enthusiasm), reporting really side-stepped the issue of violence against Stakhanovism. It may have been feared that coverage of such violence would inflame even more and also deter peasants from aspiring to be Stakhanovites. Thus silence in public arenas hung over the dimensions of violence that the movement provoked.

REACTIONS OF THE PROCURACY
TO RESISTANCE TO STAKHANOVISM

Resistance to Stakhanovism appears to have been taken very seriously by the procuracy, at least officially. Scrutiny of the *informatsionnyi doklad* (information paper or report), *otchët* (account) *soobshcheniia* (communication), *dokladnaia zapiska* (report), *informatsionnaia svodka* (information summary), *spetsinformatsiia* (special information) and *obvinitel'noe zakliuchenie* (bill of indictment) circulating within the procuracy show reports on resistance, discussions of punishments, and special meetings and conferences convened within the procuracy around these themes. While the available reports are few in number, they do nonetheless present convincing evidence that the procuracy identified behavior which they labeled "resistance to Stakhanovism" and took pains to discuss it.

In January 1936, a special *informatsionnaia svodka* "On the work of procuracy organs of the Northern Krai in the struggle with opposition to the development of the Stakhanovite movement" reported "fierce resistance on the part of class enemies, attempting through agitation and a spreading of slanderous and fictitious rumors, to discredit Stakhanovite work methods."[78] Similarly, a *dokladnaia zapiska* "On the work of the procuracy in the Belorussian Soviet Socialist Republic in the struggle against sabotage of the Stakhanovite movement in industry and in agriculture in BSSR" showed that special ten-day courses and conferences were held on the subject, involving nineteen district procuracies.[79] An *informatsionnyi doklad* from the procurator to Voronezh oblast to the republic procurator reported that there had been "sorties of the class enemy against Stakhanovites" in Tambov and Lipetskii districts as well as in the town of Voronezh. In fact, in Tambov raion there had been "a whole series of sorties of the class enemy with the aim of undermining the Stakhanovite movement."[80] Likewise, from the procurator of Sverdlovsk oblast to the republic procurator came a report "On the work of Sverdlovsk Oblast procuracy concerning resistance to the Stakhanovite movement."[81]

An *informatsionnyi doklad* from Kiev oblast in January 1936 also discussed "threats in relation to the 500ers" and broke these down into three categories: insults; systematic mocking; and beatings and slaughter.[82] Apparently in Kiev oblast, in January 1936 there were 412 cases of "hooliganism," many of which were acts in the countryside against the 500ers.[83] In January 1936, on the 7th, 8th, and 23rd, special meetings of district procuracies were convened in Kiev oblast to discuss the appropriate punishment for different forms of resistance to Stakhanovism.[84]

A detailed *otchët* sent from Kiev oblast to the infamous Andrei Vyshinskii, Procurator of the USSR, analyzed legal cases against opponents of Stakhanovism covering the period December 1935 to 15 May 1936.[85] As Table 6.1 shows, the number of offenders facing trial increased gradually in January and February 1936, peaking in April. Ninety-two of these 139 were then sent to trial and 21 of the 92 were redefined as unconnected with opposition to the Stakhanovite movement.

In analyzing these data, the *otchët* claimed that figures were higher in March and April due to "a more tense production situation."[86] By contrast, December, January, and February were "preparatory months" where tension was less. In the earlier months, it was suggested, the enemies of the 500ers tried to bring about their "psychological demoralization" through threats, slander, mockery, and humiliation, whereas subsequently there was "spontaneous wrecking of the productive activity of the agricultural Stakhanovites."[87] May constituted "the third period" and had few cases since opponents of Stakhanovism were seen to be coming to court. The procuracy considered this to be a deterrent.

Thus the procuracy collected information on resistance to Stakhanovism, categorized it, discussed it internally, wrote about it to party institutions and to the procuracy at the next administrative level up, and held meetings and conferences on it. Although particular local procuracies were often picked out by the press and accused of neglecting cases of resistance to Stakhanovism, there is evidence that in some oblasts, at least formally, discussions were held.

Table 6.1.   Cases to Be Considered for Trial by the Procurator of Kiev Oblast

December 1936	3 cases
January 1936	14
February 1936	24
March 1936	43
April 1936	46
May 1936	9
Total	139 cases

Source: GARF, f. 8131, op. 13, d. 64, l. 261.

The question of the extent to which actions matched words is hard to answer with precision. A reasonable conclusion, given the available evidence, would be that resistance to Stakhanovism was not ignored by the procuracy and itself probably varied in nature and style across republics, oblasts, and districts. It may have been practiced by only a minority of peasants but was nonetheless much discussed by the procuracy at a time of necessary mobilization against class enemies when it was imperative to be seen to be vigilant.

The People's Commissariat of Justice, moreover, would not let procuracies ignore resistance to Stakhanovism. N. Krylenko sent letters to courts at all administrative levels with the message that Stakhanovism:

> imposes upon the organs of justice the politically responsible task of struggling with what hinders the Stakhanovite movement and of defending the productive and cultural interests of Stakhanovites at work and in daily life.[88]

He made special reference to "terrorist acts," "sabotage, threats, slander and mockery" and informed procuracies that circulars were being sent out with instructions on which acts qualified for sentencing under the relevant articles of the Criminal Code. He called for particular attention to be paid to Articles 58-7, 58-8, 58-10, 58-14, 73 parts 1 and 2, 109, and 111.[89] Krylenko also noted that a conference was being convened under the Commissariat of Justice for procurators from Moscow, Leningrad, and Ivanovo-promyshlennaia oblasts, Saratov and Gor'kii krais, and Mordova and Udmurt autonomous republics. One aim was to confirm "the task had been correctly understood in oblast and krai procuracies" and that a "strict line of repression is practised by the organs of justice."[90]

The message "from above" was thus one of vigilance, action, and repression of those who opposed Stakhanovism. Within the procuracy, however, one finds an occasional sympathy for those who resisted Stakhanovism unknowingly. Indeed, in this connection, archival materials raise a question which concerns our starting definition of resistance which included a presumption of intent.

A *dokladnaia zapiska* sent to the obkom in Ivanovo-promyshlennaia oblast from the procuracy reported "On cases of opposition to the Stakhanovite movement in agriculture." This noted that as well as acts of class enemies against Stakhanovites, there were also "not a few" cases of refusal to give Stakhanovite teams help on the part of kolkhoz chairpersons and brigade leaders as well as insults meted out by other peasants. The procuracy put this down to "misunderstanding by these people of the tasks of the Stakhanovite movement" and "insufficient cultural development and backwardness" rather than "premeditated acts directed at the wrecking of the Stakhanovite movement."[91]

If these acts were not premeditated, and if harm to Stakhanovites was not uppermost in their minds, then can they be classified as resistance according to our starting definition that assumes intention? For purposes of analysis it seems that although acts may not have been consciously designed to wreck Stakhanovism, they were conducted in the knowledge that they would have an effect upon the Stakhanovites concerned, and an effect that conveyed the message that Stakhanovism was not acceptable to others. The actor may not have fully appreciated the nature of the result of his or her behavior, but nonetheless acted in such a way as to harm a Stakhanovite.

THE SIGNIFICANCE OF DIFFERENT FORMS OF OPPOSITION

This overview of different forms of resistance indicates tendencies that existed in the 1930s. Whilst one cannot know their precise extent due to lack of data and underreporting, these tendencies nonetheless prompt reflection about the relationship between rural society and state in the 1930s. Society may have been horribly repressed and suffering arbitrary terror, which should never be underplayed, but not all members of society were cowed into passivity or unable to thwart policies. Moreover, traditional cultural patterns were integral to the resistance, themselves enacted and reinforced.

The obvious point is that many rural practices and behavior patterns deviated from what leaders officially wanted *kolkhozniki* and *sovkhozniki* to be doing. Collective farmers happily criticized Stakhanovites, openly baited them, and through the "politics of dung" wrecked their manure preparations. These minor acts of humiliation and intimidation paled alongside more aggressive acts of threatening violence, burning down huts, and physical attacks. Society did not behave in an ordered way by following the cues, commands, and ideological imperatives sent down "from above." Nor did rural life match the happy smiling faces of socialist realist paintings that suggested harmony and cooperation rather than resentment, jeering, and violence. Even the advocates of the totalitarian approach recognized that resistance existed under Stalinism. Carl Friedrich and Zbigniew Brzezinski devoted an entire chapter of their classic book to the topic. They viewed resistance as coming, however, from "islands of separateness, in the totalitarian sea" and characterized it as "sporadic" at best.[92]

Archives suggest that resistance was more than "sporadic" since local procuracies ran special miniconferences on how to address the problem. The numerous examples published in *Krest'iankaia gazeta* alone, supplemented with unpublished cases in the editorial archive, suggest sharp tensions in the countryside, disrespect for official values, and frequent attempts to undermine workers who set themselves fresh work targets. Much of the opposition stemmed from the fear that if others worked harder and set new records, then pressure would hit other peasants to increase their pace. New records also disturbed the pace of rural patterns and introduced an alien tempo. In addition, the striving of particular individuals to get ahead, to become different from the others, jarred with rural collectivism. Many observers have noted in Russian culture, and in peasant culture more generally, the strain of resentment at the success of others. It is better for everyone to be the same, even if poor, than for the few to flourish. The encouragement integral to American pioneer mentality where achievement is rewarded was not part of Russian culture.

Another problem stemmed from the preferential treatment that Stakhanovites were supposed to receive. Better housing, more money, trips to Moscow, and increased status jarred with other peasants. Preferential treatment also made a material difference in the supply of farm inputs. If Stakhanovites demanded more manure or more feed for their animals in order to increase productivity, then other peasants may have had to receive less. This could become an acute problem in instances of scarce inputs. Special allocations to Stakhanovites could disrupt equanimity since they meant less manure and feed for others. In instances where Stakhanovites did receive preferential treatment, to what extent did others suffer? If others were disadvantaged, this would exacerbate their hostility to unequal patterns of allocation.

While sources do provide many illustrations at resentment of Stakhanovites' perks, they do not convincingly show the extent to which special supplies of fodder, manure, and fuel for Stakhanovites hurt others. But given what we know about farm conditions in the 1930s, it is most likely that in cases of shortages of inputs, special supplies for Stakhanovites would inevitably mean less for others. This would help to explain why many farm chairpersons refused to give Stakhanovites preferential supplies.

Another possible explanation for hostility to Stakhanovites was that they were incomers to the farm and thus perceived as outsiders and not "*nashi*" (ours). One difficulty with this hypothesis is that not all Stakhanovites were outsiders. A second is that we lack sufficient information on whether acts of hostility were meted out *only* to those who were outsiders. Lack of biographical details for the less famous Stakhanovites concerning who did and who did not suffer baiting and maltreatment make it statistically impossible to answer the question set. If seems likely, however, that outsider status may have been one factor among others that provoked resistance.

A further explanation is that peasants en masse were still angered and bitter by the experiences of grain procurements and collectivization. Although this situation in the countryside has recently been challenged by Mark Tauger, we can allow that whilst most were not about to revolt, there may indeed have been some who were still venting sufficient wrath at the system and at eager communists.[93] Stakhanovites after all epitomized the system's values.

Resistance, however, reflected more than communal values, local resentments, criticism of preferential treatment, dislike of incomers, and anger at communists. It also raised the question of why those in official positions, be they kolkhoz chairpersons, directors of machine tractor stations, raikom party secretaries, or procurators, failed to execute party policy. Was this much more than not wishing to collude in the unequal distribution of farm inputs? Whilst it was not always possible to execute party policy due to shortages of feed, fuel, and seed, enough examples suggest that reluctance to help Stakhanovites went beyond this.

Undoubtedly there was local and regional variation in the ways in which those in positions of authority behaved. But sufficient data challenge the model of a neat flow of policy from center to periphery. Guidelines issued in Moscow were frequently not followed in towns and villages. Or sometimes, as the next chapter shows, they were only partially fulfilled, thereby flouting the general spirit of policy. Obstructions, negligence, and stubborn refusal to comply with official policy characterized implementation. Inaction and reluctance to react to criticism were among the consequences. More useful than the notion of "islands of separateness" is Moshe Lewin's concept of "cultural filter" through which members of society redefined and reacted to policies sent down to them, often ignoring or reshaping the intent of leaders.[94] Not only did many ordinary peasants respond with suspicion and hostility to new pressures and demands, so too did those running farms and those in charge of local party organizations. Sources do not indicate a harmonious and even pattern of policy implementation and are rich in examples of conflict and unresolved disputes. Party policy as formulated at the center was indeed flouted and indirectly challenged by the very people who were supposed to be executing it.

Archives and newspapers more closely match Lewin's conclusion that the 1930s amounted to a "brief period" that was crammed "with shifting, intermingling social processes that moved in a chaotic and intense historical development."[95] To offer a precise operational definition of "chaos" in the relationship between society and state is hazardous. Chaos generally connotes lack of predictability, uneven patterns, disorder, confusion, and randomness. More accurately perhaps, one can see similar patterns of resistance to policy, stronger on some farms than others, more tenacious in some districts than in others. Likewise, enthusiastic support for Stakhanovism prevailed. Evidence does indicate the existence of peasants inspired to belong to the movement, to attain records and to maintain them, even in the face of opposition.

This clash of reactions to Stakhanovism was one of the social tensions that both reflected and shaped rural life. Peasants were not homogeneous mass persons as Friedrich and Brzezinski had portrayed Stalinist individuals. The "isolated and anxiety-ridden shadow" who they described does not match Pasha Angelina, the women who tried to stop her entering the fields with her tractor brigade, or the male assailants who chased her in a cart. In addition, the available social space for gossip, criticism, and opposition to the regime's heroines and heroes was greater than the totalitarian approach conveyed. Sheila Fitzpatrick has nicely illustrated the rural wrath felt toward Stalin and the quick vituperative reactions that the leader's name could provoke. Underpinning both the work of Fitzpatrick and Lynne Viola is the notion that rural resistance, in its various forms, to Stalinism was "normal."[96] Moreover, "villains" or "folk devils" on the farms and in official institutions performed a variety of politically unacceptable acts that were widespread, almost endemic in culture and system, and becoming institutionalized into the system fostered by the grindingly slow bureaucratic processes that prevailed. The keener Stakhanovites, like Demchenko and Angelina, continued to sculpt themselves in Hellbeck's sense as keen Stalinist subjects, despite the resistance that they encountered, even on occasion made more resolute by it. Arguably, the resistance could fuel a more determined "working on the self," often aided by the guidance of the *politotdel,* as well as trigger a refusal to do so by those who gave up. Even if Tauger is right that "resistance" has been much exaggerated and that peasants were more hardworking than much of the secondary literature has allowed, it remains that Stakhanovites provoked some hostility and that not all rural leaders encouraged them.

CONCLUSION

Opposition to rural Stakhanovism, then, was complex and multifaceted. In different forms it came "from below," "sideways," and "from above." No neat model captures it. Resistance cannot crudely be reduced to kulak or Trotskyite wrecking, as propaganda attempted to construct it in 1938. Communal and individual resistance to those who were different, deep cultural patterns of envy toward those doing well, patriarchal rejection of changing gender roles, ingrained patterns of rural violence, minimal rural policing topped with hostility to Stakhanovites for prompting increases in output norms, intermingled as relevant factors.[97]

More broadly, rural Stalinism was a system in which Stakhanovites as paragons of superdiligence were ready targets and bore the brunt of larger rural conflicts. They threatened different interests and provoked pent-up outbursts which were linked to some weariness after collectivization, to a hard life in the countryside, to the difficulties of delivering large enough harvests in drought years and in a centrally planned economic system with insufficient inputs, and to the emancipatory challenge to gender hierarchies, all in the context of a deeply embedded culture which did not reward success but resented it.

Inaction from the authorities likewise cannot be reduced to the univariate explanation of "political blindness." Those in positions of responsibility had to take into account prevailing social attitudes, many of which they may have shared; attitudes which went against the grain of official policies and ideology. Not only may kolkhoz chairpersons and state farm directors have disliked those peasants who wished to be significantly different from others since their special status provoked resentment among other peasants, but also upholding official policies may have on occasion been more difficult than flouting them. Farm leaders had their own popularity to take into consideration as well the unpopularity of Stakhanovites. And the high turnover among those in charge of farms reflects not only the purges, but also the undesirability of the job.

NOTES

1. GARF, f. 8131, op. 13, d. 64, l. 267.

2. Pasha Angelina, *My Answer to an American Questionnaire* (Moscow: Foreign Languages Publishing House, 1949), 26.

3. See, for example, James C. Scott, *Weapons of the Weak: Everyday Forms of Peasant Resistance* (New Haven and London: Yale University Press, 1985); and his *Domination and the Arts of Resistance: Hidden Transcripts* (New Haven and London: Yale University Press, 1990).

4. This issue is complex since anger could result from a jumble of emotions which included men angry at new women, particularly at young pioneer upstarts, and ordinary hardworking peasants who fumed at over-enthusiastic norm-busters who seemed to be working to unreasonable excess.

5. I. Vershinin, ed., *Mariia Safronovna Demchenko* (Moscow: Gosudarstvennoe izdatel'stvo politicheskoi literatury, 1938), 8.

6. Vershinin, ed., *Mariia Safronovna Demchenko*, 8.

7. Vershinin, ed., *Mariia Safronovna Demchenko*, 7.

8. Angelina, *My Answer*, 22.

9. Angelina, *My Answer*, 22.

10. Angelina, *My Answer*, 22.

11. Angelina, *My Answer*, 23.

12. GARF, f. 8131, op. 13, d. 64, l. 129.

13. GARF, f. 8131, op. 13, d. 64, l. 129.

14. GARF, f. 8131, op. 13, d. 64, l. 208.

15. GARF, f. 8131, op. 13, d. 64, l. 266.

16. GARF, f. 8131, op. 13, d. 45, l. 10.

17. GARF, f. 8131, op. 13, d. 45, l. 10.

18. *Krest'ianskaia gazeta*, 28 March 1936, 4.

19. *Krest'ianskaia gazeta*, 28 March 1936, 4. Peunkova was not the only one in the district suffering in this way, according to the same edition of *Krest'ianskaia gazeta*. "Hooligans and villains" were also hounding the Stakhanovite and *sel'kor* Tupitsin, but the procuracy had not stirred to do anything about it. Stakhanovite milkmaid Shimaraeva "had undergone every possible mockery" as well. But again this had provoked no action.

20. *Krest'ianskaia gazeta*, 16 April 1936, 2.

21. *Krest'ianskaia gazeta*, 24 April 1936, 3.

22. *Krest'ianskaia gazeta*, 16 April 1936, 2.

23. *Krest'ianskaia gazeta*, 16 April 1936, 2.

24. *Krest'ianskaia gazeta*, 30 March 1936, 1.

25. *Krest'ianskaia gazeta*, 30 December 1937, 4.

26. *Krest'ianskaia gazeta*, 30 December 1937, 4.

27. *Krest'ianskaia gazeta*, 30 December 1937, 4.

28. *Krest'ianskaia gazeta*, 6 January 1939, 2.

29. *Krest'ianskaia gazeta*, 18 March 1937, 2.

30. *Krest'ianskaia gazeta*, 16 April 1936, 2.

31. *Krest'ianskaia gazeta*, 14 October 1936, 3.

32. *Krest'ianskaia gazeta*, 14 October 1936, 3.

33. *Krest'ianskaia gazeta*, 18 March 1937, 2.

34. *Krest'ianskaia gazeta*, 10 May 1937, 1.

35. *Krest'ianskaia gazeta*, 14 May 1937, 3.

36. *Krest'ianskaia gazeta*, 14 May 1937, 3. Similarly, brigade leader Volishin who had been decorated with a medal, complained, "the leaders of Leningrad MTS do not consider it their duty to care about this brigade and do not help Stakhanovites in their work." See *Krest'ianskaia gazeta*, 16 May 1937, 2. Tractor drivers in Krutinskii raion, Omsk oblast, had similarly bitter words. The MTS director was accused of not paying Stakhanovites enough and of giving them too few products. Their tractors were also repaired late and the director showed bad leadership. See *Krest'ianskaia gazeta*, 8 March 1937, 7.

37. *Krest'ianskaia gazeta*, 18 March 1937, 3.

38. *Krest'ianskaia gazeta*, 28 March 1936, 4.

39. *Krest'ianskaia gazeta*, 18 March 1936, 3.

40. *Krest'ianskaia gazeta*, 30 March 1936, 1.

41. *Krest'ianskaia gazeta*, 16 April 1936, 2. ·

42. *Krest'ianskaia gazeta*, 30 March 1936, 1.

43. *Krest'ianskaia gazeta*, 8 April 1936, 2.

44. *Krest'ianskaia gazeta*, 8 April 1936, 2.

45. Smolensk Archive, Alexander Baykov Library, University of Birmingham, WKP 202, l. 195.

46. GARF, f. 7689, op. 11, d. 119, l. 33.

47. Smolensk Archive, WKP 202, l. 195.

48. GARF, f. 8131, op. 13, d. 50, l. 69.

49. GARF, f. 8131, op. 13, d. 64, l. 230.

50. GARF, f. 8131, op. 13, d. 64, l. 230.

51. *Krest'ianskaia gazeta*, 16 April 1936, 2.

52. P. Angelina, *Liudi Kolkhoznykh Polei* (Moscow and Leningrad: Gosudarstven-noe izdatel'stvo detskoi literatury, 1952), 13.

53. Evidence from numerous conversations with friends and acquaintances in the Gorbachev era and after.

54. Roberta T. Manning, "Women in the Soviet Countryside on the Eve of World War II, 1935–1940," in *Russian Peasant Women*, eds. Beatrice Farnsworth and Lynne Viola (New York: Oxford University Press, 1992), 220.

55. GARF, f. 8131, op. 13, d. 45, l. 9.

56. Angelina, *My Answer*, 26.

57. Iurii Il'inskii, "Iunaia Stakhanovka," in *V Budniakh Velikikh Stroek: zhenshchiny-kommunistki geroini pervykh piatiletok*, ed. L. I. Stishova (Moscow: Politizdat, 1986), 57.

58. GARF, f. 8131, op. 13, d. 64, l. 265.

59. GARF, f. 8131, op. 13, d. 64, l. 209.

60. GARF, f. 8131, op. 13, d. 64, l. 209.

61. GARF, f. 8131, op. 13, d. 64, l. 267.

62. GARF, f. 8131, op. 13, d. 64, l. 267.

63. GARF, f. 8131, op. 13, d. 64, l. 281.

64. GARF, f. 8131, op. 13, d. 64, l. 281.

65. GARF, f. 8131, op. 13, d. 64, l. 281.

66. GARF, f. 8131, op. 13, d. 64, l. 268.

67. *Krasnaia Sibiriachka*, no. 2 (January 1936): 2.

68. A letter to Ordzhonikidze from a technical director in the Donbas pointed out, "unfounded rumors" were circulating among workers about rises in norms due to Stakhanovism. See RGASPI, f. 85, op. 29, d. 704, l. 1.

69. Angelina, *My Answer*, 43.

70. Il'inskii, "Iunaia Stakhanovka," 58.

71. Il'inskii, "Iunaia Stakhanovka," 58.

72. *Krest'ianskaia gazeta*, 16 December 1936, 4.

73. Smolensk Archive, op. cit., WKP 202, l. 195.

74. For murders, see GARF f. 8131, op. 13, d. 50, ll. 88–90 and f. 8131, op. 13, d. 45, l. 27. For a curious case of Stakhanovites dying in a building that collapsed, see GARF f. 8131, op. 13, d. 40, l. 23. On suicide see f. 8131, op. 13, d. 40, l.24.

75. GARF, f. 8131, op. 13, d. 45, l. 27.

76. GARF, f. 7689, op. 11, d. 119, l. 33.

77. GARF, f. 7689, op. 11, d. 119, l. 33.

78. GARF, f. 8131, op. 13, d. 40, l. 47.

79. GARF, f. 8131, op. 13, d. 45, l. 3.

80. GARF, f. 8131, op. 13, d. 45, l. 16ob.

81. GARF, f. 8131, op. 13, d. 45, l. 19.
82. GARF, f. 8131, op. 13, d. 64, l. 208.
83. GARF, f. 8131, op. 13, d. 64, l. 279.
84. GARF, f. 8131, op. 13, d. 64, l. 207.
85. GARF, f. 8131, op. 13, d. 64, ll. 261–62.
86. GARF, f. 8131, op. 13, d. 64, l. 263.
87. GARF, f. 8131, op. 13, d. 64, l. 264.
88. GARF, f. 9492, op. 1, d. 14, l. 5.
89. GARF, f. 9492, op. 1, d. 14, l. 5.
90. GARF, f. 9492, op. 1, d. 14, l. 6
91. GARF, f. 8131, op. 13, d. 64, l. 128.
92. Carl J. Friedrich and Zbigniew K. Brzezinski, *Totalitarian Dictatorship and Autocracy,* 2nd revised ed. (New York: Praeger, 1972), 279.
93. Mark Tauger, "Soviet Peasants and Collectivization, 1930–1939: Resistance and Adaptation," *Journal of Peasant Studies* 31, nos. 3–4 (April and July 2004): 427–56.
94. Moshe Lewin, *Soviet Society in the Making* (London: Methuen, 1985).
95. Moshe Lewin, "On Soviet Industrialization," in *Social Dimensions of Soviet Industrialization*, eds. William Rosenberg and Lewis Siegelbaum (Bloomington: Indiana University Press, 1993), 272.
96. Sheila Fitzpatrick, *Stalin's Peasants: Resistance and Survival in the Russian Village after Collectivization* (New York: Oxford University Press, 1994), 287–96.
97. See Stephan Merl, "Social Mobility in the Countryside," in *Social Dimensions*, eds. Rosenberg and Siegelbaum, 41–62.

Chapter Seven

"Political Blindness" at the Local Level and Purges

Again, sneaking!

—Raikom party secretary to a Stakhanovite[1]

Many complaints lie in oblast organizations for half a year, even a year.[2]
We insist on urgent investigation.

—Editors at *Krest'ianskaia gazeta* to local procuracy[3]

Alongside the peasants who mocked and threatened Stakhanovites were two other sorts of villains whom *Krest'ianskaia gazeta* condemned. Guilty of "political blindness" (*politicheskaia slepota*) were farm leaders who through indifference and inaction held back Stakhanovites' progress and local party secretaries and governmental officials who failed to do something about this laxness when informed. "Politically blind" became an ideological label used to categorize those who did not appear to understand party policies or to grasp interpretations by the party of current events. Quite simply the "politically blind" did not "see" and so worked badly, whether through poor political education, sloth, or ineptness. Without speedy enlightenment, they were in danger of becoming "enemies" and caught up in the swirling of the purges.

STAKHANOVISM IN THE CONTEXT OF THE PURGES

Stakhanovism was used in the purge process as an indicator of loyalty to the system. Those who harmed it or who failed to promote it were ripe for investigation, job loss, expulsion from the party, arrest, trial, and punishment. If the "politically blind" who failed to help Stakhanovites did not mend their ways fast, they would be branded opponents of Soviet socialism and "enemies of the people." The Stakhanovite movement thus became a mechanism for identifying those who deserved to be purged as well as an attempt to harness peasants to work harder. Stakhanovites in industry and in agriculture became foils or weapons in struggles against the weak management of factories, farms, districts, and oblasts, and also agents of criticism and change, often to the benefit of other workers and peasants as well as to themselves.[4] Peter H. Solomon has documented how procurators received instructions to prosecute all forms of opposition to the "holy breed" of Stakhanovites and that physical attacks against them qualified as political crimes.[5]

At the district level, research by Roberta T. Manning has shown that many grass roots communists "supported, promoted and accepted" the criticisms made of officials and their persecutions.[6] There was indeed unreliability and sloppiness in the administration of many districts and a poor running of many farms, indicating that practices in the localities were in need of serious rectification. J. Arch Getty has made a case for disorganization in the regions and Chris Ward has made the point that by 1935 it had been discovered that "local files were in a mess" reflecting a degree of disorder and chaos.[7]

The *chistka*, or "cleansing," of enemies had been integral to the logic of the Leninist vanguard party, bred in its clandestine role under tsarism and confirmed in its necessity by civil war after the Revolution and by opponents of Bolshevik policies. Purges in 1921, 1924–1925, and 1928–1930 meant that expulsions from the party had become institutionalized.[8] Stalin, however, calibrated the purge to such a high level of intensity that it took on a qualitatively different form, crescendoing in the Great Purge in 1936–1938.[9]

In was in this wider context of accusation and its associated narratives on sabotage, wrecking, "terrorist attack" on Sergei Kirov, alleged plots to kill Stalin and other leaders, and on conspiracies fomented by Zinovievites, Trotskyites, and Rightists that *Krest'ianskaia gazeta* exposed inept farm managements for erecting "barriers" to Stakhanovite work methods and acted as a serious political troubleshooter against them, citing examples of neglected Stakhanovites as justifications for condemnation.

The political priorities of a given purge year and month fashioned the observations that *Krest'ianskaia gazeta*'s editors made and shaped its own scripts and narratives. In 1936, *Krest'ianskaia gazeta* labeled persistent opponents of Stakhanovism, like former kolkhoz chair Belichenko, as "kulaks" and "enemies of Stakhanovism."[10] In 1937 as the Great Purge unfolded, *Krest'ianskaia gazeta* increasingly linked the baitings of Stakhanovites to "enemies of the people" at work, in particular to Trotskyists who were also responsible for laxness in local party organizations.[11] By the end of 1937,

Krest'ianskaia gazeta blamed "irresponsible attitudes to complaints" upon the failure to look into "residues of bands of Trotskyite-Bukharin wreckers."[12] *Krest'ianskaia gazeta* informed readers that supporters of Trotsky and Bukharin were active in Donets oblast, evidenced by the fact that editors had forwarded 400 peasants' letters of complaint to raion and oblast, but only 174 had been researched.[13]

During 1938 extensive front-page coverage was given to trials of putative "spies and murderers," namely, Lev Kamenev, Mikhail Tomskii, and Nikolai Bukharin.[14] This affected the atmosphere of the paper and shaped other articles about how districts struggled badly with local enemies.[15] *Krest'ianskaia gazeta* made a direct link between the "Trotskyist-Bukharin hirelings of fascism and bourgeois nationalists" and opposition to Stakhanovism.[16] More generally, these hirelings caused "much harm in all branches of the economy and in agriculture" where "they impeded the Stakhanovite movement in every way, trying to wreck it" and tried to deter a mass movement "for a high Stalinist harvest."[17] On the third anniversary of the Stakhanovite movement, *Krest'ianskaia gazeta* announced, "We are still far from liquidating everywhere the consequences of hostile sabotage."[18] This persisted into November 1938 with claims that "The foul agents of fascism—Trotskyist-Bukharinite degenerates are trying in every way to put a brake on the Stakhanovite movement."[19] Although, on 19 January 1938, the Central Committee had adopted a resolution that condemned "excesses" in the repression of local communists and the purge process began to wind down, its concepts and discourse were still used in *Krest'ianskaia gazeta*.[20] One reason for this was the fact that the purges did not magic away the numerous problems faced by Stakhanovites.

Attacks on People's Commissariats were part of the purges. In 1937, Mikhail Chernov, Commissar of Narkomzem (*Narodnyi Kommissariat Zemledeliia*, or People's Commissariat of Agriculture), was arrested and subsequently shot.[21] In 1938 various charges were made against Narkomzem, including the criticism that in the RSFSR it openly "deceived" the state about plan fulfillment.[22] This was cited as evidence of "hostility to socialism."[23] In keeping with the barrage of criticism, *Krest'ianskaia gazeta* contended "Narkomzem of the USSR, workers of agricultural organs and agricultural science often still do not give the necessary help to Stakhanovites and to shock workers."[24] This coincided with considerable reassessment of Narkomzem within the party. A secret report on Narkomzem's apparat and local organs, sent to Andrei Andreev (then Secretary of the Central Committee), argued how "badly" they worked and held that "politically doubtful people" were still employed in it.[25] The Council of People's Commissars (Sovnarkom) and the Central Committee drew up a draft resolution on necessary changes to be made in Narkomzem.[26]

A special gathering in the Central Committee *apparat* discussed the problems of Narkomzem's structure and decision-making apparatus, indicating that it was overloaded, unwieldy, overspecialized, and overcentralized.[27] Castigations of Narkomzem by *Krest'ianskaia gazeta* were thus in keeping with the mood in top party echelons and, of course, inspired by them. Ineptness in the land departments, which were Narkomzem's local organs, did not make this task difficult for editors.

Amid the heightening tensions from waves of purges into the Great Purge, editors cast the newspaper as "folk hero" ever prepared to take up maligned Stakhanovites' causes against bungling kolkhoz chairpersons and state farm directors. Editors made peasants' complaints public for its readers by discussing them in its pages and behind the scenes they routinely sent complaints to the local party, procuracy, NKVD, land department, or whomever they deemed relevant, calling for action. If editors were not satisfied at the district level, they would refer a case of "political blindness" up to the next administrative level in the oblast, or region, noting lethargy in the district. The press presented itself as the champion of the Stakhanovites' cause. Editors constructed an image of honest reporters, there to expose wrongdoing, to chase negligence, and to battle against indifference, fear, and irresponsibility. If cadres and local officials would not "decide everything" correctly, as Stalin called upon them to do, then editors and *sel'kory* would.

Thus the role of the rural press extended way beyond that of reporter, constructor of images, and deliverer of political messages. Editors amounted to political actors who passed on information about the countryside to other institutions, checked what they did about it, and were ready to inform the secret police of inappropriate behavior. In this sense they were servants of party policy, particularly of campaigns to attack managements, purge wreckers, and cleanse the state of Trotskyites. The paper's archive does not show any direct links between editors and figures on the Politburo concerning these matters, but its vigilant eye on how district bosses behaved fitted the general atmosphere of condemnation coming out of the apex of the system. Pursuing these lines of inquiry, editors had some autonomy in deciding which cases to take seriously and which to doubt. Peasants themselves came to see the paper as an avenue of exposure and facilitator of attack against others, sometimes out of malice as well as rightful charge. *Krest'ianskaia gazeta*'s editors were well aware that attempts to settle old scores were integral to the system of informing on others. As upholders of "socialist morality" their task was to push for investigations to establish the truth.[28]

The charge of "political blindness" applied to several misdemeanors in the local party: neglecting to punish irresponsible farm leaders or to correct their wrongdoings; claiming that incriminating evidence had never reached them; failing to investigate attacks on Stakhanovites or to defend them against sabotage; making a show of supporting Stakhanovism but, in effect, of doing nothing in a practical way to help Stakhanovites attain higher targets. Emphasis in the press fell on what local leaders failed to achieve without asking the question whether the local resources were available to enable them to succeed. The widespread suggestion was that the system itself was not at fault, but those who worked in it were to blame.

Although it is extremely difficult to track all the accusations made by editors against local cadres through to their final outcomes, it is possible to identify what it said publicly, whom the press informed in the district, and how the cases were presented, enabling a categorization of complaints.

THE PRESS PUBLICLY EXPOSES LAX LOCAL LEADERSHIP

On 30 March 1936, in a front-page lead article, *Krest'ianskaia gazeta* launched a series of exposés of lax action by party officials and kolkhoz chairpersons. It called upon both "carefully to read the publication in our paper of disgraceful attitudes towards the Stakhanovite movement" and "to check" whether their farms were guilty. This was followed by a warning: "And all those who have still not understood the full seriousness of the Stakhanovite movement must hurry to change their shameful attitude towards it. The party will not tolerate facts such as those published in our paper."[29] The loud message from *Krest'ianskaia gazeta* was that those who sabotaged Stakhanovism "should be defeated."[30]

The date of this edition is important. On top of the aforementioned purges of the 1920s, the early 1930s had seen purges come in waves; a party verification procedure and exchange of party cards had already taken place. There had also been since 1928 show trials of the *Shakty* case, "Industrial case," and Menshevik trial up to the Metro-Vickers case in 1933. Robert Tucker calls these "mere curtain raisers" to the big purge trials of 1937 and 1938.[31] In mid-1930 the Sixteenth Party Congress had blamed local areas for industrial and agricultural failures and at the beginning of 1934 Stalin had complained to the Seventeenth Party Congress about sabotage and wreckers—frequently euphemisms for mismanagement—again criticizing local cadres for failing to follow party orders and for ignoring local complaints. Kirov had been murdered in December 1934 and tension seriously built thereafter. Significantly, *Krest'ianskaia gazeta*'s exposés also fell immediately before a secret Central Committee circular of 29 July "On the Terrorist Activities of the Trotskyite-Zinovievite Counter-Revolutionary Bloc."[32] Although the archive does not contain any letters from Politburo level urging editors to follow this course, it does not follow that instructions were not issued, and it is not accidental that editors launched the attack at this moment. One can interpret the newspaper's condemnations of district parties as a political signal that more was to come. Manning has also observed that crop failure in 1936 contributed to the persecution of local elites and that "political shake-ups in the localities began in earnest in June as short food supplies caused by the crop failure reached their zenith on the eve of the new harvest."[33] Purges had administrative and economic reasons underpinning their timing and orchestration, as well as political ones.[34]

THE RHETORICAL ONSLAUGHT

Krest'ianskaia gazeta began its onslaught on district party secretaries by a series of rhetorical questions. These became the hallmark of each exposure and attack. How, editors asked, should the behavior of Comrade Dobrychev in Bogorodskii raion of Gor'kii krai be assessed? Why had this local party leader done absolutely nothing about the fact that Galina Maiorova's kolkhoz chairperson had failed to give her enough animal feed to meet her target of milking on average 4,500 litres from each cow and had also scoffed at her?[35] How could such inaction be justified? "What can the secretary of Kholmzhirkovskii party committee in the Western oblast say," went on editors, to explain how they failed to praise the Stakhanovite Ruzhentsova on International Women's Day?[36] Continuing to punch across its attacks on local party cadres, editors pondered "what can the party secretary in Varvarovskii raikom of Odessa oblast say" to explain why the tractor brigade leader Shinkarchuk could not work because for "several days tractors stood idle because no one brought fuel?"[37] How, too, could the party secretary of Soldatsko-Aleksandrovskii raikom in the Northern Caucasus answer for the lack of organized study for Stakhanovites?[38]

A series of rhetorical questions like these, which quickly followed one upon the heels of the other, came across to the reader like a round of ammunition firing at its targets. Rhetorical questions became the newspaper's style when it named and shamed. Sentences were staccato in their blast, made all the more effective by the range of examples. The theme that held them together was that local party organizations had been informed about problems on farms, and then knowingly ignored them.

INACTION, "BUREAUCRATIC SHELVING,"
AND FAILURE TO INVESTIGATE IN THE DISTRICT

A usual pattern was for Stakhanovites or a group of peasants to complain to editors about farm leaders and for *Krest'ianskaia gazeta* to pass on the information to the party and procuracy. In November 1935, for instance, a group of peasants on the First of May collective farm in Uspenskii district of Azovo-Chernomore krai complained to *Krest'ianskaia gazeta* that farm leaders Zinchuk and Koriakov suppressed criticism, plundered the farm's grain, and persecuted rural correspondents. Editors accordingly informed the raikom and district procuracy on 22 November. On 3 December the raikom secretary, Comrade Saut, was sent a telegram from *Krest'ianskaia gazeta* asking what steps he had taken. Editors reported that neither the local party committee nor the secretary of the raikom had responded to this letter or to a subsequent letter.[39]

Ever vigilant, *Krest'ianskaia gazeta* informed the Party Control Commission of the krai, or territory, a higher administrative level. When questioned by the Commission, Saut claimed that he had not received a complaint from the First of May farm. *Krest'ianskaia gazeta* then sent Saut copies of all the complaints. The paper noted that "only after this" did the district procuracy take legal action against the farm leaders.[40] Little, however, had changed in the raikom. Next the party ignored a letter from the collective farm worker Bondareva. She had exposed "a whole series of scandalous abuses on the part of the collective farm leadership."[41] This information had been lying in the raikom since July. Once again, raikom secretary Saut had failed to investigate. His crime, suggested the paper, was "bureaucratic shelving" (*biuokraticheskii marinovat'*).[42]

The archive does not hold evidence of communication between editors and the top political leadership about the desirability of chasing particular district or oblast party committees. If consultation took place, or if instructions were given, records were not kept. Discussion of particular cases could also have taken place over the telephone. It is more than likely, however, that the vast majority of cases were routinely pursued as they were brought to editors' attention.

Krest'ianskaia gazeta reported numerous claims that letters of complaint had not been received by party officials when, in fact, they had.[43] Such behavior was also labeled "callous-bureaucratic" and "troublesome." Kirovskii raion was selected for being especially bad, with party, land department, oblast procuracy, and obliispolkom, or oblast soviet committee, all at fault for not reading letters of complaint.[44] Thus results from the oblast, which was meant to be overseeing the localities beneath it in the administrative hierarchy, were not necessarily any more productive than from the district. *Krest'ianskaia gazeta* moaned, "many complaints lie in oblast organizations for half a year, even a year" and "many complaints are lost."[45]

The most common instances of "bureaucratic shelving" in the district, oblast, and krai involved ignoring letters, pretending they had never been received or dealing with complaints slowly. The final charge meted out by editors that topped these three was that of a "whitewashing" of events. The party and procuracy, in these instances, would concoct false stories in their own defense.[46]

WEAK EXCUSES AND FEAR OF BOSSY FARM LEADERS

Krest'ianskaia gazeta made specific attacks on "weak excuses" given by local officials for failing to look into problems. In Korsuinskii raion, Kiev oblast, Stakhanovites' complaints were met with "we are reconstructing ourselves" as an excuse for inaction from the deputy chair of the raiispolkom (district soviet executive committee).[47] *Krest'ianskaia gazeta* observed that while "reconstructing" was going on "valuable time passes, the sowing period goes by." Then hot days come and "the land dries out," making it "hard for the 1,000ers and the 500ers to begin the sowing."[48] Moreover, without enough horses and manure the land cannot be prepared in time. "Reconstructing ourselves" suggested the paper also meant inattention to the "shameful facts of exceptional irresponsibility and slipshodness" at harvest time.[49]

The press also suggested that, in some cases, fear in the raikom of farm leaders who bullied peasants was the reason behind inaction. Kolkhoz Chairperson Skliarov, for example, had failed to organize feed for the animals on his farm, an increasing number of whom died. When peasants pressed him for feed, he cursed them. Skliarov also sold the farm's bread supply.[50] In this case, hypothesized *Krest'ianskaia gazeta*, fear of Skliarov in the raikom prevented action against him. *Kolkhoznitsa* also described how a farm chairperson had terrorized his farm for five years, beaten peasants, and suppressed all criticism. Apparently he had kept his job only because of the "lack of political concern" in the raikom.[51]

When exposing bullying by chairpersons who ran farms like violent and dictatorial fiefdoms, the press urged local party secretaries to be decisive, firm, and responsible in their actions, rather than cowed or indifferent. Indeed "indifference" to such problems was a common charge.

UNPRODUCTIVE PERSONAL VISITS

In despair about their problems, some Stakhanovites called personally on the district party secretary. This, however, could backfire. When, for example, Dar'ia Pastukhova went to the raikom, upset that her team's produce on show at a local exhibition had not been attributed to them, the party secretary greeted her with "Again, sneaking!" and told her he did not wish her ever to return to his office.[52] Prior to that the krai newspaper *Kolkhoznaia Pravda* had taken up an earlier persecution she had suffered, but district organizations had insisted on a "peaceful solution."[53] *Krest'ianskaia gazeta* exposed this chain of events and noted that as a consequence of not being taken seriously, Pastukhova left to live in a neighboring district. A personal visit had made no difference to the district's response.[54]

That Stakhanovites were branded "sneaks" indicates that they were viewed as self-righteous upholders of new rules and norms, prepared to "tell on" those who broke them to those in positions of authority and keen to highlight their own goodness.

ALL DISTRICT ORGANIZATIONS REFUSE TO HELP

It often happened that not just one local organization failed to help Stakhanovites, but everyone they approached. *Krest'ianskaia gazeta* drew attention to the fact that 500ers in Alekseevskii raion of Khar'kov oblast had complained to the kolkhoz adminstration, to the agronomist, the MTS, and the local land department that their achievements were being ignored. But none of them "paid any attention to the 500ers."[55] A regular complaint about the MTS was that its leaders failed to give spare parts or refused to permit socialist competition. The press reported, "district organizations saw all this" but failed to change local behavior, thereby "not helping Stakhanovites, as they should."[56] Similarly, in the Smolensk archive one finds letters from *Krest'ianskaia gazeta* to district party secretaries along the lines of "Such a significant flood of complaints [to *Krest'ianskaia gazeta*] indicates that the district organizations do not relate to complaints with care."[57] In this particular letter, the paper was complaining about the district executive committee, the raizo, and the procuracy.

Krest'ianskaia gazeta was hot in its criticisms when several organizations neglected spring sowing or harvesting. In Azovo-Chernomore krai, the local party and raizo in Grecheskii district were blackened for not helping collective farms. Criticism ran: "Take seed. Blame lies with the raizo that we have not yet sorted barley and maize." A trip to the district resulted in the message "Wait. The sowing does not start soon."[58] Yet again, inaction, lack of preparation, and procrastination were the accusations.

The epitome of indifference on the part of local officials, according to *Krest'ianskaia gazeta,* was when they were unaware of how many shock workers and Stakhanovites they had in the district. In Starorusskii district, for example, there were hundreds of female Stakhanovites, but the raikom and other local organizations did not have a clue who these women were.[59] Similarly, in Korsuinskii raion, Kiev oblast, *Krest'ianskaia gazeta* reported that the raizo had no record of how many Stakhanovite teams were in its district.[60] Disinterest and sloppy records were to blame, illustrating how procedures of data collection and filing had not improved.

A clear message from the press from 1936 to 1939 was that local party secretaries and procuracies sometimes colluded in the bad behavior of farm leaders by failing to check it and by ignoring many complaints sent to the raikom and to the procuracy; were slow to investigate; were rude to Stakhanovites who visited them; and, like the raizo, often did not bother to keep statistics on the number of local Stakhanovites. The message from the press was that this behavior was not what Stalin expected from his cadres and local officials in relation to Stakhanovism and the battle to produce more food.

What the press failed entirely to raise, however, was whether it was always possible for farm leaders and district officials to meet Stakhanovites' demands. Discourse covered failings rather than whether or not they could easily be addressed. This was a non-topic, but clearly a highly relevant question.

THE PARTY CELEBRATES STAKHANOVISM, THEN NEGLECTS IT

Prominent among *Krest'ianskaia gazeta*'s charges against local parties was that they would participate enthusiastically in festive celebrations of Stakhanovism at which they would publicly promise help for Stakhanovites, yet the fanfare turned out to be formal and the promises merely empty. When the pig tender Filippova returned to her village after receiving the Order of Lenin in Moscow at a Conference of Advanced Workers in Animal Husbandry, she was met with festive splendor. There to greet her were the raikom party secretary, the raikom Komsomol secretary, the chair of the district executive committee, and the head of the raizo: "Then the brass band rang out! What speeches did the district leaders deliver! They squeezed Filippova's hand, exalted her, and vowed to help her to create wonderful work conditions."[61] But when the band had stopped playing and the applause had died down, "the district leaders went home. And comrade Filippova no longer saw the leaders of the district, nor their help and concern."[62] When the party secretary was later informed of the maltreatment of Filippova by *kolkhozniki*, "he shrugged his shoulders." No one from district organizations bothered to visit her in order to discover firsthand what her working conditions were until *Krest'ianskaia gazeta* put pressure on the party secretary.[63]

More pointedly, *Krest'ianskaia gazeta* also observed that local party bosses were often happy to be in the limelight alongside Stakhanovites and to participate in any perks, but when hard work was required they made themselves scarce.[64] This was graphically clear in the case of the raikom secretary in Petrovskii district of the Northern Caucasus who was happy to take brigade leader Istoshin to give talks but when the sowing started, Istoshin regretted that he had no bedding, no trailer hands, no work norms, no fuel norms, and that "the whole brigade lived for several days in the cold on the steppe and only on the twelfth day did a sleeping wagon appear."[65] How, asked *Krest'ianskaia gazeta*, could the party secretary's behavior be vindicated?[66]

Farm leaders, specialists, directors of the MTS, district party organizations, and commissariats could all happily join in celebrations for Stakhanovites, editors noted, thereby giving orchestrated acclaim, but their promises rang hollow.

LENGTHY INVESTIGATIONS
BY THE PARTY AND THE PROCURACY

One repeated complaint was that when the party and the procuracy finally did choose to act, they conducted lengthy investigations, often too slow in their results to help the Stakhanovites in difficulty. In the case of Stakhanovite Filippova, the party secretary finally asked the procuracy to examine what had been happening. After three visits by an investigator, the work was still not complete.[67] Next came officials from the *raizo* who researched the situation on the farm and liaised with a representative from the *oblzo* (oblast land department). The procrastinating conclusion drawn was that "further investigation" was needed. *Krest'ianskaia gazeta* underscored that: "While district organizations carry out research, the persecution of Comrade Filippova is intensifying."[68]

Likewise, by the time Melan'ia Slesarenko's case finally reached the district procurator who then visited the kolkhoz and confirmed the complaints received, she had already been harassed many times. The district referred the case to the oblast procurator who requested "supplementary information." After the district procurator had carried out further investigations, the offending Belichenko was finally dismissed.[69] When, however, Belichenko subsequently burned down Slesarenko's house, the district militia proceeded slowly in its inquiries. *Krest'ianskaia gazeta* published the story two months after the fire, noting that the head of the militia, Chernyshev, was still looking into it and that "the criminals have not yet been punished. Belichenko with his drinking company continues his kulak business." Such villains were frequently branded "kulaks" in keeping with the predominant discourse of ideological slurs. Tying the episode into attacks on cadres that were part of the purges, *Krest'ianskaia gazeta* concluded, "Leaders of the district are not anxious about the acts of enemies of the Stakhanovite movement."[70] During the purges this was a serious charge since it was tantamount to accusing cadres of colluding in enemy behavior.

The Smolensk archive confirms the pattern of protracted investigations or no action. Documents illustrate how the party made lists of cases that it referred to the procuracy. A column titled "result of investigation" indicated the current stage of inquiry. In 1937, one set of maltreatments of Stakhanovites in Sychevskii raion (which included smashing Stakhanovites' windows, verbal abuse, and murder) showed a substantial number "not investigated."[71] While protracted investigations in legal cases may obtain across political systems and across historical periods, especially since evidence needs to be carefully prepared, the labyrinthine and overlapping structures of Soviet socialism acted as a brake on swift decisions, especially since officials often hesitated to act out of fear of making an error. This was one of the sharp contradictions of the Stalinist purges. Officials needed to be seen to act against wrongdoing, but the sheer fear of acting inappropriately as it could prompt their own purge itself could deter action. But this inaction carried the risk of being punishable for failing to stamp out class enemies. Officials could be damned either way. Some responded to this predicament by being hypervigilant, itself liable to be condemned for "excess."

KREST'IANSKAIA GAZETA AS SAVIOR OF STAKHANOVITES

Krest'ianskaia gazeta portrayed its *sel'kory* as "rescuers" of maligned Stakhanovites and as "saviors" of morally upright peasants who were keen to work hard but who were suffering injustice. Stakhanovites in need of protection were couched as victims, either of "resistance to Stakhanovism," of "political blindness," or of more serious action by class enemies, kulaks, lingering Socialist Revolutionaries (S.R.s), and religious sects.

Only thanks to *Krest'ianskaia gazeta*, the paper trumpeted, did the milkmaid Ol'ga Peunkova reach a hospital. She had become so distressed at the reluctance of anyone to investigate the murder of her two cows that her health started to suffer. She lay ill, but "no one from the collective farm or from district organizations came to help her."[72] Working with the procuracy of the RSFSR, *Krest'ianskaia gazeta* ensured that those responsible were arrested.[73] In the case of Stakhanovite pig-tender Filippova, *Krest'ianskaia gazeta* exposed the bureaucratic delays and inertia of investigating her situation at the district level and finally appealed to the Procuracy of the RSFSR to intervene. The clear message to readers was that without *Krest'ianskaia gazeta,* there would have been no positive outcome. In the cases of both Peunkova and Filippova, editors at *Krest'ianskaia gazeta* saw that badgering the district procuracies was unproductive. For action, the procuracy at republican level had to be called upon to sort out the inefficient districts.

Krest'ianskaia gazeta triumphantly reported the just punishments resulting from its exposés. Investigations following the newspaper's uncovering of persecution against Stakhanovites in Iaroslavl' oblast, for example, had ended in five- and three-year sentences for the kolkhoz chairperson and another farm leader. A guilty milkmaid was given two years. *Krest'ianskaia gazeta* insisted that the verdicts "were met with great approval."[74] Again, coming during the purges, these verdicts served to inform readers of what might happen to wrongdoers. The widespread approval, however, excluded farm leaders not always able to help Stakhanovites as the regime and *Krest'ianskaia gazeta* pressed them to do.[75]

KREST'IANSKAIA GAZETA PASSES INFORMATION TO PARTY COMMITTEES

Out of sight from readers, *Krest'ianskaia gazeta* liaised with the party and procuracy, informing them of cases of sabotage and negligence on farms and calling for investigation. Those letters that have been preserved indicate the sorts of issues they raised, how they were couched, and the kinds of pressures editors attempted to exert. Editors played the roles of troubleshooters, political agitators, informers, champions of justice, and even controllers since they demanded responses from the party. In the climate of purges, local parties needed to explain themselves and to account for what they had and had not done. Editors cashed in on this discourse, themselves needing to show their own vigilance in chasing a party system and procuracy that should have been defending Stakhanovites from local abuse. Moreover, to be in possession of letters of complaint from peasants and not to pass them on would have made editors themselves vulnerable to the charges of indifference and inaction that they regularly directed at others.

Although the paper's archive does not carry letters from the apex of the political system telling editors to pay special attention to particular districts, wider news of "crimes" would alert editors to which districts were vulnerable at a given time and already under scrutiny. They would know which districts were "safer" to challenge as part of a tide of exposure. It is possible

that telephone calls from on high also instructed them to follow developments in some areas rather than others, but there is no evidence of this on
record. Whether editors acted solely in response to the peasants' letters that
reached them or with political prompting as well cannot be established.

Typical of the letters available is one sent to a district party secretary in
Gor'kii oblast, informing "the kolkhoz chair and brigade leader Novikov are
impeding the work of Stakhanovites." Editors told how "in every possible
way the authority and strength of Gamazurova's Stakhanovite team is undermined, workdays are written off and sowing is done on Stakhanovites' strips
of land."[76] Editors elaborated that the kolkhoz leadership had also drawn
close relatives into the running of the farm and that "abuse, embezzlement
and self-supply" were flourishing. The newspaper's head of the Department
of Rural Correspondents and Letters, Tsybtarova, along with Instructor Bar-
sukov, requested that the party "check these signals and take measures to
bring the collective farm into a healthy state. Please inform the editors of the
results."[77] The press not only passed on information, but demanded notifica-
tion of the outcome of action. Given the severe loss of horses due to the
slaughter of animals during collectivization, anything which held back horse
teams was particularly sensitive, with copies of complaints going to the party
and the procuracy.[78]

Tsybtarova and Instructor Medvedev in the Department of *Sel'kory* and
Letters also preoccupied themselves with events on Machine Tractor Stations
(MTS). They wrote to the party secretary in Mogilevskii raion, Belorussia,
enclosing a copy of a letter from Comrade Taborko and other combine drivers on Kazumirovskii Machine Tractor Station (MTS) detailing how their
MTS director did not direct them "nor create conditions for Stakhanovite
work."[79] The editors ended with "we request that you check the facts indicated in the letter and give appropriate pointers to Comrade Bliumin, the director of the MTS. Please inform us of the measures taken."[80] In this instance,
editors are educators of the party secretary. They tell him what to do and that
he should, in turn, educate the director of the MTS in how to behave. From
one perspective, editors were part of an "educating chain" that spread from
cadre to cadre.

Sometimes the letters of complaint sent by peasants to editors were extremely long and were passed on in their entirety to the local party, generally
freshly typed at *Krest'ianskaia gazeta*. Especially clear evidence had to be
passed on if the charge involved accusations of "enemy of the people" as the
newspaper had itself to protect as well as its peasant readers to defend. Vasilii
Mavrin, on behalf of Grishin, wrote one such long letter, almost six typed
pages. The latter had been removed from his job by the collective farm management and declared "an enemy of the people and thief." Mavrin made a

long case that in his view this was "not true and a criminal act."[81] Zhukov at *Krest'ianskaia gazeta* informed Muchkanskii raikom in Voronezh oblast that Grishin was a Stakhanovite and also a candidate for the All-Union Agricultural Exhibition. In the paper's estimation there were "major abuses" here requiring "urgent measures." Zhukov asked the raikom to respond to both the newspaper and to Mavrin.[82]

Frequently complaints from the press to the raikom concerned problems broader than the obstruction of Stakhanovism, embracing drunkenness and poor behavior. Tsybtarova and Instructor Poliakov revealed to the party secretary of Ladyzhskii district in Kiev oblast that on the Bol'shevik collective farm "Comrade Svistovenko indicates that the chair of the collective farm, Onishchenk, works appallingly badly." Allegedly, "instead of [providing] keen and efficient leadership of the sugar beet harvest, he drinks heavily and conducts himself indecently among collective farmers. Such a state of affairs is patently abnormal."[83] Confirmation of Svistovenko's claims and "appropriate measures" were requested. Complaints about drunken and disorderly collective farm leaders were common and *Krest'ianskaia gazeta* regularly pressed for investigations into its consequences.[84]

The district party secretary was accountable for bad farms. If district representatives had not been seen on farms, *Krest'ianskaia gazeta* was quick to note the absence. In a letter to Fedorovskii raion of Kustanai oblast in Kazakhstan editors regretted that "no mass agitation is being conducted amongst the population" and that "for all of 1938" district representatives had not been spotted.[85] Editors commented, "there is no party organization in the village soviet, not even party members." Despite this lack, "a series of advanced collective farmers" were preparing to join the party's ranks but "the raikom extends them no help."[86] The dearth of party members in remoter rural areas did indeed mean that Soviet power was not blazoned evenly across the land.

KREST'IANSKAIA GAZETA REPRIMANDS THE PARTY

In some instances, editors at *Krest'ianskaia gazeta* harshly reprimanded the party secretary. A stern letter to the Ekaterinovskii raikom in Saratov oblast from Erionov and Uskov at *Krest'ianskaia gazeta* pointedly declared that:

> You report that "the raikom VKP/B/ is taking measures towards the elimination of abnormalities on the kolkhoz and towards the dismissal from work of incompetent comrades." This answer does not satisfy us. We request that you report specifically which measures you are taking for the removal of disgrace on the "True path" collective farm.[87]

Erionov and Uskov then objected to particular wording in the party secretary's letter. Instead of writing that the veterinary-sanitary inspector's brother had been taken by the NKVD "You apparently should have said that he was arrested for counter-revolutionary work."[88] Anger at the party secretary's response stemmed from his suggestion that Kariachin, the author of the original letter of complaint, "is a real alcoholic" who rarely works properly.[89] Here the party was querying the truth of the allegations made by *Krest'ianskaia gazeta*. So Erionov and Uskov, in turn, questioned the party's veracity.

In this instance, editors became exceedingly angry, exerting renewed pressure on the party.[90] Although the district party had claimed that kolkhoz production figures were good and that the NKVD were looking into matters, Erionov and Uskov took exception to their evidence being queried. They were, however, on fairly solid ground in tackling the party in Saratov oblast. It had been especially criticized in 1937 for harboring "enemies of the people" and party archives provide detailed statistics on the number of "Trotskyite-Zinovievites" and "Rightists" who were excluded from the party.[91]

Other letters in editorial files indicate pressure from *Krest'ianskaia gazeta* whenever its editors were dissatisfied with responses to the information that they had passed on. Typical of these is a curt letter written to the party secretary in Lukhovnitsii raion, Saratov oblast, to the effect that details had already been sent about the collective farm named after Bobkov but a reply was wanting. Thus, "We request that you immediately check the facts indicated in the letter, apply measures and inform the editors of the results."[92]

The tone and content of these letters' criticisms fit the prevailing culture of condemnation that surrounded the purges and were also consistent with the Soviet tradition of apportioning "blame." Either editors felt on extremely strong ground, or a district purge was known to be in motion, or the oblast had given approval, or all three. Editors contacted the obkom when satisfaction was not obtained from the raikom.[93] If the obkom failed to satisfy as well then it, too, was rebuked by the paper.[94]

RESPONSES FROM THE PARTY

Archival documents offer researchers very few neat cases of letters from *Krest'ianskaia gazeta* matched to responses from the party. Rather, many letters on file are either to or from a raikom or an obkom, but furnishing only half of the correspondence of a given case. Frustratingly, many incomplete stories are told.

Archives, however, are obliging in the aforementioned case of Gamazurova's Stakhanovite team. Response from the raikom came exactly one month after

Tsybtarova and Medvedev had written, informing them that the raikom had investigated the complaint and had "led a general meeting of the collective farmers" which "indicated the chair's incorrect attitude towards Stakhanovites as well as the nepotistic selection to the leadership."[95] A second meeting on the kolkhoz was scheduled for the next day to confirm matters and if the situation so demanded, then brigade leader Ageev would be dismissed.[96] This is a neat example of peasant complaint to *Krest'ianskaia gazeta*, followed by contact between editors and raikom, culminating in investigation by the party, action, and reporting back to editors.

In some instances, the raikom reported that justice would be decided in court. In response to a letter received from editors on 5 October 1938, the raikom of Shchuchenskii district in Voronezh oblast wrote in mid-November that the complaints were true. As a consequence a kolkhoz chair, members of the farm administration, and two brigade leaders were removed from their jobs for breaking the rules, for the disintegration of work discipline, for plundering collective property, and for frequent drunkenness.[97]

Sometimes editors at *Krest'ianskaia gazeta* received copies of detailed reports written after the party's investigations. A particularly colorful report from an investigator was sent to Ordzhonikidze raikom in Northern Kazakhstan oblast, with a copy to *Krest'ianskaia gazeta*. Here the "rude" behavior of Mikhailiuk Karpovich, who was given to calling *kolkhozniki* "vermin" and "loafers," was confirmed.[98] It was reported that he picked on Stakhanovite Sidorenkova, whom he called a "parasite." The evidence collected showed that everyone feared Karpovich, only whispering his or her discontent at night. Open criticism was suppressed. Nine men had left the farm due to "improper acts."[99] Karpovich threatened others with words such as "if I had a Nagan revolver, I would shoot you this and every way."[100] He also divided the peasants into two categories—Russians and Kazakhs, calling the Kazakhs "contagious Kirgiz." He would not allow Russians and Kazakhs to eat together. Predictably, many Kazakh families left the farm and the remaining ones hoped to do so as well.[101] On top of all this, Karpovich forbade *kolkhozniki* to go to the cinema or to attend Komsomol meetings. Kolkhoz meetings did not take place and "all law on the kolkhoz was Mikhailiuk" who talked about "my kolkhoz."[102] Such reports constitute excellent descriptions of the extent to which farm bosses wielded power. In this case of especially arbitrary and patriarchal power, many of the party's policies and priorities were flouted or ignored. Stakhanovite status appeared to merit little respect or encouragement. Moreover, Russian prejudices toward a nationality with whom they were meant to share a "friendship of peoples" was evident in Karpovich's discrimination against Kazakhs.

Another type of letter from party committees informed that incorrect information and empty accusations had been passed from peasants to newspaper editors. The raikom in Vinnitsa oblast dismissed one such falsehood, pointing out that the complainant had nothing to do with the farm concerned and was a member of a religious sect waging propaganda in the countryside.[103] In this case, editors accepted the party's findings.

Responses from obkomy are also available. Some of these are terse and efficient, again telling only half the story. Voronezh oblast in two sentences relayed that "the collective letter of a group of collective farmers from the farm named after Kuibyshev concerning sabotage on the kolkhoz has been confirmed. The chairperson of the farm, Churilov has been removed from his job and arrested."[104] Others can be twinned with original complaints. For example, seven months after *Krest'ianskaia gazeta*'s first letter to Voronezh obkom about the "New Life" collective farm, the obkom's Agriculture Department informed editors that a special district commission had been set up to look into the charge of plundering of farm property. Research had shown that the farm's finances were indeed not in order, there had been poor preparations for the animals as winter approached and "a low level of work discipline." As a consequence, the farm's accountant and two storekeepers faced trial.[105]

In some instances the oblast blamed the district for its slow responses. In reply to a letter from editors demanding a swift response about the Kaganovich collective farm since no reply had been forthcoming, the party committee in Vinnitsa oblast first sent a terse note that "an answer will be sent in days" adding that the raikom was responsible for the delay as all the information had been sent to the local level for investigation.[106] A full response was given four days later.[107] Being sent amid purges and turnover among party leaders, many complaints were passed to new party secretaries after the departure of the previous one, adding to delays. Occasionally the obkom informed *Krest'ianskaia gazeta* of this.

THE FLOW OF LETTERS BETWEEN *KREST'IANSKAIA GAZETA* AND THE PROCURACY

Copies of editors' letters to the raikom were usually sent to the procuracy without additional comment. So the procuracy was generally kept abreast of complaints flowing from peasants, via the press, to the party.[108] Letters written directly to the procuracy tended to chase earlier complaints, to request speedy information or, more rarely, to make the procuracy the main agent of investigation with a copy going to the party. Even more rare were cases that editors passed on to the procuracy without channeling a copy through the party as well.[109] Quite why the party was being skirted was never mentioned. It may have been due to the gravity of the situation, in which case procuracy and NKVD would have been deeply involved. It could also have been because the party was negatively implicated in developments concerned, because the local party was in a state of turmoil itself from the purges or simply because editors chose to leave a particular raikom out of the frame.

Illustrative of a direct approach to the procuracy with a copy to the party is a letter to the district procurator in Sok-Karmalinskii district of Orenburg oblast, in which editors, according to their usual formula, "request that you urgently check the facts, take measures and inform the editors of the results."[110] The letter to the procuracy took on the same style as it did in letters to the party. A long letter from peasants about the Voroshilov collective farm, which its authors titled "Chronic drunkenness," was enclosed. It described the daily drunkenness of the farm chairperson, Kirilov, and a thorough lack of work discipline that meant that no one went to work. On the November 7th holiday Kirilov organized "general drunkenness" and the horses went without feed. Whenever anyone challenged Kirilov about his behavior, he replied that he was the boss and if critics were not silent, he would smash their heads.[111]

In this instance, editors may have felt that the procuracy should take the lead over the party since the raikom was responsible for not having checked this disorderliness. The party secretary should have known about such a severe case of daily drinking and threats. Editors may also have thought that the seriousness of the offense required immediate legal action and punishment. Letters from editors to the procuracy demanding swift action on information already sent are extremely numerous.[112]

Preserved letters from the procuracy to the press came from both district and oblast levels. They report the results of investigations, give details of sentences, or query the validity of charges made. A typical example acknowledges receipt of correspondence from "Dawn of the East" collective farm concerning action against Stakhanovites and informs that it "had been sent for investigation," involving the local NKVD.[113] Seen as a serious counterrevolutionary activity, investigation of attacks on Stakhanovites invariably brought in the secret police. A typical response of the results of inquiries relayed that "for rudeness to kolkhozniki and abuse," the chairperson of the Molotov collective farm in Berezovskii village, "was condemned in trial in Bondarskii district on 22 x 1937 to five years deprivation of freedom."[114] District procuracies sent large numbers of letters with details of trial and imprisonment. Similar responses came from oblast-level procuracies.[115] Generally results were passed on without comment.

Complicated cases, however, merited more detailed treatment. A letter came from the procuracy in Vinnitsa oblast, reporting that crimes allegedly performed by Glushenko, chairperson of the Frunze farm, could not be taken to court due to "a lack of sufficient proof," but those responsible for the theft of fuel would stand trial and the veterinary surgeon was to blame for the death of the pigs and had been arrested. Investigation was still taking place into the lack of grain on the farm and this would be held up since the chief storekeeper was at a health resort for two months of treatment. In addition, Prokopenko, who had drawn attention to all of these problems, had himself been arrested, "by organs of the NKVD for counter-revolutionary activity."[116] Caught up in the purges, the complainant was suspected of being a "counter-revolutionary" and so his evidence was immediately untrustworthy. The farm, anyway, appears to have had problems with animal deaths, although in fact these were a "normal" part of rural life and whether these were any worse than the norm cannot be established. Since theft was believed to have occurred, this would be punished. This complex case resulted in some of the charges of "counter-revolutionary" being taken seriously and some pending. With the secret police involved, itself locked into a spiral of arrest and purge, some punishment was inevitable.

Whilst one cannot calculate the proportion of cases referred from *Krest'ianskaia gazeta* that resulted in arrest, trial, and punishment, evidently some did. Differences were indeed made to the running of farms and to individual lives by the newspaper's agitprop role. Where false arrest was alleged, district and oblast procuracies referred cases on to the secret police. A typical response here was "the NKVD is investigating the fact of an illegal arrest."[117] Occasionally the procuracy did not write to editors directly, but merely sent them a copy of a letter sent from one administrative level of the procuracy to another, thereby keeping editors informed of instructions within the procuracy itself.[118]

Sometimes the procuracy deviated from its normally terse style, usually when reporting detailed findings about false accusations. One complainant was found to harbor a grudge against the Rosa Luxemburg collective farm and so the Voronezh oblast procuracy wrote to say that the criticism against the kolkhoz chairperson for "unmercifully beating" peasants was unfounded. Interrogations by the district procuracy showed "absolutely nothing concrete" since bribes, beatings, and the theft of bread were not taking place. Moreover, the farm had harvested the grain in good time and the kolkhoz chairperson had not discredited Komsomol members.[119] In a context of purges, the procuracy too had to make explicit its reasons for certain actions. In a climate where arrests and trials were acceptable, even encouraged, to go against the flow could result in an accusation of lack of vigilance being brought against the procuracy itself. No institution was immune from surveillance, even those who supposedly meted out justice. Thus a careful accounting for actions was necessary.

Known "slanderers" were a nuisance to the system. Again in some detail, the district procurator felt compelled to explain that in the three years he had held his post Kostrykin had written no less than 100 different letters of complaint. In fact, he was a slanderer who falsely described himself as a *sel'kor.* He had himself once been a member of the kolkhoz administration and had been given a two-year sentence for "systematic drunkenness and the plundering of collective farm property."[120] Other peasants on the farm told how Kostrykin disrupted farm work. The procurator indicated the "absurdity" of Kostrykin's defense and commented that should more letters arrive, legal proceedings against Kostrykin would begin.[121] What is interesting about this case is why legal proceedings did not begin immediately. Discretion in individual cases is evident.

Those who complained could be self-interested, making charges that were unfounded and a waste of investigators' time. Attempts to settle old scores, hurt others, or simply create a nuisance were part of the system. Such individuals presented editors with difficulty. Their complaints had to be examined, even if editors suspected them of being groundless. In another such case, editors wrote to the local procuracy stating their dilemma. On the one hand, they were aware of Shipulin's "dishonorable" approach to the reporting of events in the countryside, but simultaneously editors "were obliged to check" his warnings and to forward them to the appropriate district organizations. Feeling vulnerable, editors insisted, "to separate what is correct from what is false—that is the business of the organization which conducts the investigation."[122] Editors asked the procuracy to specify what it had against Shipulin and then this would be used as an "official document" by *Krest'ianskaia gazeta.*[123]

Just as complaints about any aspect of farm life could be unfounded, so, too, could specific complaints about the baiting of Stakhanovites or the failure to encourage Stakhanovite labor. While many of the charges of Stakhanovites were valid, Stakhanovites could use their privileged status to make their voices heard, to urge criticism of a disliked farm leader, or to extract perks from the system. Those who wrote letters of complaint had varied motivations, ranging from altruism, concern for the collective good and a righting of unjust wrongs, to self-interest, spite, and revenge. Sheila Fitzpatrick has already drawn attention to the "pseudo-*sel'kory*" (*lzhsel'kory*), the "lingers, busybodies and cranks," embracing those who claimed to be persecuted when in fact they were simply lazy or failures, those who were gossips who delighted in information that discredited others, and those graphomaniacs who voraciously wrote letters for the sake of it and some with various delusions.[124] Not all letter writers were upright citizens interested in advancing Soviet socialism, but included the bitter, the malicious, and the mentally ill who probably could not help themselves.

KREST'IANSKAIA GAZETA EXERTS PRESSURE ON OTHER LOCAL ORGANIZATIONS

As well as putting pressure on political nerve centers of the system, namely the raikom, obkom, and district, oblast, and republican level procuraces, editors also referred complaints to district and oblast land departments (the raizo and oblzo), to district soviet executive committees (raiispolkom), and to local newspapers.

Especially prominent in letters to land departments were the twin topics of failure to promote socialist competitions and inattention to Stakhanovites. In this vein, editors urged the head of the raizo in Ocherskii raion of Sverdlovsk oblast "personally to visit Comrade Votinova and to help her fulfil her wish of organizing a socialist competition of collective farmers for a high quality of flax."[125] The background to this was that Votinova had appealed for backing but "the chairperson did not help."[126] Important about this particular example was the fact that editors also lectured the raizo on the significance of Stakhanovism and the role that socialist competitions played in its expansion.[127] The letter not only included all the usual arguments that could be found in the press, but delivered the points in a proselytizing and educational style. By implication, those in the raizo were ignorant of what Stakhanovism meant.[128]

The raizo did not always respond as editors desired. When this occurred peasants wrote to the paper a second time to bemoan the fact.[129] Editors then took the matter to the next administrative level up, to the oblzo. A letter to the head of the Riazan' oblzo narrated how on the Kaganovich collective farm "competition among milkmaids is not developed" and this was because neither the land department nor the farm management helped them to fulfill work pledges. On top of this, "the farm is not prepared for winter and the cattle are kept in filthy buildings."[130] "Necessary measures" were demanded from the oblast.

Krest'ianskaia gazeta also intervened in the training of peasants to drive tractors and combines. Another letter to the oblzo complained that the Mtsenskii school of combine driving was in a bad state. Apparently, "the hostels are cold, filthy and poorly lit; there is no papers nor exercise books; no canteen or laundry." Editors viewed it as inadmissible that as a result only 150 students remained out of the initial 300. Such conditions did not breed Stakhanovites. Editors demanded that the oblast respond to the newspaper about this and to do so over the telephone.[131] There are no recorded responses, however, to any of these complaints to the raizo and oblzo. Among archival documents are letters which respond to more technical questions concerning the preparation for spring sowing and seed quality.[132]

Different sorts of letters again went to soviet executive committees, concerned mainly with poor conditions on farms and weak infrastructure, including lack of harnesses for horses and oxen, insufficient numbers of vans, and poor tires.[133] The central message in all of these letters was that bad conditions negatively affected productivity and did not encourage shock work and Stakhanovism. Editors expected the raiispolkom to do something about local problems and to report back on what they were doing to tackle them.[134]

Finally, editors at *Krest'ianskaia gazeta* were prone to scolding editors of local newspapers, too, if they considered that they were not sufficiently vigilant in their exposés. *Kolkhoznyi Klich* (Kolkhoz Call) was reprimanded in this vein for "not once" informing district and krai organizations of the problems in Krasnodarsk krai concerning common pasture, the lack of forage reserve, and weak foddergrass cultivation. Editors pointed out that since they had received lots of letters of complaint from Krasnodarsk, they assumed that the local paper would have, too.[135] In a similar vein, *Kirovskaia Pravda* was attacked for allegedly knowing of the "disgraceful" state of affairs discussed above, but considering the matter "unimportant," did nothing about it. Editors at *Krest'ianskaia gazeta* thus berated editors elsewhere for not taking a stand against "bureaucratism and red tape."[136]

All local organizations and newspapers then were likely to receive large numbers of letters from *Krest'ianskaia gazeta* which informed, requested action, called for details of results, and berated.

CONCLUSION

Quite how effective the newspaper was in changing behavior or in instigating successful inquiries is hard to measure with precision. The proportion of referred cases which was dealt with reasonably quickly and fairly cannot be determined.[137] Editors and instructors, however, were visibly active in passing on huge amounts of information, in demanding that others act upon it, and in following ignored complaints. The large number of reported cases of subsequent investigation, dismissal from farm leadership, arrest, trial, and punishment suggest that initiatives by *Krest'ianskaia gazeta* did make a political difference. An argument can be made to the contrary only if it can be shown that

these exposés and pressures to act would have come about anyway from other
political actors in the system and would have been responded to, or neglected,
in a similar pattern.

In chasing up cases of complaint, the press often put pressure on parts of
the dominant political organ of the authoritarian state—the party itself—
demanding from it investigation, replies, or even challenging the party's
skepticism about the reliability of the paper's own peasant sources. Editors
could legitimately do this because the apex of the party had launched a growing attack on its own secretaries in the localities, often with good reason due
to ineptness, low levels of education, and lethargy. Whereas at national level,
the Old Bolsheviks were wiped out in the Great Purges, at local levels the pattern was more complex and unanswered questions remain.[138] Although the in-
nocent did get swept up in the purge process and irrationalities did occur
along with settling old scores, there often appeared to be good reason for dis-
missing the incompetent and support for this in the districts.[139]

Raikom party secretaries, however, could not always control events on
farms and machine tractor stations. Moreover, as far as farm leaders were
concerned, their task was far from easy. Apart from those among them who
were regularly drunk, a case can be made that much on the farm was out of
their control, too. Often it was hard to "encourage" Stakhanovism since soil,
harsh climate, insufficient machinery, feed, and fuel militated against it, not
helped by negative social attitudes toward the movement and anger at the new
work norms it produced. Moreover, how could perks be promised to rural
Stakhanovites if better living conditions were not there to be offered? To
these material and infrastructural barriers to encouraging Stakhanovism we
now turn.

NOTES

1. *Krest'ianskaia gazeta*, 18 March 1937, 2.

2. *Krest'ianskaia gazeta* 16 October 1937, 4.

3. RGAE, f. 396, op. 10, d. 38, l. 9.

4. For the argument that industrial Stakhanovism enhanced old tensions in factories and provoked new ones, playing a part in engendering the Great Terror, see
Robert Thurston, "The Stakhanovite Movement: Background to the Great Terror in
the Factories, 1935–1938," in *Stalinist Terror: New Perspectives,* eds. J. Arch Getty
and Roberta T. Manning (Cambridge: Cambridge University Press, 1993), 142–60.

5. Peter H. Solomon Jr., *Soviet Criminal Justice under Stalin* (Cambridge: Cambridge University Press, 1996), 303.

6. Roberta T. Manning, "The Great Purges in a Rural District: *Belyi Raion* Revisited," in Getty and Manning, *Stalinist Terror,* 170. For discussion of the significance

of local show trials, see Michael Ellman, "The Soviet 1937–1938 Provincial Show Trials Revisited," *Europe-Asia Studies* 55, no. 8 (December 2003): 1305–21.

7. J. Arch Getty, *Origins of the Purges: The Soviet Communist Party Reconsidered, 1933–1938* (Cambridge: Cambridge University Press, 1987); Chris Ward, *Stalin's Russia* (London: Edward Arnold, 1993), 111.

8. Jerry F. Hough and Merle Fainsod, *How the Soviet Union Is Governed* (Cambridge, MA: Harvard University Press, 1982), 3–191; Roy Medvedev, *Let History Judge: The Origins and Consequences of Stalinism* (New York: Alfred Knopf, 1971); David L. Hoffmann, *Stalinist Values: The Cultural Norms of Soviet Modernity, 1917–1941* (Ithaca, NY: Cornell University Press: 2003), 71–79.

9. Tens of thousands of communists had been purged during 1928–1930 tied to local failures in industry and agriculture. In a fresh wave of purges in 1933–1935 purge commissions were set up. In 1935 local party secretaries were ordered by the Party Control Commission to carry out a "verification" of party documents that was followed in the spring of 1936 by an exchange of party cards (*obmen*). All members had to hand it their cards and they knew whether they had lost their membership if a card was not received again.

The assassination in December 1934 of Sergei Kirov, Leningrad Party Secretary, was used by Stalin as a reason for accelerating the purges still further and for wiping out those whom he saw as opponents. The hunt was on for Trotskyites and Zinovievites and in January 1935 Kamenev, Zinoviev, and others were tried for the assassination. Their show trial took place in August 1937 and they were subsequently shot. In January 1937, a second show trial was staged, with sabotage and wrecking among the charges. The last show trial was held in March 1938 with Nikolai Bukharin and Genrikh Iagoda, former head of the NKVD, and other old Bolsheviks in the dock. At the All-Union level the purges amount to a wiping out of former revolutionaries and reflected both Stalin's grip on power and his own paranoia. At the local level purges involved much more than a wiping out of supporters of the revolution and showed complexity. See Manning, "The Great Purges in a Rural District" in Getty and Manning, *Stalinist Terror*, and J. Arch Getty, "The Politics of Repression Revisited," in Getty and Manning, *Stalinist Terror*, 40–64.

10. *Krest'ianskaia gazeta*, 16 April 1936, 2.

11. *Krest'ianskaia gazeta*, 18 March 1937, 2.

12. *Krest'ianskaia gazeta*, 30 December 1937, 4.

13. *Krest'ianskaia gazeta*, 30 December 1937, 4. Hiroaki Kuromiya has argued that Stalinist terror was "extensive" in the Donbas. See his "Stalinist Terror in the Donbas: A Note," in Getty and Manning, *Stalinist Terror*, 215–24.

14. *Krest'ianskaia gazeta*, 28 February 1938, 2; *Krest'ianskaia gazeta*, 3 March 1938, 1–6; *Krest'ianskaia gazeta*, 6 March 1938, 1–6; *Krest'ianskaia gazeta*, 8 March 1938, 2–3; *Krest'ianskaia gazeta*, 12 March 1938, 2–7; *Krest'ianskaia gazeta*, 14 March 1938, 1–3.

15. *Krest'ianskaia gazeta*, 1 April 1938, 2.

16. *Krest'ianskaia gazeta*, 30 August 1938, 1.

17. *Krest'ianskaia gazeta*, 30 August 1938, 1.

18. *Krest'ianskaia gazeta*, 30 August 1938, 1.

19. *Krest'ianskaia gazeta*, 14 November 1938, 1.

20. *Krest'ianskaia gazeta*, 10 January 1938, 3. For discussion of the 1939 reversal of verdicts in the district show trials and the argument that this "fits into the pattern of Stalinist policy, which was marked by sharp attacks and then partial retreats," refer to Ellman, "The 1937–1938 Provincial Show Trials," 1307.

21. For Chernov's biography, see *Gosudarstvennaia Vlast' SSSR Vysshie Organy Vlasti i Upravleniia i ikh Rukovoditeli, 1923–1991: Istoriko-Biograficheskii Spravochnik*, ed. V. I. Ivkin (Moscow: Rosspen, 1999), 585.

22. *Krest'ianskaia gazeta*, 10 January, 1938, 3.

23. *Krest'ianskaia gazeta*, 10 January, 1938, 3.

24. *Krest'ianskaia gazeta*, 18 October 1938, 1. Indifferent treatment from *Narkomzdrav, raizdravotdel*, and *oblzdravotdel* also came under attack. See *Krest'ianskaia gazeta*, 20 January 1939, 4.

25. RGASPI, f. 17, op. 123, d. 10, ll. 1–8.

26. RGASPI, f. 17, op. 123, d. 10, ll. 35–46. Andreev wrote to Mikoian commenting on this draft. See RGASPI, f. 17, op. 123, d. 10, l. 47.

27. RGASPI, f. 17, op. 123, d. 9, ll. 1–58.

28. For discussion of different types of letters to the press and for categorization of letters of denunciation, see Sheila Fitzpatrick, "Suppliants and Citizens: Public Letter Writing in Soviet Russia in the 1930s," *Slavic Review* 55, no. 1 (Spring 1966): 78–105; and her "Signals from Below: Soviet Letters of Denunciation of the 1930s," *The Journal of Modern History* 68, no. 4 (December 1996), 831–66.

29. *Krest'ianskaia gazeta*, 30 March 1936, 1.

30. *Krest'ianskaia gazeta*, 30 March 1936, 1.

31. Robert C. Tucker, *The Soviet Political Mind: Stalinism and Post-Stalin Change* (London: George Allen and Unwin, 1972), 50.

32. Merle Fainsod, *Smolensk under Soviet Rule* (London: Macmillan, 1958), 233. See, too, Medvedev, *Let History Judge*, 192–239.

33. Manning, "The Great Purges in a Rural District," in Getty and Manning, *Stalinist Terror*, 187.

34. By contrast, *Sovkhoznaia gazeta* paid less attention to the inadequacies of local party organizations. Not being a party paper, it focused rather more on state farm directors, trade unions, and people's commissariats, dealing with deficiencies in the party only in passing. Nonetheless it, too, on occasion would reprimand local party secretaries for being aware of problems and for "not taking any measures." See *Sovkhoznaia gazeta*, 14 September 1938, 2.

35. *Krest'ianskaia gazeta*, 30 March 1936, 1.

36. *Krest'ianskaia gazeta*, 30 March 1936, 1.

37. *Krest'ianskaia gazeta*, 30 March 1936, 1.

38. *Krest'ianskaia gazeta*, 30 March 1936, 1.

39. *Krest'ianskaia gazeta*, 30 September 1936, 3.

40. *Krest'ianskaia gazeta*, 30 September 1936, 3.

41. *Krest'ianskaia gazeta*, 30 September 1936, 3.

42. *Krest'ianskaia gazeta*, 30 September 1936, 3.

43. *Krest'ianskaia gazeta*, 30 September 1936, 3.

44. *Krest'ianskaia gazeta*, 16 October 1937, 4. The land administration in Kirovskii raion had "more than 200 unread complaints," the oblast procuracy had 539, and in departments of the obliispolkom, or oblast soviet committee, there were over 300.

45. *Krest'ianskaia gazeta*, 16 October 1937, 4. In the oblast land department, nine letters from *kolkhozniki* that had been forwarded by *Krest'ianskaia gazeta* were mislaid, four in the obliispolkom and five in the oblast procuracy. By comparative standards, this was actually few.

46. Accordingly, the procuracy of Ordzhonikidze krai failed to research "most important letters" written by *Krest'ianskaia gazeta*'s *sel'kory*. In cases where both district and oblast procuracies failed to satisfy, editors then wrote to the oblast Commission for Party Control. See *Krest'ianskaia gazeta*, 18 October 1937, 4; and 20 May 1936, 1.

47. *Krest'ianskaia gazeta*, 20 April 1937, 1.

48. *Krest'ianskaia gazeta*, 20 April 1937, 1.

49. *Krest'ianskaia gazeta*, 14 October 1936, 1.

50. *Krest'ianskaia gazeta*, 1 March 1936, 3. Sheila Fitzpatrick has made the point that farm leaders frequently embezzled, feathering their nest from access to the kolkhoz store. They were known as *samosnabzhentsy*, or self-suppliers, who often surrounded themselves with *podkhalimy*, or toadies, and *rastratchiki*, or squanderers. See her "From *Krest'ianskaia gazeta*'s File: Life Story of a Peasant Striver," *Russian History/Histoire Russe* 24, nos. 1–2 (Spring–Summer 1997): 215–37.

51. *Kolkhoznitsa*, no. 5 (May 1937): 2.

52. *Krest'ianskaia gazeta*, 18 March 1937, 2.

53. *Krest'ianskaia gazeta*, 18 March 1937, 2.

54. *Krest'ianskaia gazeta*, 18 March 1937, 2. The kraiispolkom (krai soviet executive committee) of Azovo-Chernomorsk had also failed to issue its decision on her case as promised.

55. See *Krest'ianskaia gazeta*, 30 December 1937, 4.

56. *Krest'ianskaia gazeta*, 30 August 1937, 1.

57. Smolensk Archive, WKP 203, l. 163.

58. *Krest'ianskaia gazeta*, 10 March 1937, 1.

59. *Krest'ianskaia gazeta*, 6 January 1939, 2.

60. *Krest'ianskaia gazeta*, 6 January 1939, 2.

61. *Krest'ianskaia gazeta*, 24 April 1936, 3.

62. *Krest'ianskaia gazeta*, 24 April 1936, 3.

63. *Krest'ianskaia gazeta*, 24 April 1936, 3.

64. In its rhetorical style, repeatedly used when blaming someone, the paper observed that a party secretary "had been when it was necessary to take Stakhanovites to different meetings and conferences," but now there was sabotage, where was he? See, *Krest'ianskaia gazeta*, 30 March 1936, 1.

65. *Krest'ianskaia gazeta*, 30 March 1936, 1.

66. Even *Sovkhoznaia gazeta* delivered this message. In an article titled "Care for Stakhanovites . . . on festive days," Ostrovskii, deputy Commissar of State Farms, was quoted at a Plenum of the Central Committee of the Trade Union of Dairy State Farms to the effect that farm directors, farm specialists, and commissariats, too, all suffered

from "political myopia." This was because "they showed an interest in Stakhanovite work on festive occasions, then quickly forgot about Stakhanovites." See *Sovkhoznaia gazeta*, 8 April 1937, 3. Another article noted that: "It often happens that after the showy stirring around this or that decorated Stakhanovite, leaders forget about him, trying to substitute banquets and verbose resolutions for efficient care and help." Although each Stakhanovite "should be surrounded by exceptional attention and care," *Sovkhoznaia gazeta* stressed, "this truth is understood by far from all leaders and social organizations of our state farms." See *Sovkhoznaia gazeta*, 16 June 1936, 1.

67. *Krest'ianskaia gazeta*, 24 April 1936, 3.

68. *Krest'ianskaia gazeta*, 24 April 1936, 3.

69. *Krest'ianskaia gazeta*, 16 April 1936, 2. After protracted investigation, then dismissal, Belichenko went on a three-day drinking binge and stole a horse from the kolkhoz. He then decided to take the horse to Slesarenko's father, intending to accuse him of the theft, but this was unmasked.

70. *Krest'ianskaia gazeta*, 16 April 1936, 2.

71. Smolensk Archive, WKP 202, l. 195.

72. *Krest'ianskaia gazeta*, 28 March 1936, 4.

73. *Krest'ianskaia gazeta*, 28 March 1936, 4.

74. *Krest'ianskaia gazeta*, 14 May 1936, 2.

75. Sometimes *Krest'ianskaia gazeta* juxtaposed "good" workers in the press against "bad" ones in the district party. In the case of Melan'ia Slesarenko, the district newspaper "Lenin's Path" was applauded for its "active defense" of Slesarenko, contrasting with the indifference of district leaders. See *Krest'ianskaia gazeta*, 16 April 1936, 2.

76. RGAE, f. 396, op. 10, d. 27, l. 202.

77. RGAE, f. 396, op. 10, d. 27, l. 202.

78. The leader of the Agricultural Department of *Krest'ianskaia gazeta*, Lishenina, wrote to a district secretary in Krasnodar krai to the effect that although Mariia Ivanova's horse team achieved "wonderful results," the Timofeev kolkhoz "hindered their work in every way." Brigade leader I. M. Shurupov "frequently hounded" them and "hampered" their work. He "transferred Ivanova's team to different work" and also "to her strip of land sent different kolkhozniki." The chairman of the kolkhoz, Lavrinenko, knew about this, but "neither does he help Ivanova's team." Lishenina had asked the district party secretary to take the necessary steps for the creation of "normal conditions" for the work of the Stakhanovite team and to aid it to perform "even better." Lishenina also asked the party to investigate whether the baiting of Stakhanovites was going on. As was generally the case, a copy of this letter was sent by editors to the raikom and also went to the procuracy. See RGAE, f. 396, op. 10, d. 70, l. 26.

79. RGAE, f. 396, op. 10, d. 9, l. 20.

80. RGAE, f. 396, op. 10, d. 9, l. 20.

81. RGAE, f. 396, op. 10, d. 19, l. 273.

82. RGAE, f. 396, op. 10, d. 19, l. 271.

83. Ibid., f. 396, op. 10, d. 48, l. 204.

84. See, too, RGAE, f. 396, op. 10, d. 48, ll. 244–49.

85. RGAE, f. 396, op. 11, d. 20, l. 7.

86. RGAE, f. 396, op. 11, d. 20, l. 7.
87. RGAE, f. 396, op. 10, d. 121, l. 6.
88. RGAE, f. 396, op. 10, d. 121, l. 6.
89. RGAE, f. 396, op. 10, d. 121, l. 7.
90. Ibid., f. 396, op. 10, d. 48, l. 122.
91. RGASPI, f. 17, op. 120, d. 289, l. 54. The agriculture department in Saratov obkom also came under heavy fire for not having liquidated "the consequences of sabotage in agriculture." See RGASPI, f. 17, op. 120, d. 289, l. 54, l. 62.
92. RGAE, f. 396, op. 10, d. 48, l. 66.
93. In January 1939, editors wrote to the agriculture department of the Saratov obkom about a letter from a schoolteacher who had complained about "a series of disgraces" on the kolkhoz named after the Seventeenth Party Congress. Copies went to district procuracy and party secretary. The latter informed editors that a penalty had been imposed on the guilty kolkhoz chair, but a second letter from the teacher claimed that "disgraces" were continuing. See RGAE, f. 396, op. 10, d. 48, l. 69.
94. When eight collective farmers wrote about "a series of abuses" and "inaction" in district organizations, editors sent a copy of the letter to the obkom. No reply came despite editors having warned that they intend to devote "special scrutiny" to this case. So editors reprimanded the agriculture department in a second letter. See RGAE, f. 396, op. 11, d. 4, ll. 379–80. For other examples concerning the obkomy in Zhitomir and Voronezh, see RGAE, f. 396, op. 11, d. 17, l. 47; and Ibid. , f. 396, op. 10, d. 19, l. 47.
95. RGAE, f. 396, op. 10, d. 27, l. 204.
96. RGAE, f. 396, op. 10, d. 27, l. 204.
97. RGAE, f. 396, op. 10, d. 20, l. 229.
98. RGAE, f. 396, op. 10, d. 38, l. 49. In fact, Mikhailiuk Karpovich regularly picked on *kolkhozniki* when drunk and picked on milkmaids in terms so vulgar that they were scratched out of the archives.
99. RGAE, f. 396, op. 10, d. 38, l. 49.
100. RGAE, f. 396, op. 10, d. 38, l. 50.
101. RGAE, f. 396, op. 10, d. 38, l. 50. One way in which peasant discontent was shown was by leaving farms. For other examples see RGAE, f. 396, op. 10, d. 38, ll. 72–77.
102. RGAE, f. 396, op. 10, d. 38, l. 50.
103. RGAE, f. 396, op. 11, d. 4, l. 329.
104. RGAE, f. 396, op. 10, d. 20, l. 273; RGAE, f. 396, op. 10, d. 21, l. 8. Letters on file variously refer to "Kariagin" and "Karagin." Misspellings and inconsistencies in spelling were common, as were grammar mistakes.
105. RGAE, f. 396, op. 10, d. 19, l. 4.
106. RGAE, f. 396, op. 11, d. 4, l. 377.
107. The answer announced that all the facts that had been forwarded in the initial complaint had been "confirmed." Furthermore, the results "had been discussed by a general meeting of collective farmers. The former kolkhoz chair, Iarov, was removed from his job by kolkhozniki and also members of the management were replaced." RGAE, f. 396, op. 11, d. 4, l. 375. These two examples are nice illustrations

of complete cases on file, both of which were chased up for faster action by newspaper editors. See also RGAE, f. 396, op. 10, d. 20, l. 50.

108. Because of this, few letters written directly to the procuracy are on file. There are far more responses from the procuracy.

109. In one such instance, editors wrote to the procurator in Monastyrshchenskii raion in Vinnitsa oblast asking for investigation of claims in an enclosed peasant's letter. The procuracy informed the paper that as a result of the investigation the farm chairperson was sentenced to four years. See RGAE, f. 396, op. 11. d. 4, l. 339 and l. 341.

110. RGAE, f. 396, op. 10, d. 104, l. 198.

111. RGAE, f. 396, op. 10, d. 104, ll. 200–201.

112. Particularly vivid cases include a letter to Krasivskii raion in Saratov oblast concerning bad management of the Seventeenth Party Congress collective farm, another to Mirzoianovskii raion in South Kazakhstan, and a third to Voronezh oblast about the maltreatment of animals which charges the management as "alien people, former kulaks and white bandits." See RGAE, f. 396, op. 10, d. 121, l. 73; f. 396, op. 10, d. 38, l. 9; f. 396, op. 10. d. 19, l. 221.

113. RGAE, f. 396, op. 10, d. 38, l. 45. Something must be said at this point about the relationship between the procuracy, the secret police, and the press. From correspondence, it is quite clear that close liaison with the NKVD was part of the process of investigation. Moreover, archives of the NKVD of the RSFSR of the late 1920s indicate that the secret police had a special Letters' Department for scrutinizing information sent to it just from *Krest'ianskaia gazeta.* For details, see GARF, f. 393, op. 74. For discussion of the relationship between the paper and secret police in the 1920s, refer to Stephen R. Coe, "Peasants, the State and the Languages of NEP: The Rural Correspondents Movement in the Soviet Union, 1924–1928 (Ph. D dissertation, University of Michigan, 1993).

114. RGAE, f. 396, op. 10, d. 20, l. 49.

115. The procuracy in Voronezh oblast, for example, informed that on the Sixteenth Party Congress kolkhoz the chairperson and the accountant were being brought to trial under Article 109 of the Criminal Code.

116. RGAE, f. 396, op. 11, d. 4, l. 345.

117. RGAE, f. 396, op. 10, d. 48, l. 182.

118. For example, Voronezh oblast procuracy wrote to the procurator in Khrenovskii raion saying, "Your response on Bel'kova's letter concerning embezzlement and abuse on the kolkhoz does not satisfy us." It instructed as follows: "Send us and the editors what you have undertaken to do regarding the letter; have you confirmed the letter—who is named, who is guilty and to what they are sentenced? Send your reply not later than 25 January 1938." This was written on 10 June, setting a fifteen-day deadline. A copy marked "urgent" went to the newspaper. See RGAE, f. 396, op. 10, d. 20, l. 70.

119. RGAE, f. 396, op. 10, d. 20, l. 239.

120. RGAE, f. 396, op. 10, d. 19, l. 87.

121. RGAE, f. 396, op. 10, d. 19, l. 87.

122. RGAE, f. 396, op. 10, d. 19, ll. 35–36.

123. RGAE, f. 396, op. 10, d. 19, ll. 35–36.

124. Sheila Fitzpatrick, *Stalin's Peasants: Resistance and Survival in the Russian Village after Collectivisation* (New York: Oxford University Press, 1994), 256–59.

125. RGAE, f. 396, op. 10, d. 125, l. 27.

126. RGAE, f. 396, op. 10, d. 125, l. 27.

127. Editors relayed that "Stakhanovites are people who are not content with their own work achievements but who try to attract other collective farmers into the Stakhanovite movement, to teach dozens of other *kolkhozniki* to work as they do. A main role in drawing in new collective farmers to the ranks of Stakhanovites is played by socialist competitions." See RGAE, f. 396, op. 10, d. 125, l. 27.

128. The *raizo* in Shostkinskii district of Chernigov oblast was sent a similar letter about a kolkhoz chairperson who did not show a Stakhanovite's team "necessary attention and help." Editors asked the land department to ensure that a better attitude toward Stakhanovites developed in which peasants "related to them with attention, valued them as the party and government value them, as the whole country values them." See RGAE, f. 396, op. 10, d. 153, l. 175.

129. RGAE, f. 396, op. 10, d. 153, l. 175. See also footnote number 43 above. Likewise, in Viazemskii district of the Western oblast, the raizo had received 400 complaints, but had ignored 130, and 100 others were "in the research stage." *Krest'ianskaia gazeta* even took pains to inform the oblast procuracy that letters sent to "a series of districts in the Western oblast" were "intolerably" ignored. And the oblast procuracy failed to act, too. See *Krest'ianskaia gazeta*, 26 June 1935, 2.

130. RGAE, f. 396, op. 10, d. 120, l. 115.

131. RGAE, f. 396, op. 11, d. 41, l. 282.

132. For example, the oblzo in Kamenets-Podol oblast replied, "preparation for the sowing campaign proceeded unsatisfactorily on several collective farms in Chererovetskii district." Only after the presidium of the raiispolkom and the raikom had intervened was the work completed. See RGAE, f. 396, op. 10 d. 44, l. 24.

133. RGAE, f. 396, op. 10, d. 153, l. 79.

134. RGAE, f. 396, op. 10, d. 153, l. 79. Another letter to the raiispolkom of Shostenskii raion of Chernigov oblast passed on that peasants were complaining that the local soviet had not honored its decision to convert a derelict church into a club. See RGAE, f. 396, op. 10, d. 153, l. 79.

135. RGAE, f. 396, op. 10, d. 70, l. 21.

136. *Krest'ianskaia gazeta*, 16 October 1937, 4.

137. The newspaper did provide some statistics on the outcomes of letters. See Fitzpatrick, "Signals from Below," 859.

138. See Ellman, "The Soviet 1937–1938 Provincial Show Trials Revisited."

139. For debate about the role of peasant support in local trials and purges and the significance of the concept of "carnival," also see Ellman, "The Soviet 1937–1938 Provincial Show Trials Revisited" and Sheila Fitzpatrick, "A Response to Michael Ellman," *Europe-Asia Studies* 54, no. 3 (May 2002): 473–76.

Chapter Eight

Inadequate Supplies and Poor Conditions

There aren't enough spare parts![1]

The cows often stand without hay, that is, hungry.[2]

A "theory" reigns that allegedly the Siberian land will not take manure.[3]

As well as "political blindness" in localities, problems of supply meant that the prerequisites for successful Stakhanovism were often wanting. If the supply of animal feed was low, how could cows produce more milk? If mechanization was not advanced, or if tractors lay idle due to lack of spare parts, how could peasants triumph over technology as Stakhanovites were supposed to do? If there was not enough manure after the slaughter of animals and if the production of chemical fertilizer was insufficient to meet agricultural needs, how could the soil improve? If living conditions were harsh, and not perceived to be improving, what incentive was there to work harder? If pay came months late, what spurred state farm workers on? If drunkenness was not uncommon, how could productivity be expected to increase? Moreover, with collectivization in such recent memory, why should those peasants who were still smarting from it wish to work heroically for the regime that had imposed it?

Although Stakhanovism was advertised as the countryside's savior, it could not be a cure-all. The paradox here is that from Stalin's point of view rural conditions necessitated something like Stakhanovism to shake them into productive action, but the dilemma for Stakhanovism's success was that often the very conditions it was meant to overcome worked against its developing.

Factors beyond the farm's control, such as an inadequate supply of spare parts or fuel, or an end to foreign imports after 1932, could not be altered by

Stakhanovite behavior, merely eased by carefully looking after machines or by economizing on fuel.[4] Likewise, poor organization on the farm, MTS, or in the local land department could not always easily be changed by Stakhanovites themselves, especially where they were in the minority. We have already seen how although Stakhanovites complained about malpractices to the press, instant rectifications were unlikely. Integral to the silences of Stalinist discourse, however, was a reluctance to openly blame the system itself. So how did the press portray what were officially known as "barriers" to Stakhanovism?

MACHINERY AND EQUIPMENT

The press discussed at length poor work, the neglect of machinery, and the relationship between the two and the press and journals often satirized problems in cartoons, as shown in Figure 8.1. One loud message was that notwithstanding the increased production of tractors and combines, they were often idle.[5] Stakhanovites could not work if they lacked the necessary fuel or enough spare parts to repair faulty machines. The sad reality, according to the press, was that tractors were often out of action. In 1936 and 1937 individual farms were criticized along the lines of "three tractors stand immobile. Around is stubble and tens of hectares of unplowed fields."[6] In this instance, the kolkhoz chair was blamed for failing to ensure a supply of fuel. Similarly in Odessa oblast, tractors stood idle for five days at a time with no fuel.[7] Farm leaders were readily targeted for failing to acquire the necessary

Figure 8.1.   "Such was the 'technical help' last year at harvest time on several MTS and state farms." Source: *Adapted from* Traktorist-Kombainer, no. 10, 30 May 1937, p. 20.

fuel. What was not said was that insufficient fuel was available for distribution and that often it was hard for collective farm chairpersons to acquire it in the first place.

Machinery lay idle either because of lack of fuel or because it was in need of repair. The press reported annual statistics on the extent to which repair plans had been fulfilled. In January 1936, just 30.1 percent of targets had been met on state farms. Out of 8,100 tractors needing major repairs, just 2,514 had received attention. Out of 10,400 tractors requiring lesser repairs, only 3,042 had been fixed. And out of 7,080 caterpillar tractors, 1,544 or 21.8 percent had been repaired.[8] A similar pattern applied to combine harvesters. By May 1935, grain state farms had repaired 1,354 combine harvesters, fulfilling the plan by 15.8 percent.[9] *Sovkhoznaia gazeta* reprimanded state farms for lax attitudes toward repairs and for neglecting to inform their People's Commissariat about the progress of annual repairs.[10]

Individual farms were also criticized for their "unsatisfactory" repair program. In Rostov oblast, the Millerovskii grain farm was exposed for having attended to only 2 of its 22 ChTZ tractors and 6 of its 20 STZ machines, and the "Five-Year Plan" pig farm in Saratov oblast was criticized for not having repaired even 1 of its 26 tractors.[11] The reason cited by state farm directors was that "there aren't enough spare parts!"[12] Journalistic investigation of the "filthy" repair shed, however, revealed disaster. Here "a disorderly scattering of parts of disassembled tractors" was encountered. A cold wind was also blowing "through chinks in the wall."[13] The general picture was one of neglect and disrepair. In fact, lack of parts and "poor work discipline" were the regularly repeated reasons for why repairs failed to take place.[14] A further problem was that machine tractor stations regularly sent poorly repaired machines back to the farms.[15]

It is worth mentioning that the press often gave a "high date" for unprepared tractors in winter.[16] Yet the figures that really mattered were those for the number of tractors still out of action when spring sowing began.[17] One reason, however, why the press stressed the lack of preparedness in December was that spring was not long off and journalists had to urge repair work soon. Castigation early was meant to prompt farms to repair in time for spring.

The general message, however, was that neglect of machines all year round was common. Grain state farms in Stalingrad oblast left all 700 combine harvesters unprotected out in the snow during winter. *Sovkhoznaia gazeta* reported that "not one" was protected by a roof. And "plentiful" autumn rain had flooded the machines. The press scolded "from such 'protection,' combine harvesters suffer more than from the most intense harvesting."[18] In addition, harvesters were not repainted, so they rusted. In sum, the message from the press was that attitudes toward machinery were "barbaric."[19] Even during periods of fieldwork, tractors and combine harvesters "on the majority of state farms" lacked attention and necessary maintenance.[20]

The problem of insufficient spare parts also received extensive newspaper coverage in *Krest'ianskaia gazeta*. Here the point was that with every new year, collective farms were being supplied with more complicated machinery. The most necessary equipment, however, often arrived without spare parts and tractors did not always have trailers.[21] Without spare parts, tractors could not be repaired. It did not help that those who repaired tractors often worked in unpleasant surroundings, offering little incentive to perform good work. Reporting on Saratov oblast revealed that on one state farm:

> The temperature in the workshop is 10–12 degrees below zero. There is no firewood. Those repairing the machines walk five kilometres to work from the village Lachinovki. There is no hostel for them on the state farm, no food.[22]

By implication, if these were the working conditions, how could high quality work be expected?

These issues are discussed in archival documents of the Central Committee Agricultural Department. At a conference of obkom agricultural leaders in December 1938, the following dialogue took place between Andrei Andreev, Central Committee Secretary, and Aleksei Demenok, head of the Smolensk agriculture department:

> Andreev: Is the supply of spare parts bad?
>
> Demenok: Bad . . . The engines are essentially repaired, but several parts are missing, consequently it is impossible to set the engine running. Several parts we manufacture ourselves, but several our factories do not make.[23]

One serious problem of using imported machines was that parts were not made at home and imports had stopped.[24] In Tula oblast, according to Nikolai D'iakonov of the Agriculture Department, coping with lack of spare parts was dealt with as follows:

> In the beginning we selected several MTS and looked at how they related to the restoration of parts. As it turned out, most old spare parts were on the dump. We gathered the directors together and began to make use of old spare parts. These helped us during repairs.[25]

It is evident that imaginative initiatives were taken to solve problems and that lethargy was not necessarily a culprit. D'iakonov added that many tractors could never have been repaired without recourse to salvaging old parts. He regretted the belief among peasants that unless old parts were thrown away, new ones would never be given. Since this worked against the repair process, D'iakonov advocated that it had to be checked.[26]

In this manner, the heads of agriculture departments came together to discuss how each obkom dealt with the deficit of parts with a view to airing issues and learning from each other how best to cope with a pressing problem. Although the press delivered the message that mechanization and Stakhanovism contributed to each other since excellent workers cared for machines and used them well, the very real lack of spare parts made it hard for all tractor drivers, especially those aspiring to become Stakhanovites. Although neglect played its part in the failure to care for machines, for which peasants could be blamed, inadequate fuel and parts could not so easily be pinned on them.

Discussions in the press of the relationship between Stakhanovism and machinery also did not dwell on the fact that the degree of mechanization varied across sectors and regions, which affected the probability of Stakhanovites emerging. For example, as shown in Table 8.1, in mid-1935 there were 2,036 MTS devoted to grain and 325 catering for vegetables and potatoes, or 49 percent of MTS for grain compared with 7.8 percent covering vegetables.[27] Regional and district variations in availability also affected the geographic probability of Stakhanovites emerging. Although an increasing number of kolkhozy were served by the MTS as the 1930s progressed, many still were not. According to Vyltsan, in 1935, 52 percent of collective farms enjoyed support from a Machine Tractor Station, 67.1 percent in 1936, and 78.3 percent in 1937. The grain growing districts fared best, in particular in Rostov, Saratov, Stalingrad, and Voronezh oblasts. In addition, argued Vyltsan, neither according to quantity or quality did machinery satisfy demand.[28] Nor would one have expected it to given the USSR's level of economic development.

Table 8.1.   MTS by Sector, 1 July 1935

Sector	Number of MTS	As % of Total Number of MTS
Grain	2,036	49.3
Cotton	452	10.9
Flax	438	10.0
Sugar Beet	550	13.3
Vegetables/potatoes	325	7.8
Simple MTS	327	7.9

Source: M. A. Vyltsan, *Zavershaiushchii etap sozdaniia kolkhoznogo stroia* (Moscow: Izdatel'stvo Nauka, 1978), 78.

LACK OF PREPARATION FOR
SOWING, HARVESTING, AND WINTER

Although Stakhanovite "lessons" were meant to overcome poor preparation for sowing, harvesting, and winter, their success was patchy. *Krest'ianskaia gazeta* identified many cases of "intolerably slow" sowing and portrayed it as a form of indiscipline.[29] Such "slackness in work discipline" in Rostov raion of Iaroslavl' oblast in late May 1936 was lambasted as "shamefully late." As a consequence, peasants "have only sown one-third of the land under cultivation."[30] The press distinguished between "advanced" machine tractor stations, which were always ready, and those in the south of the RSFSR which in 1939 "still prepare badly." Rostov oblast came under heavy fire as did Siberia.[31] Articles on "careless leadership" with respect to sowing reappeared every January, designed to trigger instant action.[32]

Other articles concentrated on a range of "mistakes" in the area served by an MTS, identifying brigades that had prepared badly, inefficient kolkhoz chairpersons, kolkhozy where tractors stood idle and where seed had not germinated.[33] The press named and shamed kolkhozy which failed to apply the lessons of agronomy. One was picked out for still sowing by hand, "hardly using the seeding machine."[34] District leaders and agronomists were also criticized for being aware that low-quality seed was being used, but doing nothing about it.[35]

Criticism along these lines was stepped up in 1938 due to a fall in temperature in the spring in some krais and oblasts. *Krest'ianskaia gazeta* commented that inclement weather had "engendered in many leaders of oblast and raion organizations a ruinous mood. Spring is delayed, it's not worth hurrying. Let's sow later, and finish later."[36] Such attitudes were branded as examples of lax standards. Procrastination also affected seed supply. Articles described how when complaints were made to the raizo, the reaction was often "Wait a bit. The sowing does not start just yet."[37] The same inattention obtained in some oblzy, as in Voronezh oblast, whose workers messed up work patterns, delayed plan fulfillment, and made the agronomists nervous.[38] Confusions also reigned in the inter-kolkhoz practice of exchanging seeds. In 1938 "scoundrels" in the district land departments upset members of the Stalin collective farm in Krasnodar by requiring additional exchanges that delayed the sowing of sunflowers.[39] In April 1938, *Krest'ianskaia gazeta* commented, "It is well-known that where there is no plan, neglect and muddle prevail."[40] The official message was that success depended upon "the self-discipline of the kolkhoz masses, upon their preparedness and the conditions of the material base."[41] The kolkhoz masses, however, could not control the local land department or everything about the material base.

The press also blamed bad sowing practices and a lack of information or decent textbooks. M. Chernenko, people's deputy and sugar beet worker, complained that although "millions of collective farmers are studying agronomy" in fact "there is not one standard textbook on sowing sugar beet." He called upon "scientific workers" to produce one so that harvests would improve.[42] The All-Union Sugar Beet Scientific Research Institute came under attack for working "unsatisfactorily" in this respect and for not helping Stakhanovites.[43]

Further problems arose at harvest time. In Vinnitsa oblast, *Krest'ianskaia gazeta* reported that a fundamental problem of sugar beet harvesting was the inability of many leaders of machine tractor stations and collective farms to combine it with other vital autumn work. Threshing and autumn plowing should have been occurring at the same time, but did not, and consequently jobs fell inappropriately out of sequence. In addition, the appropriate machinery was not always used. The June 1936 Central Committee Plenum had already decided that not less than 90 percent of the beet harvest should be gathered by a mechanical beet harvester, but this was not being practiced.[44]

Farms were frequently behind the plan for plowing. In mid-October 1936, *Krest'ianskaia gazeta* reported that Narkomzem had noted that by 5 September only 43 percent of the autumn plowing plan had been fulfilled.[45] Despite a Stakhanovite "Ten-Days" beginning on 10 October, results were inadequate. In addition, kolkhozy and MTS "stir themselves outrageously slowly."[46] Once drifting along, they fail to organize the full potential of each tractor and horse. Neither do they take advantage of the experience of advanced workers in order to guarantee a "Stakhanovite harvest."[47]

Even worse in Azovo-Chernomore krai, one MTS by 10 September 1936 had harvested only 400 hectares, a mere 6 percent of the plan, and in Kolpnianskii raion of Kursk oblast the plowing was going "criminally slowly."[48] Peasants were waiting for tractors even though the horses were doing nothing.[49] On the collective farms served by the Solntsevskii MTS in Kursk oblast, tractors had only been made use of for 54 percent of their capacity and horses for just 8 percent.[50] In Luzhskii district of Leningrad oblast, the chair of the "Red Hill" collective farm only allowed 2 horses to work in the harvest, and even then far too late.[51] Other farms were named for having plowed between only 2 and 6 hectares.[52] Whereas some articles concentrated on unused animals, others considered that the number of animals and equipment were insufficient. A *sel'kor* reporting on one farm in Balandinskii raion, Saratov oblast, noted that: "There are not enough harnesses or means of transport. There are 40 horses on the kolkhoz, ten bulls, but only twelve vans."[53] The supply of tires was also inadequate.

Party committees showed consternation about poor preparations in frequent *postanovleniia*. Saratov kraikom, for instance, argued that district leaders often exaggerated the successes of spring sowing, forgetting to encourage extensive weeding before harvest time or more general preparations. Endless talk about springtime "turns their heads and disturbs them from thinking soberly that it is no more than one-and-a-half months to harvesting."[54] The press echoed that harvesting was complicated by a proliferation of weeds. *Krest'ianskaia gazeta* instructed its readers that: "Weeds make more difficult gathering the harvest by combine harvesters and other agricultural equipment."[55] In sum, weeds made it difficult for peasants to perform well at harvest time. But many peasants failed to tackle their proliferation, despite Stakhanovite lessons.[56]

Fertile soil was important to productivity. At the very apex of the system, however, Narkomzem and Narkomsovkhozov were blamed within the Central Committee Agricultural Department for "not fulfilling the party and government's instructions on manure."[57] But even when adequate fertilizer had been available, peasants in some areas were reluctant to apply it. The press particularly scolded superstitions about the land and about what should not be done to it. Apparently, according to *Krest'ianskaia gazeta*, "a 'theory' reigns that allegedly the Siberian land will not take manure."[58]

Winter, too, was a time of year requiring preparation. Predictably farm leaders were berated for neglecting to consider it far enough in advance. On state farms, materials of the Central Committees of farm trade unions criticized political departments and local trade unions for not helping sufficiently. Trade union documents also note that all state farms lacked adequate fuel for winter. One farm, for instance, needed 150 tons of coal, but had only 50. Another wanted 359 tons of fuel but acquired just 45. These examples were apparently typical.[59] One union *postanovlenie* commented upon particular farms, such as the state farm named after Demchenko which "is not prepared for winter. Equipment is not in place. Watering is not organized. The milkmaids' working day is not sorted out. Special work clothing has not been distributed."[60]

The range of separate problems affecting sowing, harvesting, and winter was thus broad. Timing and neglect, however, were rubrics under which they could all comfortably fit. Neglect pertained, too, in the treatment of animals.

DISGRACEFUL CONDITIONS FOR
ANIMALS AND INADEQUATE FEED

We have already seen that the duty of Stakhanovites was to cater to the individual needs of their animals, to ensure that they ate appropriately, reproduced in increasing numbers, and survived after birth. Necessary prerequisites for this care were cleanliness, warmth, and sufficient feed which, if absent, acted as barriers to Stakhanovism. These issues were grave and a subject of scrutiny within the Central Committee.[61]

Stepan Sivokon', a *sel'kor* in Kazakhstan, wrote into *Krest'ianskaia gazeta* about the Red October farm in Karaganda oblast. Although it was one of the best in the district, "terrible disgrace reigns in that the cows stand in dirt, having no straw. When you go around the farm, it is possible for dirt to reach your knees." As a consequence, "the cows' uteruses are dirty." No attention was paid to the instructions of veterinary medicine and to hygiene.[62] A serious problem for the reproduction of animals was that "the cow shed for giving birth has not been repaired and there is no special warm room for newly-born calves." Moreover, "the farm is badly supplied with feed. The cows often stand without hay, that is, hungry."[63]

Given such instances, it is hardly surprising that political leaders attempted, through the Stakhanovite movement, to instill the "lessons" of hygiene, cleanliness, and care elaborated earlier. But the problem for Stakhanovism was circular. Without good conditions in the first place, the movement could not flourish until it had addressed the problems that often prevented it from igniting.

The complaint that feed was lacking or insufficient was a common one in both press and archival materials. Two *kolkhozniki,* for example, from Uzhursk raion of Krasnoiarsk krai, complained that "feed was not stored and the cattle had begun to drop from malnutrition."[64] On one of the large sheep farms in Siberia, 1,400 sheep died in the month of March 1936, also due to lack of feed.[65] To compound the issue, often there were miscalculations about animal feed. One farm had planned in springtime to have enough winter feed for five hundred sheep. By the autumn, however, it was realized that there would be one thousand sheep. *Sovkhoznaia gazeta* noted that "of course, neither feed nor animal housing were sufficient and the livestock became emaciated."[66] Trade union archives dismally observed, "on most state farms cattle are not provided with sufficient feed for winter." There was not enough roughage, food concentrates, succulent feed, or straw.[67] Conferences reiterated the problem. The First Krai Conference of Specialists on Pig State Farms of the Northern Caucasus, held in September 1935, blamed farm leaders for doing little about acquiring animal feed, albeit noting that lack of money was a problem. Even, however, on those farms where feed was sufficient, "they store it badly." Lack of albumen was a particularly widespread problem and food concentrates were not readily given. In fact, when they were, inexperienced farm workers prepared them badly.[68] There were several issues here. First, there were genuine supply shortages. Second, available supplies were often badly handled on the farm. And third, not all farm leaders made inventive use of their farm's own resources.

How well animals were fed was often linked to the work of animal specialists. If a good animal specialist left, then conditions could worsen. A brigade of Stakhanovite milkmaids wrote to *Sovkhoznaia gazeta* that for three years, theirs had been the best brigade on the farm, "but as soon as the animal specialist Comrade Tiutiaev left the state farm, the relationship of the leaders to us sharply changed. They stopped giving us concentrates and succulent feed."[69] As a consequence, milk yields fell. Of course, not all brigades were privileged to receive such special supplies. On a second farm the management "changed practically every month (this year five times)."[70] Again, this was not conducive to Stakhanovite labor.

Elsewhere animals were abused. In Orenburg oblast, young calves were "thrown out into the snow." For half an hour they would cry, then freeze.[71] On the Lenin state farm in Kuibyshev krai, the calves had extremely bad conditions in their shed:

> The doors were in disrepair and did not close. The oven burned all day, but the temperature fell to zero. Ten cows stood in the calf-house, not separated from their calves by a partition. All winter it served as a smoking room for the cattle farm workers. Typhoid broke out, killing 29 calves.[72]

Illness and disease were, in fact, common, as graphically described on a grain farm in Stalingrad krai, where "forty per cent of the calves suffer from diarrhoea." Here the "sick and healthy are kept together" in one section, "milk is not filtered," and "everyone drinks from common bowls." Because "there is not enough straw" newly born calves "are often put directly on the bare cold floor." As far as facilities went, "there is no washbasin in either the calfshed or the cowshed. There isn't even a bucket in which the calf-tenders and milkmaids might wash hands." As a consequence, "twenty-three per cent of the cows abort."[73]

In 1936, *Sovkhoznaia gazeta* insisted that conditions for animals on grain state farms were especially bad, leading to high death rates. In the first quarter of 1936, 50 percent of the younger animals on the Maslennikov state farm in Kuibyshev krai died. On the Lenin state farm in the same krai, 42 percent of the calves and 12 percent of lambs did not survive. Other examples were cited in Stalingrad krai and Orenburg oblast.[74] The official message was clear: "Scandalous figures! They show that state farm leaders have cast aside their animal farms, leaving them without any care."[75] The press regretted that animal deaths were increasing and little was being done about it. Journalists blamed the People's Commissariat, in particular grain management for its "anti-party attitude" to animal husbandry on grain state farms. Two years later, articles in *Sovkhoznaia gazeta* were still lamenting the high proportion of young animals that were dying.[76] All-Union People's Commissariats and republic level commissariats were criticized for not passing on Stakhanovite "lessons" into how to care for animals.

The lack of veterinary surgeons in many areas meant that sick animals could not be properly attended. At the December 1938 Central Committee gathering of heads of oblast agriculture departments, one speaker regretted that:

> the situation with veterinary workers is exceptionally bad. In fifteen districts we have no vets. . . . Collective farmers, of course, value animal specialists, but they strongly react to the fact that they cannot get help from a vet. It seems to them that if there had been a vet in the district, then their cow would not have died. But without a vet, loss occurs.[77]

Additional difficulties for those working with animals concerned supplies of water, towels, and other necessary items. *Sovkhoznaia gazeta* praised Comrade Savel'ev in Odessa oblast for ensuring that all his piglets lived. However, the paper reported that his brigade was not provided with water and various feeds and they had to "wipe newborn piglets with their own aprons."[78] The famous Stakhanovite pig breeder, Vladimir Zuev, also told *Sovkhoznaia gazeta,* "We still need to organize our work properly. We don't have enough sacks for grain, or tubs for kneading dough. This delays the delivery of feed." He added, "sometimes you wait hours, worrying and yourself running into the kitchen to help yourself to dough."[79] On another farm "for four pig tenders, there is only one pot. It's the same with pans for feeding the piglets. We should have three, but there is only one."[80] As a consequence, much time was spent running about trying to get the pan. Even worse, in the pig house the floor was uneven and broken, with feces everywhere.[81]

Whilst all of these factors put a brake on the development of rural Stakhanovism, the press insisted that only through better farm leadership and through the success of Stakhanovism could animal husbandry improve. Its consistent narrative was that of the "huge tasks" that the party had set state farm animal husbandry "their solution is possible only on the basis of a broad development of the Stakhanovite movement."[82] In all agricultural sectors, the official message was that the barriers to Stakhanovism could only be overcome by Stakhanovism's growth.

LIVING CONDITIONS

Better living conditions were also considered to be a vital incentive. Stakhanovites were meant to be rewarded for their heroic production efforts in various ways and better living conditions were supposed to be one of the perks. They were not always offered, however, thereby removing one material incentive to work harder. Examples are numerous in the press and in archival documents but mainly concern state farms. Here housing was supplied by the state whereas on collective farms peasants generally had their own hut but could not easily obtain timber and other materials to repair it.

State farm trade union documents are especially revealing about local conditions. Lidiia Al'tfater, for example, a "distinguished" calf tender, had to share a room with another family. The union regretted that "she has no bed, but sleeps, as she herself puts it on the 'first come' trestle bed. The room has no stove, no washbasin."[83] Sharing and cramped conditions were common. A Stakhanovite milkmaid with two children had to share a room with another milkmaid who also had a child. The room measured fifteen square meters and had a low ceiling. The Stakhanovite slept with her two children on one simple iron bed. There was no pantry and the potatoes were kept under the bed.[84] It was common for peasants not to have a table and stool.[85] Another exemplary peasant for two years had to hang a coat over the window because there was no glass.[86]

Lack of heating compounded poor conditions. According to *Sovkhoznaia gazeta*, in Dubovskii district of Azovo-Chernomore krai, seven Stakhanovites on a sheep state farm "live in exceptionally bad conditions." Here "tractor driver Liutov, with a nursing baby in the family, lived for two weeks during the winter without heating." Moreover, "the flat was so cold that it was impossible to get warm in a fur coat. The remaining Stakhanovites live in half tumbling down mud huts."[87] In such cases, Stakhanovite status had not meant better conditions.[88]

Sometimes even when it was possible to reward Stakhanovites in some way, such as sending them to sanatoria, this was not done. On a sheep farm in Dagestan, in the middle of winter the factory committee received two tickets for a sanatorium. Initially nothing was done about them. Finally, it was announced: "Stakhanovites do not have time to go to a health resort now. They must lead the sheep and work in the fields."[89] The dilemma here was that Stakhanovites were needed labor and the perks took them out of the fields. As a consequence Stakhanovites felt unrewarded.

Lack of light was an additional liability. Pig tenders in Kuibyshev krai lived in a hostel with "one lamp to three rooms. So in two rooms it is always dark—not possible to read or to study."[90] Since Stakhanovites were meant to study, this was a brake on their education and held back the development of literary *kul'turnost'*. Cleanliness was also hard for the pig tenders without washing facilities. They complained, "the bath-house works once a month. There are no washbasins or washing bowls." Promised means of entertainment had also failed to come to fruition. The chair of the workers' committee, Comrade Ukhanov, had "more than once promised to bring a radio to the hostel, to buy a guitar and a balalaika. But he did nothing. Films are rarely shown and we get bored in the evenings."[91] The pig tenders painted a grim picture of darkness, inability to wash easily, no entertainment, and boredom. There appeared to be little loyalty to the state farm.

Across farms, complaints about the bath-house were widespread. A common regret was either that it did not work or that there was not one at all. Amid numerous such complaints, a novel one from a poultry farm was that "the bath-house does not work. During the last year it was open only on 6 November."[92] This, at least, guaranteed cleanliness for the anniversary of the Revolution!

In such conditions it is not surprising that filth was a much mentioned problem—one which the *obshchestvennitsy* (public-spirited women, or female activists) were meant to confront in their efforts to raise the level of *kul'-turnost.*'[93] Archives of state farm trade unions painted a vivid picture of quite how bad it was. On one dairy farm, "unsanitary conditions reign. Flats are poorly repaired, the mud huts are dirty, ovens smoke, people sit without light. Huge overcrowding. Vegetables, pigs, chickens and people are together."[94]

It appeared common for animals and peasants to share space. On this particular farm the tractor drivers also lived in squalor. Their hostel was "in an unsanitary condition: the walls are generally filthy, there is no bedding, no bath-house." In addition, "a family of twelve lives in the bakery" and "the canteen is cold and there have been occasions when cows wandered in."[95] Such colorful examples of squalor and neglect illustrate just how far the countryside needed to develop and why enthusiastic and positive state farm workers were needed. Even if conditions were not uniformly as dire as the worst descriptions, their general improvement was pitched as both a consequence of Stakhanovism and as an incentive to work harder.

A common picture from archives is that on some farms there appeared to be no incentive to work hard at all with a lack of even the most basic food. On an animal state farm in Dnepropetrovsk oblast, not only did workers live "in unfavorable accommodation" which is "damp and cold" when autumn comes, but "food for the workers is badly prepared." Shockingly, "there are days when the chair of the workers' committee Vashkevich 'forgets' to take bread to the workers." The press criticized his "bad care of cadres" and as a consequence "several milkmaids left the state farm."[96] Thus poor living conditions prompted peasants to leave the farm rather than perform better. What one cannot deduce from sources is how representative this pattern was and what percentage of farms fit this description.

"Top secret" documents in RGASPI show in great detail movement on and off farms in the latter half of the 1930s.[97] Flux in the countryside was continuing, even if on a much reduced scale, and was a source of concern for top leaders. Memos informed Stalin, Molotov, and Andreev of the numbers of peasants excluded from farms and joining them in different oblasts.[98] Poor conditions and/or maltreatment by farm leaders, as well as the lure of industrializing towns, contributed to mobility across farms. In the closing years of the 1930s, the countryside was not as settled as conventionally thought.

Disease and ill health in the countryside were among the consequences of unsanitary living, acting as further brakes on shock work and Stakhanovism. The press was relatively quiet about this, but very occasional articles made telling points. In 1935, *Sovkhoznaia gazeta* reported that in Kalmykin, in Orenburg oblast, "malaria is widely developed. But no preventative measures against malaria are being taken on these state farms." The problem was exacerbated by the fact that "even when workers demand treatment in local hospitals and clinics, there is no quinine—the most important cure."[99] Supplementary information in trade union archives shows that malaria was especially bad in Bashkir, Kuibyshev, Saratov, Tatar, Stalingrad, and Gor'kii oblasts and krai due to ponds and bogs.[100] The press also criticized the attitudes of doctors. One peasant who went to the doctor for diagnosis and treatment complained the doctor "rudely" did not answer the questions and told the patient, "Get up . . . Somehow cure yourself."[101]

In sum, space, beds, heating, lighting, washing facilities, cleanliness, food, and medical care were perceived as serious problems on many farms, in need of drastic improvement. The rural material base, however, was too weak to make life comfortable quickly. The press made explicit that peasants deserved better and that these conditions were hardly incentives for Stakhanovite work. What the press omitted to say was that where Stakhanovites existed, they could not easily alter this predicament; at best, they could make demands on others in positions of power to do so. But local power could not necessarily deliver scarce inputs that depended upon a chain of contacts.

PAY

A more sober factor behind mediocre work was low pay. The press, archival documents of state farm trade unions, and papers of the Central Committee Agricultural Department all make the point that financial incentives for Stakhanovites were insufficient. *Sovkhoznaia gazeta* insisted that on state farms "one of the most serious obstacles in the path of Stakhanovism is incorrectly worked-out pay in most branches of animal husbandry."[102] The paper argued that the lack of bonuses for milkmaids, calf tenders, shepherds, and others "interferes with the further growth of a Stakhanovite army" and blamed "enemies of the people" lurking in People's Commissariats.[103] Trade union documents also pointed out that "a milkmaid can move from thirteen to twenty cows, but receive exactly the same pay."[104] Accordingly the call went out for an overhaul of the pay system based on the principle of "for high labor productivity—high pay."[105] Trade union documents argued for pay according to "quantity and quality of work."[106]

A conference organized by the Central Committee Agriculture Department also criticized pay on collective farms. One report drew attention to the successful milkmaid Galina Maiorova in Gor'kii oblast, but regretted that on her farm and many others, pay deterred Stakhanovism. Up to 1938:

> If pay was by the litre, then a milkmaid who got 2,300 litres from a cow received one-and-a-half work days, but one who milked 4,000 litres was given only one work day. And the more milk a milkmaid obtained, the less she was paid.[107]

The Central Committee and Narkomzem had corrected this defect with "a big result" which meant "an increase in productivity in animal husbandry." But for just over three years prior to this, wages had "held back the development of the Stakhanovite movement."[108] A conference of heads of agriculture departments concluded that the pay of animal specialists was "very low."[109] Comparisons of earnings also threw up injustices: "the work of a director of an MTS is especially complicated, but he receives less than the accountant."[110]

Another report of the Central Committee Agriculture Department written in 1939 held that MTS workers needed a new pay system, more closely tied to both the quality and quantity of work performed. It based its case on the fact that "it is necessary to stimulate the opening of virgin lands, deep plowing and use of iron blades on plow shares," but insufficient pay was not conducive to the effort required.[111] The report also declared "it is hard to reconcile with the fact that tractor drivers do not receive their pay for 4 or five months," blaming Narkomzem.[112] Tractor drivers also moaned that they had not been paid for six months, despite regularly informing the director of the MTS who "does not want to listen."[113] Trade union archives showed concern that rural workers "not having received pay for three months were not able during this time to buy even bread."[114] Documents labeled "miscalculations" in pay as "sabotage" and called for an end to arrears.[115] The period of delayed pay during Boris Yel'tsin's leadership after the collapse of the Soviet state thus had a precedent deep in the Soviet past.

The topic of rural pay was prominent in debates about what deterred Stakhanovism. The received wisdom into the 1940s was that pay incentives were necessary to boost morale and productivity.[116] One underpinning issue, not openly discussed, was that the general level of pay was inadequate due to a state squeeze on agriculture. The second issue, openly examined, was that remuneration systems were poor. The third was that remuneration systems were badly implemented, often deviating from the letter of what was expected.

DRUNKENNESS

The above problems were all compounded by drunkenness, a habit so deeply ingrained in the rural fabric that it was almost infrastructural and highly relevant to our discussion here. Discourse on drunkenness linked it to laziness, irresponsibility, and other forms of unacceptable behavior. The peasantry, including farm leaders, was castigated for drinking too much, making Stakhanovism a nonstarter.

Drunkenness affected work performance in various ways. One brigade leader in Belorussia, Petro Guk, pledged to give 600 tsentners of sugar beet per hectare. A report from Belorussia posed the question "but how did he go about fulfilling his responsibilities?" and answered "he forgot about them. Brigade leader Guk was not to be seen on the kolkhoz. He was occupied on a drinking binge."[117] Evidently, not all individual promises to meet certain work targets were taken seriously by peasants.

Krest'ianskaia gazeta received numerous letters exposing individual cases of drunkenness. Typical is one from Voronezh oblast complaining, "the management is busy with systematic drinking sprees and embezzlement of kolkhoz property."[118] Such accusations were frequently accompanied by the observation that the kolkhoz chair also failed to encourage Stakhanovite efforts.[119] We have already seen how when *Krest'ianskaia gazeta* received letters of complaint about drunkenness, editors passed them on to the raikom for investigation. Given how widespread it was, however, and a norm of rural life, thousands more instances of its harm to the farm's functioning are likely than were reported.

As an apparently eternal Russian condition, drunkenness was a predictable source of lethargy in rural areas. It may often, however, have been invoked as the main reason for bad work, when, in fact, other reasons were behind neglect, merely worsened by alcohol. Nonetheless, drunkenness's negative impact on productivity cannot be denied, even if it cannot be measured. Certainly drunkenness was not conducive to Stakhanovism. It should be noted, however, that it was the state that produced vodka and collected taxes from it.

LEADERSHIP TURNOVER

High leadership turnover on farms was one factor that seriously affected stability, the acquisition of supplies, and the encouragement of Stakhanovism and socialist competitions. Although dismissals of inept leaders were in farms' interests, the loss of leaders due to their own unhappiness about the job or the wrongful dismissal of leaders on baseless grounds complicated rural life still further.

Although the lack of appropriate skills was a main reason for high turnover, the purges ensured that turnover would not be low. In Kursk oblast in 1936, out of 8,000 collective farm chairpersons, 3,000 left their posts or were removed.[120] Inevitably turnover varied according to district and farm. As Table 8.2 shows, data on selected districts in Kursk oblast in 1937 reveal turnover ranging from 35 to 60 percent. With one-third to almost two-thirds of farm leaders leaving, there was a high degree of discontinuity throughout the seven selected raiony, making for instability in leadership.

Iakovlev was told, "people are removed mechanically" and that very often those removed, in Belgorodskii district for instance, were no different from those who were not removed.[121] If this was indeed the case, then it implied two patterns: first, that incompetent leaders were purged and also avoided purge; and second, that sufficiently adept farm leaders were unfairly swept up in the purges to the detriment of the farm.

In December 1938, the Central Committee Agriculture Department held a conference of leaders of agriculture departments of Volgograd, Ivanovo, Kalinin, Moscow, Orel, Riazan', Smolensk, Tula, and Iaroslavl' *obkomy*. Leadership turnover on farms was one of the pressing issues debated. The proceedings show that Aleksei Frolov, then leader of the agriculture department in Kalinin oblast, regretted that "in eleven months of 1938, 2,576 farm leaders were relieved of their jobs out of a total of 13,500 collective farms."

Table 8.2. District Turnover of Collective Farm Chairpersons in Kursk Oblast, 1937

District	Number of Collective Farms	Turnover in 1937	% Turnover
Besedinskii	97	45	46.4
Chernianskii	114	69	60.5
Shchebekinskii	72	36	50.0
Shchigrovskii	135	47	34.8
Oktiabr'skii	60	26	43.3
Mikhailovskii	81	49	60.5
Belgorodskii	54	29	53.7

Source: Adapted from RGASPI, f. 17, op. 120, d. 292, l. 117.

Of these, 238 left "for reasons of pay during the first months of this year," 676 "for bad management and squandering," 768 "for not providing leadership," 317 "for illness," and 430 "for simple reasons, as district workers call them."[122] These show that ill health and refusal to continue in post were problems as well as being purged for incompetence—real or alleged.

Frolov went on that in February in Turbinskii raion alone, fifty-six chairpersons from 117 farms changed, which meant turnover on almost half of the farms in the district.[123] The large numbers dismissed for failing to provide leadership underscores the huge problem of a lack of skills in the countryside and poor education levels for effective management in exceedingly difficult conditions. Although these dismissals were tangled into the purges, they were not only for political reasons or for a settling of scores.

Leaders also often chose to leave their jobs as the bleak picture in Tula oblast illustrated. Nikolai D'iakonov, head of the agriculture department in Tula oblast, reported that in its fifteen districts, out of a total of 2,200 collective farm chairpersons, turnover affected 580. Of these, 196 lost their jobs for bad management, drunkenness, and squandering. One hundred and forty, "very many" in D'iakonov's view, chose to leave of their own free will.[124]

Leadership turnover had further complexities. According to Frolov at the December 1938 conference discussed above, sometimes good chairpersons could be removed on false grounds, including the persecution of a Stakhanovite. In addition, district leaders could fail to inform the oblast about what was really happening. At the farm's general meeting, in front of visiting district leaders, peasants could vote to change their chairperson and the obkom would be entirely unaware of what had really happened. As Frolov put it, "the obkom does not know about all cases, but about some."[125] Thus, by implication, districts could go their own way and bad policy implementation could be one consequence. Evidently democratic centralism did not obtain.

Those gathered at the conference inevitably confronted the question of how to reduce turnover. Oblast leaders tended to argue that the oblast should have a greater role in the matter, enjoying an "increased responsibility."[126] In fact, the question of removal of a farm leader, in D'iakonov's opinion, should come before the oblast and not be left to the raion because the district often had its own dubious agenda. For instance, in one district of Tula oblast "instead of helping the farm chairperson, the district organized his removal." Under such circumstances, it was extremely hard for good cadres to develop on the farm.[127] Without good cadres, work discipline was often slack and Stakhanovism was not encouraged.

The drunkenness of farm leaders became a topic of amusing exchange between Iakovlev, Head of the Central Committee Agriculture Department since 1934, and farm leaders and peasants in Kursk oblast in January 1937.

Talking to peasants from the Derevenskii Truzhenik farm in Delsogorod raion about why individual farm leaders had been removed, the following ensued:

> Iakovlev: What was Ragozin removed for?
>
> Voice: Drunkenness.
>
> Iakovlev: And Merzlikin for what?
>
> Voice: For drinking.
>
> Iakovlev: Did he drink alone or in company?
>
> Voice: When alone, when there were two, when there were five.
>
> For weeks he didn't appear on the farm.[128]

Iakovlev was told that not all chairs were drunkards when they were picked for their job. So Iakovlev inquired:

> Iakovlev: That means it happens this way: as soon as someone becomes a farm chairperson, then they drink. So what about your new chair?
>
> Voice: He drinks in moderation.
>
> Iakovlev: Well, then that's okay.
>
> Voice: The state makes liquor for some reason. (Laughter)[129]

In his discussions with farm representatives, Iakovlev was given the clear message that "If you have a good farm chair, you hold onto him. With your help he can easily restore order on the collective farm."[130] Sound leadership was considered the key to success. A serious problem, however, was that the skills of good leaders were often wanting and their education levels were generally low.

Finally, the perspectives of kolkhoz chairs who chose to leave their jobs has to be considered. Evidence from Kalinin oblast suggests that the work was often unpleasant and that peasants could not always easily be roused to work hard. Comrade Kuratov, chair of the "Gigant" collective farm, explained, "I am leaving the kolkhoz because people work badly. In outside work, I'll be more relaxed and earn more."[131] Another chairperson had held his post for two years, then quit, giving the reason "it's hard work."[132] A third left one farm for another due to conditions specific to the first farm where there was "a lack of discipline and no desire to work."[133] One Grigor'ev left the Voroshilov farm after three years since it was poorly supplied with inputs.[134] A keen Komsomol member Baranov walked off the "Red Banner" farm because "the *kolkhozniki* do not listen to me."[135] And more than one farm leader left because "it is not possible to cope with the responsibilities."[136]

Pay was also a factor. One peasant refused to become a chairperson on the grounds that "pay is low, it is not worth working. You can earn more making shoes and there is no responsibility."[137] Others declined leadership jobs because "if you cannot cope, they'll judge you."[138] And indeed, some leaders also disliked the criticism they regularly received at collective farm general meetings.[139] This was indicated in my interviews with elderly peasants in 1996 on the Vladimir Il'ich collective farm in Moscow oblast. One woman in her eighties volunteered:

> General meetings occurred twice a year. They lasted half a day, or all day. There were scandals. If one man did not like what the chair did, he said so. He might say, why did you pay me so much, when someone else got this much. All the shortcomings were aired in the general meeting, like why don't we have a bath-house, or why doesn't the bath-house work?[140]

Direct criticisms, then, were hurled in the direction of the chairperson. Archives show that other farm chairpersons gave up their jobs claiming that they lacked backup from district organizations.[141] And some hesitated to take on the work since they were illiterate.[142]

Whilst political leaders regretted that the necessary leadership skills for solid work were absent from the peasantry, erstwhile farm leaders and potential ones often viewed the work as difficult and unattractive. If, moreover, peasants were reluctant to work and if farm leaders could not coax them to do so diligently, how could they easily produce Stakhanovites?

One answer in archives was that party presence needed to be higher in rural areas as weak party organization meant weak work discipline. As Comrade Makarov, deputy leader of the Agriculture Department in Vologda oblast, told other oblast leaders at a Central Committee conference:

> I want to focus on party organizations, and what party organizations we have. I do not know what the situation is in other oblasts, but in ours it is intolerable. For the entire oblast we have a total of twenty-one collective farm party organizations, but 5,967 kolkhozy.[143]

This meant a total of 121 communists spread across over 5,000 farms, topped up only by 57 party organizations on the MTS and 151 territorial party organizations.[144] So farm chairpersons generally lacked the support of communists on the farm that may, in turn, have exacerbated turnover.

Successful farms, like the Vladimir Il'ich collective farm in Moscow oblast, had an extremely low turnover of leaders. Here, according to one of the peasants whom I interviewed, "we had such organizers. Petr Andreevich was a good organizer. Then there was Shul'gin. Then Ivan Andreevich Buianov. Everything was well organized." Turnover here was indeed exceptionally low, with leaders lasting many years. "We had good chairs," another interjected. When asked what made a chairperson so good, a third answered: "We had a good chair. A good chair. He gave us work. He counted what we worked, then he paid us the correct amount. My first chair was there a very long time. He loved animal husbandry." Later in our talk, the relevance of the chair was stressed again with "It all depends upon the farm chairperson. He is the key. He must be a good organizer. A good boss. Then everything is fine." The second added:

> He threw out those who drank. He was strict. He was a good man. He under-stood us. He scolded us. But then everything was fine. Our chair saw everything. He never slept. He woke us up at 3 am. He shouted at us to get up. He gave his own wife the hardest work. She worked like a man at the hardest work. And she did it. So our kolkhoz was strong. We built new houses with iron roofs.

Consistent with Russian social and political culture, strictness was respected, even to the point of being bawled at to get up early. Collective farmers as well as top leaders viewed serious discipline on the farm as essential for success. Farm chairs with longer tenure were believed to be the most effective at se-curing this. Lack of leadership stability in rural areas, then, was one factor among several which deterred Stakhanovism.[145]

THE PEOPLE'S COMMISSARIAT OF AGRICULTURE

We have already seen how attacks on the People's Commissariats were part of the purges. Criticisms of inefficiencies within Narkomzem in particular, and on its local land departments, illustrate further problems for farms that Stakhanovites could not get close to correcting. Attacks in the press on Narkomzem intensified in 1938 and highly caustic remarks about this Peo-ple's Commissariat are found in archives of the Central Committee Agricul-ture Department.

A report sent to Andreev in 1939 blamed poor work on the inability of Narkomzem and its local organs "to solve questions which arise quickly." It ar-gued that the land organs simply could not implement party policy or control it. "Huge numbers" of orders were flowing out of Narkomzem, more than one thousand in 1938 alone, and localities were overwhelmed and impotent.[146]

On a list of Narkomzem's faults were two pertaining directly to Stakha-novism. First, Narkomzem "up until now has not fulfilled the extremely im-portant task of actually directing the Stakhanovite movement in agricul-ture."[147] Narkomzem had not taken Stakhanovism seriously and had failed to

promote it or to direct it. Second, Narkomzem had failed to promote energetic Stakhanovites into leadership positions.[148] What was needed, the report
suggested, was a "purge" of the Commissariat to rid it of "politically questionable people."[149] The message was that without solid cadres progress was
unlikely.[150]

In January 1939 a special conference under Ivan Benediktov as newly ap-
pointed Commissar after the purge of Moisei Kalmanovich, was convened by
the Central Committee to discuss Narkomzem's structural problems. One repeated point was that Narkomzem's load was "excessively large." No other
Commissariat had such a span of responsibilities or such a huge number and
variety of people working for it. One speaker underlined that at the union
level, Narkomzem was responsible for "thirty-three Narkomzem at union republic and autonomous republic level, seventy-one krai and oblast land departments, 3,560 district land departments, 6,466 Machine Tractor Stations,
and from this year 5,253 Machine Tractor Workshops." The list did not stop
there. He went on that "in Narkomzem's system are fifty-four repair factories,
and 243,000 collective farms. And recently 1,870 state farms have come under Narkomzem, that is a greater number of state farms than are brought together under the Union Commissariat of state farms."[151] In sum,
Narkomzem's scope was massive and all questions were solved "extremely
slowly" and "without consideration of actual local conditions."[152] Moreover,
Narkomzem's position at the political center was a "factor in the brake on
work in the periphery" where there were, in fact, a "colossal" number of questions to solve, resulting daily in "a stream of paper"—too weighty to be dealt
with by Narkomzem quickly.[153] In a speech delivered in February 1939 at
a meeting of party workers in Narkomzem, Kalinin also remarked that
Narkomzem was a "gigantic machine" and "one of the most political commissariats."[154] One of its main problems for him was that 80 percent of those
working in it were not party members.[155]

At the January conference, it was concluded that Narkomzem's cumber-
someness (*gromozdkost'*) and "excessively centralized leadership" were serious shortcomings.[156] Thus members of the Central Committee departments
were well aware in the 1930s of the main drawbacks of their centralized system. What they lacked was the political means to correct them.[157] Mark
Tauger has described how, before 1938, Narkomzem was also criticized for
its proliferating bureaucracy, slow decision making, contradictory directives,
mismanagement, inadequate information on regional conditions, and inability to function due to constraints placed on it from above, in particular increased grain targets.[158] There was nothing Stakhanovites in the fields could
do to solve these problems.

CONCLUSION

Factors of insufficient inputs of fuel, spare parts and animal feed, poor educational levels, instability in farm leadership, drunkenness, poor living conditions, lack of pay incentives, and overcentralized and weighty bureaucracy together worked to deter shock work and Stakhanovism. Of course, conditions varied across farms. Those which became millionaires, such as the Communist Beacon collective farm in Stavropol' krai or the Vladimir Il'ich collective farm in Moscow oblast, did not share serious problems of poor supply of animal feed or of high leadership turnover. But those in less fortunate positions had ample reasons to account for the dearth of Stakhanovites. These, moreover, were aggravated by the tendency of local leaders to pay more attention to successful farms. As a 1939 document in the Central Committee Agriculture Department on animal farms pointed out: "Little attention is given to poor farms, more to successful ones. At the centre of attention are 'advanced' farms."[159] An apparently institutionalized preferential treatment of successful farms reinforced and perpetuated their success to the neglect of weaker ones.

Paradoxically, then, what deterred Stakhanovism in reality was in propaganda to be overcome by Stakhanovism. What held productivity down, according to official lines, could best be tackled by those bent on increasing output. In circular fashion, Stakhanovites were needed in order to overcome the problems that persisted due to not having Stakhanovites. Only Stakhanovites, suggested narratives, could tackle the various causes behind Stakhanovites not existing. Yet with preferential treatment of successful farms, poorer ones struggled to produce the Stakhanovites they needed.

Stakhanovites, moreover, could not tackle the most debilitating problems and preferential treatment for advanced farms was out of their control. Supplies of spare parts, fuel, and animal feed were not determined by them, merely requested and used as efficiently as possible. Poor administration in the district and the bad running of farms was not their fault. By portraying Stakhanovism as a general corrective for the problems of the Soviet countryside, the press was implicitly blaming the failure of Stakhanovism to spread widely for the huge number of problems that remained. Thus the system itself was not at fault, implied the press, but rather the lethargy of peasants.

The very emergence of Stakhanovites, then, was difficult due a list of problems identified by the press—problems which peasants could not always themselves correct. So if the hurdles that confronted aspiring Stakhanovites were so immense, we need to consider why peasants set out to become Stakhanovites at all.

NOTES

1. *Sovkhoznaia gazeta*, 24 December 1938, 1.
2. RGAE, f. 396, op. 11, d. 21, l. 15.
3. *Krest'ianskaia gazeta*, 2 January 1935, 2.
4. R. W. Davies, *Soviet Economic Development from Lenin to Khrushchev* (Cambridge: Cambridge University Press, 1998), 44.
5. For the figures on increases in tractors and combines refer back to the section on "Industry and Five-Year Plans" in chapter 1.
6. *Krest'ianskaia gazeta*, 10 April 1937, 1.
7. *Krest'ianskaia gazeta*, 14 October 1936, 1. Kiev oblast was also criticized in 1936. See *Krest'ianskaia gazeta*, 20 March 1936, 1.
8. *Sovkhoznaia gazeta*, 8 January 1936, 2. See, too, *Sovkhoznaia gazeta*, 15 January 1935, 1.
9. *Sovkhoznaia gazeta*, 9 May 1935, 1.
10. *Sovkhoznaia gazeta*, 9 May 1935, 1.
11. *Sovkhoznaia gazeta*, 10 December 1938, 1; and *Sovkhoznaia gazeta*, 24 December 1938, 1.
12. *Sovkhoznaia gazeta*, 10 December 1938, 1.
13. *Sovkhoznaia gazeta*, 10 December 1938, 1.
14. *Sovkhoznaia gazeta*, 22 December 1938, 1.
15. *Krest'ianskaia gazeta*, 10 April 1937, 1.
16. A "high date" refers to an early date in advance.
17. I am grateful to Bob Davies for pointing this out.
18. *Sovkhoznaia gazeta*, 9 January 1935, 3.
19. *Sovkhoznaia gazeta*, 9 January 1935, 3.
20. See, for example, *Sovkhoznaia gazeta*, 12 September 1938, 2.
21. *Krest'ianskaia gazeta*, 12 September 1937, 3.
22. *Sovkhoznaia gazeta*, 24 December 1938, 1.
23. RGASPI, f. 17, op. 123, d. 6, l. 13.
24. See R. W. Davies, *Soviet Economic Development*, 44.
25. RGASPI, f. 17, op. 123, d. 6, l. 60.
26. RGASPI, f. 17, op. 123, d. 6, l. 60.
27. A *postanovlenie* of December 1935 created another 266 MTS in the non-black earth zone. See Vyltsan, *Zavershaiushchii etap*, 78.
28. *Zavershaiushchii etap*, 80–86.
29. As in Orel raion of Kursk oblast. See *Krest'ianskaia gazeta*, 18 May 1936, 1.
30. *Krest'ianskaia gazeta*, 22 May 1936, 1.
31. *Krest'ianskaia gazeta*, 6 January 1939, 1.
32. *Krest'ianskaia gazeta*, 12 January 1939, 3.
33. *Krest'ianskaia gazeta*, 20 March 1936, 1.
34. *Krest'ianskaia gazeta*, 18 May 1936, 1.
35. *Krest'ianskaia gazeta*, 18 May 1936, 1.
36. *Krest'ianskaia gazeta*, 20 March 1938, 1.
37. *Krest'ianskaia gazeta*, 10 March 1937, 1.

38. *Krest'ianskaia gazeta*, 24 March 1937, 1.
39. *Krest'ianskaia gazeta*, 26 March 1938, 1.
40. *Krest'ianskaia gazeta*, 4 April 1938, 3.
41. *Krest'ianskaia gazeta*, 20 March 1938, 1.
42. *Krest'ianskaia gazeta*, 4 August 1938, 3
43. *Krest'ianskaia gazeta*, 4 August 1938, 3.
44. *Krest'ianskaia gazeta*, 16 September 1936, 1.
45. *Krest'ianskaia gazeta*, 14 October 1936, 1.
46. *Krest'ianskaia gazeta*, 14 October 1936, 1.
47. *Krest'ianskaia gazeta*, 14 October 1936, 1.
48. *Krest'ianskaia gazeta*, 14 October 1936, 1.
49. *Krest'ianskaia gazeta*, 14 October 1936, 1.
50. *Krest'ianskaia gazeta*, 14 October 1936, 1.
51. *Krest'ianskaia gazeta*, 14 October 1936, 1.
52. *Krest'ianskaia gazeta*, 14 October 1936, 1.
53. RGAE, f. 396, op. 10, d. 121, l. 30.
54. RGASPI, f. 17, op. 120, d. 188, l. 10.
55. *Krest'ianskaia gazeta*, 18 May 1935, 1. The didactic message was that "It is impossible to call a collective farm 'Bol'shevik' if weeds flourish on its fields" and that "Sow thistle, thistle, couch grass, wild oats, field mice and other weeds—evil enemies of the collective farm." Tied to the language of the purges, "a poor struggle with weeds is directly complicit with the class enemy and his agents."
56. Refer back to the section "Lessons on Land: Soil, Manure, Seed, and Weeds" in chapter 5.
57. RGASPI, f. 17, op. 123, d. 10, l. 5–6. And on a more general level, the People's Commissariats were criticized for various problems occurring during sowing and harvesting, in particular for inadequate mechanization and the poor repair of tractors.
58. *Krest'ianskaia gazeta*, 2 January 1935, 2.
59. RGAE, f. 7689, op. 11, d. 320, l. 87ob.
60. RGAE, f. 7689, op. 11, d. 119, l. 1.
61. RGASPI, f. 17, op. 123, d. 6, l. 63.
62. RGAE, f. 396, op.11, d. 21, l. 15.
63. RGAE, f. 396, op.11, d. 21, l. 15.
64. *Krest'ianskaia gazeta*, 1 March 1936, 3.
65. *Sovkhoznaia gazeta*, 8 April 1936, 1. And in Saratov krai, a farm director who had boasted "a big store of feed" suddenly sent a telegram to the People's Commissariat about a "complete lack of feed and the catastrophic predicament of the herd." The situation on a sheep farm in Alma-Atinsk was also dire.
66. *Sovkhoznaia gazeta*, 18 April 1936, 2.
67. GARF, f. 7689, op. 11, d. 320, l. 87.
68. *Sovkhoznaia gazeta*, 28 September 1936, 3.
69. *Sovkhoznaia gazeta*, 8 December 1938, 2.
70. *Sovkhoznaia gazeta*, 8 December 1938, 2.
71. *Sovkhoznaia gazeta*, 18 April 1936, 2.
72. *Sovkhoznaia gazeta*, 18 April 1936, 2.

73. *Sovkhoznaia gazeta*, 18 April 1936, 2.

74. *Sovkhoznaia gazeta*, 18 April 1936, 2.

75. *Sovkhoznaia gazeta*, 18 April 1936, 2.

76. *Sovkhoznaia gazeta*, 4 April 1938, 1.

77. RGASPI, f. 17, op. 123, d. 6, l. 63.

78. *Sovkhoznaia gazeta*, 14 April 1936, 3.

79. *Sovkhoznaia gazeta*, 14 April 1936, 3.

80. *Sovkhoznaia gazeta*, 14 April 1936, 3.

81. *Sovkhoznaia gazeta*, 14 April 1936, 3.

82. *Sovkhoznaia gazeta*, 16 June 1936, 1.

83. GARF, f. 7689, op. 11, d. 119, l. 49.

84. GARF, f. 7689, op. 11, d. 119, l. 49.

85. GARF, f. 7689, op. 11, d. 113, l. 134.

86. GARF, f. 7689, op. 11, d. 119, l. 49. Other sources indicate that peasants had no windows due to a lack of glass. See GARF, f. 7689, op. 11, d. 320, l. 100ob.

87. *Sovkhoznaia gazeta*, 18 April 1936, 2.

88. Likewise, on a sheep farm in Dagestan, two Stakhanovites lived "in bad flats" but the farm leadership "did nothing to create better conditions for them." See *Sovkhoznaia gazeta*, 8 April 1936, 3.

89. *Sovkhoznaia gazeta*, 8 April 1936, 3.

90. *Sovkhoznaia gazeta*, 14 April 1936, 3. *Kul'turnost'* embraced literary improvement as well as a neater and cleaner way of living. Refer back to the section on "Superiority and Selflessness in the Intelligentsia" in chapter 3.

91. *Sovkhoznaia gazeta*, 14 April 1936, 3.

92. GARF, f. 7689, op. 10, d. 177, l. 5.

93. Mary Buckley, "The Untold Story of *Obshchestvennitsa*," *Europe-Asia Studies* 48, no. 4 (1996): 569–86; and Buckley, "The Soviet "Wife-Activist" Down on the Farm," *Social History* 26, no. 3 (October 2001): 282–98.

94. GARF, f. 7689, op. 11, d. 48, l. 160.

95. GARF, f. 7689, op. 11, d. 48, l. 160. The press also argued that poor living and working conditions in the fields were contributory factors to poor work. From Kamenskii raion, Cheliabinsk oblast, it was reported that, "In the fields you don't meet one well-equipped hut. They are falling down with broken windows and huge cracks. The huts have no bedding, wash basin, towel, or even simple soap." A tractor brigade leader commented, "We live as in the woods. We see no books or newspapers." See *Krest'ianskaia gazeta*, 10 May 1937, 1. The press suggested that peasants deserved better and that these conditions were hardly incentives for Stakhanovite work. What was omitted was that Stakhanovites themselves could not easily alter this predicament; at best, they could make demands on others.

96. *Sovkhoznaia gazeta*, 20 September 1938, 3.

97. See, for example, RGASPI, f. 17, op. 120, d. 277, ll. 42–55; RGASPI, f. 17, op. 120, d. 188, l. 28. Often peasants were sent off farms illegally. See RGASPI, f. 17, op. 120, d. 334, ll. 44–47; for commentary on Tadzhikistan, Kirgizia, Western Siberia, Kursk oblast, Karel'ia, Altai krai, and Novosibirsk oblast, see RGASPI, f. 17, op. 120, d. 334, ll. 21–26; for detailed All-Union statistics broken down by republic and oblast

on the extent of collectivization and the movement off farms, refer to RGASPI, f. 17, op. 120, d. 334, ll. 41–41ob.

98. See, for instance, RGASPI, f. 17, op. 120, d. 277, l. 34 on Kalinin oblast.

99. *Sovkhoznaia gazeta*, 26 November 1935, 4.

100. See, for example, GARF, f. 7689, op. 11, d. 119, l. 61; and GARF, f. 7689, op. 4, d. 81, l. 82.

101. *Sovkhoznaia gazeta*, 26 November 1936, 4.

102. *Sovkhoznaia gazeta*, 30 August 1937, 1.

103. *Sovkhoznaia gazeta*, 30 August 1937, 1.

104. GARF, f. 7689, op. 11, d. 42, l. 44.

105. *Sovkhoznaia gazeta*, 30 August 1937, 1.

106. GARF, f. 7689, op. 11, d. 119, ll. 46–47.

107. RGASPI, f. 17, op. 123, d. 14, l. 22.

108. RGASPI, f. 17, op. 123, d. 14, l. 22.

109. RGASPI, f. 17, op. 123, d. 6, l. 63.

110. RGASPI, f. 17, op. 123, d. 6, l. 64.

111. RGASPI, f. 17, op. 123, d. 10, l. 4.

112. RGASPI, f. 17, op. 123, d. 10, l. 4. For commentary on increases in 1936 in the pay of state farm tractor drivers, see GARF, f. 7689, op. 11, d. 42, l. 7.

113. *Krest'ianskaia gazeta*, 14 October 1936, 3.

114. GARF, f. 7689, op. 11, d. 119, l. 17.

115. GARF, f. 7689, op. 11, d. 119, l. 48.

116. See, for instance, RGASPI, f. 17, op. 121, d. 83, ll. 65–67. This is a letter written in March 1941 to Commissar Benediktov at Narkomzem from Vaksov in Narkomzem in the Crimea about the need to stimulate tractor drivers through higher pay. Legislation in 1941 apparently achieved higher productivity by increasing pay.

117. RGAE, f. 396, op. 10, d. 44, l. 90. This source refers to 'Petro" and not to 'Petr' which could be a misspelling.

118. RGAE, f. 396, op. 10, d. 20, l. 180.

119. Obscenity appears to have been common. See RGAE, f. 396, op. 10, d. 38, l. 50; and RGAE, f. 396, op. 10, d. 48, l. 204. Although most cases in archives and in the press concerned individual cases of bad behavior, occasionally a "socialist realist" letter painted a different picture. One *kolkhoznik* from Belorussia declared that when representatives of the sel'sovet had visited his village before the May Day holiday, they were surprised to see lots of bottles of vodka on the shelves of the village general stores. In fact, "there was an excess supply of vodka!" This was indeed "something new," especially since "drunkenness was the most usual phenomenon at weddings and funerals." This was explained by the propaganda that "now the kolkhoznik does not need vodka. With every day the collective farmer is becoming more cultured. Taste for good things is awakening, for a good cultured life. Now the collective farmer needs nice clothes, furniture and an interesting book." See *Krest'ianskaia gazeta*, 14 May 1936, 2. One vital point was to criticize the assumption that all the peasants wanted was vodka. It is conceivable that this was one element of resistance to the "peasant bashing," noted by Sheila Fitzpatrick, that had accompanied the laws of 1933 which tightened up peasants' freedom to leave the village. Peasant bashing

was a discourse that made negative remarks about peasants, sometimes in the guise of kulak bashing, but was directed at peasant attitudes and behavior. See Sheila Fitzpatrick, "The Great Departure: Rural-Urban Migration in the Soviet Union, 1929–1933," in *Social Dimensions of Soviet Industrialization*, eds. William G. Rosenberg and Lewis Siegelbaum (Bloomington: Indiana University Press, 1993), 29.

120. RGASPI, f. 17, op. 120, d. 292, l. 117.

121. RGASPI, f. 17, op. 120, d. 292, l. 118.

122. RGASPI, f. 17, op. 123, d. 6, l. 34.

123. RGASPI, f. 17, op. 123, d. 6, l. 34.

124. Detailed statistics on districts and cantons giving breakdowns of why farm leaders leave their posts or are removed intermittently appear in party archives. See, for example, RGASPI, f. 17, op. 120, d. 188, l. 28. Covering, in 1935, thirty-five districts and fifteen cantons, with a total of 1,330 collective farms, these data show a 10 percent turnover to better jobs, 3 percent due to illness, 27 percent for bad work, 13 percent for criminal activity, and 20 percent for counterrevolutionary activity, drunkenness and embezzlement.

125. RGASPI, f. 17, op. 123, d. 6, l. 36.

126. RGASPI, f. 17, op. 123, d. 6, l. 36.

127. RGASPI, f. 17, op. 123, d. 6, l. 56.

128. RGASPI, f. 17, op. 120, d. 292, l. 25.

129. RGASPI, f. 17, op. 120, d. 292, l. 25.

130. RGASPI, f. 17, op. 120, d. 292, l. 46.

131. RGASPI, f. 17, op. 120, d. 277, l. 96.

132. RGASPI, f. 17, op. 120, d. 277, l. 97.

133. RGASPI, f. 17, op. 120, d. 277, l. 97.

134. RGASPI, f. 17, op. 120, d. 277, l. 97.

135. RGASPI, f. 17, op. 120, d. 277, l. 97.

136. RGASPI, f. 17, op. 120, d. 277, l. 97.

137. RGASPI, f. 17, op. 120, d. 277, l. 97 and l. 99.

138. RGASPI, f. 17, op. 120, d. 277, l. 96.

139. RGASPI, f. 17, op. 120, d. 277, l. 96.

140. Interview conducted on 14 September 1996, Vladimir Il'ich Collective Farm, Moscow oblast.

141. RGASPI, f. 17, op. 120, d. 277, l. 98.

142. RGASPI, f. 17, op. 120, d. 277, l. 99.

143. RGASPI, f. 17, op. 123, d. 6, l. 110.

144. RGASPI, f. 17, op. 123, d. 6, l. 110.

145. Archival documents also draw attention to the high turnover of MTS directors and problems of their low educational levels. See RGASPI, f. 17, op. 121, d. 123, ll. 123–24. A letter from Benediktov to Andreev points out that in the first half of 1939, 49 percent of MTS directors were dismissed from their posts. See RGASPI, f. 17, op. 121, d. 123, l. 118.

146. RGASPI, f. 17, op. 123, d. 10, l. 1.

147. RGASPI, f. 17, op. 123, d. 10, l. 3.

148. RGASPI, f. 17, op. 123, d. 10, l. 2. The report declared, "The leadership of Narkomzem SSSR in its current composition relates extremely timidly to the promotion of Stakhanovites, of specialists completing study and of deputies of the Supreme Soviets of Union and Autonomous republics to main leadership positions."

149. RGASPI, f. 17, op. 123, d. 10, l. 2.

150. Accompanying the charges against Narkomzem were recommendations for its restructuring to overcome the defects of its functional structure. See RGASPI, f. 17, op. 123, d. 10, ll. 33–47.

151. RGASPI, f. 17, op. 123, d. 9, l. 8.

152. RGASPI, f. 17, op. 123, d. 9, l. 10.

153. RGASPI, f. 17, op. 123, d. 9, l. 10.

154. RGASPI, f. 17, op. 1, d. 782, l. 6.

155. RGASPI, f. 17, op. 1, d. 782, l. 1.

156. RGASPI, f. 17, op. 123, d. 9, l. 11.

157. For an illuminating letter to Andreev on the leadership of Narkomzem and on surprise at the appointment of Benediktov in November 1938, see RGASPI, f. 17, op. 120, d. 337, l. 59. It argues that a "much stronger" appointment was expected.

158. Mark B. Tauger, "The People's Commissariat of Agriculture," in *Decision-Making in the Stalinist Command Economy, 1932–1937*, ed. E. A. Rees (London: Macmillan, 1997), 150–75.

159. RGASPI, f. 17, op. 123, d. 14, l. 25.

Chapter Nine

Why Be a Rural Shock Worker or Stakhanovite?

Of course they gave me bonuses many times.

— Ermolai Iudin, Stakhanovite shepherd[1]

I lived very well on the state farm. I went to resorts twice—to Piatigorsk and to Eisk.

— Taisiia Prokop'eva, Stakhanovite milkmaid[2]

I already study every day. The party raikom has attached a teacher to me. Soon I shall study at the institute. What a joy!

— Pasha Kovardak, Stakhanovite tractor driver[3]

If resistance to shock work and Stakhanovism ranged from belittling to violence, why did some peasants seek Stakhanovite status? If those hostile to shock work and Stakhanovism were as unkind as the press and procuracy archives indicate, what benefits did peasants receive from becoming heroines and heroes of the fields? If *udarniki* and *stakhanovtsy* were targets of abuse for those who lived with them on the farm, how could praise from the regime compensate for torment close at hand? If becoming a shock worker or Stakhanovite required stepping outside dominant communal cultural values of "sameness," what prompted peasants to want to be "different"? If many farm leaders, directors of Machine Tractor Stations, and district party secretaries did not always help shock workers and Stakhanovites to attain their goals, why bother to strive for them against the odds?

In fact, the material attractions of shock work and Stakhanovism were several, ranging from higher wages, bonuses, and presents to promises of better housing, food, healthcare, and education. Rural workers on state farms, unlike collective farmers, could complain to a trade union if the appropriate benefits were not forthcoming and seek redress. The status of shock worker or Stakhanovite also brought recognition for hard work through invitations to congresses and conferences at which Orders of Lenin and other decorations were awarded for production feats. For many this was a psychological boost to self-esteem. Fame ensued for the most heroic, like Mariia Demchenko and Pasha Angelina. Furthermore, for some, becoming a shock worker or Stakhanovite amounted to a fulfillment of personal dreams and, in the case of women, greater self-determination in a context of traditional gender roles. Moreover, those who took pride in their work and were generally diligent anyway may have found that Stakhanovite ideals fit their nature and aspirations. More broadly, conformists who aimed to adopt the regime's priorities and those who genuinely believed in the need to construct communism, to strive down the radiant path to a glorious utopian future, to improve rural life, and to follow Stalin's calls, may have felt drawn to Stakhanovite work methods through agitprop's exhortations. Arguably, Stakhanovites were variously motivated and attracted by a range of incentives—material, emotional, and ideological.

WAGES AND BONUSES

Shock workers and Stakhanovites in industry and in agriculture were meant to earn more than non–shock workers and non-Stakhanovites. There was thus an immediate financial incentive to work harder and to attain new records. As pig breeder Tat'iana Daeva put it, "I now earn 400–500 rubles a month. My qualifications and wages are increasing."[4] Others stressed the new possibility of helping others. Milkmaid Taisiia Prokop'eva told how "I earned well which allowed me to help my mother and young brothers."[5] Men especially tended to emphasize the importance of providing well for their family. Combine driver Fedor Kolesov advertised that he was happy to earn "good wages" and that "For the summer of 1935 I earned 3,864 rubles and could provide my family with a completely satisfied life. I bought myself, my wife and children suits, shoes and bedding." He explained that his financial future was rosy because "in 1936 I shall earn even more because 751 hectares is far from the limit for a combine harvester." Promise lay in the fact that "it is the sort of machine with unlimited possibilities."[6] Those who worked on tractors and combines enjoyed the optimism that they could earn more once they had harnessed the machine's full potential.[7]

On top of higher wages came bonuses. The shepherd Ermolai Iudin acknowledged, "of course they gave me bonuses many times. So many, that it is embarrassing to say."[8] The details were as follows: "For lambs produced above the plan I received 800 rubles. For passing the winter well, 350 rubles from the Competition Commission of the Central Committee of the Komsomol." In addition, "for overfulfilling the wool clipping plan I received 700 rubles in a bonus, my helper the herdsboy Aleksei Fomin 600 rubles."[9] Two others in the brigade had been awarded 400 and 200 rubles and the brigade itself "received the natural prize of twenty lambs."[10] The most famous Stakhanovites, like Iudin and Mariia Demchenko, regularly received bonuses. In 1935, Demchenko received an advance of 867 kilos of bread and 320 rubles.[11] Reward came in rubles and in kind.

Since the wages and bonuses paid to shock workers and Stakhanovites were meant to outstrip those earned by other peasants, for those to whom this mattered, Stakhanovite status was worth the effort. The promise of more money could motivate. We have already seen, however, that pay formulas did not always reward Stakhanovites when they should have and that farm leaders did not necessarily make the appropriate payments, or else payments came late.[12] Nonetheless, knowledge that better wages were due, or had in fact been received already, was one factor that prompted Stakhanovite performances.

BETTER LIVING CONDITIONS

Stakhanovites were also meant to be given better accommodation than other peasants and trade unions on state farms particularly stressed their commitment to this, although few Stakhanovites may have attained the standard enjoyed by Pasha Angelina shown in Figure 9.1. In 1936 a Resolution of the Presidium of the Central Committee of the Trade Union of Dairy State Farms obliged directors of state farms "to create the necessary living conditions for Stakhanovites and for the best shock workers," as well as to repair their flats and hostels and to provide them with fuel.[13] The same union's Presidium adopted another Resolution to check that socialist competitions were being organized across farms and that Stakhanovites were being prepared for these, as the December Plenum of the Central Committee of the Communist party had decreed. Here "preparing Stakhanovites" included providing them with good material and living conditions. The union's Resolution called upon investigators "to check how Stakhanovites are living and what hinders their work."[14] It specifically asked how each farm's administration and workers' committee helped to improve Stakhanovites' living conditions. It instructed, "check how cooperation works and how workers are provided with clothes, shoes, articles of recreation and food products." Investigators were also to discover how the canteen worked—in particular "the quality of the food,

Figure 9.1.   Pasha Angelina, comfortable at home and praising the rewards of hard work. Source: P. *Angelina,* Liudi Kolkhoznykh Polei *(Moscow and Leningrad: Gosudarstvennoe Izdatel'stvo Detskoi Literatury, 1952).*

prices and advantages for Stakhanovites."[15] Unions, then, did gather data on the treatment of Stakhanovites on state farms.

On the farms themselves, workers' committees sometimes reiterated the importance of paying special attention to Stakhanovites. In December 1935 at a conference of workers' committees and of the best shock workers and Stakhanovites of poultry state farms in Kuibyshev krai, it was announced: "We must look after our workers in a cultured way, we must create better living conditions for them."[16] Often it was an *obshchestvennitsa* as a member of the wives' movement who paid attention to the living standards of Stakhanovites and also to the recreation facilities available to them. On the Pushkin fur state farm, for example, the wives organized a room in which Stakhanovites could rest.[17] On a bird state farm, the wives took "measures to improve the cultural/living conditions of workers, especially Stakhanovites."[18]

Archives show that trade unions took pains to record their successes. In 1936, a member of the Union of Dairy State Farms of the Central and Southern Districts congratulated the union for "in the recent past" creating "normal cultural-living conditions for Stakhanovites of the state farms." He itemized: "In the Western oblast in Shavyrina's three-room flat, the wallpaper is being renewed and at the expense of the state farm she acquired six Viennese nickel plated chairs, an iron bed and a mirror." Others had been "given nice flats with electric light and an installed radio." Two children of one Stakhanovite "are in the nursery free of charge" and "their mother's pigs are provided with feed."[19]

The list of successes went on. Comrade Novikov (state farm number 14) in Azovo-Chernomore krai had a room with a separate kitchen. The workers' committee provided the children of his dead brother with shoes and clothes.[20] In Khar'kov oblast comrade Sleptsov on "Communist" state farm "was given a good flat of two clean and light rooms, was bought two excellent beds, a soft sofa, 6 chairs and so on, given a shed and a cellar, helped to obtain boots and felt boots and three pairs of boots for the family."[21] These examples illustrate the range of ways in which Stakhanovites were helped, from more luxurious items to the most basic boots. The state farm trade unions participated actively in promoting this social differentiation of living conditions to the resentment and envy of many non-Stakhanovites. Trotsky's "revolution betrayed" was Stalin's reward to the loyal and hardworking.[22]

Orders from the People's Commissariat of State Farms regularly reminded farm leaders that their duty was to improve Stakhanovites' lives. A typical *prikaz* would begin either by drawing attention to a farm that successfully looked after Stakhanovites, or alternatively by exposing one that did not.[23] Order number seventy-two of 8 June 1936, for instance, praised the excellent work of the political department on a state farm in Sverdlovsk oblast. Advanced workers and Stakhanovites here were shown "exceptional warmth" and were surrounded with "care and attention."[24] If Stakhanovites were not looked after, they often wrote to trade unions themselves to say what they needed, effectively giving itemized shopping lists, and trade unions conducted questionnaires among the best rural workers with a view to improving their lives.[25] Stakhanovites also received special attention when ill. Ermolai Iudin suffered from rheumatism in the legs, so bad that "I simply could not walk."[26] The workers' committee and the political department immediately helped. Iudin was taken to a hospital in Rostov where he was fed "butter, eggs and different fruits."[27] He made it clear that these foods were not part of his regular diet.

In sum, daily life was meant to be better for Stakhanovites and they were supposed to be the upwardly mobile of the countryside. This logically extended to opportunities for education and self-improvement.

EDUCATION

People's Commissariats, the party and trade union Central Committees ordered special education for Stakhanovites. *Prikazy* sent down from the People's Commissariat of State Farms instructed that teachers should be attached to individual Stakhanovites. This order aimed to make illiterate Stakhanovites literate, to improve the knowledge of semiliterate and literate Stakhanovites, and to turn the most able into agronomists.

Peasants recounted how they were accorded special attention. When Ermolai Iudin was in hospital in Rostov, one Ponomarenko came from the union Central Committee and declared: "see how you work well, but you are not literate. A Stakhanovite must be literate and be thirsting for knowledge and cultural growth. We will give you a teacher so that within a year you will be literate."[28] Iudin simply narrated:

> So I study now. They gave me a teacher. Not only me, but the whole brigade studies. Vasili Shakhov is the teacher. We write down dictation and multiplication tables and we study everything in general. The Central Committee of our trade union sent 200 rubles for my studying. They sent a library, 40 little books. The literature there is varied.[29]

While Iudin was given basic education, literate Stakhanovites were taught more about their particular crop and about Russian literature and geography. Some then went on to research institutes. In 1936, for example, Pasha Kovardak was promised the opportunity to study full-time in 1937. In the meantime, she told how "I already study every day. The party raikom has attached a teacher to me. Soon I shall study at the institute. What a joy!"[30] So both local party organizations and trade union Central Committees ensured that some Stakhanovites enjoyed individual tuition from assigned teachers to suit their particular needs.

Sometimes courses were organized for those in particular sectors of agriculture as commanded by *prikaz* number 837 of the People's Commissariat of Agriculture of 10 December 1936 "On the organization of courses for those decorated with medals and for Stakhanovites in horse breeding."[31] The explicit aim of the *prikaz* was "raising" their "general educational and technical level." It called for a six-month course to be organized in Moscow for fifty peasants, beginning on 25 December and carrying a grant of 150 rubles a month.

A detailed plan of the course for horse breeders followed. For six hours a day, amounting to 900 hours over six months, the peasants would receive instruction as itemized in Table 9.1. Given the dire shortage of traction power due to the slaughter and starvation of horses associated with collectivization, such courses were designed to improve the care and reproduction of horses.[32] As well as instilling greater specialist knowledge in the horse breeder with a view to obtaining better work standards, the course inevitably delivered a dose of political education along with simple study skills.

In 1937 the Moscow Agricultural Academy named after Timiriasev organized three-year courses for Stakhanovites who had been decorated. The aim was to prepare them for further study in higher education. Combine driver Konstantin Borin took advantage of this opportunity and was later employed there as a lecturer after having attained the degree of candidate of agricultural science.[33] Many other famous names passed through this Academy. Pasha Angelina graduated in 1940.[34] Mariia Demchenko attended the Ukrainian equivalent, leaving the Kiev Agricultural Institute in 1945.[35] From then until

Table 9.1.   Study Plan for Horse Breeders' Six-Month Course

1. Political Education	100 Hours
2. Russian Language	145
3. Arithmetic	125
4. Geography	60
Total 1:	430 Hours
5. Anatomy and Physiology of Agricultural Animals	50
6. Feeding (*kormodobyvanie*) and Agronomy	60
7. Fundamentals of Animal Hygiene, Veterinary Sanitation, and Preventive Measures	90
8. Horse Breeding	200
9. Mechanizing Horse Breeding	30
10. The Basics of Planning, Organization, and Stock-taking of Production and Labor in Horse Breeding	40
Total 2:	470 Hours
Overall Total of 1 + 2:	900 Hours

Source: RGAE, f. 7486, op. 1, d. 887, l. 11.

1958 she worked as an agronomist in Kiev oblast.[36] Marina Gnatenko also continued into postgraduate study, writing a dissertation on the harvesting of sugar beet on the Comintern collective farm in Kiev oblast.[37]

Raising the education level of Stakhanovites was consistent with the image that Stakhanovites were "better" than others and part of the rural technical intelligentsia. This made them fitting delegates to conferences and congresses.

SPECIAL CONGRESSES, CONFERENCES, EXHIBITIONS, DECORATIONS, AND PRESENTS

Because they shone as good workers, shock workers and Stakhanovites were mobilized to participate as delegates to congresses and conferences. Mariia Demchenko, shown in Figure 9.2, was sent to the Second All-Union Congress of Kolkhoz Shock Workers because she "was one of the best shock workers of the district."[38] Moreover, delegates knew that they had been chosen for their outstanding achievements, a privilege which could boost their self-esteem. Such invitations were honors, not only to be near to top leaders, but also to be actively involved in the proceedings by giving a short speech on one's work or by chairing a session. Participants saw their name in the newspaper and could read about their receipt of a medal. These sparkling events also meant an excursion to the capital where they were given much better food

Figure 9.2. A delegation from Kiev oblast with Stalin, Kaganovich, Voroshilov, and Kalinin at the second All-Union Congress of Kolkhoz Shock Workers in Moscow. Mariia Demchenko is between Stalin and Kalinin (with the beard and glasses) in the row behind. Source: Vtoroi Vsesoiuznyi s"ezd kolkhoznikov-udarnikov *(Moscow: Sel'khozgiz, 1935).*

than usual. Participation was highly selective and those who attended returned to farms where the majority had never been to such a grand affair. The returning Stakhanovites were lauded in the press as local "stars."

The peasants who chaired the Second Congress's nine sessions which extended over seven days subsequently wrote pamphlets on what it felt like to assume such a huge responsibility in front of an audience of 1,100 delegates. Aleksei Zavgorodnyi from Dnepropetrovsk oblast recounted how he immediately felt that everyone was looking at him as soon as he had been asked to take the chair and how his heart sank at the idea. But he rose to the honor and after his session experienced much excitement.[39] Like others, Tat'iana Shapovalova declared that the day that she chaired "will remain a memory all my life. And all my life I shall never forget when Stalin came up to me and asked: 'Was it you who chaired yesterday? Well done.'"[40] Shapovalova described how she was especially happy to have chaired Nadezhda Krupskaia, Lenin's widow:

> With great happiness, as chairperson, I introduced Nadezhda Konstantinovna Krupskaia to the Congress. The Congress greeted her, especially the women collective farmers, in a most hearty way. Everyone stood up to meet her and there was an unusual silence in the hall as she spoke.[41]

It is not difficult to believe that Shapovalova, a field worker from Kalachevskii district in Voronezh oblast, was indeed most proud to have introduced Krupskaia, however nervous she may have been.

From even further away in the then Kazak ASSR, tractor driver Beken Tankin told how he reacted to the request to chair a session with these words: "I have never been a chairperson. I am tractor driver." When he finally chaired, he said to himself "Beken, you are on a tractor. Be careful! There must not be one breakdown, just as on the kolkhoz." He went on, "I read whom to introduce. I must not make a mistake. If you say Shankin instead of Tankin, there will be a scandal."[42] Having managed the proceedings in Russian, not his native language, Tankin then became puzzled when he lost control of the auditorium and congress participants began shouting "hooray!" As he put it: "I did not understand immediately what was happening. When Russian is spoken quickly, I do not at first grasp it. I only began speaking Russian two years ago. I thought, probably the speaker said something important."[43] The shouting, however, did not stop:

> Suddenly someone put a hand on my shoulder. I look round—Comrade Stalin. Comrade Stalin was on the Presidium! So the ovation was for him.
> Comrade Stalin is smiling, slaps me on the back with one hand and indicates towards the table with the other. . . . He is back.[44]

Stalin wanted Tankin to press a button on the table to quieten the hall. Tankin later concluded that at the time he thought, "I'll go home to my collective farm with something to talk about."[45]

While the skeptic may dismiss the words of Demchenko, Zavgorodnyi, Shapovalova, and Tankin as contrived, suiting the regime's values and the ceremonial theatricality of what Jeffrey Brooks calls "correct performance," it is quite feasible that the authors believed what they said and indeed prized highly their role in the conference and proximity to Stalin.[46] Whilst from one perspective such congresses can be viewed as "primitive ritualistic drama" characterized by "recurrent themes, stereotypical characters and symbolic settings," the stereotypical Stakhanovites, nonetheless, however outwardly similar, still enjoyed different personal histories, experiences, personalities, ages, geographic locations, and nationalities.[47] The extent and nature of the patterns of their beliefs in the system, work, perks, and Stalin will have varied somewhat. Undoubtedly they benefited from their complicity in this performance, however they appraised it.

Although this Soviet Stakhanovite chorus was here to "certify" public values and not to query them like Brooks's Greek chorus, it does not necessarily follow that they failed to treasure the fanfare that surrounded the Congress.[48] The front pages of Soviet newspapers blazoned photographs of its smiling delegates alongside Stalin, reported highlights of its speeches, and imparted great detail about the peasants who attended, the geographic spread from which they were drawn, and the number of medals awarded to them. Newsreels relayed speeches to the Soviet people. Peasants may indeed have returned to their farms with renewed vigor to play their enthusiastic part, committing themselves to higher production targets, however ritualistic and officially patterned.

Shock workers and Stakhanovites were also called to attend exhibitions of their own achievements. The importance of such events was propagandized in films. When the heroine Glasha in *Svinarka i Pastukh* (The Female Pig Rearer and the Herdsman) received her invitation to an exhibition in Moscow, she cried with shrieks of delight and in disbelief "Me to Moscow!" Once at the exhibition she took detailed notes from the different exhibits on Stakhanovite work methods, just as her grandmother had instructed, concentrating on the weight of different pigs and on how much they were fed. At the same exhibition one year later, Glasha's huge portrait adorned a billboard alongside other successful peasants. Official tours stopped at their portraits to draw attention to production records. Inevitably publicity and acclaim ensued.

Invitations to conferences and exhibitions were signs of recognition and they brought decorations, higher status, and fame for some. Advanced combine drivers, for example, were decorated in December 1935. Sixty-eight received the Order of Lenin, sixty-six the Order of the Red Banner, and sixty-three the Badge of Honor.[49] Then in February 1936, 1,373 received medals at the Conference of Advanced Workers in Animal Husbandry with Leaders of the Party and Government. Three hundred and sixty seven of these were awarded the Order of Lenin for milking more than 3,500 liters in the European part of the Union and for 3,000 liters in Eastern regions. Four hundred and twenty four peasants were given the Order of the Red Banner for between 3,250 and 3,500 liters in the European part of the USSR and for between 2,700 to 3,000 in eastern regions. Finally, 582 were decorated with the Badge of Honor for between 3,000 and 3,250 liters in European regions and for between 2,500 and 2,700 liters in the East. Decorations were carefully graded according to the extent of the output and geographical locations.[50] Over five pages of the names of recipients of medals were printed in the press.[51]

The emotion surrounding the receipt of orders was described as frequently intense. When, for example, the young Mamlakat Nakhangova received the Order of Lenin from Kalinin at an All-Union Conference of Stakhanovites, "gasping with happiness the girl was unable to thank Mikhail Ivanovich."[52] She was apparently emotionally overcome by the honor.

As well as receiving orders, shock workers and Stakhanovites were given presents for their endeavors. Praising those in attendance at a meeting of advanced collective farmers of Tadzhikistan and Turkmenistan, Stalin declared:

> The government has decided to give a lorry to each collective farm represented here and to make a present of a record player and records to each of the participants of this meeting (Applause). And watches: pocket watches for the men, and wrist watches for the women (Prolonged applause).[53]

Sometimes presents were distributed to conference participants as above, or alternatively awarded to individuals for special feats. Petrova, a female combine driver, told a Conference of Advanced Male and Female Combine Drivers, "I mowed 544 hectares and received 2,250 rubles. (Applause). Apart from what I earned, I received a motorcycle from Comrade Chernov at the People's Commissariat of Agriculture and a gramophone from the krai."[54] The receipt of presents became part of the assessment of self-worth, integral to the successful Stakhanovite's identity.

Shock workers and Stakhanovites, then, were regularly and visibly rewarded with honors and large presents out of the reach of other peasants. The same applied to special holidays and visits.

HOLIDAYS, REST HOMES, AND SPECIAL VISITS

Rewards included holidays in special sanatoria and trips to cities and the seaside. The press often reported on the building of elite rest homes, especially for Stakhanovites. *Sovkhoznaia gazeta* in 1936 revealed that near a railway station "in a picturesque spot, not far from the lake 'Sebezh,' a new rest home for Stakhanovite pig tenders is under construction." The building was for 100 people and extremely rare was the fact that "married Stakhanovites will have their own separate room."[55] Those who worked hard could thus enjoy a luxury not known to others.

Details of the holidays enjoyed were included in biographies and autobiographies. The Stakhanovite milkmaid Taisiia Prokop'eva recounted how "I lived very well on the state farm. I went to resorts twice—to Piatigorsk and to Eisk." Holidays, however, had to fit around her work schedule. She described how "on both occasions it was autumn. In summer, when my cows have just given birth, it is impossible for me to be absent."[56] The People's Commissariat of State Farms encouraged farms to send Stakhanovites to sanatoria and praised those that provided holidays in southern resorts. The commissariat was also keen for the young pioneers who joined in the harvesting to go to camp.[57]

As one of the shock workers of the First Five-Year Plan, Mamlakat Nakhangova was invited to relax in the All-Union Pioneer sanatorium "Artek." Here she enjoyed the sea "warm, blue and sweet."[58] Not only did she meet other shock workers and develop a sense of being a "special" worker but she also made international contacts. Here, too, were Spanish children "whose parents were courageously fighting fascists" in the Civil War. Among them were the daughter and son of Dolores Ibarruri, known as "La Pasionaria," heroine of Spanish communism.[59]

Trips to city tourist spots were also common for Stakhanovites, especially for delegates to conferences. The Tadzhik delegation to the All-Union Congress of Stakhanovites, for instance, afterward visited Leningrad. As a member of this group, "Mamlakat walked around the city and marvelled at the beauty of its palaces and avenues."[60] Here the delegation was invited to visit the "Red Triangle" factory. Mamlakat was impressed by its size and received a present by its workers of a rubber elephant.[61]

Visits to factories and construction projects showed rural workers industrial successes. Under the heading "Excursion of state farm shock workers to DneproGES," *Sovkhoznaia gazeta* told how thirty of the best shock workers on one farm were shown around the station and factories. The story ran that "DneproGES made a strong impression" and the peasants went back to their farm to tell everyone about the trip.[62] Probably far more exciting was a visit for combine harvest drivers to a football match. In September 1935, 277 combine drivers from the South were honored in Moscow and around 100 of these "state farm masters of the harvest were present at a football match between Moscow and Ukraine."[63] Others went to the zoo, metro, Central House of the Red Army, and in the evening "to a music hall and to the circus." As part of their treat "after talking to Commissar Kalmanovich, the combine drivers went to the Park of Culture named after Gor'kii" and some went to the opera.[64] Effort had gone into providing a varied program.

Through these special social programs, trips, and holidays in recognition of production feats, the regime gave shock workers and Stakhanovites the message that they were distinct from other peasants, worthy of praise, respect, rewards, and publicity.

SUPPORT FROM STATE FARM TRADE UNIONS

State farm workers enjoyed the support of their union in the event of grievances about not having received sufficient perks. Whilst not all cases may have been championed with equal verve and although not all farm leaderships or people's commissariats may have listened to what the union had to say, unions did nonetheless take up the causes of wronged Stakhanovites and attempted to make farm directors and administrators in high places more responsive to their needs. Trade union archives, particularly those of dairy farms, are rich in correspondence between Stakhanovites, the union, and state farm leaderships on issues concerning living standards, education, holidays, pay, and health care. There is strong evidence of attempts to accommodate Stakhanovites, to show concern for their well-being, and to bring about improvement in their lives.

One letter from the Chair of the Central Committee of Union of Dairy State farms to the chair of the Armenian Committee of the union, with a copy to the director and workers' committee of the Loriiskii state farm, listed a string of grievances, beginning typically with "Your state farm up until now has not created conditions for the work of the animal husbandry brigade of medal-winner Comrade Pogosian."[65] The union then complained that "A teacher has not been attached to comrade Pogosian and no study has been organized for him." On the most basic level, "the living conditions of comrade Pogosian are very bad: his flat has not been repaired, the roof leaks and as a consequence the flat is filthy and uncomfortable." The union scolded, "All this, inevitably, affects the productive work of comrade Pogosian and his whole brigade" and called for action on all the items mentioned.[66] The union also criticized the fact that special food concentrates were not delivered and milkmaids had to carry it in bags "over a kilometre to the cows' feeding place."[67] The union thus acted as troubleshooter and shamer.

Child care was a particularly pressing problem for state farm Stakhanovites who were sent to study in the city. A member of the union presidium wrote to an administrative head within the Commissariat of State Farms championing the case of Comrade Lobacheva. This state farm worker had already complained to the commissariat that when she studied in Sverdlovsk, there was no one to look after her children. She also had nothing with which to feed her cow since the farm director did not permit the cutting of hay. So the union asked the Commissariat to write to the farm director, demanding that he solve these problems.[68]

Sometimes complaints referred more narrowly to working conditions. A letter from the union to the head of the administration of dairy farms in the East and in Siberia pointed out that comrade Konovalov had no special work clothes for his brigade and no cans, buckets, or gauze. The union ordered the elimination of "all obstacles holding back the work of Konovalov's brigade" and then asked for a teacher "to organize regular study with him."[69] The union ended by asking for confirmation that the appropriate measures had been taken.

The union usually wrote to Stakhanovites as well, reassuring them that action was being taken and naming those who should now help them. Accordingly, Mariia Alekseevna was told that "In order to show you practical help in your productive work, we have put the question before the People's Commissar of the Dairy Industry, Comrade Smirnov, and the head of the main administration, Comrade Zalikin, who promised to help you in the near future." She was also told that the workers committee in conjuction with her farm director would "soon organize study for you."[70] Stakhanovites were given a sense of where they stood on given complaints and whom to chase if nothing happened to improve matters.

Letters from the union to Stakhanovites also commented upon living conditions. One letter to "Respected Evdokiia Iakovlevna" noted that she was concerned that there had been no repairs to her flat for two years. The union told her, "We have put this question before the administration in order for it to give the director instructions to carry out urgent necessary repairs and to check that they are done."[71] The union showed that it was doing something and state farm workers must have felt that their problems were at least being taken seriously. Other cases that were taken up included late payment of wages, care for the sick, and tickets to rest homes.[72]

Sometimes letters from the union began with praise for production feats before itemizing a huge number of ways in which the Stakhanovite would be helped. Aleksei Semenov of Leningrad oblast received the following: "We received your letter. We are very pleased that not only you, but also other horse breeders made pledges to work in a Bolshevik manner as shock workers. We wish you success." The especially fortunate Semenov was then informed that:

On the basis of your letter comrade Semenov, the People's Commissariat of State Farms and the Central Committee of the union wrote to the director and chair of the workers' committee with the recommendation to take the following measures:

1) Furnish your flat at the expense of the state farm.
2) Help you to acquire clothes and boots.
3) Improve your food (fats and butter).
4) Help you to get feed for your own cattle.
5) Attach a teacher to you to increase your general knowledge.
6) Recommend to the obkom of the union that you receive a ticket to a rest home.[73]

One can only speculate what this meant to the recipient. Did he consider it all to be his due reward, to be expected from the state for his hard work? Or was he overwhelmed by the attention, feeling proud to be treated in this way? Or was he embarrassed because of the huge distance it created between him and non-Stakhanovites? Arguably, Stakhanovites' emotional responses were several and various but according to the regime's script, they merited this. Ultimate gratitude and a boost to self-esteem are among the likely reactions. Not all offers of help were quite this extensive.[74]

Whatever the scope of rural Stakhanovites' requests, archives confirm that unions responded to the demands of Stakhanovites, attempting to help them improve their lot. One advantage for Stakhanovites on state farms was the knowledge that their union should, in theory, pursue their interests if asked. Mechanisms of support and accommodation were known to exist and could be called upon.[75]

POLITICAL CO-OPTATION

Some Stakhanovites, like the brigade leader shown in Figure 9.3, were co-opted into the more "decorative" side of politics by being named as delegates to congresses of the Komsomol and Soviets. Although in comparison with the party, the soviets wielded little power, those who sat in their gatherings were nonetheless "involved" and "mobilized" in huge political gatherings, given a sense of belonging, and accorded an official "part" in a gigantic political theater. When Mariia Demchenko became a deputy to the Council of Nationalities of the Supreme Soviet an entire half-page in the press was devoted to her biography.[76]

Milkmaid Taisiia Prokop'eva proudly announced in an essay on "My life and work" how in April 1936 she had been chosen as a delegate to the Tenth All-Union Congress of the Lenin Komsomol which had taken place in the

Figure 9.3. Praskov'ia Zeganova, who became a Deputy of the Supreme Soviet of the RSFSR, working as a brigade leader on an MTS in Smolensk oblast. Source: Adapted from Krest'ianka, no. 15, June 1938, p. 20.

Kremlin. She narrated how "At this Congress I saw great Stalin again."[77] Later she was chosen as a delegate to the November 1936 "historic" Eighth Extraordinary Congress of Soviets "which discussed the draft Stalin Constitution." Again "With indescribable joy I listened to the speech of the leader of our people, Comrade Stalin, 'On the draft Constitution of the USSR.'"[78] At this Congress, Prokop'eva was a member of the editorial commission for examining the draft constitution, a commission chaired by Stalin. Continuing in her political path, Prokop'eva was a delegate to the Seventeenth All-Russian Congress of Soviets in 1937 and finally made a candidate member of the communist party in 1937. Predictably, she imparted, "this was one of the most happy moments of my life."[79] Although Prokop'eva had to say this, we cannot assume that she did not believe it as well. One can, however, conjecture that Stakhanovites varied in the degrees of their enthusiasm according to personality, beliefs, and expectations.

Special headlines often blazoned a more general message that "Stakhanovites are joining the party and Komsomol" and the press invariably announced when the more famous Stakhanovites became members of the party.[80] On 4 July 1937, for example, *Krest'ianskaia gazeta* reported that Pasha Kovardak had entered the party as a candidate member.[81] Generally, prominent Stakhanovites were encouraged to join. Pasha Angelina became a member in 1937, followed in 1939 by Mariia Demchenko.[82]

MIXING WITH AN "ELITE" AND FAME

At congresses, conferences, and rallies shock workers and Stakhanovites mixed with each other and the idea of their "difference" from other workers and peasants was reinforced. Also by meeting leaders, sitting on tribunes with them, and enjoying short personal conversations, they were made to feel "special," accentuating their difference.

Stakhanovites also mixed with the literary intelligentsia. When Mamlakat Nakhangova visited Moscow for the All-Union Conference of Stakhanovites, she stayed in the family of writer Abdul'kasim Lakhut. He then introduced her to the writer Nikolai Ostrovskii. Allegedly Ostrovskii said to her: "What little hands you have, but they gathered so much cotton! How did that come about?"[83] Like many shock workers and Stakhanovites, she also met Aleksei Stakhanov.

Stakhanovite records guaranteed membership of this elite group of workers and peasants and a public profile, especially if the records were large. The most famous Stakhanovites received huge numbers of letters and streams of visitors. Mariia Demchenko claimed, "People began to come here from all over the Soviet Union. Every day five or ten arrived. Journalists, photographers, writers, artists, instructors from the district, the oblast and the center." The picture was an overwhelming one in which "this one takes my photograph, that one draws my portrait another writes a novel about me." She worried that "I thought that they would trample on all my beets. I even put a notice on the plantation: "Strictly forbidden for outsiders to walk on the beets."[84] Fame could bring acclaim and disruption, too.

Evidence suggests that Stakhanovites were not initially motivated by the goal of fame. According to Pasha Angelina, she had not thought about fame in advance, rather it fell upon her:

> Still less did we think of becoming famous by asserting our right to be tractor drivers. Nevertheless, in conformity with our just Soviet customs, our persevering and ardent efforts did not go unnoticed. Fame came to us. We did not hunt for it—it came to us of its own accord.[85]

Apparently fame was not a motivation for wanting to become a Stakhanovite. Nonetheless, Pasha Angelina readily acknowledged her fame, appeared to like it, and took a very positive attitude toward it:

> Sometimes I hear the word "famous" or "celebrated" uttered in connection with my name. The government has conferred high decorations and honorable titles upon me. There is even a Pasha Angelina street in Stalino; and a ship that plies the Moscow canal is named Pasha Angelina. I am proud of and cherish all this.

Figure 9.4.   Pasha Angelina wearing her medals. Source: *Praskovya Angelina,* My Answer to an American Questionnaire *(Moscow: Foreign Languages Publishing House, 1949).*

To be famous in our country means receiving the people's highest appreciation of one's labor. Such fame is great, soul-elevating happiness.[86]

Angelina, then, coped well with her acclaim and was comfortable wearing her medals, as shown in Figure 9.4. While not all Stakhanovites can have been driven by the idea of fame, indeed may not have even considered its possibility, they probably reacted differently to it when it fell upon them, according to their personality. The young Mamlakat Nakhangova, for instance, appears to have been more overwhelmed by her fame and initially shy in front of others to a greater degree than the more confident Pasha Angelina.

DREAMS

Some peasants, particularly women, expressed a passion to do well at work. Stakhanovism, if they are to be believed, was fulfillment of a particular dream. When, for example, the farm director objected to Dar'ia Garmash wanting to become a tractor driver, Garmash responded:

It is my dream to be a tractor driver, my dream! I want it, like Pasha Angelina! You understand, like Pasha Angelina, I will not back away from my dreams. I want it, I beg you, in truth, I will be like Pasha Angelina![87]

New roles for women, like tractor driving, and also Stakhanovite status in any agricultural sector, brought assertiveness and a sense of responsibility and freedom. Pasha Angelina became an official role model for women, encouraged by the regime. Whatever the cultural or gender opposition aspiring female Stakhanovites may have encountered from family, friends, and community, this did not deter some of them from aspiring to emulate Angelina. Breaking out of traditional gender roles may have been an incentive for some women rather than a deterrent, as elaborated in the next chapter.

More generally, the project of building communism was a heroic goal, a huge dream. Those peasants who strongly identified with this may have been lured by the Stakhanovite ideal. Those who were optimistic rather than cynical, those who were loyal to Stalin and to the idea of progress, readily keen to conform to the regime's priorities rather than to resist them, would have reacted positively. The benefits discussed above may have been accelerating catalysts.

Pasha Angelina expressed her loyalty to the system as follows, recounting how it felt to visit Lenin's mausoleum:

Red Square. Not breathing, I went past the mausoleum! Lenin! He dreamed of one hundred thousand tractors for Russia. I did not know of this Leninist dream when in the spring of 1930 I first sat at the wheel of a tractor, but my heart felt the Leninist idea.[88]

Inevitably, Stalin, too, earned her praise:

According to the wise decree of Comrade Stalin, giant factories for turning out tractors were built in Stalingrad, Khar'kov and Cheliabinsk. In the fields of Staro-Beshevskii district, as in the fields of the entire country, the powerful "KhTZ," "STZ" and "ChTz" tractors are already working.[89]

While many peasants may have been cynical about the system and lacking in kind words for Lenin and Stalin, certain devotees paid lip-service to their greatness and possibly even deeply believed what they said.

INTERVIEWS CONDUCTED ON THE VLADIMIR IL'ICH COLLECTIVE FARM

In-depth interviews conducted in Moscow oblast in 1996 with three elderly collective farmers who had been shock workers in the 1930s suggested that peasants did indeed cherish fond memories of their achievements in those years.[90]

They recalled that they had taken socialist competitions and higher targets seriously. One peasant, a former milkmaid, then in her eighties, recounted that:

> Not everyone can be a Stakhanovite. It depends on the person. But work is work. It was valued on the kolkhoz. I went to Kiev. I was in the Crimea. I gave speeches wherever needed. We were proud of our collective farm. I worked until I was seventy-five years old. Work is richness.

This woman excitedly pulled out of her wardrobe an old jacket covered in medals awarded to her at agricultural exhibitions. She added that her farm in Moscow oblast had competed with farms in Ukraine to attain higher output targets. She was proud of what she had achieved and pleased to have been recognized for her hard work.

Another woman of eighty-five, once a field worker, admitted that it was hard to be a shock worker. She insisted, "of course it was difficult. You had to fulfill norms one and a half times or twice." Sixty years later "I do not remember how many of us 'advanced' peasants there were, but they took the best ones to exhibitions." When subsequently asked if the work was so hard, why then become a shock worker, she answered: "To go forward. I got more. I got more workdays, so I received more produce. I sold it at the market in Moscow. I had four children. I had to clothe them."

On collective farms in the 1930s peasants' labor was measured according to the "workday" (*trudoden'*), which was calculated according to task and to productivity rather than the number of days actually worked. On this particular farm, which was a rich one, for each *trudoden'* peasants received eight kilos of potatoes, one kilo of cucumbers, two to three kilos of cabbages, one to two kilos of carrots, and varying amounts of rubles. Food that was not eaten was sold. The more workdays that peasants accumulated, the more produce they had to sell. Thus the more productive the peasant, the more work days awarded and the more money earned at market.

A third woman in her eighties, a former pig tender, was asked if the kolkhoz chairperson helped the shock workers. She burst out laughing with:

> What do you mean did the Chair help *udarniki*? He didn't help us. We tried ourselves. I got a medal at the VDNKh. I worked on the pig farm. I wanted it. It was interesting. Then I wanted more.

These peasants in the 1990s viewed the 1930s and 1940s as difficult times, but years in which they did want to do better and earn more. A fourth kolkhoz member felt, moreover, that shock workers were respected:

> Why? Because they worked better. They thought about how they could milk better. They considered new methods. They were progressive. They set examples

for others. They studied with the agronomist. They learnt. Today they say liquidate the collective farms! But they were real schools of learning.

When pressed on whether there were other reasons for aspiring to be shock workers, one quickly reacted, as though reading the as yet unasked question on my mind: "There was no *prikaz* (order). It was voluntary. You earned what you worked. It was in your interest."

These elderly women, then, stressed self-interest as the main reason for striving harder, followed by being valued by the collective farm. The one who traveled and gave speeches emphasized the value of labor, too. No one here mentioned duty to Stalin, to party, or to socialism, but there was a sense of duty to kolkhoz. If the farm did well, so did they. The sample, however, is far too tiny to be considered in any way representative. It should not automatically be assumed that elsewhere, too, duty to Stalin was wanting. These interviews are cited merely as one set of views of erstwhile shock workers.

Inevitably such interviews can be methodologically flawed by poor recall, selective memory, and reconstructions of the past. Indeed, given the hardships encountered on farms in the early 1990s, there may well have been a distorting tendency to glorify the past, showing a nostalgia for a time more cruel than would be readily admitted to a foreigner with a tape recorder. Nonetheless, sufficient evidence suggests that the peasants interviewed were hard workers, had won medals, and in the 1930s were enthusiastic peasants, ready to fulfill higher targets.

CONCLUSION

The above incentives and attractions of Stakhanovism may have been compelling for those who pursued it. Furthermore, together they may have outweighed the fears of resistance to Stakhanovism. After all, in the 1930s citizens were surrounded by the discourse of "struggle" against enemies. It may have been comforting to be on the politically correct side, even a welcome challenge. And the degree of challenge varied according to geographic location, crop, job, and farm.

On some farms and machine tractor stations, being a shock worker or Stakhanovite may have been easier than on others. If farm leaders supported, or if the farm was doing reasonably well, then the conditions for being a Stakhanovite were more propitious and resentful peasants fewer or even nonexistent. And given the instability of the 1930s, conditions could not have been assumed to be constant. An obstructive farm manager could leave or be removed. If benefits were there, or likely to be there, then why not take advantage of them? And if some kolkhoz peasants and state farm workers believed in the building of socialism and in Stalin's exhortations, then trying to be a shock worker or a Stakhanovite was officially the only way forward in 1936 and 1937. Attaining this status was the pinnacle of rural achievement. For those who wanted upward mobility both in terms of material reward and official status, then Stakhanovism was the perceived route.

NOTES

1. *Stakhanovtsy Ovtsesovkhozov o Svoei Rabote* (Rostov: Izdanie TsK Soiuza Rabochikh Ovtsevodcheskikh Sovkhozov, 1936), 17.

2. *Stakhanovtsy Sel'skogo Khoziaistva Arkhangel'skoi Oblasti* (Arkhangel'sk: Ogiz, 1939), 17.

3. *Krest'ianskaia gazeta*, 28 December 1936, 2.

4. Azovo-Chernomorskii Kraevoi Komitet Soiuza Rabochikh Svinovodcheskikh Sovkhozov SSSR, *Stakhanovtsy-svinary o svoem opyte* (Rostov: Kraikom soiuza rabochikh svinosovkhozov, 1936), 39.

5. *Stakhanovtsy Sel'skogo Khoziaistva Arkhangel'skoi Oblasti*, 18.

6. "Kombainery-stakhanovtsy o svoei rabote," *Sotsialisticheskaia rekonstruktsiia sel'skogo khoziaistva* 11, part 9 (November 1935): 20.

7. In a similar spirit, in a meeting at the Political Department of the People's Commissariat of State Farms held in 1936, amid a barrage of criticism about life on some state farms, one pig breeder nonetheless chirped up with: "On our sovkhoz there are fifteen Stakhanovites. Before conditions were bad and we earned 50–60 rubles. But now in December I earned 1,239 rubles." The clear message was that better work meant higher wages. See RGASPI, f. 349, op. 1, d. 254, l. 5.

8. *Stakhanovtsy Ovtsesovkhozov o Svoei Rabote*, 17.

9. *Stakhanovtsy Ovtsesovkhozov o Svoei Rabote*, 17.

10. *Stakhanovtsy Ovtsesovkhozov o Svoei Rabote*, 17.

11. *Krest'ianskaia gazeta*, 24 October 1935, 3.

12. Refer to chapter 8, section "Pay."

13. GARF, f. 7689, op. 11, d. 119, l. 2.

14. GARF, f. 7689, op. 11, d. 119, l. 2.

15. GARF, f. 7689, op. 11, d. 119, l. 5.

16. GARF, f. 7689, op. 10, d. 40, l. 132.

17. GARF, f. 7689, op. 10, d. 127, l. 1.

18. GARF, l. 10ob. For fuller discussion of the roles played by rural *obshchestvennitsy* see Mary Buckley, "The Soviet 'Wife Activist' Down on the Farm," *Social History* 26, no. 3 (October 2001): 282–98.

19. GARF, f. 7689, op. 11, d. 119, l. 53.

20. GARF, f. 7689, op. 11, d. 119, l. 53.

21. GARF, f. 7689, op. 11, d. 119, l. 53.

22. Leon Trotsky, *The Revolution Betrayed* (New York: Pathfinder, 1972).

23. For discussion of *prikazy* refer to chapter 2, section "Orders (*prikazy*) from Above."

24. RGASPI, f. 349, op. 1, d. 240, l. 20.

25. RGASPI, l. 50.

26. *Stakhanovtsy ovtsesovkhozov o svoie rabote*, 17.

27. *Stakhanovtsy ovtsesovkhozov o svoie rabote*, 18.

28. *Stakhanovtsy ovtsesovkhozov o svoie rabote*, 18.

29. *Stakhanovtsy ovtsesovkhozov o svoie rabote*, 18.

30. *Krest'ianskaia gazeta*, 28 December 1936, 2.

31. RGAE, f. 7486, op. 1, d. 887, l. 9.

32. According to Stephen Wheatcroft and R. W. Davies, "The number of work horses declined from 23.4 million in the spring of 1929 to a mere 12.8 million on 1 July 1934." This resulted in "an unprecedented reduction in draught power for ploughing and other agricultural operations." See S. G. Wheatcroft and R. W. Davies, "Agriculture," *The Economic Transformation of the Soviet Union, 1913–1945*, eds. R. W. Davies, Mark Harrison, and S. G. Wheatcroft (Cambridge: Cambridge University Press, 1994), 120.

33. *Stakhanovtsy polei: k piatidesiatiletiiu stakhanovskogo dvizheniia* (Moscow: Agropromizdat, 1985), 28–29.

34. *Bol'shaia Sovetskaia Entsiklopediia*, ed. A. M. Prokhanov, 8, 3rd edition (Moscow: Izdatel'stvo Sovetskaia Entsiklopediia, 1972), 582.

35. *Bol'shaia Sovetskaia Entsiklopediia*, 86.

36. *Bol'shaia Sovetskaia Entsiklopediia*, 86.

37. *Stakhanovtsy polei*, 69.

38. Valentin Kataev, "Mariia Demchenko," in *V Budniakh Velikikh Stroek: Zhenshchiny-Kommunistki Geroini Pervykh Piatiletok*, ed. L. I. Stishova (Moscow, Politizdat, 1986), 295.

39. *My predsedatel'stvuem na Vsesoiuznom s"ezde* (Ogiz: Sel'khozgiz, 1935), 21–24.

40. *My predsedatel'stvuem na Vsesoiuznom s"ezde*, 9.

41. *My predsedatel'stvuem na Vsesoiuznom s"ezde*, 8.

42. *My predsedatel'stvuem na Vsesoiuznom s"ezde*, 12.

43. *My predsedatel'stvuem na Vsesoiuznom s"ezde*, 12.

44. *My predsedatel'stvuem na Vsesoiuznom s"ezde*, 13.

45. *My predsedatel'stvuem na Vsesoiuznom s"ezde*, 39.

46. Jeffrey Brooks, *Thank You, Comrade Stalin! Soviet Public Culture from the Revolution to Cold War* (Princeton, NJ: Princeton University Press, 2000), p. 68.

47. Brooks, *Thank You, Comrade Stalin!* 66.

48. Brooks, *Thank You, Comrade Stalin!* xvi.

49. *Krest'ianskaia gazeta*, 14 December 1935, 1.

50. *Krest'ianskaia gazeta*, 24 February 1936, 8.

51. *Sovkhoznaia gazeta*, 24 February 1936, 1–4; and *Sovkhoznaia gazeta*, 26 February 1936, 2–4. Archives show that final approval for these lists went as high as the Politburo. Refer back to chapter 2 for fuller discussion. Examples are numerous. See RGASPI, f. 17, d. 972, l. 67 and ll. 159–161; RGASPI, f. 17, op. 3, d. 973, l. 30 and ll. 64–73. Medals were awarded not just at All-Union level Congresses, but also at republic and oblast levels. For instance, in February 1939 medals were awarded to

agricultural workers in the Kazakh republic and in Moscow oblast across sectors. See *Krest'ianskaia gazeta*, 16 February 1939, 1; *Krest'ianskaia gazeta*, 12 February 1939, 1.

52. Iurii Il'inskii, "Iunaia Stakhanovka," in *V Budniakh Velikikh Stroek*, ed. L. I. Stishova, 60.

53. *Bol'shevik*, no. 23–24, 15 December 1935, 7.

54. *Krest'ianskaia gazeta*, 4 December 1935, 1.

55. *Sovkhoznaia gazeta*, 18 April 1936, 2.

56. *Stakhanovtsy Sel'skogo Khoziaistva Arkhangel'skoi Oblasti*, 17.

57. RGASPI, f. 349, op. 1, d. 240, l. 20. *Prikaz* number 72, 8 June 1936.

58. Il'inskii, "Iunaia Stakhanovka," in *V Budniakh Velikikh Stroek*, 62.

59. Il'inskii, "Iunaia Stakhanovka," 62.

60. Il'inskii, "Iunaia Stakhanovka," 61.

61. Il'inskii, "Iunaia Stakhanovka," 61.

62. *Sovkhoznaia gazeta*, 30 June 1935, 1.

63. *Sovkhoznaia gazeta*, 20 September 1935, 1.

64. *Sovkhoznaia gazeta*, 20 September 1935, 1.

65. GARF, f. 7689, op. 11, d. 328, l. 1.

66. GARF, f. 7689, op. 11, d. 328, l. 1.

67. GARF, f. 7689, op. 11, d. 328, l. 1.

68. GARF, f. 7689, op. 11, d. 328, l. 9.

69. GARF, f. 7689, op. 11, d. 328, l. 6.

70. GARF, f. 7689, op. 11, d. 422, l. 39.

71. GARF, f. 7689, op. 11, d. 422, l. 77.

72. GARF, f. 7689, op. 11, d. 422, l. 78; f. 7689, op. 11, d. 328, l. 7.

73. GARF. f. 7689, op. 11, d. 51, l. 24.

74. Peasants did not always present the union with a long list of complaints. Sometimes they wrote to say how good their lives were, followed by a minor request. A response to comrade Gorshkova indicates how she had written to say her "living conditions are good," but that "the record player which was promised to you in January of this year in the People's Commissariat at a gathering of Stakhanovites has not arrived." The union had spoken to "the head of the Central Management of the People's Commissariat of State Farms, comrade Koslov, who has promised to send you a record player soon." See GARF, f. 7689, op. 11, d. 422, l. 56.

75. See, too, conclusions drawn by Lewis H. Siegelbaum from reading trade union archival materials in GARF in his "'Dear Comrade, You Ask What We Need': Socialist Paternalism and Soviet Rural 'Notables' in the Mid-1930s," *Slavic Review* 57, no. 1 (Spring 1998): 107–32.

76. *Krest'ianskaia gazeta*, 28 November 1937, 2.

77. *Stakhanovtsy Sel'skogo Khoziaistva Arkhangel'skoi Oblasti*, 18.

78. *Stakhanovtsy Sel'skogo Khoziaistva Arkhangel'skoi Oblasti*, 18.

79. *Stakhanovtsy Sel'skogo Khoziaistva Arkhangel'skoi Oblasti*, 18.

80. *Sovkhoznaia gazeta*, 30 August 1938, 3; *Krest'ianskaia gazeta*, 20 September 1938, 2.

81. *Krest'ianskaia gazeta*, 4 July 1937, 3.

82. *Bol'shaia Sovetskaia Entsiklopediia*, 86 and 258.

83. Il'inskii, "Iunaia Stakhanovka," 61.

84. I. Vershinin, ed., *Mariia Safronovna Demchenko* (Moscow: Gosudarstvennoe izdatel'stvo politicheskoi literatury, 1938), 13.

85. Praskovya Angelina, *My Answer to an American Questionnaire* (Moscow: Foreign Languages Publishing House, 1949), 30.

86. Angelina, *My Answer,* 31.

87. Dar'ia Garmash, "O Samom Dorogom," in *V Budniakh Velikikh Stroek*, ed. L. Stishova, 181.

88. Pasha Angelina, *Liudi Kolkhoznykh Polei* (Moscow and Leningrad: Gosudarstvennoe Izdatel'stvo Detskoi Literatury Ministerstva Prosveshcheniia RSFSR, 1952), 43.

89. Angelina, *Liudi Kolkhoznykh Polei*, 39.

90. These interviews were conducted on 14 September 1996 on the Valdimir Il'ich Collective Farm in Moscow oblast through the help of the farm's House of Culture and Mariia Zezina of Moscow State University. Time and resources prevented further interviews from being arranged.

Chapter Ten

Gender, Shock Work, and Stakhanovism

Comrade male tractor drivers, you did not believe that we, women, would be able to work. You did not believe, did you, that we could fulfil our plan?

— Pasha Angelina at the Second All-Union Congress of Kolkhoz Shock Workers[1]

Women do not go on drinking binges, do not play cards, do not get involved in deceit.

— Aleksandra Levchenkova at the Second All-Union Congress of Kolkhoz Shock Workers[2]

The incentives for striving to attain Stakhanovite status were material, emotional, and ideological. Women, however, had an additional incentive to men, even if it involved extra arguments, more resistance, and greater short-term difficulties in their localities. Stakhanovism gave women the possibility of asserting themselves in the village and of excelling according to criteria praised by the regime. Their successes brought acclaim and rewards from beyond the village, giving them a place in a wider world. Yet more than this, since male Stakhanovites also enjoyed a similar pattern of recognition, Stakhanovism introduced another layer of complexity into the arena of gender politics. Female Stakhanovism was a challenge to deeply embedded attitudes about appropriate gender roles.

A successful female Stakhanovite could show to others, and above all to herself, that she could achieve more than social attitudes often allowed, that she could even attain records better than many men and therefore, implicitly, query the automatic dominance of men. Since attitudes about women's inferiority were widespread, and notions of women's low intelligence and inability to be a "person" were even enshrined in proverbs, the realization by

253

women that they could outperform men in the public sphere for all to see must have been for some both refreshing and liberating. Admittedly the costs in terms of emotional wear and tear due to belittling and verbal and physical abuse from the men who could not cope with successful females must have been unpleasant. Without analyzing the phenomenon, *Sovkhoznaia gazeta* made the uncharacteristically critical suggestion that on some farms women Stakhanovites were indeed treated worse than men.[3]

Across the centuries in all political systems, some able women have been ignored, denigrated, and held back by males unable to handle female prominence. And across the centuries, some women have retreated, uncomfortable to break out of the social niche defined for them, whereas others have fought to do so, prepared to challenge rigid norms in pursuit of more honest and satisfying alternatives. Although one cannot assume that all female Stakhanovites delighted in the knowledge that their successes meant that women were not necessarily inferior to men, one must allow that some probably did. Not only do their statements back this up, they also illustrate a hitherto unrecognized discourse of the 1930s concerning the question of whether women were, in fact, not just "equal" but "better" workers than men.

SOVIET IDEOLOGY: FROM "BACKWARD" TO A "GREAT STRENGTH" AND "EQUAL"

Official Soviet ideology of the 1930s and 1940s did not explore in any depth the dynamics of gender roles. Indeed, Soviet sociology lacked a concept of "gender" until the late 1980s. Although there had been some attention before and after 1917 to issues of domestic labor and the family, Aleksandra Kollontai's call for a more thorough analysis of "the confused knot of personal relationships" was controversial among Bolsheviks and largely unheeded.[4] "Class" was the central organizing concept and so reflections upon sexual divisions were considered divisive of the proletariat and as examples of much derided "bourgeois feminism."[5]

Lively debate about female roles, nonetheless, did take place in the euphoria of the postrevolutionary situation. Under pressure from Bolshevik women like Inessa Armand and Aleksandra Kollontai, male leaders conceded the specificity of women's predicament. Special political efforts could be made to harness women's support for the revolution through the *Otdel po rabote sredi zhenshchin (Zhenotdel)*, or women's department of the party. Its existence was justified ideologically on the grounds that women were less active than men in politics, more "backward," and thus temporarily in need of different treatment. Armand also made a convincing case that peasant women in particular found themselves held back by the highly conservative and inward-looking values of the countryside. Here organizational work was very weak and daily life was, in many ways, untouched by the revolution. Moreover, illiteracy levels were much higher among women.[6]

Consistent with other changes in economy and polity, the Zhenotdel was closed in 1930 on the grounds that women were now successfully emancipated. Official ideology proclaimed that women enjoyed equal opportunities alongside men in all spheres—in the arts, science, economy, and politics. The line was that equality of the sexes was guaranteed through the economic policies of industrialization and collectivization. Stalin declared, "only kolkhoz life can obliterate inequality and put women on their feet."[7] Ideology portrayed women now as a "great might," alongside men, "shoulder to shoulder" constructing socialism. Together, women and men constituted a "great army of labor." This was the key to the "new life."[8]

Political leaders and propagandists, then, did not talk about serious differences in gender roles, in the socialization processes of girls and boys, and in divergent attitudes toward women and men. These did not constitute "problems" for Marxist-Leninist theory since the "woman question" was part of the "human question" which was an issue of "class." Working women, like working men, would be "freed" once they were part of a communist society, not oppressed in a capitalist economy. Many traditional attitudes toward women, however, were deeply intertwined in cultural patterns whose strands were often tenacious and timeless, seen as "natural" and "unchangeable." Political leaders and the people had been socialized into these values and, generally, were not ready to challenge the entire package. So although lip-service was given to some changes in gender roles, particularly in production, there was often a gap between word and deed, utterance and belief.

Furthermore, there was a sharp tension in ideology itself. Collectivization was meant to bring women's unequal position to an end, but women were now "equal" anyway. Ideological discourse implicitly acknowledged inequalities between the sexes and simultaneously explicitly propounded their equality but both could not logically obtain. The means to sexual equality, that is, industrialization and collectivization under socialism, implied a future equality. Bold socialist realist images, however, proclaimed equality now. Yet reality confirmed that equality was a distant prospect.

FROM "EQUAL" WITH MEN TO "BETTER"

Although reality starkly illustrated discrimination against women and very traditional attitudes about what women could feasibly achieve, one strand of discourse, particularly female discourse, championed that women were, in fact, on occasion better than men. This idea was expressed with varying degrees of enthusiasm at congresses, in the press, and in biographies.

A report in *Krasnaia Sibiriachka* (Red Siberian Woman) about a pig farm compared women favorably to men by reporting that "only women work on our farm and they work better than men did two years ago." Mariia Stepanova had been working there just a year, "but already in such a short time Mariia has mastered the technology of her task and provides the best examples of work."[9] *Krasnaia Sibiriachka* also illustrated how women could master technology and outstrip men. The tractor driver Usova was called to her brigade leader to hear: "You, Usova, it seems work better than men!" and "You cultivated 28 hectares and our norm is 15 hectares. For this, take this little red flag!"[10] Journals advocated that it was easy for some women to drive tractors and to exceed norms. As a reward, a red flag flew on their tractors.

Women's speeches at conferences also drew attention to the fact that they were outperforming men. In December 1935, at a Conference of Advanced Male and Female Combine Drivers attended by members of the Central Committee and government, Comrade Kofanova from an MTS in Azovo-Chernomore krai announced that: "For good work they gave me a bonus, promoted me to brigade leader. Then they put me on the red blackboard. And I was an advanced worker in the district, beating all male combine drivers (Applause)."[11] At this Klement Voroshilov, People's Commissar of Defense, let out an encouraging "That's right!"[12] Such official interjections of support reiterated the party's backing for women tractor and combine drivers. At the same gathering combine driver M. Petrova called upon all girls to enter socialist competitions against each other and then cried "Thank you Comrade Stalin for giving us an opportunity to work on such huge ships and not to fall behind men" (Applause).[13] Kofanova and Petrova appeared to think about the opportunities available to women and men and consciously to compare themselves to men. In fact, they may have contrived to use official lines and ideology to champion their cause. Given the documented opposition of both sexes to seeing women on tractors and combine harvesters, ideology could actually be used as a protector and legitimator.

Bold women like Pasha Angelina stressed with confidence that women could work better than men. In her speech to the Second All-Union Congress of Kolkhoz Shock Workers she proudly announced "Comrades, now I will tell you that my brigade for the last three years holds the red challenge banner from the political department and does not cede it to men." Provocatively, she told the men: "My women, my Komsomol tractor drivers declare: you, comrade men tractor drivers, all the same will not succeed in taking the red banner from us" (Applause).[14]

The ideological legitimacy of "socialist competitions" and the heavy emphasis on them in 1937 and 1938 enabled women's brigades safely to challenge men and to intimate that female peasants would hold their own, even shine and be unbeaten by men. Socialist competitions may unwittingly have fostered rivalry between the sexes and enabled good women workers to demonstrate their skills, be keen to publicize them, even brag about them and taunt men for not winning. A certain euphoria may have developed from being able occasionally to triumph over male labor and to receive public accolades. Pasha Angelina must have felt considerable satisfaction at her success since when she first challenged the best male team in the district to a socialist competition, its brigade leader Takhtamyshev condescendingly responded, "We don't fight women."[15]

Another message was that women could teach men—the epitome of effrontery to traditional male egos. In Pasha Angelina's autobiography she tells how Ivan Kurov came to her one day with a letter from a group of *kolkhozniki* elsewhere. They requested that Angelina's brigade be sent to them because their male tractor drivers were working badly and spoiling the sowing.[16] Angelina told the Second All-Union Congress of Kolkhoz Shock Workers that her team had been asked to help out male tractor brigades on an additional seven farms. Given how many young men had initially jeered at her that women could not handle such "complex" machines and therefore should not even try, it was not without irony that Pasha Angelina reported:

we taught the tractor drivers how to work on the machines, we showed them how women had mastered this complicated machine! We said to them: Comrade male tractor drivers, you did not believe that we, women, would be able to work. You did not believe, did you, that we could fulfil our plan? And now you study how to work from us, take from our example of how we go forward.[17]

Male tractor drivers, she mocked, needed women's help, not the other way round. The popular film *Traktoristy* echoed this point. Mar'iana Bazhan's tractor team was clearly better organized than that of the farm's male brigade whose members neglected their machines. Not until the industrious mechanic Klim came along did the men stand a chance at beating Mar'iana Bazhan in competition.

Sources of the 1930s are punctuated with evidence that on some farms the *muzhik* was not an enthusiastic worker nor keen to respect female success. Conversations in 1937 between Iakov Iakovlev, Head of the Central Committee Department of Agriculture, and kolkhoz chairs and tractor drivers from Kursk graphically illustrate the latter's indolence, lethargy, and denigration of female peasants. After hearing numerous tales of woe about poor conditions and unproductive peasants, Iakovlev asked if there were any productive peasants at all. Archives carry the following transcript:

> Voice: If I pick someone, there is Nefedova, she's not bad.
>
> Voice: She's a woman—and will remain a woman.
>
> Voice: At night it is necessary to take them by the hand and the *muzhik* has his way (*kak khochesh' kui*).
>
> Voice: Women have long hair and small intelligence (. . . *volos dlinen, a um korotok*)
>
> Voice: That's old fashioned.[18]

Even though the peasants managed to name one person who worked well, her sex immediately prompted derogatory remarks in front of one of the country's top leaders. This suggests how readily such attitudes were expressed, how deeply believed, and probably how generally acceptable among men. In fact, one wonders if much worse was edited out of the official transcript. When at other times in their conversations, Iakovlev learned that on one farm in seven years there had been nine chairpersons, and that the reason for the high turnover here and elsewhere was generally "drunkenness," no automatic comments were made denigrating male behavior.[19] Instead, there was a boyish acceptance that male workers would inevitably drink a lot.

Although ideology avoided any mention of negative "male" attributes, always linking laziness and bad work to class enemies rather than to gender divides, female shock workers and Stakhanovites at conferences were confident enough to associate some behavior patterns specifically with men. At the Second All-Union Congress of Collective Farm Shock Workers, for example, Aleksandra Levchenkova, a collective farm chairperson from Voronezh oblast, remarked that:

> Many women, they majority of them, in their work cope no worse than men. Women do not go on drinking binges, do not play cards, do not get involved in deceit. Women relate to the collective farm with care (applause) to the collective good (applause).[20]

Levchenkova does not explicitly declare that women work more efficiently than men, but that is the implication. By conveying dualities of "drinkers" and "non-drinkers," "gamblers" and "non-gamblers," "deceivers" and "honest ones," "lack of care" and "carers," she claims that men are irresponsible but women are not.

Another strand of thought voiced by women was that men were ever ready to take advantage of them, a pattern that had to be curbed. When Tat'iana Shapovalova was invited to chair a session at the Second All-Union Congress of Kolkhoz Shock Workers, she described how "I immediately led the meeting firmly, saved time and followed the procedures: fifteen speakers took to the floor under my chairing of the meeting." However, one male would not keep to time. Shapovalova regretted that "When our Voronezh Comrade Bogdanov ran over time, I telephoned him and reminded: what are you thinking, that if a woman is chairing, you need not keep order. He stopped immediately."[21] Here Shapovalova indicated that men might feel less obliged to keep to time if chaired by a woman since she was less worthy of respect and not necessarily to be obeyed.

FEMALE STAKHANOVITES SURMOUNT SOCIAL BARRIERS

Rural women entering the male-dominated mechanized preserves of tractor and combine driving, like those shown in Figure 10.1, faced various hurdles. By describing women's ability to surmount them, the literature on Stakhanovism inadvertently addressed male chauvinism. The terms "gender roles," "sexism," "male chauvinism," and "sexual discrimination" were never used and relations between the sexes were not named, labeled, or conceptualized through these constructs. However, descriptions of verbal exchanges between aspiring Stakhanovite women and male critics vividly illustrated them.

Figure 10.1.   Komsomol members M. Kosiuk and O. Demchuk responded to the call of the Central Committee of the Komsomol and the People's Commissariat of Agriculture for 100,000 women to train to drive the tractor. Source: Adapted from Traktorist-Kombainer, *no. 9, May 1939, p. 5.*

The picture on the ground, moreover, was often complex and instances of female opposition to changing gender roles illustrated that a sharp gender divide in attitudes did not always obtain. Frequently criticisms coming from men and women about new roles for women coincided. Not all men, however, were hostile to women performing new tasks. Indeed, in many cases, female Stakhanovites relied upon male support, without which they could not advance.

In her autobiography, Pasha Angelina described the opposition to her dream of becoming a tractor driver which she encountered from friends, family members, and kolkhoz workers. The first to express hostility was her friend Vasilii. He condescendingly told her "the tractor is a complicated machine" which is "easy for me."[22] When Pasha announced her seriousness about it, Vasilii retorted, "Don't think about it" and "The tractor is man's business."[23] Allegedly, Pasha responded, "perhaps women's too" to which her brother Ivan replied, "Don't be an idiot, Pasha! I am telling you, the tractor is not your business." Having the last word, Pasha declared, "You have not convinced me, my dears. Life will tell."[24]

According to the autobiography, Pasha went to see Ivan Shevshenko who was teaching her brother and Vasilii. He too was skeptical about her ambition and told her, "I cannot advise you to study how to drive a tractor. There is no such example of a woman tractor driver." Always having a ready response, Pasha pointed out, "There is a lot we did not know in our countryside before Soviet power!"[25] Although this conclusion coincided with official ideology, it was in fact an argument that worked in Pasha's favor.

Next came disagreements with her father who observed that only young men drove tractors and that "you must choose a more suitable speciality." When Pasha insisted that this was suitable for her, he announced, "I forbid it."[26] Falling ill, Pasha told her mother, "I will become a tractor driver."[27] The hallmark of the most successful Stakhanovites was stubborn refusal to drop their grand ideas whatever others said.

Vasilii persisted in his attempts to dissuade her, which included: "It will be difficult for you" followed by "it's hard for a young man to work on a tractor, even worse for a young woman."[28] Pasha's response was that "I do not search for light work. The more difficult and more complicated, the more interesting." Again echoing Soviet propaganda, she noted, "They tell me that in no country in the world are there women tractor drivers. So what? In my country there should be women tractor drivers!" Her final exasperated words to Vasilii were "why doesn't anyone want to understand me!" These no doubt echoed those of pioneering women worldwide who battled to counter rigid gender divisions of labor and the frustrating attitudes that upheld them.[29]

A prominent characteristic of Pasha Angelina was that she was a woman who dreamed. In her own words: "My dream—to become a tractor driver. I love the land. My calling is to plow the land."[30] Although critics might dismiss the authenticity of these words and label them fabricated propaganda, it is nonetheless the case that many women and men do have dreams about what they can achieve and that these dreams matter hugely to them. What is clear is that Pasha's persistence finally led to her father giving in, helped by the politically sound advice of Kurov in the political department. After seeing his sister on the tractor, even Ivan conceded, "My sister is a fine woman! She drives a tractor well."[31] Ultimately, Pasha's father congratulated her too.[32]

Once family had been won over, fresh opposition inevitably ensued from villagers. Marfa Vasil'evna, a woman of fifty-five, declared, "you should be ashamed."[33] A hostile crowd gathered and Vasilii, still opposed, asked, "What will happen?"[34] On this occasion Pasha got down from the tractor and Ivan drove it off. Vasilii took Pasha aside repeating, "I just don't want you to work on a tractor. This work is not for you. With time you will understand that I was right."[35] Vasilii's consistent pressure and nagging amounted to mechanisms of undermining which today would be called harassment. Pasha asked him to stop and informed him that he could not possibly be a friend and that she now hated him,[36] adding that "the tractor is worth it, in the fields it is quiet."[37]

Once finally trained and working on a tractor, women could not guarantee that they would be able to stay on it. Gennadii Talalaenko, director of the MTS, took Pasha off her tractor and told her to work as a storekeeper. Resenting this, Pasha sought the aid of Ivan Kurov in the political department who stood by her and went to Talalaenko with the suggestion that a women's brigade be set up with Pasha Angelina leading it. Talalaenko dismissed it with "I don't need old women (*baby*) . . . There are enough young men."[38] Under pressure from Kurov who told him that he was breaking the law, Talalaenko insisted that "I don't intend to put Angelina on a tractor. . . . The whole countryside supports me."[39] The upshot of this altercation was that the People's Commissariat removed Talalaenko from his post for "a careless attitude towards his duties" and for "bureaucratism towards the setting up of a women's tractor brigade."[40] The incident illustrates quite how hard it was for women when MTS directors mocked and ridiculed them and how vital it often was for women to have the backing and respect of senior men, amounting to a "client-patron" relationship. This has applied worldwide in all professions in situations of hiring and promotion and will continue to do so. Discrete personal mechanisms of support and patronage play huge roles in women's careers; however fair the laws, just as lack of patronage and mechanisms of disrespect can undermine women's upward mobility, confidence, and even health.

Evidence strongly backs the conclusion that tractor women encountered difficulties before, during, and after their training, exacerbated by the belief that women on machines would ruin the crop.[41] Particularly galling for women was opposition from their own sex since they more readily expected understanding, empathy, and some solidarity. Angelina regretted that "here our own women, women of the collective farm were reviling us."[42] Opposition to female tractor driving was not a simple story of men versus women but a complex one of different forms of criticism coming from men and women and also of various forms of support from both sexes. Someone from the crowd allegedly jeered, "Women can't drive machines, the machines will drive them."[43] Whenever Angelina's team worked on a different farm, as their machine tractor station served several *kolkhozy*, this pattern frequently repeated itself. She regretted how "when we move on to the next collective farm the same thing happened. The women nearly beat us up, and two of our girls were locked up in a cellar."[44] Opposition to changing gender roles was both fierce and unpleasant.[45]

Despite a very different context, there are parallels found in the 1920s in Central Asia, where some Muslim women alongside many Muslim men opposed and subverted Soviet policies of *hudzhum* (onslaught) against the subordination of women and mitigated the impact of new restrictions on men. Douglas Northrup has discussed how it was "comparatively easy to resist the new rules by ridiculing and manipulating the Soviet judicial system."[46] Female activists here, as both Gregory Massell and Northrup have shown, suffered extreme brutality that could include murder and the public dumping of their mutilated corpse.[47]

Sources indicate that Pasha Angelina was a strong role model for other aspiring tractor drivers, of whom Dar'ia Garmash's story may be typical of especially determined women. The concept of "role model" was not then in use, but descriptions of Angelina's impact on other women make it fitting. Garmash's fascination with tractors was first ignited when Vasia Lavrukhin, a tractor driver, gave her a ride and from that moment Garmash declared, "My soul sang."[48] Her dilemma was "how to do it, how to make the dream reality."[49] After working as a brigade leader in the fields, Garmash one day read in *Pravda* about the Second Congress of Kolkhoz Shock Workers, commenting "I read and re-read Pasha Angelina's speech and the dream of becoming a tractor driver was rekindled."[50] Soon after came the opportunity to enroll in a tractor course at the Rybnovsk MTS. The kolkhoz chairperson, however, objected, saying that he did not wish to lose a good field brigade leader.[51]

Persistence led to Dar'ia being sent on a course but her fiancé, Nikolai, taunted: "What are you, a young man, or what?" He argued, "It's not for you to poke your nose in there. You'll only be a hill tractor driver, enough to make you a laughing stock."[52] He lectured that "It's man's work, understand, man's work. Good tractor drivers cannot be women."[53] Nikolai insisted that he would never marry a tractor driver, even if she were the most beautiful of women. As he viewed it, "Why do I need a tractor-driving wife? I cannot look when women wear trousers; I turn away. I need a tender and affectionate wife."[54] Thereupon Nikolai promised to work hard, earn a lot, and give Dar'ia everything. Two days before the course began, he appealed to Dar'ia's mother, proclaiming deep love for her daughter, and declared that "I'm an independent man, with good earnings, and I don't bear grudges. I won't oppress Dar'ia in any way." He continued with "But not listening to me, she wants to go on a course" and asked "What sort of woman is it, for that matter, who is a tractor driver?" He pronounced, "It does not suit me." Nikolai then declared to Oksana Filippovna "I come to you like a son-in-law—order her not to go on the course. I came to you to decide how it will be."[55] Dar'ia's mother allegedly told Nikolai how much she liked him but that it was Dar'ia's choice how to lead her life.

Nikolai's own contradictory comments also show that by insisting that Dar'ia give up the tractor he could not see that he was in fact being oppressive, although he claimed the opposite. This pattern too is likely to be transhistorical and global.

As a consequence, Dar'ia did not know what to do, argued with Nikolai, and cried. Forced against her will to choose between her tractor and Nikolai who was "handsome, tall, slender, broad-shouldered . . . his entire appearance courageous and proud" and whom "it seemed impossible to love stronger," Dar'ia finally chose the tractor.[56] Heartbroken, she reaffirmed her intent. As she put it, "It was difficult for me and somehow even very offensive. And I lacked the strength to reject my dream. Holding back the tears, I said 'I am going to study the tractor.'"[57] Here we see the emotional drive to do what one wants remaining steadfast, almost strengthened by the insulting and negative responses of someone who wished to control and command.

Opposition to new roles for women was not limited to tractor driving, although especially vivid in these examples due to the fact that it involved mechanized labor. We have already seen how resistance to female Stakhanovism was often spiced with patriarchal attitudes, especially concerning the behavior of girls. In the case of the young Pioneer Mamlakat Nakhangova, the men who went to complain to her father about her records in cotton were troubled that a young girl was outshining them.[58] Here the gender dilemma seemed to be that not only a woman was performing better than men, but a very young one at that. This upset the traditional and hierarchical social structure of patriarchy in which the old and wise were to be revered, not shown up.

MEN WHO DEFENDED, ENCOURAGED, AND INSPIRED

Men were not automatically enemies in a crude way. There were those who encouraged women to pursue their aspirations and on occasions backed them as patrons. Just as Pasha Angelina could turn to Ivan Kurov for assistance and guidance so Dar'ia Garmash was especially indebted to Aleksandr Glebov. Both worked in the political department of the MTS. It was Ivan Kurov who persuaded Pasha's father to allow her to follow a course of instruction in tractor driving. Kurov also took on Gennadii Talalaenko, who had stopped Angelina from plowing. It was Kurov, too, who came into the fields to defuse the tense situation when women had barred the way of Angelina's tractor brigade to the fields.[59]

Men not only protected and defended able women but also helpfully instructed and inspired them, as suggested in Figure 10.2. Various published stories also recounted how men played crucially positive roles. One day, for example, Aleksandr Glebov came to Dari'a Garmash's field brigade and asked the women what their dreams were. After responding kindly to their embarrassed answers, he instructed them, "You must be able to dream, young girls, you must live life to the full," warning "of course, it's nice to have pretty clothes. But the most important in life is that you, your life, your work are useful to the people, to the Motherland." He stressed that "you must choose the sort of work that you will love." What mattered was that "your talents will come out, so that in your post you will feel like generals, commanders, magicians."[60] Dar'ia reflected, "He spoke so sincerely, that we all, perhaps for the first time thought about our lives, felt personal responsibility for it, for the sort of road we would choose."[61] The all-knowing Glebov then asked Dar'ia if it was true that she loved machines. He had seen her have a try on a friend's tractor and had noticed her pleasure. He posed the inevitable question: "The why don't you become a tractor driver?" He then challenged the young women to be more daring, saying "don't be timid, be persistent and we will help you."[62] For women of independent inclinations but not sure how to develop them, these may indeed have been the sorts of words which they needed to hear to spur them into action. Moreover, coming from political "gatekeepers" with some

Figure 10.2. One of the four women being trained to drive a tractor on the Labinsk MTS in Krasnodar krai. Source: Adapted from Traktorist-Kombainer, *no. 9, May 1939, p. 4.*

power in local affairs, they were encouragements that could be backed up with necessary support later.

Parents, too, could be appropriately supportive. After a group of men had visited Mamlakat Nakhangova's father to complain that she was working too fast, he supposedly laughed and commented, "Friends, you have found something to grieve about."[63] Once Dar'ia Garmash's mother had come to accept her daughter's stubborn insistence about joining the Komsomol, to which she had initially objected, she put no obstacles in the path of her daughter's tractor driving.

FABRICATION OR TRUTH?

As one reads such Stakhanovites' biographies, one inevitably questions their reliability. It was customary under Stalin to rewrite history and to portray reality in ways consistent with official ideological messages. This was indeed the case throughout most of the history of the Soviet state, although fabrication was at its crudest in the 1930s and 1940s.

The main problem here is that whereas the lies of official histories can with time be identified, the content of personal conversations among workers and peasants cannot easily be confirmed. It is one thing to match accusations of the 1939 Short Course with reality, another to be able to reconstruct a conversation held in the countryside. We can consider the merits of accusations that during the Civil War "Trotsky had disrupted the Southern Front and our troops suffered defeat after defeat."[64] But the exact sequence of points in a dialogue between Pasha Angelina and her friend Vasilii or between Dar'ia Garmash and Nikolai remain unreachable. Interviews with those concerned might clarify matters. Those, however, who were not deceased would more than likely have difficulties in recall, even muddle reality with ideology.

Should one then dismiss the utility of these reported conversations? If they cannot be verified, what can one glean from them? How can one make reliable observations about the period if the data are suspect from the start? Although these anxieties are all well-founded, they exist alongside another set of worries. Is it not foolish automatically to jettison sources of the 1930s on the grounds that they are unverifiable? Just as some stories may be fabrications, others may not. On the topic at hand, it would have been extremely odd had no male opposition to changing gender roles obtained. Indeed, if the sources err, it is more than likely that they construct a much softer opposition to new roles for women than was actually the case. In most cultures, in most periods of history, men and women have criticized changing gender roles on the grounds that they are "unnatural," "inappropriate," "unseemly," and even "offensive."

Most likely, the methodological barrier to accurate reconstruction of the resistance that occurred lies not in the content of the stories which are available, but more so in the absence of other stories. As it is, one has to delve quite deeply into a wealth of materials before encountering the stories told here. Journals and newspapers like *Stakhanovets*, *Udarnitsa Urala*, *Krest'ianskaia gazeta*, and *Krest'ianka* generally did not print articles highlighting male opposition to female production feats. One finds them tucked into occasional paragraphs in autobiographies and biographies or in a rare article in *Sovkhoznaia gazeta*. Certainly official ideology did not dwell on conflictual discourse between the sexes, instead creating a picture of happiness and enthusiasm.

The main methodological problem, then, is the paucity of information available on resistance to new roles in production for women rather than the sources that actually exist.

What can be concluded with certainty is that to be successful, shock workers, Stakhanovites, and male Stakhanovites' spouses who were in the "wives' movement" had to possess commitment, resilience, and endurance. They had to be capable of inventive reactions not only to work problems but also to critics and to those likely to inflict harm. Moreover, as Jochen Hellbeck has sensitively shown, hard workers under Stalinism would actively write themselves into the Soviet order in order to make sense of their worlds. They would derive "personal meaning and purpose" by inextricably linking their self-definition "to the cause of the state as a whole."[65] The state set the norms that defined and guided lives, which women like Mariia Demchenko and Pasha Angelina internalized. They used the concepts, phrases, and emphases that the state machine popularized which in turn fashioned their own perceptions of the world and their place in it, what Hellbeck dubs their "personal Bolshevism."[66] Thus they came to understand and order the reality around them through official prisms, even if they criticized aspects of it.

Their statements should not be automatically dismissed as fabrications simply because they may have coincided with party policy. As Alfred Meyer argued in his classic article, Soviet ideology played four main roles: it constituted the language of politics (akin to Wittgenstein's "language game"); it served as a code of communication; legitimized the political system; and acted as self-legitimation for members of the elite.[67] By furnishing the key concepts through which citizens should interpret the world, ideology provided Demchenko and Angelina and thousands like them with filters, frames of reference, and conditioned reflexes through which they had a handle on life. Although citizens could "learn" when to use the "right" concepts and notions, it does not mean that they failed to "believe" or "internalize" them, if only in part.

CONTRADICTORY GENDER IMAGES

Both the images and realities of female Stakhanovites showed determined and energetic women able to surmount challenges to their adoption of new gender roles. They strove to fulfill their own dreams and thereby pursue self-determination. This was consistent with the icon of "emancipated woman," active in production, not deterred by "vestiges of the past," belittling, opposition, abuse, or "political blindness." Figure 10.3 shows Liuba Mamrukova as such a confident woman, someone who is capable behind the large wheel,

Figure 10.3.   Liuba Mamrukova, Stakhanovite tractor driver. Source: *Adapted from* Krest'ianka, *no. 10, 1937.*

with successfully plowed fields behind her. There is no doubt here about her strength, commitment, and drive.

There was also a very different reality of Stakhanovites' wives who contributed to socialist construction by helping their husbands and by doing socially useful unpaid labor in factories, on farms, in hostels, canteens, schools, hospitals, and offices. These wives became known as *obshchestvennitsy*, meaning "public-spirited women" or "female activists," who were members of the *dvizhenie zhen*, or movement of wives. Wives' movements were, in fact, broader than Stakhanovites' wives, although all wives were cast as working "hand in hand with wives of Stakhanovites and of advanced workers."[68] An *obshchestvennitsa*'s first role was essentially a "servicing" one, a subordination of the self to another. It entailed catering to the needs of her husband and helping him to maintain his Stakhanovite status. The second role brought activity outside the home in voluntary labor. Whilst it may have been rewarding in a personal sense, it did not mean economic self-determination or the pursuit of a chosen job or profession. Rather, the Stakhanovite's wife remained dependent on her husband's income and status and was defined by his position in industry or in agriculture. Her activities, however, did draw her into the public sphere where she made a contribution to the local community and sometimes aquired skills beneficial to future employment, should she choose to take a job.

How could the Soviet state encourage two such apparently contradictory images of "socialist woman?" One was a highly enthusiastic independent wage earner striving to attain maximum productivity; the other was a dependent wife aiming to uphold her husband's status and to help boost his productivity. Whereas the former woman fit Marxist ideology, the latter did not. Leaders of the Zhenotdel, such as Inessa Armand and Aleksandra Kollontai, would have praised the spread of women's participation in the labor force as essential for women's liberation and for socialism but might have queried a servile status in the family unit.[69]

One justification for the activities of Stakhanovites' wives was that they helped to build socialism and during the 1930s, socialist construction was the top priority. Women's liberation had always received questionable support from individual leaders anyway and was generally subordinate to other goals. Thus Stakhanovites' wives contributed to the Soviet state by easing the home pressures on its best working men, by suggesting to other wives that they should encourage their husbands to be Stakhanovites, too, and by performing socially useful tasks. A second justification could conceivably have been the specificity of women's predicament. This argument had been used in the 1920s when the "political backwardness" of women merited special treatment. This justification, however, was not expressed in the 1930s, made difficult by the proclamation that men and women were now "equal." There were, nonetheless, housewives not in the paid labor force and, in effect, their lives were different from those of working women. By encouraging them to become *obshchestvennitsy*, the regime was drawing them out of the home in a "socially useful" way.

Like the Stakhanovite movement, the *dvizhenie zhen* began in industry, initially "instigated" by Vera Vesnik and Mariia Manaenkova, who celebrated their activities in 1936 at a Conference of Wives of Leaders in Metallurgy of the South. Other groupings of wives quickly formed and a flurry of conferences took place in 1936.[70] Top leaders such as Stalin, Kalinin, Ordzhonikidze, Voroshilov, and Liubimov attended these huge gatherings, giving the wives in their speeches advice on what they should be doing.[71] City and district conferences were also held. Although such large gatherings of wives of agricultural workers were less prominent, they nonetheless took place, such as when wives of rural engineering technical workers met in January 1939, organized by the Central Committee of pig state farms.[72]

At the local level wives met in a *sovet zhen* (council of wives), a *sovet zhen-obshchestvennits* (a council of wife activists) or in a *sovet obshchestvennits* (council of women activists).[73] The wives' movement also had its own journal, *Obshchestvennitsa,* which reported on wives' projects and was in print from 1936 to 1941. The local council of wives was generally set up in the husbands' workplace. Here the women decided their tasks and sought funding for their projects. Their involvement in the community ranged from rearranging the work of their husbands' canteen, aiding the kitchen staff, checking the food, providing tablecloths and flowers, establishing crèches and kindergarten, furnishing a room for workers' relaxation, helping in the local school and hospital, working to combat illiteracy, forming a choir, dramatic society, or group to study a foreign language, learning self-defense and how to shoot, or how to drive a car. All of these pursuits were adopted in towns and in the countryside.

There were, however, differences in urban and rural tasks. Wives in industry would dig the factory garden, plant flowers, help on the factory floor, and go down mines; wives in agriculture would help at harvest time in the fields, adorn tractor cabins with curtains, and clean out pigsties. Moral support and funds were sought from factory and farm directors, trade unions, and workers' committees. In the countryside the movement spread with limited success, mainly on state farms due to the presence of trade unions. While archives show that some farms had wives' groups in 1936, many did not form until 1938 and 1939. In fact, in 1938, trade unions made a special effort to encourage them.[74] In this respect, once more the countryside lagged behind the town.

STAKHANOVITES' WIVES TALK
ABOUT HELPING THEIR HUSBANDS

Whereas female Stakhanovites were regularly invited by the press and at conferences to talk about their work methods, lives, and hopes, Stakhanovites' wives were encouraged to talk about their husbands. This practice reinforced their status of "defined by another." At conferences of Stakhanovites' wives, they indulged in "husband talk" par excellence. Inessa Armand would, one suspects, have been both embarrassed and appalled. Moral support for an equal partner who gives and takes is one thing; subservience in private and public is another.

A clear illustration of "husband talk" is provided by the speeches delivered at the First Krai Conference of Stakhanovites' Wives of the Northern Krai, held in 1936. The Krai First Secretary, D. Kontorin, set the scene by telling the women present: "You, as helpers of your husbands, of Stakhanovites, of honored people in our country, must show how you surround the Stakhanovite with care and attention and create for him a comfortable, cultured, happy relaxation at home."[75] In addition, "You must teach others how it is necessary to become Stakhanovites and to help Stakhanovites advance forward on the path of high productivity."[76]

Consistent with this instruction, one engineer's wife declared: "We women must take a daily interest in how our husbands' work is going, in how they lead the Stakhanovite movement and in how to help Stakhanovites to increase productivity and the quality of their work."[77] There followed a series of tales about different men. One by one the women got up and described their husbands' careers. Their separate stories were generally prefaced by "I want to talk about my husband's work."[78] Each told of what her husband did, when he trained for more skilled work, how productive he was, and how much he earned. Some described how they helped their men to pass examinations. The conclusion reached by all was how well they now lived. Accordingly, one wife noted:

> I helped my husband to become a first class engineer. (Applause). Now he earns 800 rubles. (Retort: "Appropriate!") Now we have everything and we are beginning to live well. Workers abroad only dream of such a life, but here the dream is real. I bought our son a camera and I'm going to buy our daughter a piano.[79]

The loud message was that Stakhanovites were elite workers who gave their families a higher standard of living and *kul'turnost'*. Thus the wives had a material stake in ensuring that their menfolk remained Stakhanovites. One fitter's wife described how she conformed neatly to a rigid division of gender roles: "I aid my husband in every possible way. I try to be cheerful and do not make him worry about taking care of the home. I assume most of the chores myself." Furthermore, "At the same time I try to help my husband by advising him. Everything that I know I pass on to him." If he needed any literature to read, she looked for it "so that the time he would have spent searching for it, he can spend studying it."[80] The fitter's wife revealed nothing about her own life separate from her husband. The two lives were conflated.

Various conferences dwelled on this theme of "helper," advising wives on how best they could perform this function not just for their husbands but for the party. One strand of party ideology was that wives should be helpers of their productive men. Missing, however, from ideology was the notion that Stakhanovites' husbands should execute a similarly supportive role. Husbands, of course, were expected to be in the labor force full-time anyway. Realistically, then, they could not devote themselves to their wives' production feats in the same wholehearted way. Since wives were not necessarily employed, it was preferable that they encouraged Stakhanovite husbands and were engaged in socially useful work rather than not. Nonetheless, there was a great disparity between the lives of Stakhanovites' wives and the lives of Stakhanovites' husbands. The party, moreover, had a line on the former, not on the latter; agitprop encouraged the former but was utterly silent about the latter. Pasha Angelina's autobiography, for instance, reveals nothing about her husband until the text suddenly informs the reader that there is a husband and children as well.[81] No description is given of courtship or marriage. Her husband's relevance to her life story is constructed as no more than incidental. Neither is there any suggestion that her husband is her "helper." In fact, he appears to have been the opposite. One biography of Angelina describes how her husband pressured her to leave work to spend more time with their child and finally their marriage ended because Angelina would not quit tractor driving.[82]

After scrutinizing many sources, I have found just one reference to men helping women. This occurred in Ukraine when Khristina Baidich and Ekaterina Androshchuk gathered over 1,000 tsentners of sugar beet per hectare and "husbands came to help them."[83] It is possible that this happened more frequently than was reported since it was not an officially prominent theme. General silence, however, surrounds the topic.

"Husband talk," then, was the pivot around which wives' discourse developed. They discussed how they could contribute to the success of individual husbands and to the workplaces of all their husbands. They became preoccupied with husbands' productivity, comfort, well-being, and amusement. Newspapers and journals reiterated the theme of the duty of wives to "help" husbands, quoting wives to the effect that "All my dreams are connected with the work of my husband, for whom I want to be the first and best helper."[84]

As well as mainly supporting their men folk, on occasion wives' movements extended aid to female Stakhanovites. Although this topic was also rarely discussed, it did enjoy a sporadic presence in public discourse. *Ob-*

shchestvennitsa reported how one female Stakhanovite was grateful for the wives' help and that as a consequence: "Things became much easier for us." The wives also helped female Stakhanovites to shop for clothes and furniture.[85] The emphasis of agitprop, however, fell on help for men and also reinforced the idea that wives were moral guardians of their men, there to ensure correct behavior.

WIVES AS MORAL GUARDIANS OF
HUSBANDS AND IMPROVERS OF DAILY LIFE

In Russian culture wives had generally been subordinated to husbands in a variety of overt and subtle ways. Simultaneously, women were the organizers and decision makers in the running of the domestic sphere and also moral guardians of their menfolk. Men and women generally recognized this role of the morally superior "good" woman among whose tasks was to "save" men from themselves. This element of traditional culture persists into the millennium and effectively infantilizes the male.

Patterns of infantilizing the male served to put him down, emasculate him, and suggest that he was a hopeless creature without female guidance. The implication was that without a strong woman behind him to prop and guide, he would be lost. Infantilization can be interpreted as one way in which women could assert power over men in micro-settings and attempt to redress the prevailing misogyny. What is fascinating in the Soviet context is that male leaders themselves bought into this notion and pushed it as mechanism for social change. One characteristic of Russian culture is the paradoxical juxtaposition of men asserting female inferiority yet simultaneously requesting "save me." Processes of infantilization are thus integral to gender relations and have roles to play in both personal politics and the politics of the fields and workplace.

Discourse about wives' movements incorporated this notion of woman as moral guide and upholder of decent values. She was there to check that her husband was on the correct path and to ensure he was not tempted into antisocial acts. V. S. Molokov, leader of Aeroflot, put it this way: "it seems to me that wives must chat with their husbands about their work and influence them so that they are not accident-prone, hooligans of the air, shirkers or bad workers."[86] Wives were thus cast as upholders of work discipline. Some saw their main task as that of "relentless struggle against absenteeism and lateness."[87]

As upholders of morality, or as "snoopers" as their critics would dub them, wives even became involved in the family lives of ordinary workers and Stakhanovites. A council of wives would made it their business to talk to a comrade about the serious "lack of harmony" at home where for three years, "he had been living badly" with his wife and four young children. The "skilful and careful approach" of one of the wives "in a series of conversations" allegedly "showed him the great significance of having a strong Soviet family" and "the responsibilities of a father."[88] The council of wives thus helped this man to return to his family where life took on a "normal course."[89]

Wives also attempted to change the behavior of non-Stakhanovite males by putting pressure on their wives. One wife admitted, "We went from flat to flat to the wives of non-Stakhanovites."[90] They chatted to them and tried to win them over. The wives of Stakhanovites organized meetings in factories and on farms and invited all wives. The Stakhanovites' wives then listed which men worked well and badly: "At the meetings we explained who works well and who badly. Listening to this and not seeing her husband among the best workers, a wife begins to ask him and her neighbors why this is so." Then "having learned the reasons, she begins to work on her husband." It was deemed necessary that all wives come to know the workplace "otherwise husbands will explain away their bad work by saying that the bosses suppress initiative."[91] So Stakhanovites' wives were moral guardians of their own husbands and by extension of men who were not Stakhanovites by putting moral pressure on their wives. The notions underpinning this apparently interfering behavior were that the performance of the labor force and its productivity was everyone's business and that the "private" sphere was open for scrutiny by the collective.

As well as facilitating the productive activities of Stakhanovites, wives' movements had an extremely broad brief to improve general conditions at home, in urban and rural workplaces, in kindergartens, schools, and hospitals. This led to a range of tasks, many of them defined in terms of raising the "cultural level" and promoting cleanliness. Grigorii Ordzhonikidze (affectionately known as "Sergo"), Commissar for Heavy Industry, explained this at different conferences, making remarks relevant to industry and agriculture. His general point was that women activists were involved in "struggle for the improvement of the cultural, daily, life conditions of workers."[92] Ordzhonikidze told wives at a conference in 1936: "We demand only one thing from you today—to pay attention to improving more energetically culture." He stressed the importance of focus on "cleanliness and relaxation" for the working male and advocated "creating at home and at work such a situation that would make work and relaxation especially joyful."[93] Above all, cleanliness reflected "cultural level."[94]

Ordzhonikidze argued that traditional female skills were also called upon to make life nicer, especially sewing, by which "a good housewife can make herself a wonderful dress from simple cotton." This mattered because:

"Workers still do not earn as much as we would like, but they don't earn badly." On the one hand, "they can buy good clothes," but still "it is necessary to make them, to be able to, in order to dress well."[95] The message was clear. Until such time as high-quality clothes were sold and affordable, wives had to sew them at home. Wives also had a duty to help schools, kindergartens, and canteens attain "a neat condition." Ordzhonikidze declared: "you are obliged to help in this."[96] He also argued that wives "must" help teach children.[97] Furthermore, wives' movements should approach other women "not as patrons, but like their own sisters, giving them their knowledge to raise them to their level."[98] Thus the brief that Ordzhonikidze gave them was relatively broad.

Month-long courses brought the wives of leaders of industry together. On these they got to know each other, swapped information about their local areas, and compared how each worked. After such a course, Ordzhonikidze's advice was "having returned home, I hope you work better, and most important, instruct others in how they must work."[99] Wives of leaders of industry were implicitly cast as more advanced wives, able to pass on their knowledge and expected to do so. Their husbands' advanced status was, by extension, passed on to them. The women's social standing was thus defined not by their own independent activity but more as appendages of successful men.

OBSHCHESTVENNITSA PUTTING THE REGIME'S PRIORITIES INTO PRACTICE

Stakhanovites' wives portrayed themselves as moving abreast with all Stakhanovites in town and country with the message that everyone had paths to follow, different but complementary. Evgeniia Vesnik made an explicit link between the success of the Stakhanovite movement and the wives' activity in supporting it, although the hallmark of the latter was characterized as "modest."[100] Vesnik declared, "We still have little experience, but every one of us must find her place in the general work, however small." She suggested, "let some of us take crèches and schools, helping Stakhanovites' children to study and relax better." Others should "fight for cleanliness" in canteens, clubs, snack bars, and Stakhanovites' hostels and "let a third group organize shooting groups, sport, foreign languages, and so on."[101]

Conditions for Stakhanovites' wives were especially arduous in the countryside, however.[102] As one wife put it: "The appearance of our hostels was appalling. Trestle beds stood there, full of bed bugs. No one had ever cleaned the mattresses." So they set about "whitewashing the premises in order to rid it of bed bugs."[103] Wives in Siberia moaned, "our tractor drivers slept on dirty beds. It was impossible to look at the quilts. We heated up the bath-house and washed the lot."[104] On another farm, a wife bewailed the filthy linoleum on the floor of the canteen.[105]

As well as battling with widespread dirt, wives in the countryside were involved with sowing and harvesting. Klar Ger on a state farm in Odessa oblast told a conference of wives of pig breeders that: "Our wives started their work in 1938 at the time of spring sowing." They "mainly cleaned sowing materials" and "then equipped the tractor cabins" with "little curtains." They also brought along radios and a record player and "the wife-activists came and organized readings from the press."[106]

When the autumn came the wives put out daily field leaflets, reporting on "methods of socialist labor." They claimed that this contributed to fulfilling the plan 100 percent.[107] On other farms, wives gathered in the potato harvest. If wives worked especially well, they earned Stakhanovite status themselves. According to one wife, "We even have Stakhanovites in fieldwork. For example, the old woman Shevchenko raised the norms and every day went to work."[108]

In some parts of the country conditions were harsher than in others. Siberia saw a very short summer and a severe winter. Sowing and harvesting were therefore brief periods demanding intense labor. No woman on the farm could fail to work on the 140 hectares of root crop, 100 of which were devoted to potatoes. At this time of year, there was little free time for anyone except the sick.[109] Then before winter set in, the wives set about repairing buildings in preparation for worsening conditions.[110] Rural wives also helped in preparations for the All-Union Agricultural Exhibition.[111]

More broadly, rural wives also tried to change patterns of work, relaxation, and bathing. On one farm they wanted to see a "special cupboard" for the work overalls of female pig breeders. They also demanded "in every brigade" a special work timetable of free days, "in order to strengthen work discipline." Apparently, up until then, "the situation was bad. Female pig tenders had barely had one day off all month."[112] And conditions for washing were considered inadequate. As one put it: "The bath-house worked once a week at the start. Then, upon the initiative of the wives, the bath-house began to open twice a week: once for the men; once for the women."[113] And if peasants worked selfishly, they exposed this. For instance, one man was carrying water for the pigs. He took the bucket and attended to his pig alone. At a farm meeting, the wives told this story, causing the man to turn red.[114] Like female Stakhanovites, wives were also ready to criticize men, noting that women worked better. One declared: "We know that man working on this or that field, receives the same pay as women, but works far from how she does."

The farm's canteen had one man and one woman who worked there but "when he is on, with rare exception, there is no order, and when the woman works—another story."[115] Moreover, the male cook was a drunkard and chaos reigned.[116]

When "big epidemics" occurred in the countryside and many children went to hospital, the *obshchestvennitsa* "did not forget this and carried broth there and other food."[117] She also disciplined children if they became too wild and put a stop to a craze of playing with catapults.[118] Thus in her special care of children, *obshchestvennitsa* attended to the sick and told off the naughty. Although these sowing, harvesting, and other rural tasks differed from those of factory wives, the rural wives had other pursuits similar to those of their urban counterparts which included drama clubs, choirs, work to liquidate illiteracy, and care of small libraries.[119]

In many ways the *dvizhenie zhen* took on features adopted by the later *zhensovety,* or women's councils, promoted by Khrushchev.[120] Their goals were tailored to fulfilling the regime's priorities, which could vary according to historical period. In the 1920s and 1930s the liquidation of illiteracy was a priority of social policy. Wives of engineering-technical workers therefore "immediately undertook to get the liquidation of illiteracy going and started to work themselves as teachers."[121] And during the Stalin years citizens were pressured to make monthly payments to the state (*zaima*). These were like a loan to the state to be claimed back ten years later (or twenty or more as it often turned out). The "loan" payments were theoretically voluntary, but it was politically advantageous for citizens to make them. One task of the wives was to implement this policy by encouraging the "not organized population" to subscribe to monthly payments.[122]

From a wide range of sources, evidence suggests that the wives' movement was lively on some farms, achieving some success after 1936 in hygiene, cleanliness, child care, and harvesting, but absent on others. Of these, the "struggle with dirt" (*griaz*) was paramount, part of the wider goal of developing *kul'turnost'*. One important question is just how much initiative for individual projects came from the women themselves. While there was certainly space to conceive of projects and to make recommendations, it is also clear that some party committees, workers' committees, farm directors, and trade unions encouraged the wives to pursue particular tasks, while in other cases they ignored the women or gave variable support.[123] Just as Stakhanovism was not always greeted with enthusiasm by local officials, so, too, the *dvizhenie zhen* sometimes met tepid approval, even hostility. Archives show that just as the strength of the wives' movement varied across farms, so did support for it. One state farm wife bemoaned: "What help do the workers' committee and director give us? Absolutely none."[124] Turnover in management could also mean changing attitudes toward the women. As one wife of a pig breeder put it: "About the workers' committee. Filatov always helped us, but the new chair of the factory committee is rather haughty. He sometimes answers our wife-activist rudely."[125] In fact, the *obshchestvennitsy* were often seen by workers and peasants alike as meddling busybodies that "out of nothing to do" interfered with others' affairs both in huts and hostels and in the fields.[126]

TO BE A PAID WORKER OR AN *OBSHCHESTVENNITSA*?: AN OFFICIAL DEBATE

During the 1930s, consistent with Marxism, ideology advocated that women should enter the labor force. Resistance among women and men to this idea, however, existed. As a consequence, women's journals like *Obshchestvennitsa* debated the pros and cons of leaving the home. If a woman would not work, then the second preferred official option was for her to be a "helper" and *obshchestvennitsa*.

The debate around this issue is nicely illustrated by responses to a letter from an engineer's wife, Comrade V. She wrote in 1939 that she wished to participate in socialist construction but feared the break-up of her family, endured strong opposition to the idea from her husband, and anyway lacked help in housework.[127] One response to Comrade V. questioned how truly "Bolshevik" her husband could be if he did not participate in housework. Another letter suggested that it was wrong to go straight to work, better slowly to accommodate her husband to the idea.[128] A third advocated, "she must definitely, courageously, without fear, go to the factory. I am certain that her family life will not suffer."[129] A fourth advised Comrade V. not to go to work on the grounds that "She helps her husband in his work, is his comrade, his secretary, his helper. Creating the conditions for his work, she is in essence fulfilling a useful function for society." The importance of careful supervision of children was an additional reason.[130]

The last letter printed, seemingly the one deemed by the editors to give the "correct" response, advised that Comrade V. not enter paid work but instead devote her spare time and energy to "public work" because as an *obshchestvennitsa* "she would not bring harm to her family and it would be useful to our socialist state."[131] During the 1930s, texts indicate that given the opposition to changing gender roles, the role of *obshchestvennitsa* was second best for women. It was both useful to society and a first necessary step out of the home for women who felt unable to go straight into the paid workforce. Whilst official ideology did not emphasize its importance, "practical ideology" stressed its benefits for women and for society.[132]

The apparent clash between the images of Stakhanovite women and Stakhanovite wives is thus softened. Both categories of women helped society, but in different ways. Both categories of women participated in activities outside the home, albeit to different degrees. Both activities were instilled with the idea of "duty" and "responsibility" to socialism, party, Motherland, and Stalin.

CONCLUSION

The relevance of Stakhanovism to gender constructs was multifaceted. In terms of female emancipation, the results were decidedly mixed and contradictory. But in terms of contribution to the "new life" and to constructing socialism, heroic female workers and servicing wives had positive roles to play and each was encouraged by leaders to play their different parts. Here the priorities of the socialist state took precedence over the revolutionary goal of professional and financial independence for working women.

Paradoxically, both female Stakhanovites and members of the wives' movement may have challenged the gender status quo at a time when the party was attempting to instill discipline, order, conformity, and stability in the family and in society at large. The 1936 legislation which made divorce difficult and costly and which banned abortion coincided with "Stakhanovite Year" and was adopted just after the Stakhanovite movement was launched. So, on the one hand, the party was potentially restricting women's lives. Yet, on the other, in encouraging Stakhanovism, and in luring housewives out of the home into "socially useful work," it was unwittingly encouraging some female self-determination and possible arguments with husbands. Just as many parents, siblings, and boyfriends tried to deter women from becoming Stakhanovites, especially if this meant working on a tractor and defying the traditional division of labor, so too some husbands forbade wives to become *obshchestvennitsy*, not wanting them to leave the home.

Above all, Stakhanovism offered women opportunities to become what they had never been. Although male Stakhanovites also enjoyed these openings, Stakhanovism was additionally significant for women. This was because women could demonstrate that they were "equal" and "better" in a culture that in numerous ways told them they were "inferior" to men in the public sphere. They could show that they could perform well any task done by men, illustrate that socialist ideology on "equality" could work, and also derive some protection in their efforts from that ideology. The especially confident Stakhanovites even stood up at conferences and declared they were "better" than men, a claim alien to ideology of the 1930s. So although female Stakhanovites could not easily divorce or abort legally, they could earn more than ever before, receive decorations and presents, be awarded places in agricultural academies, and be "elected" onto the Supreme Soviet. They were part of a privileged elite, as were the wives of Stakhanovites by extension.

Thus the reality of female Stakhanovism contradicted many traditional attitudes and cultural patterns and implicitly challenged the spirit of fresh legislation. Female Stakhanovism was potentially undermining of aspects of state politics but simultaneously consistent with general ideological goals of equality of the sexes. Female Stakhanovism was a direct threat to traditional gender hierarchies and to authority relationships between the sexes. Women, too, now merited respect for their work in the public sphere and demanded recognition for it. Many a *muzhik* did not like this.

Yet the regime was prepared to offend the *muzhik* to push its policies. One reason was sheer necessity since the countryside needed women to work harder as they outnumbered men in many sectors. Moreover, as war loomed, the state needed women to take over the fields and to assume leadership positions while men went to the front. A second reason was that the party was prepared to champion the ideology of equality of the sexes over traditional male values, even though many leaders themselves could not be described as "new men." It is worth speculating, however, that leaders may not have anticipated the extent to which female Stakhanovites would blow their own trumpets and challenge men, thus stirring up resentment and prejudices.

An alternative explanation could run that in fact female Stakhanovites were a spearhead to change in the village, pushed as such by the regime. Here they would be comparable to Massell's "surrogate proletariat" in the 1920s in Central Asia in which women as the most oppressed were used through social engineering "as a potential revolutionary stratum" to shock the system into radical change which would not easily occur otherwise.[133] Whilst, however, the regime did encourage female Stakhanovism in ideology and propaganda and pushed it locally through the *politotdely,* it did not explicitly adopt the line of female superiority in work, but steadfastly held onto "equality." Even though women's arguments about being "better" than men may have suited the regime's priorities, they were never uttered by top leaders or slogans.

NOTES

1. *Vtoroi Vsesoiuznyi S"ezd Kolkhoznikov-Udarnikov Peredovykh Kolkhozov, 15–19 Fevralia 1933g: Stenograficheskii otchët* (Moscow: Sel'khozgiz, 1935), 101. For discussion of "complex and contradictory" dimensions in images of peasant women, refer to Victoria E. Bonnell, "The Peasant Woman in Stalinist Political Art of the 1930s," *The American Historical Review* 98, no. 1 (February 1993): 55–82.

2. *Vtoroi Vsesoiuznyi S"ezd Kolkhoznikov-Udarnikov*, 48.

3. *Sovkhoznaia gazeta*, 12 October 1936, 3.

4. Alix Holt, *Alexandra Kollontai: Selected Writings* (New York: W. W. Norton and Co., 1977), 237–49.

5. For fuller discussion see Mary Buckley, *Women and Ideology in the Soviet Union* (Hemel Hempstead: Harvester/Wheatsheaf; and Ann Arbor: University of Michigan Press, 1989), 44–70.

6. On the *Zhenotdel*, see Carol Eubanks Hayden, "The Zhenotdel and the Bolshevik Party," *Russian History* 3, no. 2 (1976): 150–73; Richard Stites, *The Women's Liberation Movement in Russia* (Princeton, NJ: Princeton University Press, 1978), 329–45. For Armand's writings on rural women, see I. F. Armand, *Stat'i, Rechi, Pis'ma* (Moscow: Politizdat, 1975), 60–61.

7. *Krest'ianka*, no. 1 (1936): 1.

8. Buckley, *Women and Ideology in the Soviet Union*, 113–20.

9. *Krasnaia Sibiriachka*, no. 3–4 (February 1936): 17.

10. *Krasnaia Sibiriachka*, no. 3–4 (February 1939): 17.

11. *Krest'ianskaia gazeta*, 4 December 1935, 1.

12. *Krest'ianskaia gazeta*, 4 December 1935, 1.

13. *Krest'ianskaia gazeta*, 4 December 1935, 1.

14. *Vtoroi Vsesoiuznyi S"ezd Kolkhoznikov-Udarnikov*, 101.

15. Pasha Angelina, *My Answer to an American Questionnaire* (Moscow: Foreign Languages Publishing House, 1949), 30.

16. P. Angelina, *Liudi Kolkhoznykh Polei* (Moscow-Leningrad: Gosudarstvennoe Izdatel'stvo Detskoi Literatury, 1952), 40.

17. *Vtoroi Vsesoiuznyi S"ezd Kolkhoznikov-Udarnikov*, 101.

18. RGASPI, f. 17, op. 120, d. 292, l. 29.

19. RGASPI, f. 17, op. 120, d. 292, l. 5.

20. *Vtoroi Vsesoiuznyi S"ezd Kolkhoznikov-Udarnikov*, 48.

21. S. K. Korotov et al., *My Predsedatel'stvyet na Vsesoiuznom S"ezde* (Moscow: Ogiz-Sel'khozgiz, 1935), 8.

22. P. Angelina, *Liudi Kolkhoznykh Polei*, 18.

23. Angelina, *Liudi Kolkhoznykh Polei*, 19.

24. Angelina, *Liudi Kolkhoznykh Polei*, 19.

25. Angelina, *Liudi Kolkhoznykh Polei*, 20.

26. Angelina, *Liudi Kolkhoznykh Polei*, 21.

27. Angelina, *Liudi Kolkhoznykh Polei*, 22.

28. Angelina, *Liudi Kolkhoznykh Polei*, 23.

29. Angelina, *Liudi Kolkhoznykh Polei*, 23.

30. Angelina, *Liudi Kolkhoznykh Polei*, 24.

31. Angelina, *Liudi Kolkhoznykh Polei*, 25.

32. Angelina, *Liudi Kolkhoznykh Polei*, 27.

33. Angelina, *Liudi Kolkhoznykh Polei*, 26.

34. Angelina, *Liudi Kolkhoznykh Polei*, 26.

35. Angelina, *Liudi Kolkhoznykh Polei*, 26.

36. Angelina, *Liudi Kolkhoznykh Polei*, 26.

37. Angelina, *Liudi Kolkhoznykh Polei*, 27.

38. Angelina, *Liudi Kolkhoznykh Polei*, 31. *Baba* is a rather denigrating term meaning "old hag." Of course, Pasha was young.

39. Angelina, *Liudi Kolkhoznykh Polei*, 31.

40. Angelina, *Liudi Kolkhoznykh Polei*, 32.

41. Angelina, *My Answer*, 25–26; See, too, Angelina, *Liudi Kolkhoznykh Polei*, 25–26.

42. Angelina, *My Answer*, 26.

43. Angelina, *My Answer*, 27.

44. Angelina, *My Answer*, 28.

45. Angelina, *My Answer*, 22–23.

46. Douglas Northrup, "Subaltern Dialogues: Subversion and Resistance in Soviet Uzbek Family Law," in *Contending with Stalinism: Soviet Power and Popular Resistance in the 1930s*, ed. Lynne Viola (Ithaca and London: Cornell University Press, 2002), 109–38.

47. Gregory J. Massell, *The Surrogate Proletariat: Moslem Women and Revolutionary Strategies in Soviet Central Asia, 1919–1929* (Princeton, NJ: Princeton University Press, 1974); Northrup, "Subaltern Dialogues," 134–45.

48. Dar'ia Garmash, "O samom dorogom," in *V Budniakh Velikikh Stroek: Zhenshchiny-Kommunistki Geroini Pervykh Piatiletok*, ed. L. I. Stishova (Moscow: Politizdat, 1986), 177.

49. Garmash, "O samom dorogom," 179.

50. Garmash, "O samom dorogom," 180.

51. Garmash, "O samom dorogom," 181.

52. Garmash, "O samom dorogom," 181.

53. Garmash, "O samom dorogom," 181.

54. Garmash, "O samom dorogom," 182.

55. Garmash, "O samom dorogom," 182.

56. Garmash, "O samom dorogom," 182.

57. Garmash, "O samom dorogom," 182.

58. Iurii Il'inski, "Iunaia Stakhanovka," in *V Budniakh Velikikh Stroek*, 23.

59. Angelina, *Liudi Kolkhoznykh Polei*, 24–35.

60. Garmash, "O samom dorogom," 178.

61. Garmash, "O samom dorogom," 178.

62. Garmash, "O samom dorogom," 179.

63. Il'inski, "Iunaia Stakhanovka," 57.

64. A Commission of the CC of the CPSU, ed., *History of the Communist Party of the Soviet Union/Bolsheviks/Short Course* (Moscow: Foreign languages Publishing House, 1941), 238.

65. Jochen Hellbeck, "Fashioning the Stalinist Soul: The Diary of Stepan Podlubnyi (1931–1939)," *Jahrbücher für Geschichte Osteuropas* 44 (1966): 371.

66. Hellbeck, "Fashioning," 346.

67. Alfred G. Meyer, "The Functions of Ideology in the Soviet Political System," *Soviet Studies* 17 (January 1966): 273–85; Ludwig Wittgenstein, *Philosophical Investigations*. Trans. G. E. M. Anscombe (New York: Macmillan, 1968).

68. *Stakhanovets*, no. 12 (June 1936), 24.

69. Armand, *Stat'i, Rechi, Pis'ma*; Holt, *Alexandra Kollontai*. For an overview of their arguments see Buckley, *Women and Ideology, 48–64*.

70. These included in May, the All-Union Conference of Wives of Leaders and Engineering-Technical Workers of Heavy Industry and also the All-Union Conference of Wives of Leaders and Engineering-Technical Workers of Light Industry, and in December, the All-Union Conference of Wives of Commanders and Leaders of the Red Army.

71. For further details see Mary Buckley, "The Untold Story of *Obshchestvennitsa* in the 1930s," *Europe-Asia Studies* 48, no. 4 (July 1996): 572–74. For coverage of the Union Conference of Wives of Leaders and Engineering Technical Workers, see: *Kolkhoznitsa*, no. 5 (1936): 19; and *Udarnitsa Urala*, no. 7 (1936): 12–15. Discussion of the Leningrad Conference of Wives of the Commissariat of Light Industry is found in *Obshchestvennitsa*, no. 7 (July 1939): 15. A gathering of Moscow activists reported in *Obshchestvennitsa*, no. 8 (August 1939): 20. Quite common, too, were district conferences of housewives. See *Obshchestvennitsa*, no. 9 (September 1939): 16.

72. GARF, f. 7689, op. 7, d. 146 and d. 147.

73. Different categories of "wife" came together to help their menfolk. Groupings included: the movement of engineering-technical workers' wives, the movement of wives of leaders of heavy industry, the brigade of specialists' wives, the council of wives of the management of the airforce, wives of railway workers, wives of Aeroflot workers, wives of oil workers, the movement of wives on oil tankers, buoy keepers' wives on the Volga, sailors' wives, councils of miners' wives, and wives of workers on state farms.

74. GARF, f. 7689, op. 7, d. 146, l. 150ob; f. 7689, op. 7, d. 146, l. 59.

75. *Zhenshchina—Bol'shaia Sila. Pervoe Kraevoe Soveshchanie Zhen Stakhanovtsev Severnogo Kraia, 15–17 Aprelia 1936 goda: Stenograficheskii otchët* (Ogiz: Sevkraigiz, 1936), 7.

76. *Zhenshchina—Bol'shaia Sila*, 7.

77. *Zhenshchina—Bol'shaia Sila*, 10.

78. *Zhenshchina—Bol'shaia Sila*, 17.

79. *Zhenshchina—Bol'shaia Sila*, 18.

80. *Zhenshchina—Bol'shaia Sila*, 14.

81. Angelina, *My Answer*, 4. This source indicates that Angelina had three children — Svetlana, Valerii, and Stalina.

82. Roberta T. Manning, "Women in the Soviet Countryside on the Eve of World War II, 1935–1940," in *Russian Peasant Women*, eds. Beatrice Farnsworth and Lynne Viola (New York: Oxford University Press, 1992), 219. Manning notes that Pasha's husband was the Komsomol district secretary. When his mother alleged that her granddaughter looked like Pasha, but not Pasha's husband, her husband urged her to give up tractor driving. The morals of Stakhanovites were often questioned in this manner, but Pasha refused to give up the tractor. See, too, Arkadii Slavutskii, *Praskov'ia Angelina* (Moscow, 1960), 60–67.

83. *Krest'ianskaia gazeta*, 14 October 1936, 1.

84. *Udarnitsa Urala*, no. 1 (1936): 8.

85. *Obshchestvennitsa*, November 1939, 11; *K Vsesoiuznomu Soveshchaniiu zhen khoziaistvennikov i inzhenerno-technikcheskikh rabotnikov legkoi promyshlennosti, vypusk 1, Ianvar' 1937* (Moscow: Izdanie gazety Legkaia Promyshlennost', 1937), 27.

86. *Obshchestvennitsa*, February 1939, 18.

87. *Obshchestvennitsa*, February 1939, 24.

88. *Udarnitsa Urala*, no. 10 (December 1936): 23.

89. *Udarnitsa Urala*, no. 10 (December 1936): 23.

90. *Zhenshchina—Bol'shaia Sila*, 19.

91. *Zhenshchina—Bol'shaia Sila*, 19.

92. RGASPI, f. 85, op. 29, d. 151, l.4. The first draft of the speech, later corrected, is found on ll. 1–3.

93. RGASPI, f. 85, op. 29, d. 151, l. 4.

94. RGASPI, f. 85, op. 29, d. 151, ll. 4–5.

95. RGASPI, f. 85, op. 29, d. 151, l. 5.

96. RGASPI, f. 85, op. 29, d. 151, l. 5.

97. RGASPI, f. 85, op. 29, d. 151, l. 5.

98. RGASPI, f. 85, op. 29, d. 151, l. 5.

99. RGASPI, f. 85, op. 29, d. 151, l. 5.

100. *Stakhanovets,* no. 12 (June 1936): 24. Articles about the activities of wives' movements were published in several newspapers and journals including, for industry, *Trud, Stakhanovets*, and *Udarnitsa Urala* and, for agriculture, *Krasnaia Sibiriachka, Krest'ianskaia gazeta*, and *Sovkhoznaia gazeta*. The most thorough details, however, were found in the movement's own journal, *Obshchestvennitsa*. Generally articles were written by the women activists themselves, describing their work. In other cases, their achievements were reported by journalists. Archival materials in GARF provide additional information on conferences, funding, and obstructions to the movement's smooth functioning. These are in urban and rural trade union documents and in correspondence between wives and their husbands' trade union.

101. *Stakhanovets*, no. 12 (June 1936), 35.

102. For fuller discussion consult Mary Buckley, "The Soviet 'Wife-Activist' Down on the Farm," *Social History*, 26, no. 3 (October 2001): 282–98.

103. GARF, f. 7689, op. 7, d. 146, l. 7.

104. GARF, f. 7689, op. 7, d. 146, l. 86.

105. GARF, f. 7689, op. 7, d. 146, l. 63.

106. GARF, f. 7689, op. 7, d. 146, l. 150ob.

107. GARF, f. 7689, op. 7, d. 146, l. 150ob.

108. GARF, f. 7689, op. 7, d. 146, l. 166ob.

109. GARF, f. 7689, op. 7, d. 146, l. 88.

110. GARF, f. 7689, op. 7, d. 146, l. 153ob.

111. GARF, f. 7689, op. 7, d. 146, l. 110ob.

112. GARF, f. 7689, op. 7, d. 146, l. 110ob.

113. GARF, f. 7689, op. 7, d. 146, l. 13.

114. GARF, f. 7689, op. 7, d. 146, l. 154.

115. GARF, f. 7689, op. 7, d. 146, l. 87.

116. GARF, f. 7689, op. 7, d. 146, l. 87.

117. GARF, f. 7689, op. 7, d. 146, l. 166ob.

118. GARF, f. 7689, op. 7, d. 146, l. 9.

119. GARF, f. 7689, op. 7, d. 146, ll. 150ob–151.

120. For discussion of the *zhensovety* under Khrushchev, see Mary Buckley, *Women and Ideology in the Soviet Union,* 140–55; and Genia K. Browning, *Women and Politics in the USSR* (London: Wheatsheaf, 1987).

121. *Udarnitsa Urala*, no. 7 (September 1936): 18.

122. *Udarnitsa Urala*, no. 7 (September 1936): 18.

123. *Udarnitsa Urala*, no. 7 (April 1937), 10; *Udarnitsa Urala*, no. 7 (September 1936): 15. For fuller discussion of how institutions treated the wives, refer to Buckley, "The Soviet 'Wife-Activist' Down on the Farm," 296–98.

124. GARF, f. 7689, op. 7, d. 146, l. 7ob.

125. GARF, f. 7689, op. 7, d. 146, l. 155ob.

126. *Udarnitsa Urala*, no. 7 (April 1937), 10; *K VseSoiuznomu*, 1, 28; Buckley, "The Untold Story," 577–81.

127. *Obshchestvennitsa*, no. 9 (September 1939): 25.

128. *Obshchestvennitsa*, no. 9 (September 1939): 26.

129. *Obshchestvennitsa*, no. 9 (September 1939): 26.

130. *Obshchestvennitsa*, no. 9 (September 1939): 26.

131. *Obshchestvennitsa*, no. 9 (September 1939): 26.

132. *Obshchestvennitsa*, no. 9 (September 1939): 26.

133. Massell, *The Surrogate Proletariat*, 93–127.

Chapter Eleven

What Was the Significance of Rural Stakhanovism?

The Stakhanovite movement in the vegetable fields of Belorussia has taken on a mass character.[1]

The Stakhanovite movement has not yet become a mass movement.[2]

— *Sovkhoznaia gazeta*, March 1937

Chto zhe u nas stakhanovskoe dvizhenie ili stakanovskoe dvizhenie?[3] (Do we have a Stakhanovite movement here or a drinking glass movement?)

Beyond challenging traditional gender hierarchies in villages, what was rural Stakhanovism's wider significance? How far did the images of rural shock workers and Stakhanovites projected in the press match reality? Were they really empty constructs or were some elements apt? Or rather, were they overstatements and glorifications, or in part accurate? Contrariwise, in some cases were they reasonably accurate pictures, or even understatements of the enthusiasm on the ground?

Addressing the significance of rural Stakhanovism with precision is difficult. That reality did not always match the socialist realist pictures that the press and the cinema frequently portrayed is indisputable. So something can be said about evidence that challenges propaganda and official discourse, in particular concerning the enthusiasm and resilience of Stakhanovites and their number. Not only did the press contradict itself on these topics, but also archives indicate how weak on some farms rural Stakhanovism was. Its strength appears to have varied across the vast Soviet landmass, not uniformly successful, if numbers alone define "success."

It is, moreover, methodologically easier to show when evidence subverts official images. Data that make a stark clash between the image and the reality appear immediately credible. Even though one cannot indicate how representative of reality the clash may be, one can convincingly show that the conflict did, in specific instances, exist. It is far harder to establish with certainty when evidence supports the images. This is because the skeptic can immediately retort that data that coincide with official images are themselves part of those images, and thus unbelievable.[4] The ready charge that Soviet statistics were also invariably inaccurate, inflated, and misrepresentations of reality, makes constructive use of those available awkward, especially when alternatives cannot always be estimated. Bearing these hazards in mind, what can be said with certainty about what constituted "success"?

WHAT IS "SUCCESS"?

How can success of the rural Stakhanovite movement best be gauged? This task prompts several questions: is Stakhanovism successful if it lures a particular percentage of peasants to aspire to Stakhanovite status, or is aspiration insufficient? Should success be measured not in gross numbers or in percentages of the peasantry, but rather in terms of yearly increases or decreases in the numbers of Stakhanovites? Is wide geographic spread a better indicator of a successful movement, on the assumption that a movement that is restricted to certain areas is hardly buoyant? Should perhaps success be determined by a growth of Stakhanovite lessons, their dissemination and emulation? What, moreover, is the relevance to "success" of how Stakhanovites themselves were treated? If they are not given better conditions or perks, as promised, does this mean the movement was unsuccessful, or merely differentially rewarded? Or should the only indicator of success be increased productivity? If, despite the fact that thousands of Stakhanovites existed on paper, and notwithstanding reporting of numerous new Stakhanovite "lessons," productivity failed to rise as a consequence, what would be the point of a Stakhanovite movement other than a mass mobilization of the peasantry around a certain Stalinist utopian vision? Indeed, is mobilization to toil enthusiastically for a "bright future" itself a sufficient criterion?

ASPIRING AND FALTERING STAKHANOVITES

Evidence does indeed demonstrate that a portion of the peasantry did aspire to be Stakhanovites. Motivations may have varied, but nonetheless thousands did apparently set out to emulate Stakhanov and Demchenko, if only to earn more and hopefully to live better. Rural heroes and heroines, like Vladimir Zuev,

Fedor Kolesov, Mariia Demchenko, and Pasha Angelina came forward, announced the targets they hoped to attain, generally overfulfilled them, and then challenged others to socialist competitions with a view to exceeding norms still further. In the process, they inspired other less well-known Stakhanovites to emulate them. Enthusiastic followers of the above included Tamara Riabchinskaia, Efim Kormin, Sofiia Kirilenko, and Pasha Ledovskaia.Thus, if the aspiration of some alone is an indicator, then Stakhanovism was successful. Not everyone, however, aspired to be a Stakhanovite and not everyone who tried to become one, succeeded. Since peasants also belittled the Stakhanovites and expressed hostility to them in violent ways, there were deterrents to Stakhanovism on the farm.

Another aspect of the "aspiration" indicator is whether or not aspiration can falter. Indeed, were Stakhanovites as enthusiastic and as resilient in the face of opposition as official images in the press suggested? While evidence here is patchy, procuracy archives do show that Stakhanovites who had been taunted sometimes gave up their Stakhanovite status rather than endure more hostility. Thus not all were sure enough to stand up to baiting and lack of support.

Ideology, however, portrayed them as strong, unswerving in their commitment to new production feats, and resilient in the face of criticism and bullying. Procuracy archives paint a grayer and more variegated picture. In the village of Somkov-Dolin in Ukraine, for instance, a special evening was laid on to congratulate female 500ers. Three male troublemakers, later sentenced, sat in the women's places and would not give them their seats. According to the procuracy report, throughout the entire evening the men "laughed at the 500ers," reproaching them for gathering dung and chicken droppings. As a result, "some of the kolkhoz-500ers began to refuse to fulfil the obligations they had set themselves."[5] Being ridiculed was enough to deter some women from working like Stakhanovites. This illustration is typical of many similar examples.

Although men may sometimes have given female Stakhanovites a hard time, so too did women. Recall how in Belorussia Elena Gradovkina baited the Stakhanovite Shchelkunova to such an extent that Shchelkunova ended up going to the kolkhoz chair, renouncing her Stakhanovite title, and asking for her workdays to be divided up among the other women.[6] Similarly, when two women ridiculed and threatened Stakhanovites who worked in flax, two frightened Stakhanovites stopped work in tears.[7] Patterns of intimidation by women could be just as corrosive as male bullying.

Relatives, too, had the power to turn Stakhanovites away from their work. At the extreme end of negative influence from the family, in Kiev oblast, Elisei Ruban was sentenced to five years' imprisonment for forcing his wife to give up her 500er status. Not all Stakhanovites could withstand the pressures put on them, as official images implied.[8] Others were mocked while they worked with the result that they shied away from Stakhanovism.[9]

So although some peasants aspired to be Stakhanovites and attained that status, not all of them stayed Stakhanovites due to taunting, belittling, and threats of violence. What one cannot establish is the percentage of Stakhanovites who gave up due to harassment, the percentage not put off by it, or the percentage that endured no ill treatment at all. At best one can note Stakhanovite status was not permanent. Moreover, not all Stakhanovites were apparently as determined to repel attempts to belittle them as official newspaper images suggested.

HOW MANY STAKHANOVITES WERE THERE?

If "success" cannot be measured in terms of aspirations alone, is the number of rural Stakhanovites a more useful indicator? Can one assume that the larger the percentage of Stakhanovites among the peasantry, then the more significant the movement? If so, analysis encounters an immediate problem. Whereas the trade unions produced neat tables on the number of Stakhanovites in heavy and light industry, nothing quite so useful was devised for agriculture. There appears to have been no systematic compilation of the number of Stakhanovites by sector for both collective and state farms.[10] Although archives occasionally provide statistics on Stakhanovites engaging in socialist competitions for individual farms in a given sector for the four quarters of a specified year, no All-Union tables are available. The fullest data are for state farms, collected at republican level.

The most visible statistics in the public domain are those in the press. These, however, are generally incomplete and given only in passing. For example, in December 1937, the then People's Commissar for grain and animal husbandry state farms, Ivan Benediktov, wrote a rallying piece for *Sovkhoznaia gazeta* on "Let us develop the Stakhanovite movement wider!" Almost inconsequentially, he noted that the People's Commissariat of Agriculture of the RSFSR put the number of permanent state farm workers in that republic at 185,000. Of these, just over 3,000, or 1.6 percent, were Stakhanovites.[11] This snippet from the press hardly suggests a mass movement.

Archival documents for state farm trade unions carry even patchier information, presented in different ways. Occasionally the number of rural Stakhanovites is incidentally mentioned for a given agricultural sector in a particular oblast or krai. For example, at an early gathering of Stakhanovites on dairy farms held in 1935, the following was tossed out amid a broader discussion of what constituted a Stakhanovite:

How many Stakhanovites do we have? Comrades, they say that in Khar'kov oblast there are fifteen, in Stalingrad twenty-seven, in Leningrad oblast fourteen, in Dnepropetrovsk oblast fourteen, in Kuibyshev krai eleven, in Saratov seven, in the Western oblast twelve, in Belorussia and Crimea thirteen, in Kirov oblast eight, in Ivanovo nineteen, in Gor'kii eleven, and in Azovo-Chernomore krai twenty-six.[12]

These figures apply to dairy state farms only, showing Stakhanovites to be extremely special and rare workers. Similarly, in an *otchët* of Stakhanovism in dairying in Kuibyshev krai, it was reported that up to 1936 there were only sixty-six Stakhanovites, three of whom had been decorated at a gathering in Moscow.[13] If both of these sources are accurate, then one can deduce that in dairying in Kuibyshev krai, the number of Stakhanovites increased from eleven to sixty-six from 1935 to early 1936.

Sometimes a special report "On the Stakhanovite Movement" gave the total number of Stakhanovites for a particular farm. One such report on the "Red October" bird farm announced that there were seven Stakhanovites in 1935.[14] But without data on the total number of peasants, the overall percentage of Stakhanovites cannot be calculated. At best, one knows that Stakhanovites existed and that they were in the minority. Similarly, at a gathering in 1938 of Stakhanovites and farm leaders of milk and meat state farms of Gor'kii and Kursk oblasts and of Udmurt ASSR, the head of the *politotdel* of the Kalinin state farm announced that "there are forty-one Stakhanovites on the farm and forty-six shock workers. Work is being conducted with them."[15] Again the picture is scant. The same obtains in documents of a rally in 1939 of pig state farms. One participant reports, "We have eleven Stakhanovites. Three work in the animal courtyard, eight in a field brigade, one of whom is a tractor driver."[16] Again, missing gross data make the calculation of percentages impossible, although it is evident that Stakhanovites constitute an elite minority.

Occasionally data are fuller. At a conference of heads of *politotdely*, one announced: "out of thirty shepherds' brigades we have seven which are entirely Stakhanovite and have absolutely no losses."[17] So here one can calculate that 23 percent of brigades were officially "Stakhanovite." Another volunteered, "For 320 workers on our state farm we currently have fifteen Stakhanovites."[18] So here the percentage of Stakhanovites made up 5 percent of workers. These figures, however, cannot be generalized to the entire Soviet Union because representativeness cannot be assumed. The problem of missing data also applies to comments on increases in the number of Stakhanovites. In 1938 at a gathering of Stakhanovites and farm leaders in Bashkir, it was observed that "the number of Stakhanovites on the state farm has increased: in animal husbandry it was fifteen on 1 January 1938 and on

1 April it was twenty-five."[19] Yet again, missing longitudinal gross figures limit conclusions.

Rare sources give gross figures of the number of workers on a state farm. In December 1939, V. A. Balezin, an inspector of labor protection of the Central Committee of meat and milk state farms, went on a *komandirovka* (study trip) to Ordzhonikidze krai. His brief was to investigate socialist competitions and Stakhanovism in the krai. The main conclusion of his report was that on eleven state farms in the krai, there were 5,698 workers. Of these, 2,578 participated in socialist competitions. The number of shock workers on the farms examined ranged from 30 to 121 and the number of Stakhanovites ran from 8 to 69. Although Balezin did not include any percentages himself, he provided gross figures that made such calculations possible. As can be seen in Table 11.1, the percentage of Stakhanovites varied across farms from a low of 1.4 percent to highs of 9.3 percent and 12.6 percent, averaging 6.5 percent overall. Similarly, shock workers ranged from 5.4 to 22.7 percent, averaging 10 per cent. Likewise, those on each farm engaged in socialist competitions spanned from the very low 14.5 percent on Piatigorskii state farm to 78.4 percent on the Bol'shevik Spark Farm, averaging across farms at 45.2 percent.[20] The general picture is one of immense variation within the krai.

Tables which do not give breakdowns according to individual farms, but which compare oblasts, are also moderately useful. For example, selected entries for dairying state farms in September 1936 that engaged in socialist competitions give the number of state farm workers on the farms examined and the number of Stakhanovites and shock workers among them. These, at least, permit percentages to be calculated. One can deduce, as shown in Table 11.2,

Table 11.1.   Dairy State Farms in Ordzhonikidze Krai, December 1939

State Farms	Number of Workers	Number of Stakhanovites	Number of Shock Workers	Number Competing
Borets	580	8 (1.4%)	36 (6.2%)	193 (33.2%)
Vinodelenskii	333	18 (5.4%)	32 (9.6%)	121 (36.3%)
Bol'shevistskaia Iskra	625	25 (4%)	40 (6.4%)	490 (78.4%)
Kamenno-Balkovskii	321	30 (9.3%)	45 (14%)	200 (62.3%)
KhOZO NKVD	761	52 (6.8%)	83 (11%)	250 (32.8%)
Kabardinskii	369	22 (6%)	30 (8.1%)	178 (48.2%)
Kavkazskii	785	69 (8.8%)	42 (5.4%)	313 (39.8%)
Stavropol'-Kavkazskii	576	45 (7.8%)	60 (10.4%)	270 (46.8%)
Terskii	533	67 (12.6%)	121 (22.7%)	340 (63.7%)
Piatigorskii	454	16 (3.5%)	31 (6.8%)	66 (14.5%)
Balkarskii	361	18 (5%)	48 (13.3%)	157 (43.4%)
Total	5,698	370 (6.5%)	568 (10%)	2,578 (45.2%)

Source: Adapted from GARF, f. 7689, op. 11, d. 419, l. 90.

Table 11.2. Socialist Competitions in Dairying, September 1936

Krai/Oblast	Number of Farms	Number of State Farm Workers	Number of Stakhanovites Competing	Number of Shock Workers Competing	Number of Others Competing	Total* Number Competing as % of All Farm Workers
Northern	10	3,674	302 (8.2%)	801 (21.8%)	1,153	61.4
Leningrad	9	2,582	179 (6.9%)	415 (16.0%)	883	57.2
Western	8	1,895	82 (4.3%)	197 (10.4%)	794	56.6
Moscow	7	3,062	120 (3.9%)	433 (14.1%)	1,089	53.6
Voronezh	5	1,896	45 (2.4%)	136 (7.1%)	668	44.8
Saratov	5	3,027	76 (2.5%)	77 (2.5%)	393	18.0

*In the last column the % refers to the overall percentage of state farm workers competing, thus including Stakhanovites, shock workers, and others.

Source: Adapted from GARF, f. 7689, op. 11, d. 119, l. 8.

that the lowest percentage of Stakhanovites relative to the overall number of workers competing in an oblast is 2.4 percent in Voronezh oblast, whereas the highest percentage is 8.2 in the Northern krai. The percentages of shock workers are generally higher, ranging from lows of 2.5 percent and 7.1 percent in Saratov and Voronezh oblasts respectively, to highs of 16 percent in Leningrad oblast and 21.8 percent in the Northern krai. The last column of the table shows that the proportion of all state farm workers engaging in socialist competitions varies from 27.2 percent in Saratov oblast to 61 percent in the Northern krai.[21] Even these statistics, however, are problematic. Not all state farms in the oblasts under scrutiny have necessarily been included in the table. One remains unsure of the selection process, so the range of percentages given above may not coincide with the true range. Moreover, data presented according to oblast obscure variations across farms.

More usefully, and rarely, longitudinal data are given spanning perhaps two or three years for particular oblasts. Data collected by workers' committees for pig farms in Voronezh and Kursk oblasts, shown in Table 11.3, for example, noted that in October 1937 there were 247 Stakhanovites out of 8,030 state farm workers, whereas by October 1938 there were 443 Stakhanovites out of 10,044 state farmers.[22] Thus in 1937 and 1938 the percentages of Stakhanovites were 3 and 4.4 respectively. Data for 1939 were based on fifteen farms with a total of 5,664 state farmers, of whom 446 or 7.9 percent were Stakhanovites. The table also rather curiously put data for Voronezh and Kursk together in one column, and then gave separate data for Kursk. Looking at Kursk alone, we see in 1937, fifty-one Stakhanovites out of a total workforce of 1,530, amounting to 2.9 percent. In 1938, pig state farms in Kursk had 1,512 workers, of whom 69, or 4.6 percent were Stakhanovites.

Table 11.3.   Pig State Farms in Voronezh and Kursk Oblasts

	October 1937		October 1938		October 1939	
	Voronezh and Kursk	Kursk	Voronezh and Kursk	Kursk	For 15 Farms	Kursk
Number of Workers	8,030	1,730	10,044	1,512	5,664	833
Number Competing	2,106	316	2,535	337	1,943	126
Number of Shock Workers	537	69	780	106	564	58
Number of Stakhanovites	247	51	443	69	446	56
Total of last 3 Rows	2,890	436	3,758	512	2,953	240
Last 3 Rows as % of Row 1	36.0%	25.2%	37.4%	33.9%	52.1%	28.8%

Source: Adapted from GARF, f. 7689, op. 7, d. 123, l. 7ob.

Although Stakhanovites in Table 11.3 are in the minority on pig state farms, shock workers considerably outnumber them. Their corresponding percentages are 6.7 and 4 for 1937, 7.8 and 7 for 1938, and 10 and 7 for 1939. And as Table 11.3 also illustrates, the number of state farm workers engaging in socialist competitions is considerably greater than the number who win shock worker or Stakhanovite status. Moreover, in each year covered, most peasants do not engage in socialist competition at all. This contrasts with data in Table 11.2 where in four out of six oblasts, over 50 percent of peasants are involved in socialist competitions, again underscoring varied patterns.

The most detailed statistics of all present data similar to those in Table 11.2 for socialist competitions across a large number of oblasts and krais for Russia, Ukraine, Belorussia, Georgia, and Armenia, and are broken down according to quarters of the year. Here again, one sees great variation in the number of Stakhanovites, from a low of 4.2 in Ordzhonikidze krai to a high of 17 percent in Moscow oblast. Shock workers also range from 1.6 per cent of workers in Kursk oblast to 24.9 percent in Udmurt ASSR.[23] Data on socialist competitions for the third quarter of 1939 indicate similar variations, but with occasionally changing patterns. As few as 1.8 percent of peasants competing were Stakhanovites in Kursk oblast, with as many as 17.1 percent in Arkhangel', Vologda, and Voronezh oblasts. Likewise, percentages of shock workers could vary from 5.1 to 20.1 percent.[24]

The Central State Archive of the RSFSR holds materials with the fullest aggregate picture for state farms by sector and by region. These data show that the average percentage of Stakhanovites in 1939 ranged from a high of 29.9 percent on grain state farms of the South, through 15.6 percent of dairy state farms in the center, 11 percent of pig state farms of the northwest, 8.4 percent of all sheep state farms, down to a low of 2.9 percent of dairy farms in Siberia and the East.[25] Regional variations within sectors are sharp in these data. Changes over time, however, are hard to gauge without data for earlier years.

Other archival documents, however, add that whereas on 1 January 1938, the percentage of Stakhanovites on state farms in the Russian republic was 4.1 percent, a year later it was 6.9 percent. In gross terms, numbers had gone up from 6,411 to 11,811, an increase of 84.2 percent.[26] This general rise did not mean spurts in all sectors. In central areas, for instance, the number of Stakhanovites in sugar beet had simultaneously fallen from 188 to 154. Moreover, data were incomplete and it was reported that some farms had not gathered statistics.[27]

Other materials offer more detailed breakdowns of figures according to the job performed. For example, across 83 dairy state farms in Russia, there were 2,297 Stakhanovites out of 24,901 state farmers, amounting to 9.2 percent.[28]

Table 11.4.   Breakdown of Stakhanovites by Job on Dairy State
Farms in Russia

Job	Number	Percentage
Milkmaid	748	32.5
Calf Tender	212	9.2
Tractor Driver	312	13.8
Combine Driver	162	7.0
Beet Workers, Herdsmen, Fitters, Specialists, and Others	865	37.5

Source: TsGA RSFSR, f. 317, op. 4, d. 205, l. 29.

As Table 11.4 shows, milkmaids, beet workers, herdsmen, fitters, and specialists comprised the majority of the Stakhanovites. One cannot, however,
assume that such a breakdown was representative of all farms.

All the above statistics refer to state farms.[29] Unfortunately, data on collective farms are harder to find, generally due to the absence of trade unions
that were among the main gatherers of such information. There are, nonetheless, snippets of data scattered across sources. For instance, one text notes that
in Iaroslavl' oblast in the spring of 1936, there were 3,929 Stakhanovite links,
involving 17,460 collective farmers, "mainly women."[30] In Vinnitsa oblast, in
Ukraine, there were nineteen links in 1935 that gave record harvests of over
500 tsentners of sugar beet per hectare. In the same oblast, a further 145 links
produced between 300 and 500 tsentners per hectare.[31] In 1937, in Ukraine as
a whole (but based on incomplete data) there were at least 100,000 links,
8,500 brigades, and 2,700 collective farms aiming for 500 tsentners per
hectare.[32] And in 1938 in Primorsko-Akhtarskii district of Krasnodar krai
there were "about 2,000 Stakhanovites" on collective farms.[33] Again, the picture is that Stakhanovites were an elite minority.

DISCUSSIONS OF NUMBERS

Reports in trade union archives, including materials from rallies and conferences, substantiate the above data, in particular the immense variation across
farms, which was a regularly discussed topic. A 1939 report on pig farms in
Kursk and Voronezh oblasts noted that whereas the Maslovskii state farm
boasted twelve Stakhanovites in pig breeding, and the Nachalo state farm had
eight, others such as Razdol'e, Timskii, and Ozernyi had none.[34] At a rally of
pig state farmers in Dnepropetrovsk oblast in 1935 one director rhetoricaly
asked: "Comrades, do we have individual state farms, do we have individual

brigades, do we have individual farm units which on the basis of Stakhanovite-Zuev methods of work are fighting the fulfil the plan? Yes, we do."[35] The state farms named after Ordzhonikidze, Kaganovich, Kossior, and Chervonyi were named for fitting this category, but it was far from universal. Some farms did well, others not, prompting the question, "do we have the right to come to a Stakhanovite rally when we do not have the figures for which we should be fighting?"[36] Those who stood up at rallies often regretted that the numbers of Stakhanovites were too low.

At rallies throughout the Union, directors of state farms and trade unionists admitted to the tiny number of Stakhanovites on their farms, almost like a public confession or self-criticism. In October 1937 at a gathering of Stakhanovites and shock workers on fur state farms in Novosibirsk and Omsk oblasts and in Krasnoiarsk and Altai krais, one participant announced that "we now need to have not individual Stakhanovites but entirely Stakhanovite fur farms."[37] This message came from all state farm sectors. Cast more negatively, in 1935 at a rally of pig farmers in Dnepropetrovsk oblast, one director lamented that there were meant to be tens, hundreds, and thousands of Stakhanovites, but "it is necessary to announce that this is not so" and that very few pig breeders followed Zuev's shining example.[38] In fact, on his farm there were tens, not thousands. He told how: "Today we have individual Stakhanovites. The largest number of best people on the farm are shock workers in socialist competition, but a long way off Stakhanovite-*Zuevtsy*."[39] Moreover, the difference between shock workers and Stakhanovites was both quantitative and qualitative. The deputy chair of the trade union on a pig farm was most blunt about this: "Comrades who are present here, the best people, shock workers, excellent workers, might take offence. Yes, comrades, all you best people, excellent ones, shock workers who are struggling to fulfil production tasks, it is not possible to name all of you sitting here 'Stakhanovites.'" What does Stakhanovite mean? "It is not a formal, mechanical distribution of responsibilities, not a mechanical conversion of shock worker to Stakhanovite."[40]

This trade unionist contended that Stakhanovism had become debased through the practice of awarding Stakhanovite titles to non-Stakhanovites. Pressure on farms to acquire rural Stakhanovites had resulted in the inappropriate labeling of shock workers as Stakhanovites. In order to satisfy the expectations of the party, some "Stakhanovites" were just shock workers reclassified but not necessarily working harder.

Such charges were not isolated ones. Sometimes public accusations were made about particular farms and targeted those who fudged the data. At a gathering of Stakhanovites in dairying, a speaker exposed Vanin, the chairperson of the workers' committee of the "Gigant" state farm in Ivanovo oblast, who "considers that all workers over-fulfilling norms are Stakhanovites."[41] He also damned Iur'ev of the workers' committee of the Dubovskii state farm in Azovo-Chernomore krai, for automatically including sixty-four shock workers on his farm on the list of Stakhanovites.[42] The speaker argued that some farm leaders confused *znatnye liudi* (distinguished people) with Stakhanovites. The former did well in All-Union competitions, showing high output. Stakhanovites, by contrast, broke old technical norms, making a much greater impact on productivity.[43] Sufficiently widespread evidence suggests that some farms' statistics on Stakhanovites were indeed inflated.

Union reports corroborate these findings. One along these lines revealed that on the Volzhaia Kommuna pig farm in Kuibyshev krai, of the seven workers labeled "Stakhanovite," only Tamara Riabchinskaia merited the title. It drew attention to the fact that "the production indicators of the other Stakhanovites do not give them the right to this title."[44] Indeed, sometimes quite the contrary obtained. The report exposed the practice that "Namno, brigade leader of the sows' brigade is counted as a Stakhanovite, but his brigade has a 16 percent loss of piglets."[45] Awarding non-Stakhanovites a status that they did not deserve compromised the movement in popular perceptions and rendered statistics more unreliable.

Yet these distortions were far from everywhere the case. Whereas some farms inflated statistics on Stakhanovites, others understated them. There appear to have been districts in which hundreds of Stakhanovites existed but local organizations lacked information about them because they did not seek to collect it, as obtained in Starorusskii district of Leningrad oblast.[46] This was part of the broader problem of "political blindness" in the district. Stakhanovites were there, ignored and left to their own devices, invisible statistically.

These patterns variously feed into questions of how to interpret available figures. Statistics that show few Stakhanovites, for instance, can be variously interpreted. On the one hand, they could mean inattention to Stakhanovism and a lack of interest in counting the Stakhanovites that did exist; yet on the other, assuming the figures are accurate, they could indeed mean few Stakhanovites in a given district. In the latter case, shock workers were not falsely named as Stakhanovites and Stakhanovites were openly admitted to be wanting. This sort of confession was frequent and typified in 1937 by a livestock specialist from a fur farm who regretted that: "We don't have Stakhanovites, we have shock workers, but I am certain that soon we shall have them."[47] Some farms openly admitted their lack of Stakhanovites.

To muddy the picture further, however, there were also farms where statistics on Stakhanovites and shock workers were lumped together. A report on a farm in Ordzhonikidze krai observed that:

Stakhanovites and shock workers are together. There is no separate evidence on the state farm of how many Stakhanovites and shock workers there are. They are all given bonuses. This list is held by the workers' committee.

Apparently, "the director of the farm, Comrade Nuzhdin, does not have this list and does not know how many Stakhanovites and shock workers there are."[48] Here both Stakhanovites and shock workers were known to exist, but the breakdown was not considered important by the union. Whether this was because one category outnumbered the other or because two categories were thought to be unfairly divisive is not evident. Furthermore, the farm director had no interest in the matter whatsoever. Statistical classification and analysis is especially problematic because methods of gathering data on Stakhanovism were not uniform. There were local variations, often linked to the extent to which farm leaders considered data collection on Stakhanovism to be important. In still other cases, conflicting data are available. For instance, on the Volzhaia Kommuna pig farm:

The political department does not know the state farm's shock workers. The workers' committee puts them at 80, the party committee says there are 60, and the political department does not know which figure is correct.[49]

So here the farm itself had confusing statistics that the political department was unable to sort out.

Officials and actors in the Soviet system across institutions discussed these problems of data collection and classification. Sources illustrate how their ruminations revolved around the topics of variation in collecting figures across farms, of the significance of exaggerated and understated statistics, and of what to make of categorizations and confusions. Those working in state farm trade unions readily admitted among themselves that statistics were not gathered in a uniform manner and knew that making sound comparative analysis was difficult.

NOT A WIDE MOVEMENT AFTER ALL?

Can Stakhanovism be considered a movement if the average percentage of peasants involved in it across farms was relatively small, not exceeding 6 to 9 percent? Whilst the press regularly spoke of "thousands" of Stakhanovites in an ever-growing movement, a quieter accompanying story gave a different impression. In October 1935, *Sovkhoznaia gazeta* openly admitted, "the Stakhanovite movement on state farms has not yet become a wide mass movement. Up until now Stakhanovite methods here have not really been valued."[50]

Moreover, the social attitudes of "thick-headed dullards" (*tverdolobye tupitsy*) held its possibility back because they believed that Stakhanovite methods were inapplicable on farms:

> Mechanically comparing the textile industry with the sovkhoz fields, they speak ironically, "of course Evdokiia Vinogradova can alone take on 100 machines, but a tractor driver cannot sit on two tractors at once."[51]

Evdokiia Vinogradova was a Stakhanovite textile worker who stepped up the number of machines that she attended on the factory floor. Since these reservations were expressed very soon after Stakhanov had overfulfilled his quota, one would not then have expected to see a huge Stakhanovite movement in the countryside. They might therefore be read as a call for Stakhanovism to spread and as a cue to farm authorities and local parties to mobilize the peasants around it.

Almost a year and a half later, however, *Sovkhoznaia gazeta* was delivering a variant of the same message. It argued, "One of the main reasons for bad work on the majority of dairy state farms is the weak development of the Stakhanovite movement." It observed, "The Stakhanovite movement has not yet become a mass movement on state farms. Up until now it has carried a campaign character. In many cases, it does not go beyond Stakhanovite ten days and months."[52]

Archives of the Central Committee of the trade union on dairy state farms painted a similar picture, admitting that: "The Stakhanovite movement has not taken on a mass development." Moreover, "not one union organization, not even the Central Committee, can talk about one more or less exact figure of state farm Stakhanovites." The repeated figure of "around several thousand people, says that our union from top to bottom did not lead the Stakhanovite movement," nor could it "show examples of the best Stakhanovites, take their experience and give this movement a mass character."[53] The message from the Central Committee of the union of workers on vegetable state farms was likewise.

A *postanovlenie* of the union of workers of dairy state farms described how even after Stakhanovite Five-Days and Ten-Days, "the number of Stakhanovites and Stakhanovite brigades is growing very slowly." The union blamed farm managements for skirting their responsibility to direct the movement and commented, "this stems from the fact that state farm directors shift the leadership of the Stakhanovite movement onto trade union and other organizations.[54]

In an attempt to address this problem, the Presidium of the Central Committee of the Union called for three weeks of competitions from 10 April 1936. The competitions across farms were meant to establish where conditions to facilitate Stakhanovite work were most advanced, effectively a competition of farm leaderships according to their readiness to prepare Stakhanovites. The ultimate goal of the competition was to trigger a "transition to permanent and systematic Stakhanovite work on dairy farms."[55]

The movement's slow growth was reiterated at rallies. One animal specialist of the Kommunar state farm told those present that "I view the present gathering of Stakhanovites as a turning point in the work of animal husbandry." He contrasted the more successful Stakhanovite movement in the oblast with their own efforts since "up until now we have done nothing. We are just stirring, thinking and arguing." The problem as he viewed it was that "some want to show that the Stakhanovite movement is inapplicable in our work. This Stakhanovite rally must give this opinion a firm rebuff."[56] Apparently one fear was that as a consequence of Stakhanovism, productivity would fall. The speaker continued that when the Kommunar state farm first adopted Stakhanovite methods of work, "they feared that the increase in load would lead to bad results, that the milk yield would be less." In fact, that fear had now been allayed.[57]

There was, however, one confusion. Some thought that taking on twenty-five cows automatically meant becoming a Stakhanovite. The speaker emphasized, "The task does not consist of increasing the load, but of milking more from these twenty-five cows."[58] Stakhanovism was not synonymous with caring for more animals, but with caring for more animals better and more productively. His wider message was that myths about the movement had to be dispelled. At rallies peasants occasionally expressed the view that drunkenness was the reason why the Stakhanovite movement was not developing. One admitted that instead of pursuing Stakhanovism, "on our farm, they are occupied with drinking." He told how "the head of the political department began to drink, he drank til he was drunk and was ordered to conduct his drunkenness at home." Next "the senior animal specialist also got drunk, took a horse, fell under a cart, and was pulled out." Finally, "then an animal specialist left the cattle, returned to his village also drunk, and his deputy left the field and went to town to drink."[59]

At this point another joked, *"chto zhe u nas stakhanovskoe dvizhenie ili stakanovskoe dvizhenie?"*[60] Here he used a play on words due to the similarity in sound in Russian of "Stakhanovite" and "drinking glass." The head of the political department was subsequently removed from his post and the farm was now allegedly more orderly. The seemingly eternal Russian problem of male drunkenness, however, negatively affected productivity and enthusiasm for work.

An entirely different message was that despite the lack of help for Stakhanovites and for aspiring Stakhanovites, some peasants were anyway improving their productivity. On a series of vegetable state farms, a complex picture was emerging. When leaders were asked if they had any Stakhanovites, they might answer, "No, they are only beginning to come to light." But then a trip to the farms showed some peasants overfulfilling plans by 150 to 200 per cent and others failing to meet their quotas.[61] Here the picture on the farm ranged from peasants who worked badly to those who toiled efficiently but who were unrecognized. So Stakhanovites might exist, but official statistics did not note them. A conference of chairpersons of workers' committees of the Kiev area concluded that local unions themselves needed to "reconstruct" their work in relation to Stakhanovites in order to correct "crude mistakes."[62]

Alongside this negative picture from archival sources was a more positive one. The central committee of vegetable state farms of Belorussia insisted that in that republic the Stakhanovite movement had indeed taken on a "mass character."[63] Stakhanovite rallies on farms were common and increases in productivity were evident. A list of Stakhanovites on particular farms followed, together with percentages of plan fulfillment. Yet despite the fanfare of success in the document, it concluded, "Without doubt there is a whole series of shortcomings in this work and the presidium is taking decisive measures to improve the situation of work with Stakhanovites."[64] One shortcoming noted in trade union documents for dairy farms was pay.

On the one hand, trade unions stressed the need to publicize the pay of Stakhanovites since that might boost the movement. On the other, however, in 1935 speakers at rallies argued that peasants were not paid commensurate with their workload or productivity and that this had to be investigated. As one speaker observed, "we have a series of negative aspects in the bonus system which does not pay earnings fully."[65] Calls for new pay systems were visible and unions were aware of the relevance of pay to the status of the Stakhanovite movement. Moreover, it was not just a question of whether or not Stakhanovites were paid enough. As in the 1990s, there were issues of whether farm workers were paid at all or if so, how late were the payments. In a discussion with Stakhanovites at the Political Department of the Commissariat of State Farms, one imparted that matters were so bad that on his farm we "have not been paid for three months." A visiting film projectionist had not been paid either "so he stopped coming," leaving the farmers without any films.[66] Complaints about late wages, often four months in arrears, were common.[67] So although, in theory, Stakhanovites were meant to be paid more than others, in practice, along with other peasants, their wages were months late. In these conditions, Stakhanovism was not especially attractive.

HOW SERIOUSLY WERE
STAKHANOVITE "LESSONS" TAKEN?

The press devoted a great deal of space to imparting Stakhanovite "lessons," often drawing on the findings of the research institutes that studied the minutiae of Stakhanovite output. Yet were they taken seriously, and if not, was the movement therefore unsuccessful?

Many rallies and conferences were held with the specific aim of swapping lessons. As a report on one Stakhanovite gathering of workers of fur and bird state farms put it: "the basic aim of the conference was to exchange experience." Peasants were brought together for "discussion of inadequacies hampering fulfilment of production plans, the improvement of methods and forms of leadership of the Stakhanovite movement and the attraction of new Stakhanovites."[68] Exhibitions, too, organized displays and charts on work techniques.

"Lessons," however, were not everywhere taken seriously. In the state farm trade unions, committees were sometimes berated for ignoring them. A letter written from R. Santo, Chair of the Central Committee of the Union of Workers of Vegetable State Farms, criticized the Chair of the Belorussian Committee of the same union in the following manner: "A serious deficiency in your communication of the 25th of October concerning the Stakhanovite movement in Belorussia is the absence of indications of how, by which methods they [the high records] were achieved."[69] Santo went on to say that the Belorussian union had relayed the percentages by which the plan was overfulfilled but paid no attention "to all the details of experience of Stakhanovites."[70] This meant that the Central Committee of the union was unable to pass on the experience of shock workers and Stakhanovites in Belorussia to vegetable workers elsewhere. The content of Santo's letter was very similar to that of the rejection letters written by editors at *Krest'ianskaia gazeta* to *sel'kory.* Just as some rural correspondents had focused on percentage increases in output and not on the techniques by which they were achieved, so here the message was that lessons were there to be learned, but a republican trade union was not taking them seriously enough to report.

Trade union documents sometimes criticized an oblast or krai for not paying sufficient attention to lessons, too. Commenting on dairy state farms in Ordzhonikidze krai, a union report of 1939 typically concluded, "The krai committee of the union has not conducted sufficient study of the work experience of Stakhanovites or generalized from it. The krai committee of the union does not have data on Stakhanovites and their experience."[71] So whereas some union committees were diligent in collecting information on Stakhanovite lessons, others were not. The same pattern obtained across farm leaderships.

Trade unions also castigated themselves for not organizing talks from peasants returning from agricultural exhibitions. The message was that if peasants did not pass on what they had gleaned, then there was no practical application of the knowledge acquired at exhibitions.[72] The film *Svinarka i Pastukh* touched on this problem when it portrayed Glasha returning from an exhibition. It satirized a farm meeting at which she tried to explain what she had learned. Other peasants laughed at her, refusing to take her points seriously. Trade union archives show that the official response to these problems was to urge that workers from commissariats in Moscow be sent to farms to check how lessons from exhibitions were being applied.[73]

Lessons could also be passed on but not necessarily implemented. Peasants might "know" about new techniques or "know" how to perfect old ones, but not put them into practice. Adopting new methods meant changing some established work patterns, developing fresh routines, especially if new machinery were involved. Conditions for the successful implementation of Stakhanovite lessons varied across farms and across farm leaderships. In addition, on some farms, women had specific reasons for wishing to apply new techniques or to become tractor drivers in order to break out of restrictive gender roles. The motivation, willingness, and ability to adopt new techniques or to work more diligently therefore varied.

DID RURAL STAKHANOVISM INCREASE PRODUCTIVITY?

In propaganda, Stakhanovism was meant to boost productivity and ease a series of rural woes ranging from animal losses, the negligent use of machinery and the failure to apply manure, to poor harvesting. The concept of "Stakhanovism" was elastic in meaning, loosely and conveniently linked to multiple problems. Stakhanovism was broadly supposed to instill sound work methods in "middle" and "poor" peasants after collectivization and dekulakization. But did it? Opinions on this regarding heavy industry have varied. Alec Nove boldly concluded, "no doubt the campaign had a positive effect on productivity."[74] Similar views have been held by Alexander Baykov, Maurice Dobb, and others.[75] Joseph Berliner, however, cautioned that the balance sheet for or against was hard to draw up, Solomon Schwartz maintained that Stakhanovism brought speed and wastage, Donald Filtzer contended that the consequences were disruption and the creation of a labor aristocracy, and R. W. Davies and Oleg Khlevnyuk concluded that any economic effects were at best short-term, bringing some improvements in working practices but also "disproportions and excesses."[76] Lewis Siegelbaum has preferred to see Stakhanovism as "an amalgam of practices that both impinged on and were subjected to appropriation by different groups and institutions."[77] As well as designed to increase productivity, the movement set out to discipline managerial personnel. Davies and Khlevnyuk also interpret Stakhanovism's significance at a broader level, as both "displaying and securing the unity of the nation."[78]

Arguably, the movement in the countryside added further complexities to Stakhanovism than Siegelbaum found in heavy industry. Although it was meant to be about increasing productivity through improved work practices and the skillful use of machinery, part of a grand Stalinist mobilization, it was set in a context of postcollectivization. This meant not only that the historical, political, economic, and social context in which rural Stakhanovism found itself shaped Stakhanovism's agendas, along with environmental factors, but also that these agendas had even more dimensions than their urban counterparts. Billed as a cure-all, especially from 1936 to 1939, to solve all agricultural problems from wastage at harvest time to infestations of weeds, rural Stakhanovism was about re-educating many peasants to work hard, either again or for the first time with machinery, and about prompting the non-resentful and resentful to use their machinery adeptly and to mechanize where they had not. Although agricultural techniques had "improved considerably" during the 1920s, by the end of that decade farming was "largely non-mechanised, cultivating the soil by horse-drawn implements."[79] Wheatcroft and Davies note that in 1928, as much as 44 percent of the grain area was still harvested by sickles and scythes and as much as 74 percent was sown by hand. So at the beginning of the decade, there was much room for modernization. It is significant that the production of tractors and combines just preceded the Stakhanovite movement and continued apace during it. Furthermore, as in industry, Stakhanovism attacked managements for not facilitating Stakhanovism, pointing the finger at farm leaders and at local parties for their indifference to it and their reluctance to promote new techniques.

Amid all these purposes, did productivity rise because of rural Stakhanovism? Few economic historians have tackled this question and perhaps wisely so. Part of the problem here is what Alec Nove recognized for industry: the use of new machinery and equipment plus a rationalization of labor meant "ample scope" for higher productivity.[80] This was additionally so in the countryside where requisitioning, falling productivity, collectivization, and famine, in sum "agricultural crisis," could only through efficient work be alleviated. What, then, would increased productivity in the countryside actually tell us? Would it mean that the introduction of tractors had boosted output rather than Stakhanovism per se? Although tractors were introduced into the countryside before Stakhanovism, their continued supply also coincided with Stakhanovism (and tractors were also moved out of some areas into others afresh), making it difficult to dissect their separate contributions to output. Or, in fact, did tractors facilitate Stakhanovism, rendering the former an independent variable in the productivity equation and the latter an intervening variable? And if so, how can one measure their respective contributions? Indeed, should the measurements vary by sector? If milkmaids acquire more milk from their cows, is this more easily attributable to Stakhanovite enthusiasm and care, since the complicating factor of increased mechanization is wanting? Yet, in this case, the hidden factor of how much animal feed was available renders calculation elusive again since feed and additives contributed to milk production.

Without reliable data on a series of indicators, including the availability of necessary inputs in individual cases, it is impossible to answer whether Stakhanovism brought increased productivity. At best, one can examine increases or decreases in gross output to see which trends coincided with the Stakhanovite years. Even this, however, is a very short-term analysis, overlooking the possibilities of long-term cycles. Bearing in mind the above hazards, what patterns, nonetheless, do statistics reveal?

The "most striking feature" for the years 1928–1941, according to R. W. Davies, is the "extraordinarily rapid development of industry, and particularly of capital goods, in contrast to the poor performance of agriculture."[81] This is indisputable. Paul Gregory and Robert Stuart have pointed out that decline was unmistakable, despite year-to-year fluctuations, and Nove has depicted the harvest of 1932–1933 as symptomatic of "acute crisis." [82] During the First Five-Year Plan, agricultural production declined and animals were slaughtered during collectivization and famine ensued. The excesses of collectivization together with demanding food quotas imposed upon the peasantry made for bad agricultural conditions. Rural Stakhanovism, therefore, came after falling productivity, unlike the situation in industry. Moreover, recovery was "slow."[83] Davies points out that average agricultural production in 1937–1939 exceeded the 1928 level "by at most 9.5 per cent" and the 1909–1913 level "by at most 25 per cent." But agricultural production per head of population in 1937–1939 was lower than in 1928.[84]

After famine, there was a "relatively better harvest" in 1933 and during 1934–1936 agriculture began to improve at a time of fantastic industrial development.[85] Peasants had also been accommodated by the policy of allowing again the private ownership of livestock. In addition, collective farmers' markets had been legalized in 1932, permitting peasants to gain income from the sale of produce of their private plots (and also from the sale of produce received as payment in kind for work days on collective farms). Earlier brutalities, therefore, were being softened in the interests of peasant and state alike. Positive results included productive toil on private plots and increases in live-

Table 11.5.   Animals in the USSR: State and Private (in Millions of Heads)

	January 1934		January 1938	
	State and Collective Farm	Private Plots	State and Collective Farm	Private Plots
Cattle (all)	12.3	21.2	18.0	32.9
Cows	4.6	14.4	5.5	17.2
Sheep and Goats	16.3	20.2	29.3	37.3
Pigs	6.2	5.3	8.8	16.9

Source: Nove, *An Economic History of the USSR,* 239. Drawn from *Sel'skoe khoziaistvo SSSR,* 1960, 263–4.

stock numbers both collectively and privately owned, as shown in Table 11.5.[86] Stakhanovism tout court, then, is unlikely to have been responsible for more animals being born, although so-called "Stakhanovite work methods" and the appropriate care of animals may have contributed. The settling down of the countryside after turmoil, the official sanction of private plots and animals, plus a generalized need for some normalcy were all positive factors which coincided. Peasants, however, worked intensively on their private plots with the result that by 1937, as much as 25 percent of all collective farm production came from them.[87] Many peasants were thus keener to work on their private plots than to become Stakhanovites on collective land. Arguably, the rewards were more immediate and often vital for family subsistence.

If, however, we examine the revised figures on grain harvests discussed by Nove, the picture is one of falling yields. The year 1936 was climatically unfavorable, followed by good weather in 1937. Total grain harvests fluctuated from 67.6 million tons in 1934, 75.0 million in 1935, 56.1 million in 1936, and 97.4 million in 1937.[88] A case can be made that climate was an important variable, although approaching poor weather conditions with "Stakhanovite preparation" may have made for better results rather than worse. But the extent to which Stakhanovite "lessons" were applied in good and bad conditions cannot be known. Statistics presented by Roger Clarke for all grains confirm this pattern showing no substantial increases from 1925 to 1941, although there are fluctuations.[89] Davies and Wheatcroft attribute these only in part to bad weather conditions, which were particularly poor during 1930–1934 and 1935–1939.[90] They conclude that whilst weather played a "significant role" in low yields, it was "not the major factor."[91] Other factors such as inexperience on the part of political leaders and farmers of collective agriculture and of large-scale mechanized farming, together with inflexibility in the system regarding the need for different techniques in different regions, militated against efficiency.

How do other yields compare with grain? Clarke's statistics show consistently better cotton yields in the 1930s than in the 1920s, although a good yield in 1925 was not improved upon until 1935. The increased yield in 1935, however, cannot be put down to Stakhanovism because it just predated it. The average yield of 10.2 tsentners per hectare in 1935 rose to 12.1 in 1937 and fell to 10.8 in 1940.[92] So even if Stakhanovism made a contribution to increases, it was unable to prevent falls. Average sugar beet yields also fluctuated, from a high of 170 tsentners per hectare in 1925, 132 in 1928, down to 64 in 1932, thereafter increasing to 96 in 1934, 132 in 1935, up to 181 in 1937, only to fall again to 146 in 1940.[93] What one cannot answer with certainty is how much of the increase after 1935 was due to stabilization of the countryside, how much was due to good weather in 1935, and how much stemmed from more enthusiastic work on the part of peasants like Mariia Demchenko and Pasha Angelina.

Taking these different statistics together, it seems reasonable to conclude that at best Stakhanovism may have contributed to the increased productivity of some peasants, but never alone was it a determining factor in overall yields. Moreover, fluctuations suggest that Stakhanovism was unable to prevent falling yields. It appears, then, that first one cannot calculate the impact made by Stakhanovism on overall yields; and second, if Stakhanovism did make a difference, it was unlikely to be huge. This was because, as shown earlier, most peasants were not Stakhanovites. Whilst the productivity of individual Stakhanovites and particular Stakhanovite brigades may well have increased, as Andreev described in detail at the Eighteenth Party Congress, it did not do so sufficiently to raise overall productivity. Moreover, proportionally greater commitment was shown to private plots rather than to collective agriculture.

WERE STAKHANOVITES ALWAYS PRIVILEGED?

Although many peasants may have been attracted to Stakhanovism for material reasons as well as for increased status, did they, however, always receive the perks that were publicized? We have seen how pay on some farms was months in arrears. Were perks part of a broader fiction, promised but not delivered?

Evidence conclusively demonstrates that many shock workers and Stakhanovites benefited from more workdays, presents, holidays in elite sanatoria, and medals. So privileges were given to known individuals. If, moreover, Stakhanovites complained about not receiving what was due to them, state farm trade unions and editors at *Krest'ianskaia gazeta* would back their demands for attention. Simultaneously, not all shock workers and Stakhanovites considered that the appropriate privileges came their way. So they used the opportunity of Stakhanovite rallies to make their complaints known.

At one very early rally in October 1935, for example, the Lenin state farm in Smolevicheskii raion of Belorussia was criticized for not repairing the flat of Stakhanovite Metlitskii.[94] Mechanisms of complaint like this, however, suggest a movement with successful methods of drawing attention to Stakhanovite problems and demanding action. A dynamo of naming and shaming integral to the movement attempted to install effective redress. Central Committees of state farm trade unions also played a positive role in this respect. For instance, the Central Committee of fur and bird state farms wrote to Narkomzem of the RSFSR to regret that on certain farms peasants lacked beds, washbasins, bowls, and huts with boiling water.[95] Often the bath-house did not work, hostels were not repaired, and special work clothes were not provided.[96] Far worse conditions, however, were reported elsewhere. A meeting of workers' committees exposed extremely bad conditions on bird state farms in Kuibyshev krai: "Stakhanovites Malykhina, Surkova and Gur'ianova live in terribly bad conditions. Not having beds, they sleep near the threshold of the kitchen."[97] Trade unions put in place mechanisms for blaming the chairs of workers' committees for doing nothing to improve living conditions. We have already seen that documents held that inaction interfered with the development of the Stakhanovite movement since peasants with high productivity deserved good living conditions.[98] Arguably one success of the movement was wider discussion of bad rural living conditions more generally—for Stakhanovites and non-Stakhanovites. Although they could not be addressed overnight, they were defined and lamented, even if improvement in the first instance was meant to be for Stakhanovites only. Criticisms were often leveled at "they" who did not "study questions of caring for living people."[99] Here "they" referred to the "triangle" (*treugol'nik*) of power on the farm—party, trade union, and farm management. Where the party was absent, the trade union, management, and *politotdel* on state farms were accountable.

Illustrative of the most basic complaints about living standards, shock workers and Stakhanovites in numerous sources moaned about the lack of an operating bath-house. Typical was: "I do not know when the bath-house works—either once a year, or not at all. I have not washed there once."[100] The elderly peasants whom I interviewed in the 1990s also joked about problems with the bath-house.[101] Yet it was evident that a roof over one's head and food in the belly mattered considerably more.

Evidence discussed earlier indicates that ways of treating Stakhanovites varied across farms. Whereas unions made special efforts to accommodate state farm workers and listened to complaints about poor living conditions, some Stakhanovites nonetheless enjoyed better standards of living and perks than others. Stakhanovite status, therefore, did not automatically mean a better

living standard. In terms of delivery, results were mixed. There were successful results for some Stakhanovites and little improvement for others. In both
cases, however, outcries were common, along with demands for attention and
change. Arguably, complaint procedures served ultimately as generally beneficial motors of social change, but as divisive ones in the first instance.

EFFORTS TO SPREAD STAKHANOVISM

Although rural Stakhanovism may not have developed to the extent that party
enthusiasts desired, there were indeed efforts on the ground to expand its
scope. Despite lack of rigor in the collection of statistics and notwithstanding
numerous organizational problems, state farm trade unions regularly discussed
the Stakhanovite movement and what they should be doing for it. In 1936, a
large union gathering brought together representation from Kiev, Zhitomir,
and Chernigov. Prior to this, local events had built up into the large meeting,
mobilizing sets of fifteen state farms to discuss what trade union members
should be doing to promote Stakhanovism.[102] The main item under discussion
was: "Expansion (*razvorachivanie*) of the Stakhanovite movement." Official
trade union documents, invariably titled "On the development of the
Stakhanovite movement," also listed a series of problems to be overcome. A
common theme was that the "main deficiency" in developing Stakhanovism
was the failure of political departments, workers' committees, and farm leaders to tackle illiteracy and semiliteracy.[103] There were repeated calls for the organization of study for peasants and special instruction for Stakhanovites.[104]
The illiterate would find the "lessons" blazoned in *Krest'ianskaia gazeta*'s
pages remote, best relayed to them through the literate.

Trade unions regularly issued *postanovleniia* for "concrete measures" to be
taken to improve socialist competitions and for shock workers and
Stakhanovites to be organized to further this goal. Typical of the general pattern was the call issued in late 1937 by the reindeer section of the trade union
concerned with fur and bird state farms.[105] Slightly differently, but with a similar aim in mind, the Presidium of the Central Committee of Milk and Meat
State Farms called for competitions of farm leaderships according to criteria
of preparing the best conditions for Stakhanovite labor.[106] Not only were
Stakhanovites to compete, but farm leaders' direction and handling of the
competitions were under scrutiny. The Presidium described this effort as
"workers' control" to establish that the decisions of the 1935 December
Plenum of the Central Committee of the Communist Party were being put
into practice. It entailed a "mass political measure" which meant the formation of special brigades on every farm. Each "controller" in the brigade would

investigate a particular question and the brigade would be helped in its work by an *aktiv* of Stakhanovites and union members.[107] Allegedly every "short-coming" and "scandal" had to be noted in a report together with suggestions for overcoming them. The report then had to be presented to a general farm meeting. The workers' committee would consider results and give bonuses to the best controllers.[108] Similarly, with 1938 being the first year of the Third Five-Year Plan, renewed efforts at the end of 1937 went into reflections about the meaning of Stakhanovism for the following year.[109]

Numerous local rallies of shock workers and Stakhanovites were also convened with a view to encouraging harder work. The repeated call from these was that: "Each shock worker must strive to become a Stakhanovite. They must follow already existing Stakhanovites." This was based on the unswerving assumption that "the Stakhanovite movement opens up rich un-tapped possibilities for increasing labor productivity."[110] Animal specialists, agronomists, and anyone with expertise were called upon to inspire, facili-tate, drive, and fashion the Stakhanovite movement. A line that never fal-tered was that "the specialist must be an organizer of the Stakhanovite movement, take pride in it."[111] The most repeated message, however, was that of the first oblast rally of pig farm Stakhanovites in Dnepropetrovsk oblast that "Comrades, it is necessary that at the second rally we will not be 40 Stakhanovites, but 10 times more."[112] This mantra was at the core of ef-forts to spread Stakhanovism widely, propagated and designed to be inter-nalized and acted upon.

Although diligence in collecting statistics varied across farms and districts, those who did attain Stakhanovite status were often known to the more effi-cient local unions since the latter compiled numerous lists of Stakhanovites on different farms by name, job, number of years on the farm, and production feats.[113] Many files include formal *kharakteristiky* (testimonials) and also per-sonal biographical statements of individual Stakhanovites.[114] So some effort was made to keep track of the growth of Stakhanovism, even if the complete All-Union picture was wanting. In fact, there are thousands of pages of archival documents that list Stakhanovites and give brief biographies, with some describing how Stakhanovism began on particular farms.[115]

In the same vein, new Stakhanovites were encouraged to stand up at rallies and explain how they set about becoming Stakhanovites. As milkmaid Kosheleva described it:

We pledged to join the Stakhanovite movement and improve our care of the cat-tle. We took on more cows in order to fulfil the plan better. This month I had to give 800 litres, but I milked 1000 litres. In 1933 we had fifteen record-giving cows; today we have thirty-nine and forty-nine "elite" cattle.[116]

Kosheleva announced that now she earned 300 rubles a month whereas previously the figure had been 180. So rallies informed non-Stakhanovites of how to proceed in order to increase productivity and earn more money.

Rallies also tried to make Stakhanovism look attractive by declaring that attention was indeed paid to Stakhanovites' living conditions. Whilst evidence strongly suggests that on some farms Stakhanovites did not live better than others, on others efforts were definitely made to improve the quality of daily life for hard workers. One participant asked the rhetorical question: "How were conditions created for carrying out the Stakhanovite movement on our farm?" The process started when "we went round all the flats, looked at how each male and female worker lived." Then, as a consequence, "we repaired flats, looked at the inventories (which often do not exist)." Then finally, "we gave the best of Stakhanovite calf-tenders and milkmaids good flats. We sent the best Stakhanovites to rest homes and gave them bonuses."[117] Discourse held that efforts were made, rendering it indeed worth trying to become a Stakhanovite since rewards could follow. So although archival documents readily expose organizational and statistical deficiencies with Stakhanovism, they also show the variety of methods adopted to encourage Stakhanovism to spread, ranging from rallies and conferences to various *postanovlennia*.

For social movements to persist and expand, they require commitment, organization, and resources.[118] Evidence suggests that these varied across farms. If commitment was high, but organization weak, then Stakhanovites found themselves without support. If resources were scant, then their performance was affected. And if commitment was low, then resources would not necessarily inspire or boost involvement. The most propitious conditions for the movement obtained when motivation from sufficient peasants and the farm leadership existed, when organization was strong, and if resources were available or managed to be obtained. Having all three in the second half of the 1930s was not easy or automatic. Taken together, primary sources indicate that rural Stakhanovism was not a coherent movement spread evenly across the USSR. Rather, there were pockets of success on some farms and in some districts, with uneven distributions within oblasts and krais. It is worth adding, however, that social and political movements are rarely evenly distributed and even less so in countries of large geographic spread.

CONCLUSION

Notwithstanding the fact that a minority of peasants aspired to become Stakhanovites and despite the fact that its "lessons" were not everywhere received with enthusiasm, the movement nonetheless occasionally peaked at around 17 percent of peasants engaged in socialist competitions. Moreover, a sufficient number of rural workers were inspired to achieve productive feats that made Stakhanovism as a phenomenon much discussed in a range of institutions from the party, procuracy, and secret police to trade unions and collective farm meetings. Worldwide, social movements do not have to involve the majority of a given population for them be considered politically, socially, or economically significant. Moreover, certain individuals, whether peasants, members of state farm trade unions, or kolkhoz chairs, did encourage Stakhanovism. Although patterns of resistance did obtain, mechanisms of support prevailed, too, with accompanying campaigns to urge its spread. And while some campaigners did not take it seriously, others approached it with verve and appeared to internalize its goals as stated by the party.

In a complex manner, rural Stakhanovism could also be simultaneously "successful" and "fictitious" on different farms and also, paradoxically, on the same farm. In the former more straightforward case, one farm with a respectable reputation for Stakhanovism was Mariia Demchenko's Comintern collective farm in Kiev oblast. Other farms, such as Gigant in Ivanovo oblast and Dubovskii in Azovo-Chernomore krai, claimed to have respectable numbers of Stakhanovites, but in fact large numbers of them were really shock workers. Still others, such as Razdol'e, Timskii, and Ozernyi in Kursk and Voronezh oblasts, had no Stakhanovites at all. In the second case, where Stakhanovism was both success and fiction on the same farm, Stakhanovites did exist but neither in the number proclaimed nor with the resilience suggested.

Weighing up all the data, one can best conclude that rural Stakhanovism was more significant ideologically, socially, and politically than economically. Ideologically, Stakhanovites were beacons of successful labor, icons of socialist production in all its glory. In socialist realist terms, they were perfect peasants, diligent, keen, and able to overcome all obstacles. Here success and fiction intermingled in ideologically constructed images and fiction was a very real part of reality. Official images, repeated daily in the press, blended elements of daily life with fictions about daily life. So the reality of the regime's icons was simultaneously true and untrue.

Socially, Stakhanovism was a mixed "success." For some Stakhanovites, but not all, it brought better accommodation, food, presents, holidays, and widening opportunities. For some, but not all, it provoked the hostility of others and unpleasant violence. Some Stakhanovites endured this, others backed away from Stakhanovism altogether. For some women, it brought a redefinition of gender relations on the farm, with both its positive and negative consequences. More broadly, rural Stakhanovism gave the countryside an elite group of peasants, officially superior to others. It was thus socially divisive.

This can also be interpreted as a way of reinventing kulaks in a more politically correct guise for the system or in a more objectionable guise for those peasants who resented Stakhanovites' perks.

Politically, Stakhanovism was both success and failure. Its heroines and heroes illustrated that enthusiasm for socialist production had reached the fields. Moreover, technology had spread, symbolized by the tractor, and the role of science had grown, witnessed by the attention paid to fertilizer and new techniques. It was not, however, an overwhelming political success. Not all peasants were as keen to boost socialist production as were Stakhanovites. Not all peasants bothered to change their work patterns, especially if farm leaders did not encourage this. Many peasants, nonetheless, were mobilized politically, whether in socialist competitions, rallies, conferences or huge congresses with top leaders. Visibly, Stakhanovism had an impact on rural life, but greater on some farms than on others. Again, it was members of a minority elite who participated in the political fanfare of huge conferences and who were co-opted by the political system. Mobilizations around the monumental purposes of Stakhanovism may have attempted to advertise the unity of the nation that R. W. Davies and Oleg Khlevnyuk perceive in Stakhanovism, but the displays of what Jeffrey Brooks" calls "rituals of theatre" were not synonymous with "securing" that unity.[119] Arguably, at best a minority was united and, even then, one defining dimension of that unity was competition amongst them.

In economic terms, the success of rural Stakhanovism is controversial, clearer in individual cases of increased productivity documented at length by the All-Union Scientific Institute of the Agricultural Economy than in general trends, therefore of minimal impact overall. Although Soviet sources firmly linked the two, claiming that Stakhanovism boosted productivity, in fact good organization on the farm, mechanization, fuel, good weather, fertilizer, new techniques, and animal feed were crucial independent variables. Moreover, the incentives to work hard on private plots were higher. Rural Stakhanovism, then, played its most important role in political mobilization, ideology, and social differentiation than it did in boosting overall yields.

NOTES

1. GARF, f. 7689, op. 4, d. 80, l. 51. This was declared on 26 October 1935 by Berkovskii, Chairperson of the Belorussian Union of Vegetable State Farms, in an official document reporting on successful Stakhanovites.

2. *Sovkhoznaia gazeta*, 6 March 1937, 3.

3. GARF, f. 7689, op. 11, d. 43, l. 53. This is a play on words. Here the Russian word "glass," or "*stakan*," is given an adjectival ending making it "*stakanovskoe*," which is very close in sound to "Stakhanovite" as an adjective: *Stakhanovskoe*.

4. *Sovkhoznaia gazeta*, 14 April 1936, 3; *Krest'ianskaia gazeta*, 24 October 1935, 3; *Krest'ianskaia gazeta*, 8 December 1935, 1; *Krest'ianskaia gazeta*, 10 February 1937, 8. On the methodological problems of dealing with fragmentary data, see Miles Fairburn, *Social History: Problems, Strategies and Methods* (Basingstoke and London: Macmillan, 1999), 39–57.

5. GARF, f. 8131, op. 13, d. 64, l. 231.

6. GARF, f. 8131, op. 13, d. 45, l. 10.

7. GARF, f. 8131, op. 13, d. 45, l. 11.

8. GARF, f. 8131, op. 13, d. 64, l. 232.

9. GARF, f. 8131, op. 13, d. 64, l. 266.

10. Sheila Fitzpatrick cites several statistical sources on Stakhanovism. They do not, however, provide rural data as she implies. See Sheila Fitzpatrick, *Stalin's Peasants* (New York and London: Oxford University Press, 1994), p. 266 and footnote 13 on p. 267.

11. *Sovkhoznaia gazeta*, 22 December 1937, 2. Benediktov subsequently became deputy minister of agriculture of the RSFSR, followed by first deputy minister of agriculture, then in November 1938, minister of agriculture of the USSR.

12. GARF, f. 7689, op. 11, d. 42, l. 28.

13. GARF, f. 7689, op. 11, d. 119, l. 236.

14. GARF, f. 7689, op. 10, d. 40, l. 112.

15. GARF, f. 7689, op. 11, d. 320, l. 97ob.

16. GARF, f. 7689, op. 7, d. 81, l. 11ob.

17. RGASPI, f. 349, op. 1, d. 253, l. 6.

18. RGASPI, f. 349, op. 1, d. 253, ll. 12–13.

19. GARF, f. 7689, op. 11, d. 320, l. 19.

20. GARF, f. 7689, op. 11, d. 419, l. 90.

21. GARF, f. 7689, op. 11, d. 119, l. 8.

22. GARF, f. 7689, op. 7, d. 123, l. 7ob.

23. GARF, f. 7689, op. 11, d. 460, l. 13.

24. GARF, f. 7689, op. 11, d. 460, l. 15.

25. TsGA RSFSR, f. 317, op. 4, d. 69, l. 6.

26. TsGA RSFSR, f. 317, op. 4, d. 69, l. 3.

27. TsGA RSFSR, f. 317, op. 4, d. 70, l. 1.

28. TsGA RSFSR, f. 317, op. 4, d. 205, l. 29.

29. Refer back to Table 1.4 for statistics on state farms.

30. M. A. Vyltsan, *Zavershaiushchii etap sozdaniia kolkhoznogo stroia, 1935–1937* (Moscow: Nauka, 1978), 128.

31. Vyltsan, *Zavershaiushchii etap*, 126. See also *Sotsialisticheskoe Zemledelie*, 26 October 1935.

32. Vyltsan, *Zavershaiushchii etap*, 127.

33. *Krest'ianskaia gazeta*, 4 April 1938, 2.

34. GARF, f. 7689, op. 7, d. 125, ll. 8–9.

35. GARF, f. 7689, op. 7, d. 16, l. 8.

36. GARF, f. 7689, op. 7, d. 16, l. 10.

37. GARF, f. 7689, op. 10, d. 170, l. 14.

316	*Chapter Eleven*

38. GARF, f. 7689, op. 7, d. 16, l. 8.
39. GARF, f. 7689, op. 7, d. 16, l. 8.
40. GARF, f. 7689, op. 7, d. 16, l. 78.
41. GARF, f. 7689, op. 11, d. 42, l. 28.
42. GARF, f. 7689, op. 11, d. 42, l. 28.
43. GARF, f. 7689, op. 11, d. 42, l. 29.
44. RGASPI, f. 349, op. 1, d. 239, ll. 155–159.
45. RGASPI, f. 349, op. 1, d. 239, ll. 155–159.
46. *Krest'ianskaia gazeta*, 6 January 1939, 2.
47. GARF, f. 7689, op. 10, d. 170, l. 17.
48. GARF, f. 7689, op. 11, d. 419, l. 95.
49. RGASPI, f. 349, op. 1, d. 239, l. 156.
50. *Sovkhoznaia gazeta,* 14 October 1935, 1.
51. *Sovkhoznaia gazeta,* 14 October 1935, 1.
52. *Sovkhoznaia gazeta*, 6 March 1937, 3.
53. GARF, f. 7689, op. 11, d. 119, l. 23. A gathering of trade union committees in Gor'kii and Kazan concluded that the Stakhanovite movement "is not developed" and that "there is an incorrect understanding of the Stakhanovite movement by workers' committees and by administrations." This resulted in the absence of help for Stakhanovites from both workers' committees and farm leaders. Refer to GARF, f. 7689, op. 4, d. 81, l. 2.
54. GARF, f. 7689, op. 11, d. 119, l. 4.
55. GARF, f. 7689, op. 11, d. 119, l. 4.
56. GARF, f. 7689, op. 11, d. 43, l. 84.
57. GARF, f. 7689, op. 11, d. 43, l. 84.
58. GARF, f. 7689, op. 11, d. 43, l. 85.
59. GARF, f. 7689, op. 11, d. 43, l. 53.
60. GARF, f. 7689, op. 11, d. 43, l. 53.
61. GARF, f. 7689, op. 4, d. 81, l. 3.
62. GARF, f. 7689, op. 4, d. 81, l. 100.
63. GARF, f. 7689, op. 4, d. 80, l. 51.
64. GARF, f. 7689, op. 4, d. 80, l. 52.
65. GARF, f. 7689, op. 11, d. 42, l. 44.
66. RGASPI, f. 349, op. 1, d. 254, l. 1.
67. See, for instance, RGASPI, f. 349, op. 1, d. 254, l. 10; and RGASPI, f. 349, op. 1, d. 254, l. 12.
68. GARF, f. 7689, op. 10, d. 350, l. 9.
69. GARF, f. 7689, op. 4, d. 80, l. 53.
70. GARF, f. 7689, op. 4, d. 80, l. 53.
71. GARF, f. 7689, op. 11, d. 419, l. 90.
72. TsGA RSFSR, f. 317, op. 4, d. 205, l. 2.
73. TsGA RSFSR, f. 317, op. 4, d. 205, l. 3.
74. Alec Nove, *An Economic History of the USSR* (Harmondsworth, Middlesex: Penguin, 1984), revised edition, 234. See, too, R. W. Davies, "Stakhanovism and the Soviet System: A Review Article," *Soviet Studies* 41, no. 3 (July 1989): 484–87.

75. Alexander Baykov, *The Development of the Soviet Economic System: An Essay on the Experience of Planning in the USSR* (Cambridge: Cambridge University Press, 1946); Maurice Dobb, *Soviet Economic Development Since 1917* (London: Routledge and Kegan Paul, 1966).

76. Joseph Berliner, *Factory and Manager in the USSR* (Cambridge, MA: Harvard University Press, 1957); Solomon M. Schwartz, *Labor in the Soviet Union* (London: The Cresset Press, 1953); and Donald Filtzer, *Soviet Workers and Stalinist Industrialization: The Formation of Modern Soviet Production Relations, 1928–1941* (New York: Ardmonk, 1986); R. W. Davies and Oleg Khlevnyuk, "Stakhanovism and the Soviet Economy," *Europe-Asia Studies* 54, no. 6 (September 2002): 867–903.

77. Lewis Siegelbaum, *Stakhanovism and the Politics of Productivity in the USSR, 1935–1941* (Cambridge: Cambridge University Press, 1988), 6.

78. Davies and Khlevnyuk, "Stakhanovism," 897.

79. S. G. Wheatcroft and R. W. Davies, "Agriculture," in *The Economic Transformation of the Soviet Union, 1913–1945*, eds. R. W. Davies, Mark Harrison, and S. G. Wheatcroft (Cambridge: Cambridge University Press, 1994), 112.

80. Nove, *An Economic History of the USSR*, 234.

81. R. W. Davies, *Soviet Economic Development from Lenin to Khrushchev* (Cambridge: Cambridge University Press, 1998), 43.

82. Paul R. Gregory and Robert C. Stuart, *Soviet Economic Structure and Performance*, 3rd ed. (New York: Harper and Row, 1986), 112; Nove, *An Economic History of the USSR*, 239.

83. Davies, *Soviet Economic Development from Lenin to Khrushchev*, 45.

84. Davies, *Soviet Economic Development from Lenin to Khrushchev*, 45.

85. Nove, *An Economic History of the USSR*, 239; Davies, *Soviet Economic Development from Lenin to Khrushchev*, 54.

86. Nove holds that it was in part due to the government's willingness to allow private plots and the private ownership of livestock that the livestock population could recover from earlier losses through slaughter and hunger. See Table 11.5: It cites Nove's statistics for the numbers of animals on private plots and on state and collective farms.
For the argument that saying that private plots were more productive than collective farms amounts to an attack on socialism, and does not hold up since the same criticism can be made by comparing small garden plots with relatively lower yields of "capitalist" farms, see Mark Tauger, "Modernization in Soviet Agriculture," paper presented at a Conference on Modernization and Russian Society in the Twentieth Century, University of Birmingham, 17–18 October 2003.

87. Wheatcroft and Davies, "Agriculture," 127. According to Soviet estimates, in 1937, household plots of collective farmers produced just 1.1 percent of grain, but 38.4 percent of vegetables and potatoes and 67.9 percent of dairy produce and meat. Moreover, in 1938, 64.6 percent of the cattle, 75.1 percent of pigs and 56 percent of sheep and goats were on the private plots.

88. Nove, *An Economic History of the USSR*, 240. For further detail, see R. W. Davies, "A Note on Grain Statistics," *Soviet Studies* 21, no. 3 (1969–1970), 314–29.

89. Roger Clarke, *Soviet Economic Facts, 1917–1970* (London: Macmillan, 1972), 114–15.

90. Davies and Wheatcroft, "Agriculture," 125.
91. Davies and Wheatcroft, "Agriculture," 126.
92. Clarke, *Soviet Economic Facts*, 116.
93. Clarke, *Soviet Economic Facts*, 117.
94. GARF, f. 7689, op. 4, d. 80, l. 51.
95. GARF, f. 7689, op. 10, d. 177, l. 5.
96. GARF, f. 7689, op. 10, d. 177, ll. 5–6.
97. GARF, f. 7689, op. 10, d. 40, l. 132.
98. GARF, f. 7689, op. 10, d. 40, l. 132.
99. GARF, f. 7689, op. 10, d. 40, l. 73. The conditions referred to were of Volkov on the Krasnyi state farm who lived in a "bad room," shared with two other families. Zaretskii's room was "all right" but still "the roof leaks and there is no radio."
100. RGASPI, f. 349, op. 1, d. 254, l. 3.
101. Interviews conducted on 14 September 1996 with elderly women on the Vladimir Il'ich Collective Farm, Moscow oblast, about the 1930s.
102. GARF, f. 7689, op. 4, d. 81, l. 77.
103. TsGA RSFSR, f. 317, op. 4, d. 205, l. 29.
104. TsGA RSFSR, f. 317, op. 4, d. 205, l. 29. See, too, TsGA RSFSR, f. 317, op. 4, d. 69, l. 3.
105. GARF, f. 7689, op. 10, d. 170, l. 1.
106. GARF, f. 7689, op. 11, d. 119, l. 4.
107. GARF, f. 7689, op. 11, d. 119, l. 7.
108. GARF, f. 7689, op. 11, d. 119, l. 7.
109. GARF, f. 7689, op. 10, d. 170, l. 2.
110. GARF, f. 7689, op. 10, d. 40, l. 73.
111. GARF, f. 7689, op. 10, d. 40, l. 74.
112. GARF, f. 7689, op. 7, d. 16, l. 52.
113. See, for example, GARF, f. 7689, op. 10, d. 170, l. 13.
114. For instance, GARF, f. 7689, op. 10, d. 40, ll. 31–33 and ll. 78–79.
115. Illustrative of this pattern is bird farm number three on Krasnyi state farm. Here "from 10 November" 1935, dated precisely, "the Stakhanovite movement began to develop." Among the first were M. Mezentseva and N. Nikitenko "who went onto Stakhanovite work methods, adopting pledges to care for 2,400 birds instead of 1,150." Stakhanovism for brigade leaders here, such as E. Belova, meant a pledge "to oversee two brigades, with 24,000 birds instead of one brigade with 12,000 birds." Other peasants followed by making similar pledges. Allegedly "success" here was fast since by 1 December 1935, "the farm moved to Stakhanovite methods completely." See GARF, f. 7689, op. 10, d. 40, l. 81.
116. GARF, f. 7689, op. 11, d. 43, l. 39.
117. GARF, f. 7689, op. 11, d. 43, l. 52.
118. Anthony Oberschall, *Social Conflict and Social Movements* (Englewood Cliffs, NJ: Prentice-Hall, 1973); John McCarthy and Meyer Zald, "Resource Mobilization and Social Movements: A Partial Theory," *American Journal of Sociology* 82 (1977): 1212–41; Charles Tilly, *The Politics of Collective Action* (Cambridge: Cam-

bridge University Press, 2003); Sidney Tarrow, *Power in Movement*, 2nd ed. (Cambridge: Cambridge University Press, 1998).

119. Davies and Khlevnyuk, "Stakhanovism"; Jeffrey Brooks, *Thank You, Comrade Stalin! Soviet Public Culture from Revolution to Cold War* (Princeton, NJ: Princeton University Press, 2000).

Chapter Twelve

Conclusion

Lyushka's real ascent began when a reporter wrote a sensational article (either it was based on her own words or else he made the whole thing up himself) which reported that Lyushka had broken with the age-old way of milking cows and from now on was going to grab four udders at the same time, two in each hand.

— Vladimir Voinovich[1]

Is Vladimir Voinovich's suggestion that Stakhanovism was an absurd movement of sweated labor propagandized through a false journalism entirely fair? Certainly, he captures nicely the "sensational" dimension of Stalinism, its exaggerated praise of achievements and the requirement that journalists produce such material and "find" Stakhanovites. Voinovich also conveys the irrationality of some work practices stemming from the frenzied pressure to "break" with methods of the "past" and to become "new" women and men. These, indeed, were all elements of Stakhanovism. What he overlooks, however, is Stakhanovism's relevance to the countryside at a time when leaders wished to inject diligence, dynamism, and technology into agriculture in order to produce more food and to offer peasants the opportunity for self-advancement in the grand Stalinist project and identification with it. The kulaks, having been dispossessed, displaced, and exiled, needed to be replaced in a new politically correct guise. Hard-working and successful peasants were sorely needed, although the meaning of their work had to be for the collective, not for the individual family farm. Productivity had to be raised, animal losses made up, and new machinery mastered. The fact that Stakhanovism did not necessarily result in the above is a separate question. What matters is that Stakhanovism was pitched in propaganda as a means to these ends and that some peasants aspired to become Stakhanovites. Much of Stakhanovism's significance lay in its intents — intents that were continually redefined and fashioned by leaders, accepted and shaped by some peasants.

Crucial to the campaign to "make" Stakhanovites were its multiple intents that included the creation of role models like Mariia Demchenko. At their broadest, the intents were about solving all rural ills — an impossible task in the short term, but through Stakhanovism, rural problems were named, put on agendas, and made public. In being called upon the tackle them all, Stakhanovites were being used by the regime as mobilized motors of change, there to spearhead transformations not just in agricultural production, but also in battles with lax local officials and farm leaders over management and administration. In the process, they became unwitting participants — some willing, some not — in the purge process as saboteurs of Stakhanovism were meted out punishments as "enemies of the people" and Stakhanovites were foils against them. They were simultaneously among the Soviet Union's new "cultured" elite consumers, testimony that life was becoming "better and merrier." In this sense, the interventionist state attempted to promote its goals by harnessing Stakhanovism to serve its multiple causes and by differentially rewarding and privileging the best workers and peasants, testimony to Soviet advances.

From this perspective, rural Stakhanovism was wielded as a tool or instrument by the state's leaders with the broad objective of transforming the countryside. The purpose was monumental, stretching way beyond incremental changes into a huge project ranging from the generation of new work patterns to sculpting peasant belief patterns and psyches. In the momentum, leaders wanted to shape and manage peasant attitudes, moods, actions, and ambitions. For Peter Holquist this would amount to "gardening" a purer society populated by new persons who were "conscious" and "superior" individuals, their souls engineered by the regime, with Marxism-Leninism bringing a "moral urgency" to the project.[2] Amir Weiner has similarly talked of the Soviet enterprise as approaching society as a "malleable construct" in a broader context of a "continuous purification campaign" whose aim was to "eliminate divisive and obstructive elements."[3] The "urge to maximize" the management of society was what in his view produced surveillance and "physical and mental cataloguing" necessary to grand visions and transformations.[4] In the process "new sites of excision" were ordained which disposed of "human weeds." In this sense, Stakhanovism could be interpreted as one site of excision.

Some especially keen peasants, however, as self-determining subjects as well as objects of policy and circumstance, did choose to work harder, whether complying with party pressures, enticed by material rewards, or cajoled by farm leaders, made possible by available inputs and opportunities, because they always had worked well, out of a wish to be called "Stakhanovite," out of an ideological or psychological desire for full involvement in the Stalinist utopian dream or simply as testimony that they were becoming Sovietized, or out of a combination of these. A central conclusion here is that peasants received Stakhanovism in various ways and for several reasons, not neatly reducible to one alone. Stakhanovites' various motivations interacted with the Stalinist regime's push for Stakhanovism to develop, spread, and transform. Rural Stakhanovism became part of "micro-politics" on the farm in which peasants fashioned its content and contours and had a definite input into what precisely societal "purification" and engineering of their souls meant. With Hellbeck and Halfin one can concur that many keen Stakhanovites may have attempted to sculpt their own souls along official lines as they understood them, but then again, not all Stakhanovites and shock workers may have done this and those who did, will have done so in differing patterns.[5] Self-sculpting will inevitably have been shaped by setting and been affected by other variables such as generation, gender, personality, support mechanisms on the farm, and so on. In short, local context mattered hugely and one cannot assume particular patterns a priori. Here the thorny question of how representative certain patterns of sculpting the self were cannot be answered.

Categories of peasant, moreover, were various. At its simplest, on collective and state farms, peasants can be subdivided into Stakhanovites, shock workers, and other peasants, each with distinct behavior patterns and aims.[6] Each subdivision can be further divided. There were grand and keen Stakhanovites, routine or ordinary Stakhanovites, and faltering Stakhanovites. The same applied to shock workers. Non–shock workers and non-Stakhanovites were not homogeneous either. Some chose to oppose Stakhanovism, others did not; and those who opposed it, did so in a multitude of ways, with varying degrees of belligerence and lethargy. Farm leaders, too, were not all efficient, effective, or necessarily in charge for long, and their high turnover was not conducive to Stakhanovism. Some supported Stakhanovites as best they could in a situation of shortages, others did not attempt to do so. Farms poor in resources were less able to produce Stakhanovites and in any case, the divisiveness of Stakhanovism ran against the grain of collective values. Egalitarian peasant culture was hostile to those attempting to be "different" and "better." Excising this attitude into something ideologically purer was no easy task for the state or its Stakhanovite engines.

Diverse "interests" alone cannot account for the variation in Stakhanovite numbers across farms. Organization on the farm was a crucial variable. Whether or not machines were repaired, whether attitudes to hard work were positive, and above all whether the effort was seen to be worth it mattered.

Peasants who fall into Sheila Fitzpatrick's category of "passive resistance" to the collectivization of agriculture exhibited indifference to *prikazy* and decisions, if they were even aware of them. Exertion, for these peasants, was decidedly not worth it. In Fitzpatrick's view, most peasants followed passive resistance "to a greater or lesser extent."[7] This strategy contrasted with "positive accommodation," according to which peasants sought to make the best of collectivization and to benefit from it if they could. Pursuing Stakhanovism was one form of "positive accommodation," which in Fitzpatrick's view entailed becoming adept at Potëmkin scripts of Stakhanovism's purpose.[8] Peasants who were ready to work hard to attain Stakhanovite status must have seen a point in so doing. In between these two strategies was "passive accommodation" which meant acceptance, "however grudging," of the collective farm, and an attempt to use it to one's advantage.[9] Exuberance, however, was wanting.

While Fitzpatrick's categories are compelling, they do not allow for any peasants to be genuine supporters of collectivization and/or Stakhanovism. Her peasants are resentful of the former and adopt varied strategies for relating to the latter. Yet some citizens, as Stephen Kotkin, Jochen Hellbeck, and Igal Halfin contend, did support the system, being loyal to its enthusiastic projects, to its "special mission," or to what Moshe Lewin has described as its "spectacular" feats.[10] Kotkin criticizes both Fitzpatrick and Lewin for interpreting the Second Five-Year Plan as a period of "retreat" or variant of "revolution betrayed," contending instead that Stalinism was not a partial retreat or throwback to the past, but "remained forward-looking and progressive throughout."[11] Whilst one hesitates wholeheartedly to embrace Kotkin's notion that Stalinism cannot be understood without reference to the eighteenth-century European Enlightenment promoting rationality (since irrationalities can be readily identified), or to perceive Stalinism as wholeheartedly "progressive," he is accurate to note its great forward looking swirls and its appeal for some citizens, including peasants.[12] Among that minority were Mariia Demchenko, Pasha Angelina, and many others. Poor peasants, moreover, had most to gain from the collective project. Through shock work and Stakhanovism they could strive for upward mobility, recognition, and perks and be participants in a huge "spectacular" show, involved collectively with others, even join a labor elite, in a grand purpose of huge proportions, regularly given ideological reinforcement. In the process of mobilization, they worked on themselves, striving to become new persons, better to match communist ideals. Those who took to Stakhanovism had to exert themselves in the fields, often working long hours, even round the clock at harvest time. That thousands of such workers existed makes it hard to make a sustained case that the entire peasantry opposed Stakhanovism.

Nicholas Timasheff has argued that in 1934 a "great retreat" marked the abandonment of communism, as a significant break from the socialist offensives of revolution, First Five-Year Plan, and collectivization. The spirit of retreat, in his view, was embodied in Stakhanovism "more clearly than in anything else."[13] The "miracle" of Stakhanovism in industry came, in Timasheff's view, from two directions: first, from rediscovery of the rational organization of labor; and second, from a "friendly conspiracy" around Stakhanovites, created by their superiors, which provided excellent working conditions, guaranteeing that "theatrical performances" could follow.[14] Increased purchasing power for Stakhanovites due to wage differentials was part of what Timasheff dubbed "the restoration of freedom of consumption." Not everyone could buy available items, making this a "complete retreat since the system introduced was identical with that used in capitalist society, except for the fact that the shops were mainly State agencies."[15]

What Timasheff, however, ignores here is that the "friendly conspiracy" was not always so cozy. Many Stakhanovites complained that better wages, housing, and perks were not forthcoming and so they were not treated as expected. In sum, some Stakhanovites criticized the state for not implementing a successful conspiracy. Evidence shows that Stakhanovites were differentially rewarded by the state, with famous names receiving more perks and presents than "average," ordinary, or unrecognized Stakhanovites; at best, the conspiracy allowed the unrewarded publicly to moan about it. Timasheff is also oblivious to the fact that rural Stakhanovism was embraced by the more heroic women as a means to their own emancipation and as a challenge to gender hierarchies in the village. In this sense, it was not a retreat at all but a progressive advance, albeit disruptive and contentious.[16]

In some respects, Timasheff's views are similar to Trotsky's on the "revolution betrayed." Trotsky, too, felt that Stalinism deviated from a revolutionary path, arguing that a Soviet Thermidor had set in because the bureaucracy had conquered the Bolshevik party and defeated the program of Lenin. In short, "the leaden rump of the bureaucracy outweighed the head of the revolution."[17] Thus "democratic centralism gave place to bureaucratic centralism."[18]

Certainly, the study of rural Stakhanovites' records and "lessons" became bureaucratized, as the files of the Narkomzem and the All-Union Scientific Institute of the Agricultural Economy attest. Trotsky, however, unlike Timasheff, was not critical of Stakhanovites as one might have expected. Rather, he found their achievements "extremely interesting as evidence of the possibilities open only to socialism."[19] The problem for Trotsky was not in their existence but in the difficulty in spreading their feats to large numbers of workers and peasants. As Trotsky put it: "to raise millions to a small degree of technical skill is immeasurably harder than to spur on a few thousand champions."[20] Just as Trotsky was sensitive to the overwhelming hurdles that needed to be surmounted in order to change traditional family life and to revolutionize relations between the sexes, so, too, he appreciated the enormity of the task of persuading workers and peasants to transform their attitudes toward labor and to perform better.[21] We have seen how many peasants were indeed reluctant to engage in socialist competitions. Moreover, most peasants were not Stakhanovites and those who did perform well were more likely to be shock workers than Stakhanovites. The incoherent muddle in the countryside over how to count Stakhanovites, or whether to bother at all, reflected in some areas indifference, lethargy, and chaos rather than Sovietized "forward looking" commitment to a "special mission."

Above all, Trotsky showed wisdom about the intractable practicalities of translating revolutionary dreams—whatever the dreams—into reality. Although Kotkin is right that Stalinism meant special missions, the missions themselves glittered more in ideology, in the scripted texts of *Krest'ianskaia gazeta* and in the fanfare of huge conferences with leaders in Moscow, in Jeffrey Brooks's "rituals of theater," than in the fields without dung, with insufficient animal feed and lacking in spare parts for idle and rusting machinery.[22] Notwithstanding the fact that keener Stakhanovites hurled themselves into production pledges, challenged other farms to competitions, and found themselves whirling in praise, presents, and sudden fame, this Sovietized minority was not the rural norm.

That Stakhanovites were a minority of peasants does not mean that the phenomenon was insignificant for the Soviet state. It was a characteristic element of Stalinist mobilization for higher output, for involvement in the system itself, and for proof that under Stalin life was happier and more "cultured." In fact, modernization theorists could logically claim that the introduction of pay differentials and move away from revolutionary utopia, as they understood it, in favor of managerial modernizers was part of a broader and inevitable process of change.[23] Stakhanovites, however, did not necessarily promote efficiency or higher productivity overall, which were often the result of other factors combined.

Above all, Stakhanovism on the ground involved an interaction between the practices and actions of peasants and the exhortations of the state. What peasants gave and what they demanded in return from farm leaders and the local party was part of the construction of what Stakhanovism became. As a movement it was shaped by peasants' willingness and receptivity, peasants' hostility, and peasants' indifference. Patterns of peasants' reactions varied according to farm, district, and region, producing a variegated picture across the Soviet landmass. None of the classic theoretical approaches quite captures this diversity. Totalitarian approaches imply too much uniformity and give insufficient credit to peasants as social and political actors, as agents of their own fate within the parameters of an oppressive one-party state.[24] Totalitarian frameworks inadequately appreciated the weakness of the state in some rural areas and the disrespect for ideology. The group approach paid too much attention to elites, failing to consider that peasants and workers had interests too, varied ones at that, and that they might act accordingly, and in so doing actually make political differences—if by political we allow the shaping of the contours of a social movement.[25] Fitzpatrick's more empirical work is far more in tune with the practical relevance of peasants' action, but shies from the conclusion that a part of the peasantry may actually have supported collectivization or embraced Stakhanovism with a verve that reflected Sovietization rather than a calculated reaction to making the best out of a collectivized reality. Here some credit must be given to the totalitarian approach's emphasis on the importance of ideology as an independent variable. Kotkin allows for Sovietization, but gives insufficient play to self-interest without Sovietization and without concern for the grand "special mission." Indeed, a blend of Fitzpatrick and Kotkin comes closer to rural reality, allowing for a broader range of both local interests and possibilities than each alone would sanction. In fairness to Kotkin, Stakhanovism in rural life, the most backward and demoralized sector, was distinct from the construction of Magnitogorsk, a huge and high-prestige Stalinist urban and industrial project. Moreover, peasants were not concentrated in one geographic space as in Magnitogorsk, but stretched out from each other in peasant islands, making the best of what they had locally. The number and nature of the factors affecting rural life were more diverse and unpredictable.

In size the rural Stakhanovite movement was smaller than its industrial leader, both on paper and in reality. Stakhanovite highs, such as 58 percent of trade unionists in oil refining and 42 percent in electrical power workers, did not obtain in rural sectors.[26] In many respects, however—such as propaganda, rallies, conferences, socialist competitions, and production pledges—rural Stakhanovism mirrored its industrial counterpart and Stakhanovism as movement was a bridge between town and country, a link between otherwise diverse settings. Both had grand Stakhanovites, the icons of the system, much propagandized and most privileged and also average ones, rewarded or not by the system. The rural scene had faltering Stakhanovites, too, those ready to give up when taunted and threatened by others. Those who have written on industry do not discuss the waverers, but do acknowledge the hostility toward Stakhanovites in general. Yet since in some industrial sectors, the majority of workers were Stakhanovites, Stakhanovism was much more the norm than in rural areas. The faltering were perhaps more likely when in a minority.

Some issues surrounding industrial and rural Stakhanovism are similar, too, such as whether the party's role in pushing Stakhanovism "from above" or "sideways" was more important than spontaneity and enthusiasm "from below." With Lewis Siegelbaum, I concur that the party was not necessarily a unitary body with one harmonious aim or one mode of behaving.[27] Even the Central Committee in December 1935 had to reflect upon what Stakhanovism "meant." Rural examples also exhibit diversity in the way in which the party reacted to Stakhanovism across local levels. Concerning initiative from below, even if peasants were "prompted" by the *politotdel* or Komsomol to increase productivity, motivations for diligence varied and Stakhanovite behavior did not exist in isolation but in interaction with farm leaders, other peasants, the local party, and others. The contours of Stakhanovism were fashioned by the system, local setting, and personal goals.

The nature of this interaction, however, could be more complex and chaotic in rural than in urban contexts. Weather, for instance, affected sowing, harvesting, and the length of growing seasons, all of which had a bearing on productivity. There was nothing comparable in industry that had seen heroic upturns in the First Five-Year Plan of 1928–1932 and Stakhanovism followed on from these. The urban tale was more upbeat. The rural story, by contrast, coming after a serious low in productivity and morale, was set in a sadder context and Stakhanovism was pitched in propaganda as the savior of all rural woes. So Stakhanovism's brief was huge—to make up animal losses, to combat weeds, to care for machinery, and a host of other specific tasks. Thus the meaning of rural Stakhanovism became that of saving the countryside from everything that was wrong.

Such a job description was unattainable. Not only did the countryside lack the economies of scale possible in some industrial sectors and in transport, but Stakhanovism in the fields could not shape the supplies of necessary inputs, such as fuel, which were required for it to be successful. Certainly some successful farms were privileged in the supplies they received, but this was not the norm. Energetic farm leadership helped, but the job of farm chairperson was not enviable and tenure was unstable. Continued instability in the countryside, despite its new "quieter" state after 1935, did not contribute to Stakhanovism. Statements from farm leaders show that they often left their jobs highly disgruntled and/or unable to perform them well. The benefits that came to them were not as lavish as those enjoyed by some heads of industrial plants and not necessarily an incentive to stay. Farms, however, invariably needed the boss to remain rather to suffer yet another new one. As in industry, as Siegelbaum has noted, it was not just skill that set Stakhanovites apart, but "the opportunity to apply their skills."[28] In many rural contexts, easy Stakhanovite opportunities were wanting and local conditions were often to blame. As a consequence, as in industry, attacks were made on managements for failing to provide peasants with the necessary prerequisites for Stakhanovite feats.

Successful rural Stakhanovites who did exist, then, like Mariia Demchenko, made full use of the opportunities available to them but in so doing often found the going tough and highly arduous. In a short report for the magazine *Kolkhoznitsa,* Demchenko referred back to her pledge to Stalin to harvest 500 tsentners of sugar beet per hectare. She noted how difficult it had actually been to attain due to frosts, dry spells, and pests.[29] Her simple message was that hard and careful work and a huge amount of determination were the keys to success. Whilst not all peasants were gripped by her persistence and tremendously eager resolve, a Sovietized minority did champion Stakhanovite feats in the fields, taking Fitzpatrick's "positive accommodators" of collectivization along with them.

Evidence overwhelmingly shows that within the confines of the one-party state, despite communalities, various local "realities" on the ground obtained, contributing to the different shapes that a social movement took. The variables that contributed to the outcome of Stakhanovism were several. Crucial among them, however, were the attitudes and actions of the peasants concerned. Based on the numerous "thick descriptions" and stories of discrete microlevels or "micro-politics," this study holds that the relationship between society and state in the 1930s was rather more complex than established theoretical approaches have suggested and that aspects of many perspectives rather than one alone best capture the dynamics and states of rural worlds.

Finally, the story of rural Stakhanovism, in all its dimensions, reveals a huge amount about the attitudes, atmospheres, textures, and hurdles of rural society under Stalin. The possibilities and limits of the processes of transformation in the countryside were part of the frustrating rural legacy to late-Stalinism and to the leaderships of Khrushchev, Brezhnev, Chernenko, Andropov, Gorbachev, Yel'tsin, and Putin. In the twenty-first century, the Russian Federation has a rural inheritance with deep and pained roots, stretching back through Stakhanovism, collectivization, and the Stolypin reforms from 1905 to the village commune, the emancipation of the serfs in 1861, and serfdom. Domestic, regional, and international contexts have greatly changed since the late 1930s, but the huge challenge to refashion the countryside is still on the political agenda.[30] Some historians have recently bewailed the dominance of what they dub "1930s studies" in the Soviet field on the grounds that it amounts to a "dictatorship of the decade" and a "bundled set of strands that typify an arbitrary slice of time" which telescope the study of Russian history into the Stalin period.[31] Whilst all periods merit serious analysis, the point that they underplay is that these years, as well as being among the most historically gripping, tumultuous, and tragic, not only boomed out hope for glittery futures, but hammered down foundations for much that followed.

NOTES

1. Vladimir Voinovich, *The Life and Extraordinary Adventures of Private Ivan Chonkin* (Harmondsworth: Penguin, 1978), 144.

2. Peter Holquist, "'Information Is the Alpha and Omega of Our Work': Bolshevik Surveillance in Its Pan-European Context," *The Journal of Modern History* 69 (September 1997): 417 and 447.

3. Amir Weiner, "Nature, Nurture, and Memory in a Socialist Utopia: Delineating the Soviet Socio-Ethnic Body in the Age of Socialism," *The American Historical Review* 104, no. 4 (October 1999): 1114.

4. Weiner, "Nature," 1118.

5. Jochen Hellbeck, "Fashioning the Stalinist Soul: The Diary of *Stepan Podlubnyi* (1931–1939), *Jahrbücher für Geschichte Osteuropas* 44 (1996): 344–73. Igal Halfin, *Terror in My Soul* (Cambridge, MA: Harvard University Press, 2003).

6. This excludes the *edinolichniki*, or individual peasant farmers, on neither collective nor state farms, who constituted about 10 percent of peasant households by the mid-1930s, on around 6 percent of cultivated land.

7. Sheila Fitzpatrick, *Stalin's Peasants: Resistance and Survival in the Russian Village after Collectivization* (New York: Oxford University Press, 1994), 10.

8. What Sheila Fitzpatrick dubs the "potëmkinism" of rural Stakhanovism was a false and glossy image of its success scripted by party ideologues. It did not follow that peasants' conversations on the farms reiterated official narratives.

9. Fitzpatrick, *Stalin's Peasants*, 10.

10. Stephen Kotkin, *Magnetic Mountain: Stalinism as a Civilization* (Berkeley and Los Angeles: University of California Press, 1995), 12; Hellbeck, "Fashioning"; Halfin, *Terror in My Soul*; Moshe Lewin, *The Making of the Soviet System: Essays in the Social History of Interwar Russia* (London: Methuen, 1985), 33.

11. Kotkin, *Magnetic Mountain*, 6.

12. For discussion of those who did not see Stalinism as forward looking, see Lynne Viola, *Peasant Rebels under Stalin: Collectivization and the Culture of Peasant Resistance* (New York: Oxford University Press, 1996), preface and 9.

13. Nicholas Timasheff, *The Great Retreat: The Growth and Decline of Communism in Russia* (New York: Dutton, 1946), 136.

14. Timasheff, *The Great Retreat*, 138.

15. Timasheff, *The Great Retreat*, 140.

16. Other moves away from the revolutionary goals of 1917 for Timasheff included the replacement of internationalism with nationalism and reinstatement of bourgeois specialists.

17. Leon Trotsky, *The Revolution Betrayed: What Is the Soviet Union and Where Is It Going?* (New York: Pathfinder, 1972), 94.

18. Trotsky, *Revolution Betrayed*, 98. Milovan Djilas in Yugoslavia held similar views about the ascendancy of a "new class" composed of "the political bureaucracy" with special privileges derived from their administrative monopoly. Tony Cliff also echoed Trotsky, depicting the bureaucracy as a ruling class that had accumulated capital in a state capitalist system. See Milovan Djilas, *The New Class* (London: Thames and Hudson, 1957); Tony Cliff, *State Capitalism in Russia* (London: Pluto, 1974). Other theorists, however, have not dwelled so heavily on bureaucracy. Isaac Deutscher, for instance, stressed that the revolution was unfinished and Roy Medvedev held that problems stemmed from revolution in a backward country. Coming from different directions, Jean-Paul Sartre portrayed the very notion of socialism in one country as an "ideological monstrosity," while Rudolf Bahro in the former German Democratic Republic bewailed the subaltern status of citizens, arguing that their alienation could be overcome only through cultural revolution harnessing the massive "surplus consciousness" or energetic mental capacity. See Isaac Deutscher, *The Unfinished Revolution: Russia 1917–1967* (Oxford: Oxford University Press, 1967); Jean-Paul Sartre, "Socialism in One Country," *New Left Review*, no. 100 (November–December 1976): 143–63; and Rudolf Bahro, *The Alternative in Eastern Europe* (London: Verso, 1981).

19. Trotsky, *Revolution Betrayed*, 83.

20. Trotsky, *Revolution Betrayed*, 83.

21. Leon Trotsky, *Women and the Family* (New York: Pathfinder Press, 1970).

22. Jeffrey Brooks, *Thank You, Comrade Stalin! Soviet Public Culture from Revolution to Cold War* (Princeton, NJ: Princeton University Press, 2000).

23. Theorists such as Richard Lowenthal and John Kautsky argued that industrialization demanded managers and efficiency, not revolutionaries and Marxist ideology. In their perspectives, the goals of modernization and communist utopia clashed. As the former was pursued, the sway of the latter declined and rationality triumphed over doctrine. Or as Joseph Berliner would put it, industrial maturation demanded the triumph of material modernizers over dialecticians. See Richard Lowenthal, "Development vs. Utopia in Communist Policy," in *Change in Communist Systems*, ed. Chalmers Johnson (Stanford, CA: Stanford University Press, 1970), 33–116; John H. Kautsky, *Communism and the Politics of Development* (New York: John Wiley and Sons, 1968); Joseph S. Berliner, "Marxism and the Soviet Economy," *Problems of Communism* 13 (September–October, 1964): 1–11.

24. Carl J. Friedrich and Zbigniew K. Brzezinski offered the "totalitarian syndrome of six defining characteristics in their *Totalitarian Dictatorship and Autocracy*, second revised edition (New York: Praeger, 1965), 22. See, too, Hannah Arendt, *The Origins of Totalitarianism*, 2nd ed. (Cleveland: Meridian Books, 1958), 242–46; Merle Fainsod, *How Russia Is Ruled*, revised ed. (Cambridge, MA: Harvard University Press, 1963), 300. An early critique was provided by Robert Burrowes, "Totalitarianism: The Revised Standard Version," *World Politics* 22 (January 1969): 272–94.

25. H. Gordon Skilling and Franklyn Griffiths, *Interest Groups in Soviet Politics* (Princeton, NJ: Princeton University Press, 1971), 25.

26. Lewis H. Siegelbaum, *Stakhanovism and the Politics of Productivity in the USSR, 1935–1941* (Cambridge: Cambridge University Press, 1988), 170.

27. Siegelbaum, *Stakhanovism*, 66.

28. Siegelbaum, *Stakhanovism*, 79.

29. *Kolkhoznitsa*, no. 11–12 (November 1935): 14–15.

30. For discussion of contemporary rural issues see Stephen K. Wengren, David J. O'Brien and Valeri V. Patsiorkovski, "Russia's Rural Unemployed," *Europe-Asia Studies* 55, no. 6 (September 2003): 847–867; Louis Skyner, "Property as Rhetoric: Land Ownership and Private Law in Pre-Soviet and Post-Soviet Russia," *Europe-Asia Studies* 55, no. 6 (September 2003): 889–905; and Grigory Ioffe, "The Downsizing of Russian Agriculture," *Europe-Asia Studies* 57, no. 2 (March 2005): 179–208.

31. The Editors, "1930s Studies," *Kritika: Explorations in Russian and Eurasian History* 4, no. 1 (Winter 2003), 1–4; and the Editors, "Really-Existing Revisionism?" in *Kritika: Explorations in Russian and Eurasian History* 2, no. 4 (Fall 2001): 707–11.

Appendix I:
Resources and Methodology

Research for this book was conducted after 1991 at a time when party archives were finally open to Westerners and state archives were much more accommodating than in the past. Although the story of rural shock work and Stakhanovism could have been told without access to archives, it would have been a far more skeletal tale.

The Central Party Archive, or TsPA (*Tsentral'nyi partiinyi arkhiv*), soon renamed itself the Russian Center for the Preservation and Study of Documents of Recent History, or RTsKhIDNI (*Rossiiskii tsentr khraneniia i izucheniia dokumentov noveishei istorii*), often referred to as the former party archive. It subsequently became the Russian State Archive of Socio-political History, or RGASPI (*Rossiiskii gosudarstvennyi arkhiv sotsial'no-politicheskoi istorii*). Its holdings drawn upon in this book include Politburo protocols and minutes, texts of Central Committee Plenary Meetings, *postanovleniia* (decisions), discussions at regional party committee meetings, documents of Central Committee party departments (particularly the Department of Agriculture and Department of Agitation and Propaganda), protocols of the Orgburo and Secretariat, *prikazy* (orders) of the People's Commissariat of State Farms, and stenographic reports of All-Union Congresses of Kolkhoz Shock Workers. The private papers of Mikhail Kalinin and Andrei Andreev were especially useful and those of Grigorii Ordzhonikidze, Lazar' Kaganovich, Iosif Stalin, and Andrei Zhdanov were of some relevance.

The Komsomol, or youth group of the party, played a role in encouraging rural Stakhanovism. Its materials were held in the Center for the Preservation of Documents of Youth Organizations, or TsKhDMO *(Tsentr khraneniia dokumentov molodezhnykh organizatsii)*, better known as the former Komsomol archive and later moved to come under the umbrella of RGASPI. All references cited here, however, use the original TsKhDMO classifications. Of special importance were documents and resolutions of the Komsomol's Central Committee and reports on the Komsomol's role in spring sowing, socialist competitions, and in mechanizing female labor.

A particularly rich holding of letters from shock workers and Stakhanovites on state farms is found in the archives of the Central Committees of state farm trade unions, located in the State Archive of the Russian Federation, or GARF (*Gosudarstvennyi arkhiv Rossiiskoi Federatsii*), which was formerly the Central State Archive of the October Revolution, or TsGAOR (*Tsentral'nyi gosudarstvennyi arkhiv Okt'iabrskoi Revoliutsii*). These materials are divided according to sector: dairy; pigs; vegetables; and fur and poultry. They also include trade union reports on rural shock work and Stakhanovism and on how best to spur the movement to spread.

Documents from local and oblast procuracies and from the People's Commissariat of Justice were essential for discussion of resistance to shock work and Stakhanovism. These are also held in GARF. The Central State Archive of the RSFSR, or TsGA RSFSR (*Tsentral'nyi gosudarstvennyi arkhiv RSFSR*), which is affiliated to the aforementioned larger GARF (and known as "*malyi* GARF," or "little GARF"), has similar procuracy materials for the Russian republic. Documents of the Russian Commissariat of State Farms are also housed here and carry useful aggregate statistics on rural Stakhanovism in the Russian republic.

Other illuminating sources are found in the Russian State archive of the economy, or RGAE (*Rossiiskii gosudarstvennyi arkhiv ekonomiki*), previously known as the Central State Archive of the Economy, TsGANKh (*Tsentral'nyi gosudarstvennyi arkhiv narodnogo khoziaistva*). Here the fascinating editorial archive of *Krest'ianskaia gazeta* (Peasant newspaper) contains letters from peasants written in 1938 and 1939 to newspaper editors. Some of these are complaints from Stakhanovites about farm life, which editors forwarded to the local party and procuracy. There is correspondence as well between editors and rural reporters, discussing how stories on Stakhanovism should be framed. RGAE also houses papers of the secretariat of People's Commissariat of State farms and of the All-Union Scientific Research Institute of the Agricultural Economy.

Recordings of Stakhanovite rallies, speeches at congresses, recollections and greetings can be listened to in RGAF (*Rossiiskii gosudarstvennyi arkhiv fonodokumentov*), or the Russian State Archive of Phonograph Documents. These include speeches and commentaries of Stakhanovites such as Pasha Angelina, Dar'ia Garmash, and Pasha Kovardak, addresses from Nadezhda Krupskaia on women's work, and greetings to shock workers from Mikhail Kalinin.

Nonarchival primary sources for this study are also extensive and include documents from party and Komsomol congresses, speeches from Stakhanovites' rallies, conferences and congresses, the rural press from 1935, in particular *Krest'ianskaia gazeta* and *Sovkhoznaia gazeta*, Stakhanovites' memoirs, Soviet books on the countryside and on rural Stakhanovism, popular magazines and journals which include *Krest'ianka* (Peasant woman), *Kolkhoznik* (Collective farmer), *Kolkhoznitsa* (Female collective farmer) and *Udarnitsa Urala* (Shock worker of the Urals), and also specialist journals such as *Sotsialisticheskaia Rekonstruktsiia Sel'skogo Khoziaistva* (Socialist Reconstruction of Agriculture), *Sotsialisticheskoe Zemledelie* (Socialist Agriculture), *Stakhanovets* (Stakhanovite), *Traktorist-Kombainer* (Tractor driver, combine driver), *Sovkhoznoe proizvodstvo* (State farm production), *Sotsialisticheskaia Zakonnost'* (Socialist Law), and *Obshchestvennitsa* (wife-activist).

The methodology adopted here is interpretative and eclectic, drawing on a range of sources and attempting to answer several different but interrelated questions. Since one central aim is to discuss how Stakhanovism was officially presented to the Soviet people, I dissect official speeches, newspaper articles, ideology, and propaganda of the period in order to determine the constant and changing features of the image of "Stakhanovite." Additional light is shed on the contours of Stakhanovism that the regime wished its journalists to emphasize by scrutinizing rejection letters from editors at *Krest'ianskaia gazeta* sent to rural correspondents. An inductive trawling of sources for answers to guiding questions is adopted. Every available issue of *Krest'ianskaia gazeta* and *Sovkhoznaia gazeta* held in Moscow in the State Public History Library of Russia has been read. Relevant articles were laboriously copied out by hand since photocopying was not permitted. Other journals were read here and in the Russian State Library, or former Lenin Library. The Smolensk Archive was read in the library of the Centre for Russian and East European Studies (CREES) at the University of Birmingham, and numerous excellent pamphlets on Stakhanovism and Stakhanovites' memoirs (many uncatalogued) were found in the library of the University of Glasgow along with Soviet secondary sources.

Building an accurate picture of what life was like on the farm from 1935 is fraught with methodological challenges. Ideology is visible and loud, which makes its concepts and notions accessible for analysis. Quite how representative opposition to Stakhanovism from other peasants was, however, is harder to establish with precision. The same applies to problems of feed supply and to "obstacles" created or suffered by farm directors. Moreover, once instances have been found, one is haunted by questions of the reliability of sources. Did Pasha Angelina really suffer resistance in the way she describes it in her autobiography? Is the story she tells a distortion that better fits ideology than reality? Are the numbers of Stakhanovites claimed by farms mere fictions to placate local party leaders? Were farm directors and chairpersons who failed to "help" Stakhanovites really so unreasonable, or just singled out in advance to be purged anyway for other reasons? And how valid are the conclusions drawn from the instances available if they do not constitute a representative sample? At best, one can categorize "tendencies," humbly acknowledging that their precise extent cannot easily be known. And on possible exaggerations and distortions, such as those found in memoirs, one can highlight their interest as examples of Stalinist discourse.

The picture of rural reality is pieced together from a range of press, archival, and secondary sources. Themes which affected Stakhanovism, such as the behavior of kolkhoz chairpersons, leadership turnover on the farm, the purges, drunkenness, and the politics of manure are selected as topics for discussion. I am not testing narrow hypotheses here, rather attempting to locate Stakhanovites in the context in which they found themselves and to which they contributed.

Appendix II: *Krest'ianskaia gazeta*

Krest'iankskaia gazeta was one of the main newspapers for peasants in the 1930s, published under the auspices of the Central Committee of the party. The decision to launch it had been taken at the Twelfth Party Congress in 1923 and the first edition appeared on 25 November 1923. *Krest'ianskaia gazeta* came out fifteen times a month, reaching a circulation of one million by the time it ceased publication in 1939. Quite why the paper closed down is shrouded in mystery. Mention of its closure can be found in Politburo minutes that claimed that the paper had ceased to satisfy rural readers in different districts. At the same time, it was decided that *Sovkhoznaia gazeta* would come out only every third day, rather than every second. Other papers, too, were cut back, although *Pravda*'s circulation was to increase by 100,000. Problems with paper supply may have contributed to a desire to streamline news, thereby further enhancing *Pravda*'s status as *the* authoritative source.

Krest'ianskaia gazeta played several important roles. First, it imparted crucial information about party policy, in particular concerning agriculture. It was thus a propaganda arm of the state, instructing readers in priorities for the countryside and describing rural successes and failures. Second, in its related but broader agitprop role, the paper aimed to mobilize peasants, farm leaders, and local authorities to act appropriately throughout the agricultural cycle. This might entail observations on what needed to be done for the spring sowing, the autumn harvest, or prompt advice on how best to combat weeds or how to use manure. Part of this agitprop function concerned the mobilization of peasants into shock work and Stakhanovism and the exerting of pressure on farm directors and chairpersons to help Stakhanovites. Third, *Krest'ianskaia gazeta* was an exposer of social injustice in the countryside. Its journalists drew attention to the maltreatment of Stakhanovites and championed their causes where necessary. Often this meant referring Stakhanovites' complaints to another organization for action. Fourth, the paper involved peasants in its work and encouraged them to become *sel'kory*. Although the *sel'kor* enjoyed the opportunity of reporting news from his or her locality, editors played highly interventionist roles when it came to subject matter and style of presentation. Thus rejection letters from editors are one useful source for gleaning what was expected of reporters. Fifth, *Krest'ianskaia gazeta* encouraged peasants to write in about various aspects of rural life. Peasants sent in millions of letters about achievements, failures, lazy or drunken collective farm chairpersons, and attempts to sabotage Stakhanovism. *Krest'ianskaia gazeta* performed a highly political role in championing peasants' causes when they fit party priorities for agriculture.

In its internal structure, *Krest'ianskaia gazeta* had a special Department of Rural Correspondents. This was set up at the beginning of 1924. The department pursued several tasks: it generally looked out for new cadres to draw into *Krest'ianskaia gazeta*, doing so by working through the journal *Sel'kor*; it liaised with existing *sel'kory*, attempting to instruct them in appropriate ways; and guided the work of Circles of Friends of the Newspaper (*Kruzhki Druzei Gazety*). By 1925, there were already 5,000 *sel'kory*, of whom 3,843 were in the RFSFR, around 400 in Ukraine, more than 150 in Belorussia, and the remainder from elsewhere. By 1926, there were 1,450 *kruzhki*.

The paper's archive suggests that *Krest'ianskaia gazeta*'s editorial structure changed over the years. In 1925 there were four main departments: the Department of Peasants' Letters, the Department of *Sel'kory,* the Information Department, and the Legal Advice Department. After 1925, these four became the Legal Department, Department of *Sel'kory,* Information Department, and Bibliographic Department. E. B. Derusova, who wrote a foreword to the archive, regrets that it is hard to reach firm conclusions about the tasks and functions of different subdivisions within departments due to a lack of documents. See E. B. Derusova, "*Predislovie' k f. 396, Redaktsiia 'Krest'ianskaia gazeta'*" (Moscow, 1990), f. 396, 2–3. It is evident from reading letters to the newspaper from *sel'kory* that by 1938 the Department of Peasants' Letters and the Department of *Sel'kory* had merged into the Department of *Sel'kory* and Letters. Correspondence is also on file from departments not mentioned by Derusova, such as the Agriculture Department, Department of Party Construction, and Department of Agitation and Propaganda.

Above all, *Krest'ianskaia gazeta* came to be seen as one of many authoritative places to which letters of complaint could be sent with the possibility of action being taken by the editors. Due to the huge number of letters received, editors established special links with twenty-two central institutions and people's commissariats (some sources say twenty-six). A portion of letters was sent directly to other organizations. By 1925, Narkomzem had fifty people examining letters, and soon after 100. In Narkomfin, fifteen people dealt with letters. In other organizations, one or two people scrutinized mail. Different organizations received varying quantities of mail. According to E. B. Derusova, by 1925 Narkomzem was receiving up to 70,000 letters a month, Narkomfin up to 10,000, the NKVD between 10,000 and 12,000 and other institutions rather fewer, such as Tsentrosoiuz with just 10 to 12 a day.

For further details on the history of the paper, consult Sheila Fitzpatrick, "Readers' Letters to *Krest'ianskaia gazeta*, 1938," *Russian History* 24, nos. 1–2 (Spring–Summer 1997): 149–70; for its role in relation to other Soviet newspapers, see *Jeffrey Brooks, Thank You, Comrade Stalin! Soviet Public Culture from Revolution to Cold War* (Princeton, NJ: Princeton University Press, 2000), 3–53.

Glossary

aktiv	chosen group of activists
batrak	agricultural laborer
batrachka	female agricultural laborer
bedniak	poor peasant
brigade	collective farm work unit
Comintern	Communist International
dekulakization	expropriation of the kulaks
demchenkovtsy	emulators of Mariia Demchenko
dvadtsatipiatitysiachniki	25,000ers
gusevtsy	emulators of Petr Gusev
hectare	a measurement equal to 2.471 acres
kolesovtsy	emulators of Fedor Kolesov
kolkhoz	collective farm
kolkhozy	collective farms (plural)
kolkhoznik	collective farm member
kolkhoznitsa	female collective farm member
kolkhozniki	collective farm members (plural)
Komsomol	All-Union Leninist Communist League of Youth
konkurs	competition as individual activity
krai	large administrative territory within a republic
kraikom	krai party committee
kulak	rich peasant
kul'turnost'	culture
link (*zveno*)	subunit within a brigade
Gosplan	State Planning Commission
mesiachnik	monthers

MTS	machine tractor station
muzhik	male peasant
Narkomzdrav	People's Commissariat of Health
Narkomzem	People's Commissariat of Agriculture
NKVD	People's Commissariat of Internal Affairs, or secret police (from 1934)
Obkom	oblast party committee
oblast	region
Oblzdravotdel	oblast health department
obshchestvennitsa	public-spirited woman or female activist
obshchestvennitsy	plural of *obshchestvennitsa*
OGPU	*Ob'edinënnoe gosudarstvennoe politicheskoe upravlenie*, or secret police
partorg	party organizer
People's Commissar	Head of a People's Commissariat or government ministry
peredoviki	advanced workers
piatiletka	Five-Year Plan
piatisotnytsy	500ers (those who gathered 500 tsnentners of sugar beet per hectare)
Politburo	political bureau of the communist party's Central Committee
politotdel	political department of state farm or MTS
pood	16.38 kilograms
postanovlenie	resolution or decision
postanovleniia	resolutions or decisions
prikaz	administrative order
prikazy	administrative orders
raikom	district party committee
raion	district
RSFSR	Russian Soviet Federated Socialist Republic
raizdravotdel	district health department
raizo (raionnyi zemel'nyi otdel)	district land department
sel'kor	rural correspondent
sel'kory	rural correspondents (plural)
sel'sovet (sel'skii sovet)	rural soviet

semisotnitsy	700ers (those who gathered 700 tsentners of sugar beet per hectare)
seredniak	middle peasant
sorevnovanie	competition as a group activity
soviet	council (elected in no-choice elections)
sovkhoz	*sovetskoe khoziaistvo*, or state farm
sovkhozniki	state farm workers
Sovnarkom	*Sovet Narodnykh Komissarov*, or Council of People's Commissars
Stakhanovite	normbuster par excellence
stakhanovets	Stakhanovite
stakhanovka	female Stakhanovite
stakhanovtsy	Stakhanovites
Sverdlovtsy	pig breeders on Sverdlov state farm
tridtsatniki	30ers (in cotton)
trudoden'	a labor day, according to which collective farm work was measured and paid, varying across jobs
tsentner	a tsentner is 100 kilograms
Tsentral'nyi Ispolnitel'nyi Komitet (TsIK)	Central Executive Committee of All-Union Congress of Soviets
tysiachniki	1,000ers (those who gathered 1,000 tsentners of sugar beet per hectare)
udarnik	shock worker (male)
udarnitsa	shock worker (female)
udarniki	shock workers (plural)
VDNKh	Park of Economic Achievements
VTsSPS	All-Union Central Council of Trade Unions
zagotovki	grain procurements
zagotoviteli	those attempting to implement the *zagotovki*
zemel'nye organy	land organs
znatnye liudi	distinguished people

This book uses the Library of Congress transliteration system with the exception of names and words whose more customary English forms are now widely adopted. Thus Komintern is here Comintern, Trotskii becomes Trotsky, and El'tsin is written as Yel'tsin. Soft signs at the end of some words have also been dropped, but retained where convention tends to keep them. So oblast' is simply oblast, whereas *kul'turnost'* remains true to the original.

Selected Bibliography

KEY ARCHIVAL MATERIALS

1. RGASPI (*Rossiiskii gosudartsvennyi arkhiv sotsial'no-politicheskoi istorii*)

Fond 15, opis' 2 (*Plenumy TsK VKP (b)*)

F. 17, op. 2 (*Zasedaniia plenumov TsK VKP (b), 1918–1941*)

F. 17, op. 3 (*Protokol zasedaniia politburo TsK VKP (B)*)

F. 17, op. 10 (*TsK VKP (b), Otdel po rabote sredi zhenshchin*)

F. 17, op. 21 (*TsK VKP (b), Otdel rukovodiashchikh partiinykh organov sektor informatsii*)

F. 17, op. 79 (*Upravlenie delami TsK KPSS, 1935–1956*)

F. 17, op. 85c (*Sekretnyi otdel TsK, 1926–1934*)

F. 17, op. 114 (*Protokoly zasedanii Orgbiuro i sekretariat*)

F. 17, op. 121 (*Sekretariat Orgbiuro TsK VKP (b), 1939–1948*)

F. 17, op. 120 (*TsK KPSS obshchii otdel*)

F. 17, op. 123 (*Sel'skokhoziaistvennyi otdel TsK VKP (b), 1937–1946*)

F. 17, op. 125 (*Upravlenie propagandy i agitatsii TsK VKP (b), 1938–1948*)

F. 17, op. 129 (*Upravlenie delami TsK VKP 9(b), 1938–1948*)

F. 73, op. 2 (*Andreev, Andrei Andreevich*)

F. 77, op. 1 (*Zhdanov, Andrei Aleksandrovich*)

F. 78, op. 1 (*Kalinin, Mikhail Ivanovich*)

F. 81 (*Kaganovich, Lazar' Moiseevich*)

F. 82 (*Molotov, Viacheslav Mikhailovich*)

F. 85 (*Ordzhonikidze, Grigorii Konstantinovich*)

F. 349 (*Politupravlenie Narkomata Sovkhozov SSSR, 1933–43*)

F. 558 (*Stalin, Iosif Vissarionovich*)

2. TsKhDMO (*Tsentr khraneniia dokumentov molodezhnykh organizatsii*)

F. 1, op. 2 (*Plenumy TsK VLKSM*)

F. 1, op. 3 (*Protokoly zasedaniia biuro TsK VLKSM*)

F. 1, op. 5 (*Stenogrammy Soveshchanii TsK VLKSM, 1920–1965*)

F. 1, op. 10 (*Protokoly, stennogrammy*)

F. 1, op. 23 (*Dokumenty TsK VLKSM; Protokoly, postanovleniia TsK, tkirkuliary, svodki, and perepiska*)

F. 1, op. 33 (*Orgotdel, 1932–1975*)

F. 1, op. 32 (*Otdel Propagandy, 1941–1965*)

F. 37 (*Vsesoiuznye konferentsii VLKSM*)

3. GARF (*Gosudarstvennyi arkhiv Rossiiskoi Federatsii*)

F. 393 (*Narodnyi Komissariat Vnutrennykh Del RSFSR, 1917–1930*)

F. 3316 (*Tsentral'nyi ispolnitel'nyi komitet SSSR, 1922–1937*)

F. 5515 (*Narodnyi Komissariat Truda*)

F. 5548 (*Vsesoiuzno mezhsektsionnoe biuro inzhenerov i tekhnikov, VMBIT/ VTsSPS*)

F. 5451 (*Vsesoiuznyi tsentral'nyi sovet professional'nykh soiuzov*)

F. 7689 (*Tsentral'nye komitety profsoiuzov rabochikh i sluzhashchikh sel'skogo khoziaistva i zagotovok (Ob'edinennyi Fond)*)

F. 7689, op. 4 (*TsK profsoiuza rabochikh ovoshchnikh sovkhozov*)

F. 7689, op. 7 (*TsK profsoiuza rabochikh svinovodcheskikh sovkhozov*)

F. 7689, op. 10 (*TsK profsoiuza rabochikh pushnykh i ptitsevodcheskikh sovkhozov*)

F. 7689, op. 11 (*TsK profsoiuza rabochikh molochno-miachnykh sovkhozov tsental'nykh i iuzhnykh raionov*)

F. 7860 (*Tsentral'nye komitety professional'nykh soiuzov rabotnikov miasnoi i molochnoi promyshlennosti, 1931–1953*)

F. 7924 (*TsK Profsoiuza rabotnikov zemorganov; TsK Profsoiuzov MTS iuga i tsentra*)

F. 8131 (*Prokuratura SSSR, 1924–1962*)

F. 8131, op. 13 (*Prokuratura SSSR, 1935/1936*)

F. 8131, op. 14 (*Prokuratura SSSR, 1937*)

F. 8131, op. 15 (*Prokuratura SSSR, 1938*)

F. 8131, op. 16 (*Prokuratura SSSR, 1939*)

F. 9432 (*Narodnyi Kommisariat Iustitsii SSSR, Sekretariat*)

F. 9492 (*Ministerstvo Iustitsii SSSR, 1936–1956*)

F. 9506e (*NKVD*)

4. TsGA RSFSR (*Tsentral'nyi gosudarstvennyi arkhiv RSFSR*)

F. 310 (*Ministerstvo zemledeliia RSFSR, 1917–1946*)

F. 317 (*Ministerstvo sovkhozov RSFSR, 1936–1946*)

F. 328 (*Glavnoe upravlenie ptitsevodcheskikh sovkhozov, 1934–1955*)

F. 353 (*Ministerstvo iustitsii, 1917–1963*)
F. 428 (*Verkhovnyi sud RSFSR*)
F. 461 (*Prokuratura RSFSR s 1936*)

5. RGAE (*Rossiiskii gosudarstvennyi arkhiv ekonomiki*)

F. 260 (*Vsesoiuzny nauchno-issledovatel'skii institut ekonomiki sel'skogo khozi -aistva/VNIIESKh, 16 Iulia 1934–1937 Fevralia 1938*)
F. 396 (*Redaktsiia Krest'ianskoi gazetii, 1938–1939*)
F. 7486, op. 18 (*Ministerstvo sel'skogo khoziaistva SSSR. I: Glavnoe upravlenie podgotovki massovykh kadrov; II: upravlenie rukovodiashchikh kadrov*)
F. 7799, op. 1 (*Uchrezhdeniia po rukovodstvu miasnymi i molochno-miasnymi sovkhozami Narkomzema SSSR, Narkomata zernovykh i zhivotnovodcheskikh zhivotnovodstva SSSR*).
F. 7803 (*Narkomat-Ministerstvo sovkhozov SSSR*)
F. 7803, op. 1 (*Sekretariat Narkomsovkhozov SSSR i Ministerstva Sovkhozov SSSR*)
F. 9477, op. 1 (*Uchrezhdeniia po rukovodstvu zhivotnovodcheskoi otrasl'iu sel'skogo khoziaistva*)
F. 9489, op. 1 (*Vse-soiuznyi nauchno-issledovatel'skogo instituta sveklovicheskogo polevodstva*)
F. 9495 (*Narodnyi Komissariat Zemledeliia SSSR*)
F. 9495, op. 1 (*Uchrezhdeniia po rukovodstvu sveklovichnoi otrasl'iu sel'skogo khoziaistva, 1932–1953*)
F. 9481, op. 1 (*Narodnyi Komissariat Zemledeliia SSSR, glavnoye konevodcheskoe upravlenie*)
F. 9495 (*Narodnyi Komissariat Zemledeliia SSSR*)

6. RGAF (*Rossiiskii gosudarstvennyi arkhiv fonodokumentov*)

7. CREES, University of Birmingham

Smolensk Party Archive, Microfilm copy

RELEVANT FILMS

Bogataia Nevesta (The Rich Bride)
Traktoristy (Tractor Drivers)
Skazanie o zemle sibirskoi (Tales of the Siberian Land)
Svinarkha i pastukh (The Female Pig Rearer and the Herdsman)
Svet'lyi put' (Radiant Road)
Utomlennye solntsem (Burnt by the Sun)
Vesëlye rebiata (The Happy Lads)
Volga Volga (Volga, Volga)
Zerkalo (The Mirror)

NEWSPAPERS AND JOURNALS

Bol'shevik
Izvestiia
Kolkhoznik
Kolkhoznitsa
Krasnaia Sibiriachka
Krest'ianka
Krest'ianskaia gazeta 1935–1939
Obshchestvennitsa, 1936–1941
Pravda
Rabotnitsa
Sel'kor
Sotsialisticheskaia Rekonstruktsiia Sel'skogo Khoziaistva
Sotsialisticheskaia Zakonnost', 1934–1939
Sotsialisticheskoe Zemledelie
Sovkhoznaia gazeta, 1935–1939
Stakhanovets
Trud
Udarnitsa Urala

STENOGRAPHIC REPORTS OF
CONFERENCES AND CONGRESSES

Labor in the land of socialism: Stakhanovites in Conference (Moscow: Co-operative publishing society of foreign workers in the USSR, 1936).

Obrashchenie 2-go Oblastnogo S"ezda Kolkhoznikov-udarnikov, Sotsialisticheskoe zemledelie Urala, no. 5–6 (May–June, 1935): 7–11.

Pervyi Vsesoiuznyi S"ezd Kolkhoznikov Udarnikov Peredovykh Kolkhozov, 15–19 Fevralia 1933g: Stenograficheskii Otchët. Moscow-Leningrad: 1933.

Pervyi Vsesoiuznyi S"ezd Udarnykh Brigad (k tridtsatiletiiu s"ezda): Sbornik Dokumentov i Materialov. Moscow: Izdatel'stvo VTsSPS, Profizdat, 1959.

Pervoe Vsesoiuznoe soveshchanie Rabochikh i Rabotnits-stakhanovtsev, 14–17 Noiabria 1935: Stenograficheskii Otchët. Moscow, Partizdat TsK VKP(b), 1935.

Udarniki zavodov—Udarnikam Polei: Rechi predstavitelei Delegatsii Fabrik i Zavodov na 2-om Vsesoiuznom S"ezde Kolkhoznikov-Udarnikov. Moscow: Gosudarstvennoe izdatel'stvo kolkhoznoi i sovkhoznoi literatury Sel'khozgiz, 1935.

VseSoiuznoe Soveshchanie Rabochikh i Rabotnits-Stakhanovtsev, 14–17 Noiabria 1935: Stenograficheskii otchët. Moscow: Partizdat TSK VKP (b), 1935.

Vtoroi Vsesoiuznyi S"ezd Kolkhoznikov-Udarnikov, 11–17 Fevralia 1935 g: Stenograficheskii Otchët. Moscow: Sel'khozgiz, 1935.

BOOKS AND ARTICLES (IN RUSSIAN)

Afanas'ev, Iu. N. ed., *Sud'by Rossiiskogo Krest'ianstva*. Moscow: Rossiiskii Gosudarstvennyi Gumanitarnyi Universitet, 1996.

Angelina, Praskov'ia N. *Liudi Kolkhoznykh Polei*. Moscow and Leningrad: Gosudarstvennoe Izdatel'stvo Detskoi Literatury, 1952.

Angelina, Praskov'ia, N. *O Samom glavnom: moi otvet na amerikanskuiu anketu*. Moscow: 1948.

Armand, Inessa. *Stat'i, Rechi, Pis'ma*. Moscow: Politizdat, 1975.

Azovo-Chernomorskii Kraevoi Komitet Soiuza Rabochikh Svinovodcheskikh Sovkhozov SSSR. *Stakhanovtsy-svinary o svoem opyte*. Rostov: Kraikom soiuza rabochikh svinosovkhozov, 1936.

Bil'shai, V. *Reshenie zhenskogo voprosa v SSSR*. Moscow: Gosudarstvennoe izdatel'stvo politicheskoi literatury, 1959.

Danilov, V. P. *Ocherki istorii kollektivizatsii sel'skogokhoziaistva v soiuznykh respublikakh*. Moscow: Gosudarstvennoe izdatel'stvo politicheskoi literatury, 1963.

Danilov, V. P., M. P. Kimma, and N. V. Tropkina, *Sovetskoe krest'ianstvo: kratkii ocherk istorii (1917–1970)*. Moscow: Politizdat, 1973.

Chukhno, A.V., I. K. Martovitskii, and Iu. A. Bocharnikov, *50 let kolkhoznoi zhizni*. Moscow: Kolos, 1971.

Ezhova, V. P., V. I. Lopatova, and N.N Slastukhin. *Zhenshchiny Sovetskoi Mordovii*. Saransk: Mordoveskoe knizhnoe izdatel'stvo, 1964.

Gasanov, R. M. *Stakhanovskoe dvizhenie v Dagestane*. Makhachkala: Dagenstanskoe knizhnoe izdatel'stvo, 1975.

German, M. E. *Stakhanovskie zhenskie brigady na peregruzochnykh rabotakh*. Moscow: Rechizdat, 1940.

Ivin, I. A. and P. P. Masalov. *Na bor'bu za rekordnyi urozhai sakhsvekly: opyt piatisotnits-ordenonosok Dadykinoi i Kirichenkoi*. Kursk: Kurskaia Pravda, 1936.

Kolkhoz—krepost' nashei rodiny. Ogiz: Sel'khozgiz, 1935.

Korotkov, S. K. et al. *My predsedatel'stvuem na Vsesoiuznom S"ezde*. Moscow: Sel'khozgiz, 1935.

KPSS v Rezoliutsiakh i Resheniiakh S"ezdov, Konferentsii i Plenumov TsK, 6. Moscow: Politizdat, 1985.

Laptev, I. *Sovetskoe krest'ianstvo*. Moscow: Gosudarstvennoe izdatel'stvo kolkhoznoi i sovkhovnoi literatury, 1939.

Liashenko, I. V. and B. F. Kniazevskii. *Stakhanovtsy zernovykh kul'tur Kirgizii*. Frunze: Kirgizgosizdat, 1937.

Nefedova, V. K., ed. *Stakhanovtsy polei: k piatidesiatiletiiu stakhanovskogo dvizheniia*. Moscow: Agropromizdat, 1985.

Obrashchenie 2-go oblastnogo s"ezda kolkhoznikov-udarnikov, Sotsialisticheskoe zemledelie Urala, no. 5–6 (May–June, 1935): 7–11.

Osokina, Elena. *Za Fasadom "Stalinskogo Izobiliia."* Moscow: Rosspen, 1998.

Panfilova, A. M. "Iz istorii stakhanovskogo dvizheniia." *Vestnik Moskovskogo Universtiteta*. Ser. 8. *Istoriia*. No. 1 (January–February, 1987): 18–31.

Petukhov, I. and A. Shushakov. *Dasha Garmash i ee podrugi*. Moscow: 1943.

Pod znamenem Stalina. Novosibirsk: Zapadno-sibirskoe kraevoe izdatel'stvo, 1935.

Rubinshtein, M. *Novye formy stakhanovskogo dvizheniia*. Ogiz: Gosudarstvennoe izdatel'stvo politicheskoi literatury, 1940.

Sakharov, V. A. *Zarozhdenie i razvitie stakhanovskogo dvizheniia*. Moscow: Izdatel'stvo Moskovskogo Universiteta, 1985.

Stakhanovskii opyt uborki urozhaia v zernosovkhozakh Povolzh'ia i Sibiri. Moscow: Narodnyi komissariat zernovykh i zhivotnovodcheskikh sovkhozov SSSR, 1939.

Stakhanovtsy ovtsesovkhozov o svoei rabote. Rostov: Izdanie TsK soiuza rabochikh ovtsevodcheskikh sovkhozov SSSR, 1936.

Stakhanovtsy polei: k piatidesiatiletiiu stakhanovskogo dvizheniia. Moscow: Agrpromizdat, 1985.

Stakhanovtsy sel'skogo khoziaistva Arkhangel'skoi oblasti. Arkhangel'sk: Ogiz, 1939.

Stakhanovtsy-svinari o svoem opyte. Rostov: Kraikom soiuza svinosovkhozov, 1936.

Stishova, L. I., ed. *V Budniakh Velikikh Stroek: Zhenshchiny-kommunistki geroini pervykh piatiletok*. Moscow: Politizdat, 1986.

Vershinin, I., ed. *Mariia Safronovna Demchenko*. Moscow: Gosudarstvennoe izdatel'stvo politicheskoi literatury, 1938.

Viola, L and T. Macdonald, S. V. Zhuravlev, and A. N. Mel'nik. *Riazanskaia Derevnia v 1929–1930 gg: Khronika Golovokruzheniia*. Moscow and Toronto: Rosspen, 1998.

Vorozheikin, I. E. *Letopis' trudovogo geroizma: kratkaia istoriia sotsial'isticheskogo sorevnovaniia v SSSR*. Moscow: Politizdat, 1984.

Vyltsan, M. A. *Ukreplenie material'no-tekhnicheskoi bazy kolkhoznogo stroiia vo vtoroi piatiletke (1933–1937)*. Moscow: Izdatel'stvo Akademii Nauk SSSR, 1959.

——. *Sovetskaia derevnia na kanune Velikoi Otechestvennoi Voiny*. Moscow: Politizdat, 1970.

——. *Zavershaiushchii etap sozdaniia kolkhoznogo stroia 1935–1937g*. Moscow: Nauka, 1978.

Zelenin, I. E. *Zernovye Sovkhozy SSSR, 1933–1941 gg*. Moscow: Nauka, 1966.

Zvezdin, Z. K., I. I. Bel'nosov, and M. I. Khluev. *Sotsialisticheskoe sorevnovanie v SSSR, 1918–1964: dokumenty i materialy profsoiuzov*. Moscow: Izdatel'stvo VTsSPS, 1965.

BOOKS AND ARTICLES (NON-RUSSIAN)

Angelina, Praskovya. *My Answer to an American Questionnaire*. Moscow: Foreign Languages Publishing House, 1949.

Bartlett, Roger, ed. *Land Commune and Peasant Community in Russia*. Basingstoke and London: Macmillan, 1990.

Berliner, Joseph. *Factory and Manager in the USSR*. Cambridge, MA: Harvard University Press, 1957.

Blum, J. *Lord and Peasant in Russia from the Ninth to the Nineteenth Century*. Princeton, NJ: Princeton University Press, 1961.

Brooks, Jeffrey. *Thank You, Comrade Stalin! Soviet Public Culture from Revolution to Cold War*. Princeton, NJ: Princeton University Press, 2000.

Buckley, Mary. "The *Nagornovskoe Dvizhenie*: A Stakhanovite Movement in Ploughing That Was Not." Pp. 39–47 in *Edinburgh Essays on Russia*, edited by Elspeth Reid. Nottingham: Astra Press, 2000.

Clark, Roger. *Soviet Economic Facts, 1917–1970*. London: Macmillan, 1972.

Conquest, Robert. *The Harvest of Sorrow: Soviet Collectivization and the Terror-Famine*. London: Hutchinson, 1986.

Davies, R. W. *The Socialist Offensive: The Collectivisation of Soviet Agriculture, 1929–1930*. London: Macmillan, 1980.

———. *The Soviet Collective Farm, 1929–1930*. London: Macmillan, 1980.

Davies, R. W., Mark Harrison, and S. G. Wheatcroft. *The Economic Transformation of the Soviet Union, 1913–1945*. Cambridge: Cambridge University Press, 1994.

Davies, R. W. *Soviet Economic Development from Lenin to Khrushchev*. Cambridge: Cambridge University Press, 1998.

———. "Stakhanovism and the Soviet System: A Review Article." *Soviet Studies* 41, no. 3 (July 1989): 484–87.

——— and Oleg Khlevnyuk. "Stakhanovism and the Soviet Economy." *Europe-Asia Studies* 54, no. 6 (September 2002): 867–903.

Davies, Sarah. *Popular Opinion in Stalin's Russia: Terror, Propaganda and Dissent, 1934–1941*. Cambridge: Cambridge University Press, 1997.

Eklof, Ben and Stephen P. Frank, eds. *World of the Russian Peasant: Post-emancipation Culture and Society*. Boston: Unwin Hyman, 1990.

Fainsod, Merle. *Smolensk under Soviet Rule*. London: Macmillan, 1958.

Farnsworth, Beatrice and Lynne Viola, eds. *Russian Peasant Women*. New York: Oxford University Press, 1996.

Figes, Orlando. *Peasant Russia; Civil War: The Volga Countryside in Revolution (1917–1921)*. Oxford, Clarendon, 1991.

Filtzer, Donald. *Soviet Workers and Stalinist Industrialization: The Formation of Modern Soviet Production Relations, 1928–1941*. New York: Ardmonk, 1986.

Fitzpatrick, Sheila. *Stalin's Peasants: Resistance and Survival in the Russian village after Collectivization*. New York: Oxford University Press, 1994.

———. "From *Krest'ianskaia gazeta*'s Files: Life Story of a Peasant Striver." *Russian History* 24, nos 1–2 (Spring–Summer 1997): 215–37.

———. *Everyday Stalinism: Ordinary Life in Extraordinary Times: Soviet Russia in the 1930s*. New York: Oxford University Press, 1999.

———, ed. *Stalinism: New Directions*. London and New York: Routledge, 2000.

Garros, Veronique, Natalia Korenevskaya, and Thomas Lahusen, eds. *Intimacy and Terror: Soviet Diaries of the 1930s*. New York: The New Press, 1995.

Getty, J. Arch and Roberta Manning, eds. *Stalinist Terror: New Perspectives*. Cambridge: Cambridge University Press, 1993.

Halfin, Igal. *Terror in My Soul: Communist Autobiographies on Trial*. Cambridge, MA: Harvard University Press, 2003.

Hellbeck, Jochen. "Fashioning the Stalinist Soul: The Diary of Stepan Podlubnyi (1931–1939)," *Jahrbücher für Geschichte Osteuropas* 44 (1996): 344–73.
———. "Working, Struggling, Becoming: Stalin-Era Autobiographical Texts." *The Russian Review* 60, no. 3 (July 2001): 344–73.

Hindus, Maurice. *Red Bread: Collectivization in a Russian Village.* Bloomington: Indiana University Press, 1988.

Hobsbawm, Eric. "Peasants and Politics." *Journal of Peasant Studies* 1, no. 1 (1973): 3–22.

Hoch, Steven L. *Serfdom and Social Control in Russia: Petrovskoe, a Village in Tambov.* Chicago: Chicago University Press, 1986.

Hoffman, David L. *Stalinist Values: The Cultural Norms of Soviet Modernity, 1917–1941.* Ithaca, NY: Cornell University Press, 2003.

Hough, Jerry and Merle Fainsod. *How the Soviet Union Is Governed.* Cambridge, MA: Harvard University Press, 1982.

Hughes, James. *Stalinism in a Russian Province: A Study of Collectivization and Dekulakization in Siberia.* Basingstoke and London: Macmillan, 1996.

Kenez, Peter. *The Birth of the Propaganda State.* Cambridge: Cambridge University Press, 1985.

Kingston-Mann, Esther, and Timothy Mixter. *Peasant Economy, Culture and Politics of European Russia, 1800–1921.* Princeton, NJ: Princeton University Press, 1990.

Kotkin, Stephen. *Magnetic Mountain: Stalinism as a Civilization.* Berkeley and Los Angeles: University of California Press, 1995.

Lewin, Moshe. *Russian Peasants and Soviet Power: a Study in Collectivization.* London: George Allen and Unwin, 1968.
———. *Making of the Soviet System: Essays in the Social History of Interwar Russia.* London: Methuen, 1985.

Medvedev, Roy. *Let History Judge: The Origins and Consequences of Stalinism.* London: Spokesman Books, 1976.

Moon, David. *The Russian Peasantry 1600–1930: The World Peasants Made.* London: Longman, 1999.

Nove, Alec. *An Economic History of the USSR.* Harmondsworth, Middlesex: Penguin, 1984.

Pallot, Judith, ed. *Transforming Peasants: Society, State and Peasantry, 1861–1930.* Basingstoke and London: Macmillan, 1998.

Rosenberg, William G. and Lewis H. Siegelbaum, eds. *Social Dimensions of Soviet Industrialization.* Bloomington: Indiana University Press, 1993.

Scott, James C. *Weapons of the Weak: Everyday Forms of Peasant Resistance.* New Haven, CT: Yale University Press, 1985.

Shanin, Teodor. *The Awkward Class.* Oxford: Oxford University Press, 1972.

Siegelbaum, Lewis H. *Stakhanovism and the Politics of Productivity in the USSR, 1935–1941* Cambridge: Cambridge University Press, 1988.

Solomon Jr., Peter H. *Soviet Criminal Justice under Stalin.* Cambridge: Cambridge University Press, 1996.

Stakhanov, Aleksei G. *The Stakhanovite Movement Explained.* Moscow: Foreign Languages Publishing House, 1939.

Stites, Richard. *Russian Popular Culture*. Cambridge: Cambridge University Press, 1992.

Tauger, Mark B. "The People's Commissariat of Agriculture." Pp. 150–75 in *Decision-Making in the Stalinist Command Economy, 1932–1937*, edited by E. A. Rees. London: Macmillan, 1997.

——. "Soviet Peasants and Collectivization, 1930–1939: Resistance and Adaptation." *Journal of Peasant Studies* 31, nos. 3 and 4 (April and July, 2004): 427–56.

Tian-Shanskaia, Olga Semyonova. *Village Life in Late Tsarist Russia*, ed. David L. Ransel. Bloomington, Indiana University Press, 1993.

Tilly, Charles. *The Politics of Collective Action*. Cambridge: Cambridge University Press, 2003.

Viola, Lynne. *The Best Sons of the Fatherland: Workers in the Vanguard of Soviet Collectivization*. New York: Oxford University Press, 1987.

——. *Peasant Rebels under Stalin: Collectivization and the Culture of Peasant Resistance*. New York: Oxford University Press, 1996.

——, ed. *Contending with Stalinism: Soviet Power and Popular Resistance in the 1930s*. Ithaca and London: Cornell University Press, 2002.

Yaney, George L. *The Urge to Mobilize: Agrarian Reform in Russia, 1861–1930*. Urbana: University of Illinois Press, 1982.

Index

abortion, 25, 279
accommodation to Stakhanovism, 324
advanced workers (*peredoviki*), 42–43,
 50–51
Ageev (brigade leader), 181
alcohol. *See* drunkenness
Alekseevna, Mariia, 240
Alieva, Almaz, 71
All-Ukraine Conference of Stakhanovites
 in Animal Husbandry, 103
All-Union Agricultural Exhibition, 105,
 276
All-Union Conference of Advanced
 Workers in Animal Husbandry
 (1936), 54
All-Union Institute of Manure,
 Agrotechnology and Soil Science,
 118
All-Union Leninist Communist Union
 of Youth, 52–53
All-Union Scientific Institute of the
 Agricultural Economy, 117, 314
All-Union Scientific Research Institute,
 121
All-Union Socialist Competition of
 Women's Tractor Brigades (1937),
 70
All-Union Sugar Beet Scientific
 Research Institute, 203

Al'tfater, Lidiia, 208
Andreev, Andrei, 50–53, 167, 200, 209,
 217, 308
Andreevich, Petr, 216
Andreev-Khomiakov, Genadii, 9
Andreichenko, Akulina, 151
Andrle, Vladimir, 6, 21
Androshchuk, Ekaterina, 4, 72, 272
Angelina, Praskov'ia (Pasha), 5, 53, 69,
 76, 77, 81, 84, 122, 125, 126, 137,
 139–40, 147–48, 151, 159, 228, 230,
 233, 242–45, 244, 253, 256–57,
 260–62, 264, 272, 283n82, 289
Angelina, Praskov'ia (Pasha), father of,
 78, 260–61
Angelina, Praskov'ia (Pasha), husband
 of, 272, 283n82
animals: conditions for, 204–7;
 declining numbers of, 22; in films,
 87; lessons on, 130–32; numbers of,
 314; sabotage against, 145–46;
 slaughter of, 21
animal specialists, 206
Anisimov, N., 104–5
anniversary of 1917 revolution, 57–58
Antichrist, 21
Apocalypse, 21
Armand, Inessa, 254, 269, 271
Artiukh, Ivan, 100

Index

About the Author

Mary Buckley is Visiting Fellow at Hughes Hall, Cambridge. She has taught Soviet and post-Soviet politics and society for over twenty years and is author or editor of numerous books and articles. She has written on Soviet ideology, gender, state and society under Gorbachev, Stalinism, Russian domestic and foreign policy, terrorism, and human trafficking. Since 1978 she has been a regular visitor to the Soviet Union and Russian Federation through the British Council, the Soviet Ministry of Higher and Special Education, the British Academy, and the Russian Academy of Sciences.

ALSO BY THE AUTHOR

Redefining Russian Society and Polity (1993).
Women and Ideology in the Soviet Union (1989).
Soviet Social Scientists Talking: An Official Debate About Women (1986).
The Bush Doctrine and the War on Terrorism: Global Responses, Global Consequences, co-edited with Robert Singh (2006).
Global Responses to Terrorism: 9/11, Afghanistan and Beyond, co-edited with Rick Fawn (2003).
Kosovo: Perceptions of War and Its Aftermath, co-edited with Sally N. Cummings (2002).
Post-Soviet Women: From the Baltic to Central Asia, ed. (1997).
Perestroika and Soviet Women, ed. (1992).
Women, Equality and Europe, co-edited with Malcolm Anderson (1988).